Management Live:
The Video Book

Robert Marx
University of Massachusetts at Amherst

Todd D. Jick
Harvard University

Peter J. Frost
University of British Columbia

Prentice-Hall, Englewood Cliffs, NJ 07632

Library of Congress Cataloging-in-Publication Data

Marx, Robert (Robert D.)
    Management live : the video book / Robert Marx, Todd D. Jick,
  Peter J. Frost.
        p.   cm.
    Includes bibliographical references.
    ISBN 0-13-946781-5 (paper bound) :
    1. Organizational behavior. 2. Management.   I. Jick, Todd,
  . II. Frost, Peter J. III. Title.
  HD58.7.M375 1991
  658.3--dc20
                                                    91-11851
                                                    CIP

Credits:

Acquisitions Editor: Alison Reeves
Development Editor: Jane Ritter
Editorial and Production Supervision: Lisa Kinne
Cover Design: Marianne Frasco
Page Layout: Art Kleiner
Manufacturing Buyer: Robert Anderson
Prepress Buyer: Trudy Pisciotti
Keyboarder: Faith Tansey

 © 1991 by Prentice-Hall, Inc.
A Paramount Communications Company
Englewood Cliffs, New Jersey 07632

Printed in the United States of America

10 9 8 7

ISBN 0-13-946781-5

Prentice-Hall International (UK) Limited, *London*
Prentice-Hall of Australia Pty. Limited, *Sydney*
Prentice-Hall Canada Inc., *Toronto*
Prentice-Hall Hispanoamericana, S.A., *Mexico*
Prentice-Hall of India Private Limited, *New Delhi*
Prentice-Hall of Japan, Inc., *Tokyo*
Simon & Schuster Asia Pte. Ltd., *Singapore*
Editora Prentice-Hall do Brasil, Ltda., *Rio de Janeiro*

(Copyright acknowledgments appear on page 377, which constitutes a continuation of the copyright page.)

TABLE OF CONTENTS

The marriage of video and management education has been slowly occurring in the last few years. With the publication of this new experiential video book, the full benefit and excitement of this marriage will surely be realized. It is a bold pedagogical innovation and one that many of us have awaited. And it has been put together with great teaching care by three instructors — Bob Marx, Todd Jick and Peter Frost — who have dedicated much of their professional time to creating engaging and stimulating classroom experiences.

Management Live!: The Video Book shows us how to integrate the power of the visual — the video — with thoughtful exercises, readings, self-assessment and theory material. Each of the topics in this book is centered around the video clip. These clips are sometimes very serious documentaries, but more often they are segments of films and TV shows that creatively, and often playfully, demonstrate key management issues. The videos really bring things to life, but the educational value has been significantly deepened by the surrounding materials — such as the "Ready for Class" preparation and the "Coming to Our Senses" follow-on.

There are also underlying values that are being conveyed in this book. There is an unmistakable tone and point of view. The authors clearly want to underscore the importance of fairness and ethical behavior in the work place, the appreciation for diversity and for understanding all perspectives (for example, labor and management, the drivers of change and the recipients of change, etc.), and the need to have a sense of humor. But they are also dead serious about helping us build better functioning and healthier organizations.

Perhaps more than anything else *Management Live!* demands us all to be forward looking and leading edge. We are directed towards the twenty-first century over and over throughout the book. We are urged to ponder how things will be different, and must be different, as we approach the future. And we are given the confidence and hope that while the new challenges are indeed going to be more formidable than ever before experienced in management, they can be managed effectively with integrity and fairness.

As you move through this book, you will never feel a sense of sameness or redundancy. Each chapter not only has its own unique subject matter but also a unique combination of learning experiences and stimulation. You will read some short cases, you will have to go out and do some interviewing, you will be asked to look inward within yourself as well as outward at the world you live in, you will work on some team projects, you will have to debate and defend your point of view with others, you will be asked to make decisions and you will be asked to listen and watch others.

And yet one thing remains constant throughout the book. The authors have made each chapter "customer/learner-friendly." They want all students of management to find themselves enticed and engaged by the challenges of management and organizations, and each chapter does this for us. In essence, students will be asked to behave in the same way that organizations of the future must — to be learning all the time.

If this were an old-style conventional book, I would now urge you to simply read on. This book, however, will be different. You will not only have to read on, you will now have the chance to enjoy a book for your "viewing pleasure." You will not be passively participating in someone else's classroom but you will be proactively contributing and shaping your own learning. Indeed, what Professors Marx, Jick and Frost have done is to bring education alive, as well as management.

Boston, Mass.
February 1991

Leonard Schlesinger
Associate Professor
Harvard Business School

DEDICATION

This book is dedicated to the great teachers
of our lives who taught us that everywhere
we looked there was something to learn.

Especially

Mitzi and Martin Marx

Leon and Millicent Jick

Felix and Mary Frost

It is also dedicated to our students who have
inspired us to try new ways of teaching and
urged us to teach with values and with
feelings.

ACKNOWLEDGMENTS

We started to work on this book at the Organizational Behavior Teaching conference held at Bentley College, Waltham, MA, in 1987. Bob Marx and Todd Jick had just presented a session on the use of video in the organizational behavior classroom featuring the now infamous David Letterman clip on the merger of General Electric and NBC, which has become one of the many provocative videos in this book.

Following the session, Peter Frost who had been in the audience suggested that it might be fun to combine our experiences and ideas for using videos in the form of a book that would make the video medium more easily accessible to faculty and students as a tool for teaching management principles. The three of us met again over a sumptuous New Orleans dinner at the Academy of Management's National Meeting in August of that year, brainstorming ideas late into the night and the project was launched. While we have produced this book as three equal partners, it has in many ways been influenced by the efforts of many others. We wish to thank the many talented and generous people who have supported this project. At the same time we assume complete responsibility for any errors, omissions or flaws in the book.

We are deeply indebted to the Organization Behavior Teaching Society, for it was at their annual conference in Bentley that the idea for this book was born. The OBTS is a magical organization and the meetings have been a special place to share our thoughts about teaching, test new and risky ideas among supportive but honest colleagues, heal our tired minds after an intensive year in the classroom and renew our excitement and love for teaching. It was the creative and playful atmosphere of the Organizational Behavior Teaching Conference that created the synergy required to make this book a reality. Thank you David Bradford for founding and supporting this organization for so many years.

Once the idea of a book based on video segments was developed, it took the courage and vision of Alison Reeves, our editor at Prentice Hall, to make it a reality. Using her multiple talents as a hard-nosed negotiator, riverboat gambler, video fanatic, and group therapist, Alison Reeves ventured into uncharted territories when she became the product champion of a book never before tried in the higher education marketplace, a book based on video segments. Her many hours of negotiating with film and television industry officials is an important reason for the high quality of video segments contained in this book. Her support of this project in so many ways is deeply appreciated.

Fiona Crofton, a doctoral student at Simon Fraser University, played an important role in shaping the tone of this book. She was instrumental in keeping our book values-oriented and emphasizing the feeling side of management. She helped us to title exercises in ways that students could understand. Her probing questions helped us to improve the organization and flow of exercises and her thoughtful comments will have spared readers from innumerable errors, glitches and unpardonable lapses of consciousness suffered by authors with small children and frequent bouts with jet lag. In addition, Chapter 15 was written in close collaboration with Fiona Crofton. We are grateful to her for her contributions.

There are many other colleagues who have made substantial contributions to the development of this book. We want to thank Mark Maier of SUNY Binghamton for sharing his NASA video segment with us. His dedication and persistence at bringing out the story of the Challenger tragedy has created a powerful learning experience for students of management. Lee Bolman of Harvard University was an early supporter of our video project and contributed the idea of using the Martin Luther King video segment as an example of leadership in action. This segment never fails to touch students and instructors in many ways. Lee's recent book *Reframing Organizations: Artistry, Choice and Leadership* (written with Terry Deal of Vanderbilt University) has inspired us to find video segments that show how managers lead from very different sets of assumptions about organizations.

We want to thank Tom Peters, author of *In Search of Excellence,* for going out onto the factory floor to interview Pat Carrigan, in one of our favorite video segments. It is still difficult to find video segments of excellent women managers in action. This video segment and Tom's article included in our chapter on race and gender in the work place helps our book express a deeply felt value of a fair and humane workplace.

Sim Sitkin of the University of Texas at Austin and Jack Brittain of the University of Texas at Dallas contributed "Carter Racing," a superb exercise for helping students simulate the decision-making experience.

Robert Quinn of the University of Michigan generously allowed us to include portions of his provocative book *Beyond Rational Management,* especially the story of the "Journey from Novice to Master Manager" and the "Management Practices Survey" which helps students identify how their values translate into managerial role behavior.

Ken Blanchard of Blanchard Training and Development and author of the *One Minute Manager* was an inspiration to us as an early user of feature films such as *Twelve O'Clock High* to teach management concepts, and his use of humorous film segments to make management training a positive experience.

Steve Meisel of Lasalle University and Larry Michaelsen of the University of Oklahoma have been charter members of the video group. Their OBTC workshops on video were always full of new ideas that fueled our excitement for this project.

Robert Lussier of Springfield College, Springfield, MA, generously contributed several questionnaires that helped apply the lessons from the videos and the text to each reader's unique constellation of abilities and values. Self assessment forms on motivation and decision making were adapted from his recently published book, *Human Relations in Organizations: A Skill Building Approach.*

Allen Ivey of the University of Massachusetts and author of numerous books on counseling and communications skills played an important mentorship role in the professional development of the first author. His pioneer work with videotaped training of counselors resulted in the video literacy that was so helpful in recognizing how video segments could be used to teach management. His micro-training concept comprises the core of the chapter on communication.

Much of the writing of *Management Live: The Video Book* was accomplished during the first author's sabbatical leave at Western Washington University in the spring of 1990. The hospitality, support and professional interchanges that were offered by Bruce Wonder, Chairman of the Department of Management, and colleagues Joe Garcia, Ken Keleman, and Christopher Taylor helped the final product immeasurably. The second author wishes to thank Susan Rosegrant for her continuous support and able assistance of this project.

The journey from an idea to a published book requires the technical assistance of many dedicated people behind the scenes. Without their expertise, and creativity, our scratches and doodles would not have evolved to the polished form seen in the finished product. We wish to thank Sandra Van Duyn of the University of British Columbia, Meredith Jacobson of Western Washington University and the Word Processing Center at the University of Massachusetts for their patience in typing the many drafts of these chapters.

Tim Hodges of Harvard Business School was always there to assist us and flawlessly accomplished all tasks he tackled.

Prentice Hall staff who contributed enormously were Lioux Brun, Alison Reeves' administrative assistant, Jane Ritter, development editor, and Faith Tansey, keyboarder. Art Kleiner, our desktop publisher, deserves special thanks for his ability to artistically display the printed word in a style that invites the reader to join in the experience of *Management Live: The Video Book*. Finally, our families deserve credit for enduring our video addiction. They often gave up their right to the VCR so that we could record yet another video segment for this book.

Chapter 1

Managing and Learning

in the 21st Century

As we approach the twenty-first century, the business world is going through a revolution as dramatic as the political upheaval in the Soviet Union, Eastern Europe and South Africa. The successful manager of tomorrow will be someone who is prepared for changes, and who even thrives on them. The manager of the future will likely be a woman or the member of a minority group, leading a work force that consists of a larger percentage of women and minorities. Changing demographics and changing values in the United States will place greater value on fairness in hiring and promoting people based on their abilities rather than their race, ethnicity or gender. When managed well, greater diversity in the work force will yield dividends for organizations. You are likely to be among those twenty-first century managers who will make this happen.

The manager of the twenty-first century will be influencing a work force that will expect to have input on decisions. You will probably recall some years from now how you were unwilling to work for companies that did not encourage full participation in the important decisions. As a twenty-first century manager, employee input and creativity at all levels of the organization will be valued.

Tapping employee creativity will require new ways of leading that build flexible networks to fit the changing business environment.[1] As the twenty-first century manager you will teach others how to manage themselves and will empower employees to flout conventional wisdom in search of better ways to do things.

You will celebrate the demise of rigid hierarchical structures that have too many layers for effective communication to take place. Under your leadership, your employees will be able to respond quickly to embrace new projects, educating themselves continuously about the technical and managerial tasks necessary to be at the cutting edge.[2]

The twenty-first century manager will be a global citizen.[3] In the next decade you will see talented managers passed over for promotions because they had not become fluent in the language and cultures of other countries. In the global economy of the twenty-first century you will be managing business transactions with the Soviet Union, China, Eastern Europe and a new South Africa, as well as with the more traditional U.S. trading partners such as Canada, Western Europe, Central and South America and the Far East. And as you become comfortable with these changes, new political and economic alliances will force you to be continuously innovative. Your ability to understand the customs and needs of every trading partner will be essential to success in the global market.

The manager of the twenty-first century will be a master of changing technology. Rapid change in management information systems, travel and communication, robotics and production processes will be the norm. Your ability to understand change and to help your employees adapt to it will determine your success as a manager. Organizations that cannot adapt to rapid and continuous change will not flourish.

The twenty-first century manager will be a person who considers ethics and social responsibility to be an important part of her job. As the earth's natural resources diminish and its population grows and strives for a higher standard of living, business decisions will be heavily influenced by their effects on the environment and on the health and safety of the work force. Managers with impressive histories of ethical decisions will be the heroes of the twenty-first century.

Many students are already preparing for being managers in the twenty-first century. Women and minorities are increasingly enrolling in management courses. Classes are designed to teach the important advantages of participatory decision making. Computer literacy is now taught in elementary school. Many of you will be spending a semester or summer abroad learning about business in another culture, while taking foreign language courses at your college or university. Business ethics courses will help you avoid personal and environmental catastrophes such as those seen in the Exxon Valdez oil spill, the Bhopal chemical contamination, the Wall Street insider trading scandals, and discriminatory labor practices. Your management education should help you handle the ethical dilemmas you will face as a twenty-first century manager and help you build a more honest and humane work place.

1. Adapted from Tom Peters, "The Challenges Businesses Face in the 90s," appearing in the *Bellingham Herald,* July 22, 1980, p. 83.
2. Ibid.
3. Ibid.

At the same time that the content of management education is changing, the ways that students learn about management are changing. Just as the compact disc and the cassette tape have replaced the record album, so have portable video cameras and inexpensive videocassette recorders begun to supplant traditional educational films in the classroom. Modern video technology allows any student or instructor to record a timely television broadcast and have it shown in class the next day.

In many universities today students learn management skills by practicing them in front of the video camera, then observing and critiquing their performance by viewing the tape with a partner. With special effects such as stop action and slow motion to help analyze behavior and with the timeliness of instant playback, we are on a threshold of a video-based approach to learning. It is hardly surprising that video recordings are playing an increasing role in education.

Recalling the adage "A picture is worth a thousand words," the moving image of video may be worth many thousands of words. Because we are a generation brought up on television, we are familiar with its entertainment capabilities. However, video is also a formidable teaching tool, and the topic of management is particularly amenable to its use. As a behavioral science that requires rational, quantitative and intuitive interpersonal skills, management is often a delicate balance of science and art. There are theories about how to manage and skills necessary to do it. But sometimes those who have mastered the theories have difficulty implementing them. Meanwhile, others who are quite effective managing people may make technical mistakes or operate from erroneous assumptions. Our task is to bring the scientific, factual side of management and the artistic, skillful side of management together.

Management Live: The Video Book is based on our 10 years of experience using brief carefully selected video segments in the classroom. Video can show the subtleties, the emotions and the context of managerial behavior. It can show management as it really is. Using this book, you will see video segments that capture the excitement, tension, and humor of management as only video can. These segments will offer you a glimpse of people "caught in the act," showing us what management is all about. The video segments will supplement more traditional lecture and textbook teaching technologies by vividly enhancing the written word with pictures and movement.

Important facts and theories about managing will become more meaningful to you when you can explore the feelings and skills associated with management in action. You will observe management activity outside of the office and factory as well as that which takes place behind closed doors in the organization. *Management Live: The Video Book* will bring the essence of management to your classroom through scenes from well-known films, such as *Broadcast News, One Flew Over the Cuckoo's Next* and *Nine to Five*. You will observe legendary and historic figures who can teach us much about management, such as Martin Luther King and Hyman Rickover. You will see others, less famous, but with important messages, such as Pat Carrigan, Ben Cohen, and Jerry Greenfield. Much of life is filled with humor and management is no different. From the *David Letterman Show, Saturday Night Live,* and the film *Nine to Five* you will learn about management with a smile. *Management Live: The Video Book* is based on a strong value system. It emphasizes a work place that is productive because the work force is treated with fairness and respect. You will see the pain caused by job discrimination. You will also experience optimism for the work place of the future as you watch segments that highlight the growing impact of women and minorities in business. You will watch companies such as Ben and Jerry's Ice Cream that are committed not only to a quality product but to asking how business can help the environment and even contribute to world peace. You will *be there* as video technology shows you the directions to twenty-first century management.

Management Live: The Video Book Users Manual

Each module, or chapter, in *Management Live: The Video Book* highlights a different topic that is central to effective management. *Management Live: The Video Book* differs from other books written about management in that it is based on the video segments. Each video segment introduces you to the module's topic in a way that involves you personally in that topic. The video segments were chosen to illustrate the *essence* of managerial activities rather than simply show managers talking to subordinates at a desk.

Each feature presented in *Management Live: The Video Book* requires you to be prepared, active and reflective about the module's main topic. You will be expected to attend class having thought about the current topic and having made a decision, or described a personal work experience. *Management Live: The Video Book* offers provocative exercises to help you become involved with each topic. There will be significant action and interaction using this book. The video segments and class preparations will often lead to in-class small-group discussions and problem-solving tasks.

The results of these activities will help you diagnose your own skills and knowledge about management and reflect on how you can strive for greater competence. Finally, carefully selected articles will point the way to how the best organizations and managers of today are preparing for the twenty-first century.

Each module in *Management Live: The Video Book* contains most or all of the seven sections described below. The sections will help you learn about management in several ways. Because each module is tailored to a specific video segment and topic, the order of the sections in each module may vary slightly.

Ready for Class: This section will help you prepare for the video and class exercise by completing a questionnaire, case, or related assignment. The "Ready for Class" sheets can be taken out of the workbook and handed in during class.

Textbook Tie-In: This section describes theories and knowledge that comprise the core of the chapter topic. "Textbook Tie-in" is designed to introduce and integrate information available in traditional textbooks with the experiential information learned from video segments, class discussion and self-reflective exercises.

Mirror Talk: Focussing on Me: An important part of twenty-first century management will be self-assessment and self-awareness. In Mirror Talk: Focussing on Me you will ask yourself probing questions about your management skills and values. The results of your "Ready for Class" exercises and classroom interactions will help focus on you, the manager of tomorrow.

Lights, Camera, Action: Management Live: "Lights, Camera, Action" introduces, shows and discusses the videos that make up the core of this learning experience. The "Lights" section introduces the video segment. The "Camera" section is the video clip itself. The "Action" section typically includes questions the viewer should consider while viewing the video segment.

Making Connections: In-Class Interactions: Participation in group discussion and decision making is a basic skill for twenty-first century managers. "Making Connections: In Class Interactions" is a small-group exercise that will be based on the video segment or "Ready For Class" exercise. In this part of the learning sequence, you and your fellow students will compare your perceptions about the topic. You will learn from the interactions of ideas and will attempt to make group decisions.

Coming to Our Senses: Making a Difference: This section of the chapter asks you to review what you have experienced in "Ready for Class," "Mirror Talk," "Lights, Camera, Action," and "Making Connections." You will be asked to step beyond the traditional intellectual questions about the topic, and focus on your feelings and sensations. What did these experiences collectively say to you? The final portion of "Coming to Our Senses: Making a Difference" asks you what you will do different or how the topic has become personally meaningful to you.

Dateline 21st Century: Headlining each topic are timely articles of importance to the manager of the future. Dateline 21st Century will be your glimpse into the future, today.

You will be using *Management Live: The Video Book* in many ways. You will be watching, interacting, reflecting and changing how you think about things. We have designed this workbook to reflect the skills you will need to be a leader who possesses direction, awareness and competence. We hope *Management Live: The Video Book* helps transport you toward enlightened twenty-first century management.

We begin our glimpse into your future as a manager by transporting you to the year 2010. The following *Wall Street Journal* articles takes some educated guesses about what life will be like in tomorrow's workplace.

Reading 1.1

DAY IN THE LIFE OF TOMORROW'S MANAGER[4]
He, or She, Faces A More Diverse, Quicker Market

By Carol Hymowitz, Staff Reporter of the *Wall Street Journal*

6:10 a.m. The year 2010 and another Monday morning has begun for Peter Smith. The marketing vice president for a home-appliance division of a major U.S. manufacturer is awakened by his computer alarm. He saunters to his terminal to check the weather outlook in Madrid, where he'll fly late tonight, and to send an electronic-voice message to a supplier in Thailand.

Meet the manager of the future.

A different breed from his contemporary counterpart, our fictitious Peter Smith inhabits an international business world shaped by competition, collaboration and corporate diversity. (For one thing, he's just as likely to be a woman as a man and — with the profound demographic changes ahead — will probably manage a work force made up mostly of women and minorities.)

Comfortable with technology, he's been logging on computers since he was seven years old. A literature honors student with a joint M.B.A./advanced communications degree, the 38-year-old joined his current employer four years ago after stints at two other corporations — one abroad — and a marketing consulting firm. Now he oversees offices in a score of countries on four continents.

Tomorrow's manager "will have to know how to operate in any-time, any-place universe," says Stanley Davis, a management consultant and author of "Future Perfect," a look at the 21st-century business world.

Adds James Maxmin, chief executive of London-based Thorn EMI PLC's home-electronics divisions: "We've all come to accept that organizations and managers who aren't cost-conscious and productive won't survive. But in the future, we'll also have to be more flexible, responsive and smarter. Managers will have to be nurturers and teachers, instead of policemen and watchdogs."

7:20 a.m. Mr. Smith and his wife, who heads her own architecture firm, organize the home front before darting to the supertrain. They leave instructions for their personal computer to call the home-cleaning service as well as a gourmet-carryout service that will prepare dinner for eight guests Saturday. And they quickly go over the day's schedules for their three- and six-year-old daughters with their nanny.

On the train during a speedy 20-minute commute from suburbs to Manhattan, Mr. Smith checks his electronic mailbox and also reads his favorite trade magazine via his laptop computer.

The jury is still out on how dual-career couples will juggle high-pressure work and personal lives. Some consultants and executives predict that the frenetic pace will only quicken. "I joke to managers now that we come in on London time and leave on Tokyo time." says Anthony Terracciano, president of Mellon Bank Corp., Pittsburgh. He foresees an even more difficult work schedule ahead.

But others believe that more creative uses of flexible schedules as well as technological advances in communications and travel will allow more balance. "In the past, nobody cared if your staff had heart attacks, but in tomorrow's knowledge-based economy we'll be judged more on how well we take care of people," contends Robert Kelley, a professor at Carnegie Mellon University's business school.

8:15 a.m. In his high-tech office that doubles as a conference room, Mr. Smith reviews the day's schedule with his executive assistant (traditional secretaries vanished a decade earlier). Then it's on to his first meeting: a conference via video screen between his division's chief production manager in Cincinnati and a supplier near Munich.

4. *The Wall Street Journal*, (March 25, 1984), p. B-1, reprinted by permission of *The Wall Street Journal*, © 1989, Dow Jones & Company, Inc. All rights reserved worldwide.

The supplier tells them she can deliver a critical component for a new appliance at a 10% cost saving if they grab it within a week. Mr. Smith and the production manager quickly concur that it's a good deal. While they'll have to immediately change production schedules, they'll be able to snare a new customer who had been balking about price.

While today's manager spends most of his time conferring with bosses and subordinates within his own company, tomorrow's manager will be "intimately hooked to suppliers and customers" and well-versed in competitors' strategies, says Mr. Davis, the management consultant.

The marketplace will demand customized products and immediate delivery. This will force managers to make swift product-design and marketing decisions that now often take months and reams of reports. "Instant performance will be expected of them, and it's going to be harder to hide incompetence," says Ann Barry, vice president-research at Handy Associates Inc., a New York consultant.

10:30 a.m. At a staff meeting, Mr. Smith finds himself refereeing between two subordinates who disagree vehemently on to promote a new appliance. One, an Asian manager, suggests that a fresh campaign begin much sooner than initially envisioned. The other, a European, wants to hold off until results of a test market are received later that week.

Mr. Smith quickly realizes this is a cultural, not strategic, clash putting a let's-do-it-now, analyze-it-later approach against a more cautious style. He makes them aware they're not really far apart and the European manager agrees to move swiftly.

By 2010, managers will have to handle greater cultural diversity with subtle human-relations skills. Managers will have to understand that employees don't think alike about such basics as "handling confrontation or even what it means to do a good day's work" says Jeffrey Sonnenfeld, a Harvard Business School professor.

12:30 p.m. Lunch is in Mr. Smith's office today, giving him time to take a video lesson in conversational Chinese. He already speaks Spanish fluently, learned during a work stint in Argentina, and wants to master at least two more languages. After 20 minutes, though, he decides to go to his computer to check his company's latest political-risk assessment on Spain, where recent student unrest has erupted into riots. The report tells him that the disturbances aren't anti-American, but he decides to have a bodyguard meet him at the Madrid airport anyway.

Technology will provide managers with easy access to more data than they can possibly use. The challenge will be to "synthesize the data to make effective decisions," says Mellon's Mr. Terracciano.

2:20 p.m. Two of Mr. Smith's top lieutenants complain that they and others on his staff feel a recent bonus payment for a successful project wasn't divided equitably. Bluntly, they note that while Mr. Smith received a hefty $20,000 bonus, his 15-member staff had to split $5,000, and they threaten to defect. He quickly calls his boss, who says he'll think about increasing the bonus for staff members.

With skilled technical and professional employees likely to be in short supply, tomorrow's managers will have to share more authority with subordinates and, in some

cases, pay them as much as or more than the managers themselves earn.

While yielding more to their employees, managers in their 30s in 2010 may find their own climb up the corporate ladder stalled by superiors. After advancing rapidly in their 20s, this generation "will be locked in a heated fight with older baby boomers who won't want to retire," says Harvard's Mr. Sonnenfeld.

4 p.m. Mr. Smith learns from the field that a large retail customer has been approached by a foreign competitor promising to quickly supply him with a best-selling appliance. After conferring with his division's production managers, he phones the customer and suggest that his company could supply the same product but with three slightly different custom designs. They arrange a meeting later in the week.

Despite the globalization of companies and speed of overall change, some things will stay the same. Managers intent on rising to the top will still be judged largely on how well they articulate ideas and work with others.

In addition, different corporate cultures will still encourage and reward divergent qualities. Companies banking on new products, for example, will reward risk takers, while slow-growth industries will stress predictability and caution in their ranks.

6 p.m. Before heading to the airport, Mr. Smith uses his video phone to give his daughters a good-night kiss and to talk about the next day's schedule with his wife. Learning that she must take an unexpected trip herself the next evening, he promises to catch the SuperConcorde home in time to put the kids to sleep himself.

Chapter 2

What Do Managers Do?

Beginning students of management often envision themselves a few years after they leave school as successful leaders, with productive work teams, the respect of their colleagues and a good shot at higher office. At the same time, they may have a very cloudy notion of how to reach their vision. "What do successful managers actually do?" is a frequently asked question among management students. Marketing students market, and accounting students crunch numbers, but how does one manage? Students of management often begin to learn the answers to such questions with textbook descriptions and definitions of managerial life.

Definitions

Managers use organizational resources to accomplish organizational goals. Managers get things done by planning, organizing, leading and controlling.

Categories of Managers

Managers may be at the top, middle, or lower level of an organization. They may be *functional managers* who are responsible for particular departments, *general managers* who oversee many departments in a division, or *project managers* who coordinate people across functional lines to complete a specific project.[1]

Managerial Skills

Effective management requires technical, human and conceptual skills.

Technical skills equip managers to perform specific tasks and teach them to employees. Thus, first-line managers are close to hands-on service delivery or production. They are valued especially for their technical competencies.

Human relation skills are necessary for managers at all levels of the organization. Because managers spend so much time interacting with others, the ability to lead, motivate and communicate is essential at all levels of management. Employees will become more committed to organizational goals when they perceive that the organization values their input and is considerate of their needs. High motivation and morale provide a competitive edge for companies that attend to human relation skills.

1. Adapted from R. L. Daft, *Management* (Chicago: Dryden Press, 1988), pg. 12-18.

Conceptual skills require managers to see the big picture. Successful upper level managers are able to combine information about people, technology, finance, competition, past performance and present circumstances to make good management decisions. While lower level managers may be called upon more for their technical expertise, middle managers for their human relations expertise, and upper level managers for their conceptual expertise, all managers must be able to use any of these skills at any moment.

Myths and Facts About Managerial Activity

A day in the worklife of a typical manager includes a broad variety of activities. Noted management researcher Henry Mintzberg follwed a large number of managers around and observed their daily routines.[2] He discovered that people outside the profession had erroneous beliefs about managerial activities. His observations revealed the following four myths about managerial behavior.

Myth	Fact
1. Managers are reflective systematic planners.	Managers jump from one problem to the next, responding to pressures of the job with little time for reflection and planning.
2. The effective manager has no regular duties to perform, but engages in primarily planning and delegation.	Managers have many duties, including presiding over ceremonies, securing "soft" information and seeing important customers.
3. Managers prefer to receive data from formal management information systems.	Managers strongly favor verbal media, especially phone calls and meetings.
4. Management is quickly becoming a science and a profession.	The manager's job is very complex and each manager has a unique system for making decisions that they themselves may not understand.

The observations and definitions presented here begin to describe the roles and activities of managers. But even after absorbing some of these textbook descriptions and observations of managerial behavior, most students still seem dissatisfied. "We understand the importance of accomplishing organizational goals through effective use of resources," they say, "but how does that happen?" Or, "We realize that successful managers must understand the big picture, the people they work with and the technical aspects of their work, but when should each be emphasized?" And, "What about me?" an inquiring students ask, "Do I have the ability to manage successfully?"

These questions go to the very core of the issue. Managing is not a static or sterile occupation. It combines rationality and order with emotion and intuition. Management is an emerging science and an activity that requires artistry and skill.

2. Henry Mintzberg, *The Nature of Managerial Work* (New York: Harper & Row, 1973).

Effective managers, it appears, must have an impressive array of attributes. They must be systematic, flexible, intuitive, self-aware and strategic. How can one person learn to do all these things well?

January 1, 2001

"The Journey from Novice to Master Manager" by Robert Quinn introduces you to the process by which one manager mastered some of the complexities of management in today's business world.

Reading 2.1
THE JOURNEY FROM NOVICE TO MASTER MANAGER[3]
By Robert Quinn

As I listen to the man sitting in front of me, my mind ran backwards across the interviews that I had just completed. His subordinates and peers had given him glowing reviews: "Born to manage," "A great role model," "He is one person I am glad to work for."

As I tried to ask him questions that would unlock the mystery behind his success, an interesting story began to unfold. It seemed to involve both a crisis and a transformation.

After graduating from a five-year engineering program in four years, he had taken a job with his current organization. He had made a brilliant start and was promoted four times in eight years. He had the ability to take a complex technical problem and come up with a better answer than anyone else could. Initially he was seen as an innovative, action-oriented person with a bright future.

After his last promotion, however, everything started to change. He went through several difficult years. For the first time he received serious negative feedback about his performance. His ideas and proposals were regularly rejected, and he was even passed over for a promotion. In reflecting on those days he said:

It was awful. Everything was always changing and nothing ever seemed to happen. The people above me would sit around forever and talk about things. The technically right

3. Adapted from R. E. Quinn, *Beyond Rational Management* (San Francisco: Jossey Bass, 1988), pg. 1-2. Reprinted with permission.

answer didn't matter. They were always making what I thought were wrong decisions, and when I insisted on doing what was right, they got pissed off and would ignore what I was saying. Everything was suddenly political. They would worry about what everyone was going to think about every issue. How you looked, attending cocktail parties — that stuff to me was unreal and unimportant...

On several occasions, the engineer's boss commented that he was very impressed with one of the engineer's subordinates. Finding the comment somewhat curious, the engineer finally asked for an explanation. The boss indicated that no matter how early he himself arrived at work, the subordinate's car was always there.

The engineer went to visit the subordinate and relayed that he had noticed that the subordinate always arrived at work before he did. The subordinate nodded his head and explained: "I have four teen-agers who wake up at dawn. The mornings at my house are chaotic. So I come in early. I read for awhile, then I write in my personal journal, read the paper, have some coffee, and then I start work at eight."

When the engineer left his subordinate's office, he was at first furious. But after a couple of minutes, he sat down and started to laugh. He later told me, "That is when I discovered perception." He went on to say that from that moment everything started to change. He became more patient. He began to experiment with participative decision making. His relationships with superiors gradu-

ally improved. Eventually he actually came to appreciate the need to think and operate in more complex ways at the higher levels of the organization...

In the end, the frustration and pain turned out to be a positive thing because it forced me to consider some alternative perspectives. I eventually learned that there were other realities besides the technical reality.

I discovered perception and long time lines. At higher levels what matters is how people see the world, and everyone sees it a little differently. Technical facts are not as available or as important. Things are changing more rapidly at higher levels, you are no longer buffered from the outside world. Things are more complex, and it takes longer to get people on board. I decided I had to be a lot more receptive and a lot more patient. It was an enormous adjustment, but then things started to change. I think I became a heck of a lot better manager.

As a manager this man was not perfect. Clearly he had his share of bad days, and during the preceding year, a bad one for the industry, he had his share of defeats. There were occasions when he got discouraged and there were times when his subordinates felt he still acted too impulsively. Nevertheless, he had a wide range of capacities and most of the time displayed an ability to call upon them in successful ways. For the most part, he had become, with considerable effort, a master of management — a person with the capacity to create excellence.

Roles That Managers Play[4]

Because the world and its organizations are changing so rapidly, the pathways to mastering management are varied and sometimes contradictory. The manager described in Robert Quinn's book *Beyond Rational Managment* had started out as a master of technical problems, but as he got promoted, this single framework was no longer sufficient for effective management. While consistency is generally regarded as a positive trait, a single strategy for managing complex organizations can omit many options that could help resolve an ongoing problem. Many of us have worked for managers who believed that all problems could be resolved through rational thinking, or friendly interaction, or political maneuvering. While these single-solution strategies sometimes work, they often result in frustrated employees who understand that several sets of values and skills are necessary to accomplish most managerial tasks. Quinn introduces the ***competing values framework,*** which stresses that managers must operate from several values that appear to be contradictory in our minds. Managers must be creative, but pay attention to detail. They must be attentive to the external environment, but maintain stability within the organization. They must support and listen to employees and also know how to use power and influence when required. Master managers are more likely to be able to behave in flexible, and sometimes contradictory ways. They can move quickly from the technical, rational thinking required to analyze computer output to the more emotional response required to empathize with the intensely personal feelings of an insecure subordinate.

We now turn our attention to your journey toward mastery of management. We will begin by exploring your values and how they translate into managerial roles that you prefer and avoid. Because each of us has different life experiences and values, we differ in ways that we play each managerial role and our ability or inclination to try each one. We tend to play roles that we are good at rather than the role that may be required in a particular situation. The first step in the journey from novice to mastery is self-awareness.

In the following exercise, please describe how you behave in several managerial situations. The resulting score will help you diagnose which managerial roles you use most frequently and which ones may be underutilized. These results will suggest certain skills that you have developed and and recommend other skills to be developed further. Because there is no "best set" of roles for a manager to play, answer the questions as honestly as possible. If a situation appears that you do not typically encounter, answer the question as if you were dealing with a similar situation that you do handle. For example, if you currently do not manage others in a work setting, you may be a member of a club, living unit, or project where you are responsible for accomplishing tasks with other people. Please answer the following questions as honestly as you can and have your answers "Ready for Class."

4. R. E. Quinn *Beyond Rational Management* (San Francisco: Jossey Bass, 1988).

Name _____

ID# _____

Section _____

Managerial Practices Survey[5]
Self Assessment

Listed below are some statements that describe behaviors that managers often use. Whether or not you have had managerial experience, indicate how frequently you might engage in the following behaviors. As a student, you may apply these statements to your activities at jobs, class projects, student organizations or interactions with roommates.

Please use the following scale to respond to each statement. Place a number from 1 to 7 in the space to the left of each of the items.

1	2	3	4	5	6	7

Very
Infrequently

Very
Frequently

As a manager, I would...

_____ 1. listen to the personal problems of subordinates.

_____ 2. keep track of what goes on in the work group.

_____ 3. influence decisions made at high levels.

_____ 4. do problem solving in creative, clever ways.

_____ 5. clearly define areas of responsibility for subordinates.

_____ 6. display a wholehearted commitment to the job.

_____ 7. hold open discussions of conflicting opinions in groups.

_____ 8. anticipate workflow problems; avoid crises.

_____ 9. compare records, reports, and so on to detect any discrepancies in them.

_____ 10. show empathy and concern in dealing with subordinates.

_____ 11. set clear objectives for the work unit.

_____ 12. search for innovations and potential improvements.

_____ 13. work on maintaining a network of influential contacts.

_____ 14. bring a sense of order and coordination to the group.

_____ 15. see that the work group delivers on stated goals.

_____ 16. encourage participative decision making in work-group sessions.

5. Adapted from R. E. Quinn, *Beyond Rational Management* (San Francisco: Jossey Bass, 1988), p. 131.

What Do Managers Do?   15

Name _____

ID# _____

Section _____

Computing Your Scores[6]

A simple worksheet will allow you to compute your scores.

A. Record on Figure 2.1 all the scores from the self-assessment exercise. For example, suppose on items number 7 and 16 you gave yourself scores of 5 and 6 next to numbers 7 and 16. On the lines under "facilitator," you would write a *5* and a *6*. Do this for all 16 items.

B. Total the two scores under each role. In the illustration given, you would add 5 plus 6 to get a total of 11. Compute the total for eight roles.

C. Divide each total by two. Continuing with the same illustration, you would simply divide 11 by 2, obtaining a result of 5.5. Put 5.5 on the blank line after the word total. Follow the same procedure for all eight roles.

6. Ibid.

Figure 2.1: Computational Worksheet for Self-Assessment

The Facilitator	The Mentor	The Innovator	The Broker
# 7 _____	# 1 _____	# 4 _____	# 3 _____
# 16 _____	# 10 _____	# 12 _____	# 13 _____
Total _____	Total _____	Total _____	Total _____

The Producer	The Director	The Coordinator	The Monitor
# 6 _____	# 5 _____	# 8 _____	# 2 _____
# 15 _____	# 11 _____	# 14 _____	# 9 _____
Total _____	Total _____	Total _____	Total _____

Name _____

ID# _____

Section _____

Self-Assessment: Drawing Your Profile[7]

Drawing your own profile is also a fairly simple process. It involves transferring your score from the worksheet to Figure 2.2 and then connecting the scores by drawing lines between them.

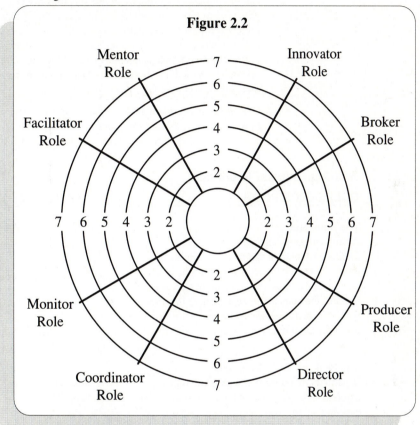

Figure 2.2

First, locate your final score for a given role. Following the example from the last set of instructions, let us assume that it is 5.5 for the facilitator role. Go to the line labeled "Facilitator Role" on the diagram. Find the circles marked with the numbers 5 and 6. Make a dot halfway between these circles.

Repeat the process for each of the remaining scores. When you are finished, there should be a small mark representing a score for each of the eight roles.

To complete your profile, draw straight lines connecting the eight scores around the circle. You should then have a complete profile.

7. Ibid.

Self-Assessment Feedback

You have completed, scored, and visually plotted your Managerial Practices Survey. Now what do your scores mean?

Each of the eight roles that managers play require different skills and each are an important aspect of managerial effectiveness. As you read the descriptions of each role and look at your completed profile, a picture of your most preferred and least preferred roles should emerge.

In general, roles in which you have scored 5 or above are most preferred roles, and those where you have scored 3 or below are least preferred roles. Any role above 5 can be considered a strength, unless it is the only very high score and is coupled with several scores under three. This may indicate that you over-utilize your most preferred role at the expense of other necessary roles. In general, roles scoring below 3 may be seen as less preferred roles and may cause difficulties on the journey to master management. A cautionary note: This is an abbreviated version of a more detailed questionnaire and should be interpreted as only a very general indicator of your relative role strength.[8]

8. Those interested in a more detailed version, consult R. E. Quinn, *Beyond Rational Management* (San Francisco: Jossey Bass, 1988).
9. Adapted from R. E. Quinn, *Beyond Rational Management* (San Francisco: Jossey Bass, 1988).

What is most important as you explore your personal role analysis is to explore how closely it coincides with your values and skills at work, and how you can become more fluent in those roles that are difficult for you to enact.

Self-Assessment Feedback[9]

ROLE DESCRIPTION	STRENGTHS	DIFFICULTIES
The Innovator Your score: _____ As an innovator, a manager is expected to facilitate adaptation and changes. Unlike the monitor role, where deduction, facts and quantitative analysis rule, the innovator role requires the manager to be a creative dreamer who sees the future, envisions innovation and packages them in inviting ways.	Ability to innovate, change, adapt	Too much: Disastrous experimentation Too little: Too conservative, oblivious to external factors
The Broker Your score: _____ Is particularly concerned with maintaining external legitimacy and obtaining resources. In carrying out this role, the manager is expected to be politically astute, persuasive, influential and powerful. Image, appearance and reputation are important. As a broker, the manager is expected to meet with people from outside the unit, to represent, negotiate, market, act as a liaison and spokesperson and to acquire resources.	Ability to influence, negotiate, acquire resources	Too much: Political expediency, lack of values Too little: Too unassertive, your ideas not implemented

Both Innovator and Broker roles are essential for managing the external environment in a flexible manner, by using power and managing change. Growth and change are accomplished in a creative manner.

ROLE DESCRIPTION	STRENGTHS	DIFFICULTIES
The Producer Your score: _____ A producer is expected to be task-oriented and work-focused and to have high interest, motivation, energy and personal drive. In this role a manager is supposed to encourage subordinates to accept responsibility, complete assignments and maintain high productivity. This usually involves stimulating unit members to better accomplish stated goals.	Ability to accomplish goals, make profit, initiate action	Too much: Low morale, human exhaustion Too little: Low productivity, weak problem solving
The Director Your score: _____ As a director, a manager is expected to clarify expectations through processes such as planning and goal setting and to be a decisive initiator who defines problems selects alternatives, establishes objectives, defines roles and tasks, generates rules and policies, evaluates performance, and gives instructions.	Ability to plan, prioritize, clarify, provide structure	Too much: Over-regulation, lack of attention to human needs Too little: Indecisive, policies unclear

Both the Producer and Director role are essential for accomplishment and productivity. The Producer and Director roles stimulate achievement through rational planning, goal setting and problem solving.

ROLE DESCRIPTION	STRENGTHS	DIFFICULTIES
The Coordinator Your score: _____ As a coordinator, a manager is expected to maintain structure and flow of the system. The person in this role is expected to be dependable and reliable. Behaviors include protecting continuity, minimizing disruptions, doing paperwork, reviewing and evaluating reports, writing budgets, and writing and coordinating plans and proposals.	Ability to provide stability, control and continuity	Too much: Perpetuates status quo without question, insensitive to change Too little: No stable systems in place
The Monitor Your score: _____ As a monitor, a manager is expected to know what is going on in the unit, to determine whether people are complying with the rules and to see if the unit is meeting its quotas. The monitor must have a passion for details and be good at rational analysis. Behaviors in this role include technical analysis, dealing with routine information and logical problem solving.	Appropriate measurement systems in place, state of the art management	Too much: procedural, sterility, careful measurement of the wrong things Too little: Inadequate information available to make decisions and measure progress

Both the Coordinator and Monitor roles are essential to the internal stability of an organization. Carefully designed internal data collection systems allow facts to be analyzed and decisions made.

ROLE DESCRIPTION	STRENGTHS	DIFFICULTIES
The Facilitator Your score: _____ The facilitator is expected to foster collective effort to build cohesion and teamwork and to manage interpersonal conflict. In this role the leader is described as process oriented. Expected behaviors include mediating interpersonal disputes, using conflict reduction techniques, developing cohesion and morale, obtaining input and participation, and facilitating group problem solving.	Ability to manage conflict, build teamwork through open discussion and participation in decision making	Too much: Unproductive group decision making, too many meetings Too little: Low morale, demotivated employees, poor communication
The Mentor Your score: _____ The mentor is expected to engage in the development of people through a caring empathetic orientation. In this role the leader is expected to be helpful, considerate, sensitive, approachable, open and fair. In acting out this role, the manager listens, supports legitimate requests, conveys appreciation and gives compliments and credit. He or she sees people as resources to be developed. The leader helps with skill building, provides training opportunities, and helps people develop plans for their own individual development.	Ability to inspire high commitment in employees, concern for developing supporting employees	Too much: Extreme permissiveness, everyone does their "own thing" without considering effect on the organization Too little: Absence of role model, development of employees not emphasized

The Facilitator and Mentor roles emphasize the flexibility of the organization to respond to the needs and motivations of its employees. Effective interaction and trust are central to developing human resources.

Roles Managers Play

Lights: Introduction to the Video Segments

Twenty-first century managers will require great flexibility to succeed in a changing work environment. Yet each individual is likely to maintain preferred roles, those they see as more valuable or appropriate for their work situation or those at which they are more skilled. In the following two video segments you will observe two managers, each with a very different basic approach to managing, yet similar in many respects.

Camera: Description of the Video Segments

1. Pat Carrigan is not your typical General Motors plant manager. For one thing she is a women in a profession dominated by men. Her background as a psychologist and researcher is unusual in this position. In Pat's factory, hourly employees are supervising themselves and helping to make crucial management decisions normally reserved for top management. Carrigan says, "It's a step toward building the factory of the future..." How does she achieve such extraordinary efficiency and maintain the loyalty and respect of hardened automobile workers? Video segment #1 will explain.

2. Hyman Rickover, the father of the nuclear submarine, was interviewed on *60 Minutes* in 1984. Admiral Rickover had almost single-handedly managed the nuclear submarine fleet, including the design, production and deployment of this crucial component of our nuclear deterrent capabilities. This Navy legend, who died in 1987, managed in some rather unorthodox ways. He refused to allow a book of Navy regulations on his ship. "If people knew their job they didn't need a book of regulations to tell them how to do it," he exclaimed in the 1984 interview. Rickover also made cadets who gave "stupid answers" sit in a broom closet for a few hours to think about their answers. He was able to stay in his job 20 years past his retirement date, even though several presidents tried to retire him. The Hyman Rickover video segment illustrates a successful manager who was most capable at specific managerial roles. What were they?

Action: What to Observe

On the following worksheet, identify which roles Pat Carrigan and Hyman Rickover use most frequently and those they use most infrequently. Describe behaviors or comments in the video segments that are the basis of your judgment.

	PAT CARRIGAN	HYMAN RICKOVER
Most Used Role:		
Least Used Role:		

Role Analysis

As you watch the two video segments, describe actions or statements that support each manager's use of thevarious management roles. Be prepared to identify what you believe to be the most used role and least used role for each segment.

Roles	PAT CARRIGAN	HYMAN RICKOVER
	Behaviors or Statements to Support Role Use	
Innovator: facilitates change		
Broker: influential negotiator		
Producer: accomplishes goals		
Director: plans & prioritizes		
Coordinator: provides stability		
Monitor: measures progress		
Facilitator: builds teamwork		
Mentor: develops employees		

Name _____

ID# _____

Section _____

Exercise 1

In your small group:

1. Choose a spokesperson.

2. Have each person share their views of the roles Carrigan and Rickover used most frequently and least frequently.

3. Your ideas about these roles may differ. Arrive at a group decision for your answers.

Support with behaviors and statements.

	PAT CARRIGAN	HYMAN RICKOVER
Most Used Role:		
Least Used Role:		

Now that you have completed your "Ready for Class Self Analysis" and watched the Pat Carrigan and Hyman Rickover video segments, please reflect on your scores, observations and discussion and what they mean to you.

Role analysis

1. My strongest role: (name of role)

2. What managerial strengths does this role offer me?

3. What is the potential difficulty that I can expect from using this role too frequently?

4. My lowest scoring role:

5. What is the potential management difficulty I can expect from using this role too infrequently?

6. What strengths can I gain from learning how to use this role more frequently?

7. How do these self-assessment scores and their accompanying strengths and weaknesses fit with your perceptions of yourself?

1	2	3	4	5
Extremely Inaccurate		Moderately Accurate		Extremely Accurate

8. Identify a boss who you thought was very good to work for. What was his/her strongest and weakest role?

Boss's name:

Organization:

Boss's strongest role:

Your strongest role:

Boss's weakest role:

Your weakest role:

Were this boss's role scores similar to yours or different?

CIRCLE ONE:	Both similar	One similar	Neither similar

Explain how the high and low role scores for each of you made it easy to work well together.

COMING TO OUR SENSES: MAKING A DIFFERENCE

 You have observed managers Pat Carrigan and Hyman Rickover in action, assessed your own role profile, talked to your classmates, and looked and read about what managers do. What have all of these images and interactions meant to you? How can these experiences help you move more quickly toward becoming a master manager? As you watched Carrigan and Rickover, which one did you identify with most closely? Are there parts of both you wish to emulate?

- What did I see that helped answer the question, What do managers do?

- What did I hear?

- What did I feel?

- What did I think?

- And now, what will I do to make a difference?

We have started our exploration of the subject of management by asking what managers do. Much of what managers do depends on their values, skills and the specific nature of the job. By observing your values and skills you can begin to take pride in your strengths and assess how you wish to develop yourself further.

For some, this chapter raises more questions about management than it answers. *Management Live: The Video Book* will introduce you to the wide variety of roles, skills and values that will result in effective management for the twenty-first century. You will be challenged to make these images and ideas meaningful for your personal and professional growth.

Chapter 3

Organizational Culture

At 3M the 11th commandment is: "Never kill a new product idea." This emphasis on innovation is supported by a story about the discovery of transparent cellophane tape. The story relates how an employee accidentally discovered the tape but was unable to get his superiors to buy the idea. Marketing studies predicted a relatively small demand for the new material. Undaunted, the employee found a way to sneak into the boardroom and tape down the minutes with his transparent tape. The board was impressed enough with the novelty to give it a try, and the cellophane tape was an incredible success.[1]

Peggy McDonald was hired on April 1st, 1984, to work in the design department of the Los Angeles Olympic Organizing Committee (LAOOC). This organization's purpose was to organize and operate the Games of the XXIIIrd Olympiad in Los Angeles, California, in 1984. Peggy wrote of her observations about the LAOOC culture during the life of that organization. (It ceased to exist at the end of the games.) She described several aspects of organizational culture. For example:

1. Alan Wilkins, *Exchange* (Fall 1981)

Dress code. The dress code stipulates that women should wear dresses and always wear stockings and "proper undergarments." Men must wear neckties at all times and should not have beards. ...One woman who was wearing long shorts one day in preparation for moving heavy boxes to the warehouse was told by an older woman in a "gross polyester floral muu-muu" that she was attired inappropriately.

The "Peter test" (named after Peter Ueberroth, the president of the LAOOC). At the time of hire, each person, no matter how comparably important or insignificant her or his position appears, is randomly assigned a country. People are told that at any time, Peter Ueberroth...could call someone into his office and ask the person to tell him everything about Somalia or Mozambique or whatever his or her assigned country is. The alleged purpose of this exercise is to have a ready source of current information should a delegate show up unexpectedly, but it clearly forces the new recruit to do homework and feel potentially pivotal to the organizaion.

Another sort of "Peter test" was announced at orientation, striking fear into the hearts of most present, especially those many years removed from school and tests. All new staff members were required to take a test administered by the president himself. The material to be tested included "everything" about the history of the Olympic Games, current, international and local news and infinite details about the LAOOC. Horror stories were told about unexpectedly being required to name the countries in Africa, the council members in Los Angeles, and the sports commissioners for 23 events at the 1984 Games. Those being tested were give 24 hours' warning.

Staff Lunches. The staff is encouraged to eat "on campus" at the "Cafe de Coubertin" named for Baron Pierre de Coubertin, founder of the modern Olympic Games. It has standard cafeteria fare, varied by the day and thoroughly unexciting. The staff, though, is offered a $2 per day subsidy to eat at the Cafe, which makes for cheap, or sometimes, free lunch. Keeping the staff in the same location for lunch presumably reduces downtime caused by lengthy drives or too many errands. It does increase camaraderie among staff, with common food to complain about. Additionally, the Cafe is used as a site for information dispersal. It sports a "Days to Go" calendar; a route map of the Torch Relay's progress, which is updated daily; and a screening room which shows inspirational Olympic newsreels at lunch. Uniforms for the Games are modelled at lunch and sports demonstrations occur weekly. It is impossible to eat regularly at the cafeteria without being genuinely excited about the Olympic Games and, by transference, the LAOOC.[2]

2. Excerpts from Peggy McDonald, "The Los Angeles Olympic Organizing Committee: Developing Culture in the Short Run," in Michael O. Jones, et al., eds., *Inside Organizations: Understanding the Human Dimension* (Newbury Park, CA: Sage, 1988) pp. 165-177.

The cellophane story is about a hero in the 3M organization, someone who persevered but took chances, who displayed loyalty but also broke corporate rules (for example, going unauthorized into the boardroom and tampering with top-management documents). It is one story among many others at 3M that tell the listener (especially the newcomer) what is valued in the corporation. It communicates that "We expect you to put your life on the line for a product, to bend the rules, to stay the pace to get things done. If you do and you succeed, you will be rewarded." It is a powerful way to tell members of the organization what some of the key values, norms and behaviors are at 3M.

This kind of story is likely to have much more impact on listeners than a written description in an employee handbook that sets out in dry technical language what 3M believes in, sanctions and rewards. Of course, such organizational and job descriptions will also be a part of the formal communication system of the organization. Dress codes, tests and challenges that psyche people up and out, activities and rituals that involve and stimulate the whole group in the organization are all part of the stuff we call **organizational culture**. We can see in Peggy McDonald's report that there also is a story aspect about the dress code and the "Peter tests" that make each of these cultural communications to anyone interested in "how we do things around here," about what is valued, punished and ignored.

So what is organizational culture? People studying the subject are discovering its complexities, and some researchers even disagree about what it is, how it can be studied and what its role in managing organizations can and should be. However, the most common view of organizational culture is that it is a set of important understandings and assumptions shared by a group of people about what is done and said in that organization in order to cope with the oportunities and problems that the group faces in getting the organization's work done and in adjusting to the environment. These cultural patterns of an organization are not usually stated directly. People in the culture may not even be aware of them. It may take an outsider's questions about why certain things are done the way they are in an organization to focus on the shared understandings that make the organization's members perceive, or think or feel or act in the accepted manner. The clues are hidden in the stories about heroes, in the manner of dress and in the strategies of the organization — especially those that tell you what is rewarded and punished, who gets the resources to do things and who does not.

Newcomers often blunder into realizing the significance of organizational culture when they do something that seems perfectly innocent or well intentioned and then find that someone else takes offense. Sometimes, the newcomer is taken aside by a fellow worker and told: "Hey, buddy, that's not the way we do things around here! You are working too hard!" or "Nobody talks to the store manager that way!" or "You cannot wear a brown suit around here!" (Remember the woman in the long shorts who was reprimanded by the woman in the muu-muu at the LAOOC.) When the newcomer recovers from his embarrassment or anger, he typically finds there is nothing in the written manual of procedure, or even in the formal briefing by his boss that hinted at the newly learned rule. It is "in between the lines," part of the fabric of the culture in the organization. Some of an organization's culture is on the surface — in the logo, the dress code, the jargon of the company, the stories. It is fairly easy to see, although only through careful detective work will its meaning be clear. The more powerful aspects of culture are typically buried much deeper beneath the surface of daily organizational life. Some of this can be teased out of the organization's language and the focus of its policies, strategies and practices. They can be discovered when we see what people in the organization define as important, when we examine what they do in a crisis.

Even more difficult to detect, even for the members of the culture themselves, are the basic beliefs and assumptions they share even without being conscious of them. These are beliefs about the way the world works, about what is truly important in life and what is not. Even though these underlying assumptions are hidden and taken for granted, they often play out in the day-to-day activities of an organization.

For example, 3M's attitudes towards taking risks and being innovative may tell us something about the organization's deep-seated beliefs about human nature, how people are motivated and how best to harness individual creativity. Those beliefs are likely to include a view that people are self-starters, can be trusted to do creative work if they are challenged and encouraged and given permission to take risks. If these beliefs were not fundamental to the organization (if, for example, the core beliefs are that people can't think for themselves, can't be trusted, must be monitored and guided every step of the way, and that the world is too dangerous a place to let people take risks), then we would probably find that even if people were told by managers to take risks, even instructed in the manuals to do so, the real messages in the culture and in the consequences for action would be, "If you step out of line, bend or break rules you will be punished." While this all sounds logical, cultural underpinnings to organizational actions are rarely obvious to members of the culture. Managers in a "suspicious" culture may say they favor risk-taking, and may even believe this to be true at a superficial, conscious level, but may be unaware of the deeper shared beliefs in the organization's culture that people can't be trusted, the world is dangerous and controlling behavior is a must. They may also wonder why there is no innovative behavior in their organization.

Corporate attitudes can lead to major contradictions between what is said and what is done. It is likely, for example, that one of the difficulties in getting equality of treatment between men and women in many organizations is because the core values and beliefs of such organizations emphasize men's contributions and roles over those of women. The assumption that a woman's place is in the home may be deeply rooted in the core values of the company.

Organizational culture often reflects earlier events and crises in the life of the organization. What is stressed as valuable in the organization is what has worked well in the past when a crisis or a major event was encountered. The early history of 3M was of a company that made a major mistake which, through innovation and risk taking, it converted into a success. The 3M company was founded to mine corundum. The quality of the ore was very low and 3M was stuck. In desperation, the owners hit on the idea of making sandpaper, which was used in Detroit automobile plants. They then invented masking tape and turned the initial mistake into a success. This theme of taking risks and overcoming mistakes runs through much of 3M's history. (The invention of Post-it Notes is a more recent example of the process by which 3M employees can champion a new idea that may benefit the company.)

Organizations do not Necessarily have Single Cultures

While many discussions of organizational culture treat it as if it were a single phenomenon — that is, there is one, homogeneous culture for a given organization (IBM or Proctor and Gamble are often given as examples) — this is not typically the case. Usually there are several subcultures, some of which may even conflict. An organization in which there appears to be a high degree of agreement about how it operates — with shared values, norms and attitudes — may, on careful investigation, be discovered to have important subcultures as well. Most notably we may find one subculture that managers share and another subculture that workers, or nonmanagement, have in common. (Workers, however, will often give lip service to the management culture.) Or, we will find a clear subculture for one department or division in a company and a different one for another department or division. This is sometimes seen when visiting, say, the engineering group and then talking to people in the marketing department of a company. There may be a distinct culture in each group and members of each culture may be hostile toward those in the other. Reports about the tensions between the Apple-II and the Macintosh groups at Apple Computer in the 1980s reveal some important differences in terms of their subcultures, even though the overall culture of Apple was strong.

Why do we Bother with Organizational Culture?

If we do not pay attention to the culture in the organizations we work in, we are likely to stumble, to miss cues, to be ignorant of much that is going on around us (and to us) in our daily lives at work. Much like power and politics in an organization, culture cannot be ignored without missing much that is subtle but important in the way things work in organizations. If we assume that being a manager and an employee in a company is solely a rational, logical experience, we are in for many surprises. In a culture, there are important codes, and attending to them draws our attention to many of the feelings expressed at work. It helps us understand the emotional side of organizational life. Culture shapes and reinforces perceptions, what we see, attend to and believe in. We need to recognize that what we might see as isolated acts or expressions of belief in an organization are often bits and pieces of larger patterns of action or more substantial clusters of what is believed to be important in the organization. We need to see the context of an act or a belief to understand its meaning. Paying attention to culture helps us do this.

Finally, culture is about *shared* assumptions and values. If we want to change what is done in an organization, we might want to change the way decisions are made, say from "tell and sell" tactics to participative decision-making. To make such changes, we need to understand the effects of the changes on the culture of the company. We must try to understand how such changes will be received by the culture. If the change seriously threatens the culture, the desired change may well fail.

READY FOR CLASS: UNDERSTANDING AN ORGANIZATION'S CULTURE

Name _____

ID# _____

Section _____

3. Adapted with permission from Gareth Morgan's *Creative Organization Theory* (Newbury Park, CA: Sage, 1989).

As you get ready to further study organizational culture, start by thinking about the culture of one of your current organizations: your business school or the business department in your college or university. Look for evidence of the culture in the images, metaphors, artifacts, beliefs, values, norms, rituals, language, stories, legends, myths and other symbolic constructs that decorate and give form to the experience of everyday life.

How would you describe the culture of your business school or major department? Try to be systematic in your analysis by identifying specific examples. Use the following worksheet to aid your analysis.[3]

1. What are the principal images or metaphors that people use to describe the organization?

2. What physical impression does the organization and its artifacts create?
   Does this vary from one place to another?

3. What kinds of beliefs and values dominate the organization? (officially, unofficially...)

4. What are the main norms (that is, the do's and don'ts)?

5. What are the main ceremonies and rituals and what purposes do they serve?

6. What language dominates everyday discourse (for example, buzzwords, cliches, catch phrases)?

7. What are the dominant stories or legends that people tell? What messages do they convey?

8. What reward systems are in place? What messages do they send in terms of activities or accomplishments that are valued?

9. What are the favorite topics of informal conversation?

10. Think of three influential people: In what ways do they symbolize the character of the organization?

11. Are there identifiable subcultures in the organization? Are they in conflict or in harmony?

12. What impacts do these subcultures have on the organization? What functions do these groupings serve for their members? Is the overall effect on the organization positive or negative?

MIRROR TALK: FOCUSSING ON ME

Following your examination of the organizational culture within your business school or major department, you may have had an opportunity in class to share your analysis with fellow students. As you dicussed the various views, you may have noted areas of both agreement and disagreement. In addition, you may have felt surprised or amused at some of the points raised by others. Talking about an organization's cultures can be fun. It can be comforting and can show us that we are in something together. It can also be disturbing, leading people to question whether they really fit in.

To further examine your school's culture do the following:

1. Review the notes you made on the culture of your business school or major department as well as any notes you made in class when you discussed the topic with fellow students.

2. Add to those notes any additional thoughts you now have about the culture of your business school or major department.

3. On a sheet of paper answer the following questions. Take a few minutes to think about each question before you write an answer.

1. Which of the major beliefs and values that you and your class identified in the class exercise:
    a. Are most important to you?
        (That is, you identify with, believe in, strongly.)
    b. Are least important to you?
        (That is, you do not feel that they matter much to you.)
    c. Why do you think these are very important
        or very unimportant beliefs and values?

2. which of the main norms (do's and don'ts) that you and your class identified in the class exercise:
    a. Have the most impact on you (on what you do; on what you feel)?
    b. Have the least impact on you (on what you do; on what you feel)?
    c. Why do you feel this way about these norms?

3. Which of the rewards and punishments in your business school's culture do you feel:
    a. Are fair to you and to others?
    b. Are unfair to you and to others?
    c. Why do you feel this way about the rewards and
        punishments in your business school's culture?

4. In what ways is the culture of your business school
    a. A help to you achieving your aims and activities?
    b. A hindrance to you achieving your aims and activities?

Finally, look over your answers to these questions and think about one issue you have been finding difficult to understand or cope with in your business school culture (for example, getting your ideas across to others; getting recognition for your work from an instructor; feeling irritated with other students whose ideas and viewpoints make them seem like they come from another planet). Note in what ways you might better understand this issue as a result of now having a better understanding of the organization's culture.

Lights

The videoclip you will see in class today is taken from a 1986 episode of the David Letterman show (a popular late-night talk show on NBC). In these scenes you will see what happens to David Letterman when he visits the General Electric corporate office in New York City shortly after GE acquired NBC, Letterman's employer. Letterman tries to enter the GE building, carrying a basket of fruit to present to GE's board of directors. He encounters resistance from GE employees and learns some interesting lessons about the parent company's culture (including a glimpse of the "GE Corporate Handshake"). To say more would spoil the experience of watching this classic episode. Enjoy the viewing!

Action: Analyzing the Cultures of GE and NBC

We get only clues about GE and NBC cultures from viewing this videoclip. It is only a snapshot of each company, seen through the eyes of the NBC cameras and scriptwritiers. However, we can become sensitized to these cultures by reflecting on what we have seen. We can form some hunches and can begin to think up questions about the cultures (especially of GE) that we might want to ask of their employees. Careful observation of even a brief display of a company's culture is important each time you enter an organization for any serious purpose such as a job interview, project consultation or study assignment. With these thoughts in mind, jot down your impressions and observations related to the following questions.

1. What artifacts (such as logos, buildings or office layouts) did you observe in this video clip?

GE:

NBC:

What might these artifacts tell you about the cultures of each company?

GE:

NBC:

2. What were the dress codes in each company?

GE:

NBC:

What might these codes tell you about each company?

GE:

NBC:

3. What seem to be important norms (do's and don'ts) in each culture?

GE:

NBC:

4. What evidence can you deduce about how things are done at NBC and GE from the video clip?

GE:

NBC:

What can you tell about each culture from these behaviors?

GE:

NBC:

5. What might be the meaning of the GE Corporate Handshake when you look at it from a   cultural perspective? (Stretch a bit here. List as many ideas as you can.)

GE:

NBC:

6. What questions would you like to ask David Letterman about NBC to get a better fix on its culture?

7. What questions would you like to ask the employees of GE, say security man Alano Ramos, about GE to get a better fix on its culture?

MAKING CONNECTIONS: IN-CLASS INTERACTIONS

In small groups in class, share your analysis of the culture of your business school or major department. After each group member has shared his or her analysis, talk about what there is in common and what is different in your analysis of the culture.

Discuss in your group ways to represent visually, in creative and informative ways, the consensus you reach about the culture of your business school or department. Include in your image any minor differences in the way various members of your group see the organization's culture.

Consider using flipchart paper to present the visual image and information you have agreed on. Record major points and use images to portray the organizational culture. Do not clutter the picture with masses of information. Let your imaginations run. Complete the image with a single symbol that, in your group's opinion, captures the essence of the culture you are describing.

Share your chart with the rest of the class. With the help of your instructor, compare and contrast the charts prepared by each group.

COMING TO OUR SENSES: MAKING A DIFFERENCE

One Organization's Culture

Organizational culture is really about language — the language that tells us about life in organizations. This language helps us hear, speak, read and see important things that go on in organizations. Such things are often forgotten or taken for granted when we focus only on the work we do or the machines we operate. It is a complex and subtle language. We need to learn it, just as we must learn other work languages, such as those for computers, accounting, marketing, production or human resources. It is a language that challenges, teases, frustrates and educates us. It is never fully understood by people in organizations, and it is constantly changing. It is perhaps best approached through a combination of intuition and logic, playful images and serious analysis, paying attention to feelings as well as facts. When exploring an organization's culture or cultures, you are looking for patterns rather than isolated features, although it may be the single aspects (a story, a slogan, a logo, a layout of offices) that you first focus on. To conclude this study of organizational culture, do the following:

1. Read the instructions that follow. If you think it will help you, put the instructions on an audiotape so you can play them and then act on them without having to refer to notes. Alternatively, make a few notes on a card of the steps involved, so you can move through them smoothly. It is important to do the exercise in the sequence noted and to give some serious time to it. The exercise can be done in 20 to 30 minutes. Use more time if you wish.

2. Find a quiet place to sit where you will not be interrupted. Have with you a sheet of paper, and the "Coming to our Senses" Worksheet, some colored pens or pencils and if you wish, your notes from the class discussions. You can put on some of your favorite music if you want to do so. When you have all this together and are comfortably seated, take a few moments to relax. Close your eyes. Feel your body's weight in the chair. Feel your feet on the floor. Kick off your shoes. Clear your mind of the issues and tensions of the day. When you are ready start to play with some ideas about organizational culture.

Without moving from where you are, or writing down or drawing anything yet, try to get a picture in your mind's eye of what your ideal organizational culture would be like, the one you would most like to work and live in when you graduate. What would be its main values and beliefs? What would be the norms for behavior? What would it reward? What kinds of artifacts would you like it to emphasize? What would a good slogan for it be? What would its hero stories focus on? What kinds of people would be heroes? When you have played around with these ideas and questions, open your eyes and pick up one of the pens and this paper.

3. Sketch a picture on the worksheet that represents your ideal organization. In other words, show what your ideal organizational culture looks like. You need not be an artist to do this. Just draw something that conveys to you what your ideal organizational culture is all about. You can use both words and drawings. You can look around later for cartoons or materials in magazines or newspapers to make a collage if you like. Is your ideal culture best captured in several colors? Does it resemble some particular animal or mix of animals, or a person or persons? Sketch your ideas with a sense of ease and enjoyment, but try to make the drawing a reflection of how you see, in your mind's eye, your ideal organizational culture.

4. Write on the worksheet the emotions you feel or imagine you will feel being in that ideal culture. List the words or phrases that capture this for you (happy, comfortable, exciting, whatever). Try to capture what your organizational culture would feel like.

5. Jot down the name of a song or some lyrics from a song or write your own song words to represent the culture you would ideally like to work in. In other words, describe what your ideal organizational culture would *sound* like.

6. Put on this worksheet the symbol or image that could stand as a shorthand summary of what your ideal organizational culture is. This could be the image you keep in your mind to remind you of your preferences when you are out interviewing for a job. The symbol will remind you to pay attention to culture when you are in organizational settings.

7. Finally, list on the worksheet three steps you will take in the next month to make yourself more skillful in paying attention to the culture(s) of organizations you interact with. (An example might be to look for indicators of organizational culture in the next movie you watch.) Leave space next to each step to record your actions when you take them.

Many books and articles have been written about corporate culture. It has been a hot topic in management circles for almost a decade. We are becoming increasingly aware of how complex the concept is and how difficult it is to see and understand, let alone manage. Most of the writing on corporate culture focusses on large organizations, and on the managers within these organizations. The following article, "Creating a New Company Culture" from *Fortune* magazine, is about just such an organization. The article emphasizes the company's realization that change must incorporate and even begin with inputs from and consultation with people doing the lower level tasks in the company.

As the world of organizations becomes more complex and diverse, the importance of organizational culture will become increasingly significant. People with different personal values, beliefs and practices have always come together to act out the culture of the work place. However, when we add diversity of national cultures, as organizations go international and global into the next century, we will witness effects that will require a sensitivity to managing culture that is much more prevalent than is the case today.

Reading 3.1

CREATING A NEW COMPANY CULTURE[4]

by Brian Dumaine

So it has come to this: You've automated the factory, decimated the inventory, eliminated the unnecessary from the organization chart, and the company still isn't hitting on all cylinders — and you've got an awful feeling you know why. It's the culture. It's the values, heroes, myths, symbols that have been in the organization forever, the attitudes that say, Don't disagree with the boss, or Don't make waves, or Just do enough to get by, or For God's sake, don't take chances. And how on earth are you going to change all that?

If your company is like a great many others, it will have to step up to this challenge. The changes businesses are being forced to make merely to stay competitive — improving quality, increasing speed, adopting a customer orientation — are so fundamental that they must take root in a company's very essence, which means in its culture.

This news depresses those who remember corporate culture as the trendy concern of the mid-Eighties, when consultants ranging from the super-sober to the wacky tried to change companies' cultures and almost always found they couldn't. But take heart. An increasing number of enterprises are at last figuring out how to alter their cultures, and more than ever are doing it.

The basic lesson sounds like a Confucian principle: Cultural change must come from the bottom, and the CEO must guide it. Despite the apparent contradiction, Du Pont, Tandem Computers, and many others are making that idea work. Says Du Pont CEO Edgar Woolard: "Employees have been underestimated. You have to start with the premise that people at all levels want to contribute and make the business a success."

The CEO must show the direction of the change to make sure it happens coherently. But a cultural transformation is a change in the hearts and minds of the workers, and it won't happen if the CEO just talks. David Nadler, the president of Delta Consulting Group, warns of the plexiglass CEO syndrome: "CEOs encase their mission statement in plexiglass, hand it out, and people laugh. You have to change the way the person who assembles the machine or designs the product acts." This means the CEO must live the new culture, become the walking embodiment of it. He must also spot and celebrate managers and employees who exemplify the values he wants to inculcate.

No cultural change happens easily or quickly. Figure five to ten years for a significant improvement — but since the alternative may be extinction, it's worth a try. Here's how the most successful companies are changing their cultures today:

• **BEYOND VISION.** Yes, a CEO must promulgate a vision, but the most brilliant vision statement this side of Paraguay won't budge a culture unless it's backed up by action. At a major manufacturer, a manager who preached quality found that a part in the tractors coming off his assembly line was defective and would burn out after 300 hours of use rather than the specified 1,000 hours — a problem the customer wouldn't notice for quite a while. The manager could ship the tractors and make his quarterly numbers, or he could fix the flaw. He decided to fix the flaw. His people now know he's serious about quality.

Du Pont CEO Woolard, who preaches that "nothing is worthwhile unless it touches the customer," understands that communicating isn't enough. At a number of his plants he has a program called Adopt a Customer, which encourages blue-collar workers to visit a customer once a month, learn his needs, and be his representative on the factory floor. As quality or delivery problems arise, the worker is more likely to see them from the customer's point of view and help make a decision that will keep his "adopted child" happy.

Management at Florida Power & Light is changing its culture from that of a bureaucratic backwater to one that worships quality and service. The company shows it is serious by giving even the lowliest employees extraordinary freedom to practice that religion. Example: The utility discovered that its meter readers suffered more on-the-job injuries than any other type of employee, and they were nasty ones — dog bites. The meter readers in Boca Raton wanted to form a team to study the problem. Under the old culture, management would have scoffed at such a notion as a waste of time. Says executive vice president Wayne Brunetti: "It would have been so easy for us to reject this kind of idea." But the new ethos allowed the meter readers to take the initiative. They formed a team of ten who surveyed households, found out which ones had fierce Fidos, and then programmed hand-held computers to beep just before a visit to a dangerous address. Dog bites (and absenteeism) are down, and morale (and service) is up.

• **ALTER HISTORY.** A company with the wrong history and myths can get itself in big trouble. For years after Walt Disney's death his ghost stalked the halls of the company's studios in Burbank, California, causing executives to freeze in their tracks and wonder, "What would Walt have done?"

These hero worshipers were driving the studio into the ground with an outdated line of family flicks. Realizing that sometimes history can't be changed without changing the players, CEO Michael Eisner came aboard and cleared the deck, bringing in new managers, most of whom had never met Disney. The new crew, freed of the spectral overseer, began to create a culture that was more sophisticated than stodgy, more adventurous than cautious, more ambitious than content. They have turned the company around by (among other moves) daring to make grown-up films like The Color of Money and Ruthless People, which would have irked old Walt.

Can something as amorphous as history be changed without spilling blood? Consider what a FORTUNE 500 manufacturer did with a factory that had a history of poor quality, hostile labor relations, and terrible productivity. The company hired a consultant who started out by talking with the employees. They eagerly told him about Sam, the plant manager who was a 300-pound gorilla with a disposition that made King Kong look like Bonzo the chimp.

One time Sam examined a transmission, didn't like the work he saw, picked up a sledgehammer, and smashed it to pieces. A worker summoned to Sam's office threw up on the way. Another time Sam drove his car into the plant, got up on the roof, and started screaming at his workers. One worker, fed up, poured a line of gasoline to the car and lit it.

The stunned consultant made an appointment to see the plant manager. When he walked into the office he saw a slim, pleasant-looking man behind the desk; his name was Paul. "Where's Sam?" asked the consultant. Paul, looking puzzled, replied, "Sam has been dead for nine years."

From then on Paul and the consultant realized they had a serious problem. For years Paul had been trying to instill a sense of fairness and participation, but the plant's nightmarish history was so strong his efforts had failed. To cope, Paul and his supervisors sat down with groups of eight or ten assembly workers to discuss the plant's history — 300-pound Sam and all. Just discussing it helped clear the air. Paul also tried hard not to do anything Sam would have done. Once, while on the noisy shop floor, he abruptly pointed at a worker, commanding him to throw away a coffee cup left near a machine. Paul merely thought he was taking care of a safety hazard. The workers on the floor, mindful of the hateful Sam, thought something like, "Ah, he's just another militaristic S.O.B. who loves spit and polish." Better for Paul to have tossed the cup away himself — a small gesture, yet that and a thousand other subtle messages will eventually help transform a culture. After four years of effort, Paul's plant this fall won his company's top award for quality.

• SYMBOLS, SYMBOLS, SYMBOLS. As Paul learned, executives often underestimate the power symbolic gestures have on workers. Taking the corporate jet to a Hawaiian retreat to discuss cost cutting isn't exactly going to send the right message to the troops.

At Tandem, the computer company in Cupertino, California, a general manager once told CEO Jimmy Treybig that he wanted to fire an employee. Treybig said OK, but first find out why the person wasn't performing. The general manager discovered the employee had serious family problems and decided to give him another chance, sending a signal to everyone else in the company that we treat people around here with consideration. Says Treybig: "You have to keep remembering what your company is. All your work is done by your people."

Something as simple as an award can help make a culture more innovative. In Japan, Sharp rewards top performers by putting them on a "gold badge" project team that reports directly to the company president. The privilege instills pride and gets other employees scrambling for new ideas and products in the hope that they too may make the team.

Awards can also encourage risk taking. About a year ago, the people in Du Pont's relocation department — who help move executives to new cities — thought they could boost productivity by installing a new computer system. The experiment failed, but rather than chastise those who suggested it, the company in November presented them with a plaque that told them. We're proud of your effort and hope you try again as hard in years to come.

• CREATE UNIVERSITIES. Michael Beer, a Harvard business school professor, urges CEOs to identify models within the corporation. Scour the company to find some maverick manager who has figured out how to do it right — achieving high quality, good morale, innovative products. Then hold up this department or factory as a kind of university where employees can learn how others have succeeded. It's important not to force managers to adopt everything the university offers. Let them choose what works best for them.

In a study of six FORTUNE 500 companies that wanted to change their cultures, Beer found the only one that truly succeeded used the model approach. "With this one," says Beer, "the change began way before the CEO became fully aware of it. It was started in a small plant by some innovative managers. The top learned about it from the lowest level and spread the best practices around the company."

A caveat: The model concept works only when top management believes that all its employees have the ability to learn and grow. Too often a company stereotypes its blue-collar workers as dumb, inarticulate, and mindlessly loyal to archaic values like macho exhibitionism and anti-intellectualism. Shake it. Says Du Pont group vice president Mark Suwyn: "These people manage their lives well outside the factory. They sit on school boards or coach Little League. We have to create a culture where we can bring that creative energy into the work force."

Du Pont considers its plant in Towanda, Pennsylvania, which makes materials for printed circuitboards and other products, a model of the kind Beer is talking about. The plant, organized in self-directed work teams, lets employees find their own solutions to problems, set their own schedules, and even have a say in hiring. Managers call themselves facilitators, not bosses. Their main job is to coach workers and help them understand the tough, external market forces that demand a dedication to quality, teamwork, and speed. Over the past four years productivity at Towanda is up 35%.

Last spring Du Pont surveyed 6,600 of its people, including some at Towanda, and found that flexible work hours were a top priority. Working mothers and single parents said it was hard to cope with the kids while keeping to a rigid plant schedule. A team at Towanda got together and devised a novel solution: Take vacation time by the hour. During slack times when three of the four team members could easily handle the job, one could take off a few hours in the afternoon to go to a school play or bring a sick kid to the doctor. Today other Du Pont workers and managers visit Towanda to learn about flextime. A few have already borrowed it for their own plants.

Getting the most out of the university idea, CEO Woolard has found it helps to assign different goals of excellence to various Du Pont factories. He may tell the manager of one plant to be the best in team building, another the best in employee benefits, and a third the safety leader. As they improve, he holds up their accomplishments as examples to others. Says he: "It's win-win. You don't have to say one plant is a dog."

• **TRUST STARTS FROM WITHIN.** After a decade of restructuring, layoffs, and astronomical CEO salaries, worker trust has taken it on the chin. One of the biggest cultural challenges is to persuade workers to get religion again. It won't be easy. Making an angry, distrustful worker a believer requires fiddling with deep-rooted values. As almost any psychiatrist will tell you, it's a Herculean task to change a single individual. So imagine what it takes to change the beliefs of thousands.

Stephen Covey, a consultant to IBM, Hewlett-Packard, and other major companies, and author of The 7 Habits of Highly Effective People, believes every individual from the CEO down must realize that trust starts from within himself. Says he: "It's ludicrous to think that you can build trust unless people view you as trustworthy." In his seminars Covey gets managers to examine their deepest motives and to realize the importance of integrity and openness. And it's not all touchy-feely. Says Covey: "The best way our clients save money is to increase the span of control. When people trust you, you don't have to ride them, and that means fewer managers can oversee more people."

A manager can destroy a lot of trust by acting as if he's better than the people who work for him. Tandem CEO Treybig remembers suggesting that a couple of visiting managers spend a half day on the assembly line. They balked, thinking it a waste of time to mingle with blue-collar workers. "It was like you offered them syphilis," Treybig says.

He thought the idea made sense because much of Tandem's long-term success, he believes, comes from treating people as equals. For the past 15 years Tandem every Friday afternoon has put on its legendary get-togethers, once known as beer busts but now called popcorn parties (the Tandemites don't drink like they used to). Here Treybig and his top managers mix with the troops and exchange ideas about what's bad, what's good, and what can be done better in the company. As a bonus, employees from different parts of the business share ideas about the latest technologies. Four times a year Treybig spends five days in different resorts around the country with a couple of hundred people from all levels of the corporation. They talk business, play, drink beer until 2 A.M., and generally learn to trust each other. Says Treybig: "They'll go back and tell fellow employees that you care about people."

Du Pont CEO Woolard argues that the best way to create a more trusting environment is to reward the right people. "The first thing people watch," says he, "is the kind of people you promote. Are you promoting team builders who spend time on relationships, or those who are autocratic?"

Covey agrees, adding that managers should tailor reward systems to recognize team effort rather than individual accomplishment. As the wrong way to do it, he cites a CEO who would call his managers into his office each week to talk about team spirit. At the end of the meeting he'd point to a large painting of racehorses with photos of the managers' faces pasted over the thoroughbreds' heads. Then he'd announce, "So and so is ahead in the race to win the trip to Bermuda." Says Covey: "It nullified everything he said earlier."

Trying to change an institution's culture is certain to be frustrating. Most people resist change, and when the change goes to the basic character of the place where they earn a living, many people will get upset. Says the University of Pittsburgh's Kilmann: "If you talk about real change and people aren't getting uptight and anxious, they don't believe you." Some will fight. After months of working on cultural change with employees of a company, Kilmann asked the group to write down what they were doing differently. One manager wrote: "I wore a different color tie."

Managers seeking a way to think about the process might reflect that a company trying to improve its culture is like a person trying to improve his or her character. The process is long, difficult, often agonizing. The only reason people put themselves through it is that it's correspondingly satisfying and valuable.

Chapter 4

Organizational Theory

> Bureaucracy tends to be position-centered in that authority derives from position and status or rank is critical. Post entrepreneurial organizations tend to be more person-centered, with authority deriving from expertise or from relationships.[1]

We live most of our lives in organizations. They provide the context for our careers and for many of our social activities. The YMCA is an organization, as are environmental groups like the Sierra Club, a corporation like General Motors and the fraternities and sororities on your campus. While organizations differ in their goals, size and wealth and structure, all organizations seek to accomplish things through the arrangement and coordination of tasks and people. Where we can do things by ourselves, we do not need organizations. However, very few situations do not call for some organizational contact or arrangement.

The purposes of organized efforts are influenced by those in the organization who wield power. Organizational goals are also affected by events of the past, the history and culture of the organization, the environment in which it operates and the organization's future prospects.

1. Rosabeth Moss Kanter, *When Giants Learn to Dance* (New York: Simon & Schuster, 1989), p. 353.

Analyzing the ways in which organizations work helps us understand the activities and events in our daily lives in and around organizations. For example, it is probably not too difficult for you to recall at least one time that you were treated rudely by a department store clerk. "I'm sorry," the clerk may have said with obvious annoyance. "We can't replace that item... it is out of stock;... it is against company policy;... it is not my responsibility to make a decision, please take it to the supervisor on the fourth floor!" You know, of course, what can happen when you find the supervisor on the fourth floor. "No, that is not my responsibility, please....!" Why do you think the clerk was unpleasant and avoided helping you? Was he or she simply a poor communicator? Possibly, or was the clerk just having a bad day? That is also possible. Except you may be aware that your acquaintances have had similar unpleasant encounters with this clerk or with other clerks in the same store. Are the clerks poorly trained, then? That is a reasonable explanation. However, if such behavior is the rule among both supervisors and clerks, an organizational issue may be at the root of the problem. What might these organizational causes be? One possible explanation is poor channels of communication in the organization. Another name for this problem is an ineffective communication structure. It can be enlightening to talk to senior managers of a department store like the one in our example. They might tell you that the customer is their primary concern, that they want to do everything possible to keep customers happy and are continually sending memos to department heads to emphasize this point. Trouble is, the message gets blocked along the way, or is distorted when translated into instructions sent (often again by memo) through the chain of command to those closest to the customer — the sales clerk.

Another possibility is that the senior managers are saying one thing in their memos — treat the customer well — but are doing something else. What happens when the clerks accept returns of damaged or unacceptable merchandise from customers? If the organization is striving to control costs and, therefore, considers returned merchandise an unacceptable expense to the company, it is likely that management will reward the uncooperative behavior of the sales clerks. What the organization may actually *punish* would be pleasant and quick handling of a customer's complaint. So the organization may state official goals such as serving customers well but operate according to other goals such as controlling costs.

Many organizations are sufficiently complex that their senior managers may not realize the existence of contradictions between stated policies and actual practice. The contradictions may escape notice among the many goals, the multiple levels of hierarchy and the many different perspectives within the organization. A slightly different explanation for the poor customer service is the existence of a battle over the customer service policy. The sales department may be encouraged to sell, sell, sell and may be criticized when returned goods hurt the sales record. The buying department, meanwhile, may have a goal of purchasing high quality merchandise and want to know what is not up to standard. That department's interest would be to have clerks accept faulty merchandise so it can be examined. The accounting department might be aligned with sales, wanting to discourage returns to keep costs down. The result is an internal struggle over the company's policy toward its customers. The outcome of the conflict will be influenced by which senior managers have the most power. Can the sales vice president be more persuasive than the merchandising vice president? Is there a workable coalition between sales and accounting managers to defeat the merchandising department's goals? Does the chief executive officer have a process for resolving these differences, for pulling the different goals of the departments together to minimize conflict and keep the company moving forward? These are all organizational issues. And we thought that one uncivil sales clerk just needed training in communications skills!

Organizational theory and analysis focuses on the way tasks and people are arranged to get work done — to accomplish the goals and serve the interests of people in and around the organization. An important question is whether people exist to serve organizations or whether people are the resources that organizations need to function and survive. This is not a trivial issue. People join organizations to accomplish things they cannot do alone. They join organizations to work toward their dreams, to make a living, to make things happen. It might seem obvious then that organizations exist for people. However, many people's experience in organizational life does not bear this out. Some members of organizations feel like no more than cogs in a giant machine. We will illustrate this later in the video clip from the movie *Modern Times*. Even as a student you may identify with this cog-in-a-machine feeling when you are in the middle of a school term bouncing from one midterm exam to another!

Whatever the answer to this question of organizational purpose, a fundamental issue of organizational design regards how the arrangement and coordination of people and tasks affect the people in the organization. Much of the current work in the design of organizations is focussed on making them more fit to compete in a global environment, more adaptable to rapid changes in the economic and political environment and more compatible with work forces that are increasingly diverse and well educated.

Our textbook tie-in will focus on organizations as processes rather than "things" or concrete realities. Organizations are only in a limited way the buildings, plants and offices that we associate with them. It is the managing of the processes of organizing that are important. Organizations evolve as they interact with their environments, and their evolution occurs in the context of economic and social history. Successful economic activity requires that individuals coordinate their activities. This can be done through markets, where coordination is effected through the way people influence each other through prices they will pay for goods and services. Coordination can also be accomplished through contract negotiations. In small organizations, coordination can be accomplished through personal interactions such as the leadership of managers and interpersonal communications. Formal organizations are a means of coordination that involves efforts to minimize dependence on any particular individuals or situations. It is a way to get things done in a predictable way.

In the last 40 years, researchers have identified and labelled two basic building blocks of organizational design: the mechanistic and the organic systems of coordination. North American automobile manufacturing plants with their highly routinized assembly lines are excellent examples of mechanistic organizational systems. In contrast, the early versions of many successful electronics firms, such as the Apple Computer organization, have been described as organic, free-flowing organizations. Organizations are never purely mechanistic or purely organic in design; all are hybrids of these basic forms. Some parts of an organization may be mechanistic (for example the manufacturing plant) and others may be organic (for example, the research and development department). Coordinating these differences usually requires some blend of organic and mechanistic system components.

Your text will likely discuss the characteristics of mechanistic and organic systems of coordination. We will briefly outline some of them here. Mechanistic forms of organization typically have routine technologies that are easy to understand. Activities of workers are highly specialized, with each individual doing a specific task over and over again. The workers' activities are also programmed, with each step (usually there are only a few and they are easily learned) laid out in a fixed sequence. The technology and operation of a fast food restaurant provides a good picture of this form of organization. The organization is arranged in a formalized hierarchy and is governed by a policy manual — possibly called the "Company Bible" — that prescribes all the responses people are to make to situations that arise in the course of a typical work day.

Communication is both formal and unidirectional in the mechanistic form of organization. Orders flow down from the top of the hierarchy and information on activities flow back up the organization through designated channels. The roles of individuals, workers, supervisors and managers are prescribed and are not expected to be tampered with. One works almost exclusively in one's role at one's task. Stepping outside these boundaries does not make sense to the senior management and may be seen as disruptive. The machine runs most smoothly when all the parts function according to plan. The mechanistic form of organization make more sense when the organization's technology is predictable and well understood, and the environment is stable and contains no surprises.

In organic systems, there is much less emphasis on prepackaged and stable technologies. In fact, the way tasks are done and the manner in which supplies are transformed into products or services is often unpredictable and difficult to understand. There is a dynamic interaction between people and the organization's production process. A "Company Bible" would make no sense in this kind of organization. Events and ideas change too rapidly to have a policy manual that tries to address every eventuality in the organization. (Imagine the size of the manual — assuming people had time to compile it, let alone be able to read through it!)

There is no formal hierarchy in the organic system. People come together in teams to figure out what needs to be done and how to do it. Communications flow up, down and sideways in the organization. Meetings are a central mechanism for coordinating information and activities. Jobs shape themselves, people create and change roles to meet the needs of the situation. Emphasis is on expertise and knowledge rather than position in a hierarchy and seniority. Whereas mechanistic organizations use departmentalization as a way to coordinate, organic organizations rely on collaboration to define and redefine roles as the task requires. The organic system is a response to unpredictable technology and a rapidly changing environment.

The environment that an organization functions in helps shape the way its activities are coordinated. As companies grow, they tend to segment, with different parts of the organization doing different tasks. Each component of the organization faces its own environment, develops its own system of coordination, sets its own goals and attracts its own kinds of people with compatible expertise and styles of work. These components, or subsystems, typically resemble either mechanistic or organic forms of organization depending on the technology of their work and the environments they face. While most organizations require some departmentalization, the resulting challenge to managers is to integrate the subsystems so that each can do its job while still contributing to the overall aims of the organization.

This is an essential challenge for managers of systems. They need to allow growth and flourishing of different specialties, while ensuring that the whole operation thrives. In a simple, stable environment, the mechanistic approach to integrating the subsystem can work. In a complex, turbulent environment, however, the management team needs to also use organic system processes. Instead of a manual and a hierarchy, these managers must use teams of specialists, troubleshooters, intensive leadership and even specific permanent structures such as the matrix structure to make things happen effectively for the whole organization. (The reading, "Managers of Meaning: From Bob Geldof's BandAid to Australian CEOs", at the end of this chapter, brings these management issues alive.)

Name _____

ID# _____

Section _____

Your university or college is one example of an organization. So is the faculty or department in which you've chosen to major. The latter is a component of the larger organization. However, we can easily see that what we call our organization, where we draw its boundaries, depends on our perspective and the questions we want to answer. The president of the university sees the university's business school as a department of his or her organization. The dean of the business school can agree that this is a college department, but views it as central to many of the dean's management concerns and it is the organization for his or her faculty members and the students in the B-school.

As preparation for this module on organizational theory and analysis let us focus on the business school in your university or college. Answer the following questions, using what you know about your business school:

1. What are the goals of the business school?

2. Note and define four common ways an organization's activities can be coordinated. (Check your text for details about coordination strategies if you need to.)

3. How are the activities of your business school coordinated? (Make some guesses if you do not know this precisely.)

4. Suppose you were a student in a B- school where you were covering the same material in different courses or were frequently writing seven midterms in two-day bursts, what might you infer about the structure and design of the organization? Why might this occur in B-school organizations?

MIRROR TALK: FOCUSSING ON ME

Name _____

ID# _____

Section _____

Suppose you could design an organization that perfectly matched your abilities and needs and your views of what organizational life should be for people in the 1990s. Imagine that you could set it up any way you wished and were not constrained by limited resources or past history and culture. Write a paragraph below that describes that ideal organization. What would be its goal, its structures, its setting? What kind of people would it hire? Where and how would you fit into the organization?

Now that you have written about your ideal organization, read it over and answer the following questions.

1. What can you infer from this paragraph about what you value in a real organization? Note the key points for yourself, the purposes, activities and outcomes that are important to you.

2. What do you not value in real organizations? That is, what purposes, activities and outcomes that you do not want to be involved in or associated with?

3. Write a slogan or draw a picture that summarizes or captures the essence of what you want out of your organizational life when you graduate. Let your imagination flow. (You might want to keep this slogan or picture somewhere to remind you or your ideal for the future.)

MAKING CONNECTIONS: IN-CLASS INTERACTION

2. Excerpted with permission from Peter J. Frost, "Experiencing Mechanistic versus Organic Systems: Adding Affect to Students' Conceptual Grasp of 'Abstract' Organizational Concepts," *Organization Behavior Teaching Review*, 14, III (1989/ 90), pp. 87-90.

Your instructor will give you some instructions to "warm up" to the concepts of mechanistic and organic systems. Following this warm up you will be assigned to either a mechanistic, an organic or a judging subgroup. Then follow these instructions:[2]

Mechanistic and Organic Subgroups

Think about the concept you have been assigned to deal with. Take note of its characteristics. You will be asked in 20 minutes to act out this concept in front of the other groups and the judges. Your presentation should convey to those watching the demonstration the characteristics and nuances of the concept. Your presentation will be a maximum of 5 minutes. Judges will assess your presentation in terms of accuracy to the definition of the concept, the creativity with which you represent the concept and the quality of the presentation itself.

Judges' subgroup: You will be given your instructions by the class instructor.

At the close of the exercise, you will be given an opportunity to discuss the exercise.

LIGHTS, CAMERA, ACTION: MANAGEMENT LIVE!

Name _____

ID# _____

Section _____

This video segment is the opening sequence of *Modern Times*, a classic movie starring Charlie Chaplin, one of the greatest comedians of the twentieth century. The focus of this sequence is Chaplin's experiences as a worker on the assembly line of a huge manufacturing plant in the 1930s. While the story is set in another era, the social commentary about life in an organization has many parallels to our contemporary work scene. At times the actions in the movie are hilarious; at other times, Chaplin's adventures evoke sadness and anger.

Action

As you view the video segment answer the following questions:

1. What is the structure of the organization Charlie Chaplin works in?

2. What issues about organizational life are emphasized in this sequence?

3. What are the parallels between this slice of organizational life and the experience of work in modern manufacturing organizations?

4. What have we learned about managing organizations in recent years that might prevent the work experiences that Charlie Chaplin had?

Name _____

ID# _____

Section _____

Suppose you have been asked to summarize the purposes and consequences of systematically organizing tasks and people to get work done. Your views will appear on a TV special on the "Organized World of Work." As you prepare for this presentation, you mentally review what you have learned about organizational theory and analysis from your text and your class lectures and exercises. You also reflect on your own experiences as a worker or a participant in various organizations (for example, as a student in college). Out of these thoughts will come the essence of your presentation in front of the TV cameras.

1. What have you identified as the most important things about when someone wants to manage the design of an effective organization?

2. What does it feel like to work in:

    a. A well designed organization? Why?

    b. A poorly designed organization? Why?

3. Give one brief example that describes for you (and, of course, for your TV listener) the best organization you have worked in or heard about. (This will be the example you can draw on for your TV interview!) Sketch the example in a way that shows clearly why this is/was such an effective organization.

Organizations of the twenty-first century will need to be competitive, flexible and compassionate if they are to survive the challenge of that era. They will need to harness the ingenuity and inventiveness of individuals while at the same time capturing and delivering the synergy that comes from team efforts within or even across organizational forms. David Limerick captures this tension with the term "collaborative individualism." Organized activity will be more like baseball than basketball, if Limerick's vision is correct. We will need strong individual efforts aimed at strengthening the output of the whole team and we will need collaborative efforts to get difficult tasks accomplished.

Twenty-first century managers will need a sophisticated sense of organizational design and a willingness to lead others through new forms of coordination to accomplish organizational goals, rewarding the successful efforts of others along the way. David Limerick's article on Australian CEOs gives a good sense of what this world of leaders and organizations looks like.

It will not be an easy world in which to be a manager. In some senses it is the manager who may find herself caught in some of the pressures and dilemmas that Charlie Chaplin displayed so evocatively for the assembly line worker. By this we mean, that for managers, like Chaplin's worker, life seems to be moving ever faster to a seamless world of never-ending activity. This can create stresses and strains that leave people exhausted and hooked on their work, just as Chaplin was "hooked" on his. The real challenge may be to design organizations that control this relentless pressure on managers and others and give people a chance to balance their lives between work and other activities. It cannot be done by intention alone. We need to design our organizational systems to make it happen.

Rosabeth Moss Kanter captures this tension in an amusing way in her book *When Giants Learn to Dance*.[3] The organizational game, as she describes it, puts heavy and often conflicting demands on people:

> Think strategically and invest in the future — but keep the numbers up today.
>
> Be entrepreneurial and take risks — but don't cost the business anything.
>
> Continue to do everything you're currently doing even better — and spend more time communicating with employees, serving on teams and launching new products.
>
> Know every detail of your business — but delegate more responsibility to others.
>
> Become passionately dedicated to visions and fanatically committed to carrying them out — but be flexible, responsive and able to change direction quickly.
>
> Speak up, be a leader, set the direction — but be participative, listen well and cooperate.
>
> Throw yourself wholeheartedly into the entrepreneurial game and the long hours it takes — and stay fit.
>
> Succeed, succeed, succeed — and raise terrific children.

3. New York: Simon and Schuster, 1989, pp. 20-21.

The challenge is there for the twenty-first century manager as designer and manager of the process of organizing.

Reading 4.1

MANAGERS OF MEANING: FROM BOB GELDOF'S BAND AID TO AUSTRALIAN CEOS

by David C. Limerick

An Irish pop singer, Bob Geldof may be remembered more as a quintessential leader of the 1980s and 1990s then as a musician. Outraged by the ineffective response of governments worldwide to the Ethiopian famine, he decided to make a record. Not just any record, however. He enlisted the support and participation of many great pop artists, and the record made millions of dollars. He then arranged a concert. Again, not just any concert, but a concert on a scale never dreamed of by anyone else — performed by an array of pop stars never before assembled and watched by billions of people throughout the world. The money generated by "Band Aid" and "Live Aid," as those two projects were called, helped relieve starvation in Ethiopia.

Geldof's participation in the relief effort did not end with fund raising. He maintained a vivid public image, meeting public figures worldwide and urging, bullying and cajoling them until relief got through to Ethiopia. "Band Aid" and "Live Aid" were followed by "Sports Aid" and a host of other "Aids," which orchestrated interest groups throughout the world toward the same cause and kept up the momentum of aid to Ethiopia.

What Geldof achieved and the way he did it provide insights into the new challenges facing strategic managers. In a study of 50 Australian chief executive officers (CEOs), two colleagues and I found that they face the task that Geldof faced — of cutting across loosely coupled groups and individuals (who very often are stars in their own right) and getting them to collaborate in a common cause. Strategic managers

no longer are the rational analysts of a few years ago; they are managers of vision, of mission, of identity, of culture. They are managers of meaning.

The research project on which I base much of my current thinking began in 1984. My colleagues and I set out to look at linkages between strategy, structure, and culture in 50 Australian business and government organizations selected on the basis of either financial success over a number of years or reputation for good management. Although we analyzed newspaper and journal articles, company reports and other literature on each of the organizations studied, the heart of the study was a series of in-depth interviews with their CEOs during which we teased out strategic and structural changes in their organizations and the CEOs' perceptions of the core values they would like to see their organizations have.

I have used the experiences of those Australian CEOs to look at (1) the social and organizational changes that have occurred during the past decade or so, (2) the new managerial priorities they imply, and (3) the techniques and competencies required for meeting those priorities. (See Exhibit 4.1 for a summary of the characteristic and demands of the Geldof era.) I believe that the Australian CEOs and Geldof are not alone in their management approach. Rather, their experiences will, I believe, strike a familiar chord in managers of other Western organizations as well.

Organizational and Social Changes During the Geldof Era

During the 1960s and 1970s, managers and academics alike drove organizations hard toward "inter-

locking group" structures — organizational forms that were tightly linked and tightly controlled (sometimes the euphemism "facilitated" was used). More often than not, even divisionalized organizations had a sizable number of controllers/facilitators at their headquarters to keep the organization integrated. ITT, with a 300-member staff at its Brussels headquarters alone, exemplified organizations of that time.

In contrast, the CEOs my colleagues and I talked to in the Geldof era deliberately rejected most of those models in favor of very loosely coupled systems with high levels of individualism. Most of them were transforming the tightly interlocked structures of their organizations into decentralized and cellular ones. As one CEO commented, "I don't want more relationships between people; I want fewer."

The CEO of an engineering firm provided, perhaps, the most complete expression of this change in direction: "So we decided to identify segments of the industry and to literally create free-standing units to deal with each. We said to them. This is your baby; you tell us what your market is, the resources you need, the strategy you're going to develop, the market share you're aiming at. Then we would turn a bunch of fellows loose on a dedicated speciality."

Loosely Coupled Organizations

In general, loosely coupled organizations have three key characteristics. They have (1) smaller, autonomous units that are (2) innovative, proactive, and market-oriented and (3) led by a lean corporate headquarters.

4. Reprinted by permission of publisher, from *Organization Dynamics*, Spring 1990. © 1990 American Management Association, New York. All rights reserved..

EXHIBIT 4.1 Characteristics of the Geldof Era

Social and Organizational	New Managerial Priorities	Requiring the Use of	Requiring New Competencies
Loosely coupled organizations	Management of identity	Language and slogans	Holistic, empathetic abilities
Collaborative individualism	Management of corporate culture	Legends and models	Metastrategic vision
		Systems and sanctions	Mature, internal locus of control
			Networking skills

One CEO expressed the views of most in our survey when he argued, "You have to be decentralized; the more we can create cells of people with a lot of autonomous delegated authority, the more successful we are." Those cells have to be customer-oriented, with "a determination to be in control of the environment instead of being pushed around by it," according to the CEO. Although they are smaller units, the cells are dedicated to specified market niches and are able to focus on "controlling" or, more realistically, influencing the environments of those niches.

To ensure autonomy and responsibility for action, loosely coupled organizations have to keep corporate headquarters very small. In many cases, widespread decimation of central staff positions may be needed. As one CEO remarked, "We discovered that we could not afford two personnel officers at $35,000 each; we could only afford one at $70,000!"

Geldof's fundamental management philosophy is very similar. In his autobiography *Is That It?* (Penguin, 1986), he stated, "Band Aid must never become what I have always most detested — an institution." Instead, he created a network

of loosely coupled, dedicated units: "I told Kevin we could extend the value of what we did by setting up various 'Aids' in the industries most of our essential purchases for Africa would come from." He thus stimulated the formation of "Truckers for Band Aid," "Builders for Band Aid," and a host of special-interest groups such as "Sports Aid," "Actor Aid," and "Bush Aid." As Geldof observed, the list went on "longer than the alphabet."

The Australian CEOs we interviewed were developing organization structures much closer to Geldof's Band Aid than to the integrated bureaucracies of the 1970s: They were transformational leaders dedicated to needs and to doing something about them. They were supported by a lean, organic executive group as they attempted to orchestrate decentralized, autonomous individuals and groups toward a common vision and goal. Those parallels fascinated me but also raised a fundamental question: Why should such a widespread movement toward "chunked" organizations have emerged in Australia during the 1980s?

The notion that such movements are fads did not seem to make much sense. Indeed, most of the CEOs claimed to have invented the movement for themselves. A better answer lies in systems theory itself. *Loosely coupled systems handle change and turbulence more effectively.* Such systems have emerged as a pragmatic response to the extreme rate of change during recent times. Tightly coupled systems simply cannot adapt fast enough.

Geldof makes a similar point about Band Aid: Compared with larger, conventional charities, Band Aid was infinitely more adaptable. He wrote, "We were flexible and could look around to see where gaps were left by the other agencies and then plug them."

The very responsiveness of a loosely coupled organization enables it to pursue strategies of nichemanship. That characteristic, moreover, is reinforced by a second development within the organization — the emergence of collaborative individualism.

Collaborative Individualism

Contrary to my expectations, the Australian CEOs did not mention teamwork during intensive questioning about the effectiveness of their organizations. In fact, only three or four references to teamwork were made during the entire series of interviews. We therefore broached the issue with the CEOs at the end of each discussion, at which point they usually reported that teamwork was vitally important to their organizations.

According to the CEOs, teamwork had been their dominant problematic issue during the 1970s, and during the decade they had poured resources into team development. However, by the 1980s teamwork had receded to the status of a *sine qua non* of effectiveness; the dominant problematic issue had become individualism. The CEOs were far more concerned about developing mature, proactive individuals with a self-driven capacity to transform systems. As the CEO of a large government organization put it: "I am looking for someone who will keep asking questions when the rest of the team has stopped."

Such individuals had to be collaborative, however. The CEOs desired a form of individualism that stood on the shoulders of teamwork. As another CEO stated, "I am looking for a team of individuals."

In this sense, collaborative individualism lies on the other side of teamwork. It stresses the need for individuals who are not imprisoned by the boundaries of the group and who will transform the group when the interests of the organization so dictate. Transformational leadership, as distinct from transactional leadership, is an important characteristic of the collaborative individual. As J. Burns in his book *Leadership* (Harper and Row, 1978) pointed out, transactional leaders work by increment, contracting and

transacting with others to maintain a stable organization, whereas transformational leaders create new situations and processes. Independent, transforming individuals, they create a new vision of the possible and inspire others to follow.

Although individualistic values are part of the historical consciousness of Anglo-American-colonial society, the individualistic value of the 1980s are subtly different. The CEOs we interviewed did not seek the return of the corporate buccaneer of the 1960s, clawing his or her way through four levels of management to get to the top. Yet they did not want servants of collectivism either. They saw the collaborative individual as (1) individualistic, yet collaborative; (2) proactive, with an internal locus of control; and (3) politically aware and skilled. The CEO of a large Australian bank captured this image when he stated that he did not want a team of football players but rather a team of cricketers.

For American readers, baseball players can be substituted for cricketers in the CEO's metaphor; the meaning is the same. The CEO wanted individuals who would confront that 100-mile-an-hour- ball on their own yet adjust their styles — collaborate — when their teams were in trouble. They had to be able to solve their own problems as well as those of the group.

"The need is for... the will to *manage*... and so we are saying to people that you do not have to be reactive, you must go out and plan and act on the business," he explained.

Collaborative individualism applied to relationships with governments, too. As one CEO noted, "Our big breakthrough was in developing techniques for dealing with government." Another pointed out that such political responsiveness demanded that managers have "political skills" and a capacity for political infighting.

Bob Geldof: The Collaborative Individual

The characteristics of the collaborative individual are very close to those of Bob Geldof: individualistic yet collaborative, proactive, and internally driven but with rugged political skills. He values those same characteristics in the people he admires, as his recounting of a meeting with Mother Teresa in Africa demonstrates: "There was a certainty of purpose which left little patience. But she was totally selfless; every moment her aim seemed to be, how can I use this or that situation to help others....She held my hand as she left and said, 'Remember this. I can do something you can't do and you can do something I can't do. But we both have to do it.'"

And Geldof did. His vision was clear. When asked why he was trying to organize something as impossible as a global telethon, he replied, "Because people are dying."

At the same time, Geldof was skilled at using political guile, or even force, when necessary. For example, he blocked the British government from taxing his Band Aid record sales by taking the matter into the public arena. And when a catering company at his charity concert wanted a profit, he threatened to tell everyone to pack their own meals and boycott the company.

The characteristics of the collaborative individual and the task that confronted Geldof are essentially congruent. The "organization" he brought together was loosely coupled in the extreme, consisting of mature, proactive individuals, many of them stars, with the potential for collaboration. However, a collaborative individual, Geldof, was needed to transform this aggregate into a collaborative enterprise.

Other managers have confronted similar situations. Jimmy Pattison and Llew Edwards, for example, had to get hundreds of independent contributors to collaborate toward a common goal at the Vancouver and Brisbane Expo sites. Perhaps they, too, can be seen as pioneers of a new managerial era. Most of the organizations we studied were not as atomistic or as diffuse as Band Aid or the Vancouver and Brisbane Expos, but many seem headed in that direction. Some were beginning to franchise parts of their businesses or to engage in toll manufacturing (a process of subcontracting parts of, or even the whole of, manufacturing to other independent organizations).

A number of American and European companies have adopted similar structures. Lewis Galoob Toys Incorporated, for example, sold $58 million of "Golden Girl" action figures at a time when the company had only 115 employees. Galoob farmed out all manufacturing to contractors in Hong Kong and did not even collect its own accounts, selling receivables instead to a credit corporation. Sulzer Brothers Limited, a Swiss manufacturer of diesel engines, now licenses engine design to other firms and services engines made by licensees. Even large, long-established companies such as Firestone Tire & Rubber, Minnesota Mining & Manufacturing Co., and General Electric Co. sell finished products bought from foreign companies. Such organizations together with more loosely coupled organizations with widespread autonomous units (such as Johnson & Johnson, which has more than 130 business units) are facing many of the same challenges to strategic management as those confronted by Geldof. Thus we are at the beginning of a Geldof era, not the end.

New Managerial Priorities and Techniques

The problem with loose coupling and individualism is that they represent a centrifugal force that can endanger the survival of the whole. Whereas tightly coupled organizations can rely on a myriad of strategic and operational control systems to achieve integration, loosely coupled organizations have to rely on bottom-line information to evaluate divisional performance. That information, however, may come too late to prevent dangerous actions or even alert the organization to them. The recurrent nightmare of a natural-resource-based company, for example, is that one of its divisions will act irresponsibly, destroying public confidence in the entire company and thereby endangering the long-term survival of the enterprise.

In the absence of more operational controls, CEOs of loosely coupled organizations have to rely on shared goals, values and meanings to secure collaborative action. That is, they have to create "value-driven" systems. Our study suggests that the CEOs of loosely coupled organizations face two major interrelated challenges: the management of identity and the management of corporate culture.

Management of Identity

Recent thinking on corporate strategy has focused on identification of the organization's "mission" and the "vision" on which that mission is based. At the heart of these two issues is the very identity of the organization — its unique shape, boundaries, purpose and values that differentiate the organi-

zation and its members from other organizations. I do not believe that this concern is an accidental fad. On the contrary, loosely coupled organizations depend for their very survival on a widespread acceptance of a clear vision and mission.

In the course of our interviews, most of the CEOs provided a cogent picture of the linkages between strategy, structure and culture within their organizations, all of which were linked to deep-seated image of the identity of the organization. For a few, this "metastrategy" was perfectly conscious and coherent. The CEO of a large chemical company, for example, linked disappearing trade barriers and the maturating of the chemical industry to his company's attempts to move away from an engineering-oriented bureaucracy toward autonomous, market-oriented business units governed by a small corporate headquarters. His picture was a coherent; the vision of the entrepreneurial organization, clear. For many of the other CEOs, the image was less accessible, although I was impressed by the fit between the elements of the identity they each espoused.

In many of the organizations we looked at, we spoke to senior managers who reported directly to the CEO. These managers did not always understand their organization's metastrategy as clearly as the CEO did. For the most part, the CEOs seemed aware of their failure to clearly communicate their overall vision of the organization.

During the interviews, no one statement or phrase communicated the CEO's vision. Rather it was revealed through a whole series of allegories, metaphors, slogans, legends and myths. I have come to the conclusion that such a concept of identity is so much an empathetic and holistic phenomenon that it defies the linear logic of speech. As one CEO complained, "Every time I try to communicate the image, I cheapen it."

The difficult task that confronts strategic managers today parallels the one surmounted by Geldof — reaching across loosely coupled, autonomous individuals and providing a basis for collaboration by identifying and communicating a common vision and mission. For Geldof, the mission of Live Aid was clear: People were dying. He communicated this mission fearlessly to others. In trying to persuade the pop group The Who to participate in Live Aid, for example, he resorted to the ultimate argument: if they played, they would be responsible for saving a few people's lives. "It was true, but it sounded so corny," he wrote about the incident. "It came down in the end to personal responsibility."

It was difficult for Geldof not to cheapen his vision, not to make it sound corny. This same task confronts each CEO of loosely coupled systems. He or she has to establish and communicate the very *identity* (vision, mission) of the organization and manage the field of shared meanings, values and beliefs that surround the identity to make the vision credible and persuasive.

Management of Corporate Culture

Our study provides abundant data on the continuing and almost obsessive attempts of CEOs to come to grips with and mold the field of meaning within the organization — to manage its culture. Many of those attempts were related to crises that had demanded not only radical structural change but also massive cultural change for the organization. For a major Australian bank facing the trauma of deregulation of the finance industry, a major problem was, in the CEO's words "the shape of our people." As he explained, "We have a culture which goes back 150 years. Now we are a financial conglomerate acting globally. And so now we are asking people to change their shape, to change their culture."

In moving toward new organizational forms and missions, the CEOs we interviewed were expanding and in some cases redefining the identity and shape of their enterprises. What did these new organizations look like? Almost all of them emphasized autonomy and proactivity, two characteristics central to loosely coupled systems and collaborative individualism. Companies had to move away from uncertain introspection and the reactivity that accompanies it. Said one CEO, "We definitely tend to be too inward looking. Somewhere deep down in our gut is an unspoken feeling that we can't do it as well as those other people." Instead, the companies had to move toward confident innovativeness. As one CEO noted, "We have to be entrepreneurial. It was almost a *cri de coeur* from members of an organization which had recently merged and was looking for a new identity."

For most CEOs we interviewed, the task of managing and transforming the values of their organizations was a challenge undertaken at an overt, conscious level. The strategies and variables they used to manage culture, however, were often more subtle, more elusive and less conscious. They included language and slogans, legends and models, systems and sanctions, as well as self-modeling.

Language and slogans The CEOs used a variety of images couched in rich, expressive language to approximate the values they sought. Many of those images recurred a number of times during a CEO's interview. It became clear that the images had assumed the status of slogans and in all probability were used frequently in everyday contact with others in the organization.

For example, one CEO said, "One in five acquisitions don't work out, and there are lots of managers who look to me to make their divestment decisions for them. In effect, they continue to hold the dead baby to the breast." That rather shocking image of holding a dead baby to the breast recurred a number of times during the interview. Such phrases and slogans tend to become institutionalized. Managers at a large finance company we studied were dominated by the notion of "stretch objectives," a term inspired by Cecil Rhodes's (and Robert Browning's) maxim "Let every man's reach exceed his grasp." To the analytical outsider, such phrases may seem trite. Yet, when Brian Loton, CEO of Australia's largest company, BHP, said "Big is out. Good is in," I noted that he had an almost visceral identification with the phrase. The executives around him, too, nodded intensely.

Such identification may penetrate far down the line, according to the CEOs we interviewed. Yet it is not won easily. The CEO of a computer company commented, "The biggest danger is apathy...(but) there is a real dedication to this set of values. While to a certain extent apathy and cynicism blow them apart, respect for the values is stronger and more typical of the organization as a whole."

Language, on its own, is not enough to secure shared meaning. It has to be represented and reinforced in other organizational processes and symbols.

Legends and models Many organizations in the study had key figures in their history who had assumed legendary status and who were held up to others as models for action. The CEOs we interviewed were intimately aware of those legends and eager to tell us about them. A mining company's deeply held values of care for people in the organization were neatly wrapped up in the following legend told during our interview with its CEO: "There is the story that George Fisher, in the half an hour it took him to get to the gate of his factory from his car, would get to know absolutely everything that was happening simply by talking to various people. Legend also has it that Sir James, too, in driving down the streets of, say, Mt. Isa, would suddenly stop the car and say 'Isn't that so-and- so who was involved in training the winning cricket team yesterday?'"

A retail chain revered its founder as "a genius." An oil company hailed its founding explorer as "a dreamer" who created the "exploration culture" of the organization. Whether such stories are true in every detail is irrelevant; they are models and persuasive symbols of deeply held values.

Systems and sanctions The number of systems and sanctions available in loosely coupled organizations is not as great as the number of systems and sanctions availablein more bureaucratic organizations. Nevertheless, the systems that are available are widely used to institutionalize values. In our study, organizations that had retained some staff strength at corporate headquarters used such human resources systems as orientation and training programs and performance appraisal to back up their values. Some regularly distributed throughout the organization videotapes of executives giving briefings or morale talks. Others used credos and charters to institutionalize their core values. Many moved employees around the organization to diffuse values.

Most CEOs, however, ultimately had to back up core values by resorting to the strongest sanctions of all: promoting, demoting or firing. They used such sanctions only when all else had failed. One CEO, for example, had taken his highest-performing manager and put him into the "sin bin" (a research laboratory) because his behavior was not quite ethical enough. The CEO said he intended to keep him there until the manager learned "better manners" — that is, until the manager learned to conform to the central values of the organization.

Self-modeling Most of the CEOs preferred not to resort to such sanctions and attempted to use positive modeling whenever possible. Since the systems available to them were so scarce, most of them in the end relied on personal example. They networked extensively within their organizations, asserting their values and attempting to represent core values and meanings personally. Although some frustration could be sensed behind these limitations, not one of the CEOs was prepared to centralize to gain greater control. As one of them rather desperately said, "I just have to use the force of my own personality and style."

The extent of such networking was typified in one CEO's description of a senior manager's typical week at his company: "Thirty percent attending small, informal meetings; 20 percent visiting plants and project sites; 20 percent talking on the telephone; 10 percent attending scheduled meetings; and 5 percent on answering correspondence and reading."

As I listened to CEOs talking about their techniques for managing meaning, I was reminded most strongly of Bob Geldof — his traveling, networking, cajoling, building images of the possible and, despite a lack of access to sanctions, succeeding in building a landmark collaborative enterprise. Overall, I gained a clear picture of the overwhelming attention given by CEOs to the task of creating and communicating meanings and values, a task they believed was central to the achievement of the organization's objectives.

The CEOs reported that in most organizations the chief executive plays a key role in the management culture. One CEO reflected, "The influence of the top person in the organization is quite frightening, really." Yet our data also suggest that this influence is not exerted from an isolated position. Most of the CEOs we spoke to had built around them a tight cohort of senior executives with whom they shared the problem of managing change. These groups aimed at creating a culture with its own momentum. Ideally it would "get to a point that even if the leader is not there, the culture will go on," as one CEO noted. The task of communicating a new vision and identity to even that group of senior executives, however, can be formidable and frustrating for the CEO.

From our study, we simply have no knowledge of how effective the CEOs and managers actually were at managing corporate culture (that is the subject of a second study now under way). For some analysts there is a question of whether culture can be there is a question of whether culture can be managed at all. Certainly CEOs are not the sole influencers of fields of meaning in organizations; there are many other actors and subcultures and counter-cultures at work. But our CEOs are undeterred by the debate. They see themselves as being a vital force in the development of the values of their organizations, and our study gives ample evidence of the overwhelming amount of their time devoted to attempting to manage culture.

To create and sustain corporate cultures, even with the help of a top management cohort, is an enormous challenge that demands the exercise of competencies not generally considered centrally important to management in past decades. The sheer magnitude of the networking task can tax personal energy reserves to the point of exhaustion. The public image of the tired, emotional Geldof provides an index of how hard the road is to travel.

New Competencies for Managers in the Geldof Era

The managers of the Geldof era are not the rational contingency analysts of past decades. Their roles as managers of meaning place a new emphasis on holistic, empathetic skills. Such skills, to be sure, have always been important to management, but they are vitally, critically important to managers of meaning. We explored with the CEOs in our study the competencies required by senior managers in today's organizations. The clusters they helped us identify reflect the new managerial role:

• *Skills in empathy.* The CEOs stressed that managers should be empathetic, warm, and able to supervise autonomous individuals. The capacity to communicate, often symbolically, also was important.

• *Skills in transformation.* The rapid pace of change requires skills in changing systems and values. Thus managers require transformational leadership skills; they have to be strong and able to both mold and change their organizations.

• *Proactivity.* Using such phrases as "self-driven," "doers," "bias for action" and "ambitious," the CEO stressed the need for an ability to get things done. Pragmatic common sense, reflected in such phrases as "smell for the dollar," "common business sense" and "good knowledge of what the business is about," also is required.

• *Political skills.* Managers have to be able to understand the political climate and deal with the political environment.

• *Networking skills.* Managers need the capacity to network between the elements of the broader organizational picture, interpreting for them the mission and identity of the organization.

• *Intuitive, creative thinking.* The CEOs stressed creativity, intuition, imagination, innovation, lateral thinking and the ability to ask "what if" questions rather than linear logical abilities.

• *Personal maturity.* The task of networking throughout very different autonomous systems makes enormous demands on the maturity of the individual, who is no longer able to cling to a specific role within a coherent structure for a sense of identity. Thus managers need both self- understanding and a commitment to the values of the larger system. They must understand their strengths and weaknesses, continue learning by self-evaluation and have the capacity to cope with stress. They also must be mature, professional, loyal and ethical in business practice.

The skills described above are characteristic of Geldof. He is empathetic but proactive, as his reaction to first seeing the dying children of Ethiopia demonstrates: "The eyes were looking at me. I began to cry. I was angry. Crying was useless and a waste of energy." He used his energy and political skills to transform the efforts of others and to achieve what others said could not be done. His actions were brilliant, creative, quirky and entirely intuitive. As he explained, "but it *was* different. It *was* extraordinary. I am too close to it now to stand back and see it in all its unlikely power and glory, but in future years I know I will wonder how the hell it was possible and what it was that enabled me to do it. I never once stopped to consider what happened next. I acted intuitively all the time."

According to Geldof, these abilities were forged and tempered by his early experiences. But can they be developed through formal training and education? This was an issue we explored with the Australian CEOs.

In general, the CEOs cited the focus on rational analysis in traditional M.B.A. programs as inadequate for imparting empathetic skills. Many argued that the skills described above are *process* skills, distinct from the knowledge areas covered by most Australian management schools. The CEOs wanted more action-learning strategies, such as in-company M.B.A. programs or an emphasis on in-company projects and experiences.

Moreover, the CEOs were puzzled by the emphasis on conventional OD techniques preoccupied with teamwork — techniques they considered inadequate. They wanted increased attention focused on programs that help individuals map and understand themselves; stimulate symbolic thinking, intuition and empathy; encourage the capacity to tolerate ambiguity and paradox; and develop networking and political skills. These characteristics are hard-won, and people with them are difficult to find. Thus, while the CEOs most frequently mentioned the "quality of human resources" as the key strength of their organizations, they also most often nominated it as their key area of threat and vulnerability.

The task of managing meaning is difficult and demanding, to be sure. Why else would chief executives need to devote so much of their time to it? Yet we sensed among the Australian CEOs in our study a certain confidence, even perhaps a touch of arrogance, in their capacity to conceive of and move their organizations toward new identities and new values. Without such confidence, "Saint Bob," as Geldof sometimes was called, could not have achieved what he did either.

A Final Note

Not all transformational leaders are as socially contributive as Geldof was. There must of necessity be a fine line between transformational leadership and autocracy. We believe that when there is a large power gap in organizations, transformation means autocracy. However, the essence of the loosely coupled system is the autonomy of the parts, and the essence of collaborative individualism is the empowerment of the individual. That, too, was the essence of the situation Geldof faced. Under such circumstances, the identification of mission and the mobilization of values are a contributive social act.

Implicit in this analysis is a warning. Management theorists and practitioners alike must think more overtly about the management of corporate culture, about the social conditions in which it takes place and about the controls and checks on "transformers" in our organizations and our societies. The odds are that we will see the emergence of more managers of meaning, not fewer. As noted earlier, we are at the beginning of the Geldof era, not the end of it. It deserves very close attention.

Chapter 5

Power and Politics

Those who have the gold make the rules! But consider also that those who make the rules get the gold!!

On Thursday, August 21, 1980, at 6:13 p.m., ABC's *World News Tonight* ran a four-and-a-half-minute segment detailing allegations of criminal fraud, conspiracy and conflict of interest against a number of executives in a large United States corporation. The fact that a network news program would run an exposé on an organization or its leaders surprised no one. But the news report was, nevertheless, news in itself, because the corporation involved was ABC, Inc.

The so-called *Charlie's Angels* scandal was uncovered originally by the *New York Times*. *ABC News* subsequently investigated it in more depth, turning up additional damaging information. The overall accusations made against ABC, Inc. basically boiled down to this: (1) that executives at ABC were involved in a scheme to defraud the "profit participants" in *Charlie's Angels* of close to $1 million, diverting a large part of that money to Spelling-Goldberg Productions via "creative accounting"; (2) that a lawyer in ABC's West Coast contracts division was fired when she tried to bring this to the attention of ABC executives; and (3) that a very close friend of Aaron Spelling and Leonard Goldberg, a friend whose children all worked for either Spelling or Goldberg and who was a partner in some real estate deals, was none other than Elton Rule, the president of ABC.

In November 1980, *Fortune* ran a follow-up article on the story, adding one new dimension not in the *ABC News* report. It seems that ABC's chairman, then seventy-four years old, was expected to retire sometime soon. Rule was his most likely replacement. Among other top executives, the most aggressively ambitious was believed to be Roone Arledge. Arledge and Rule were, in the words of one ABC employee, " about as friendly as Iran and Iraq." Roone Arledge was in charge of *ABC News*.[1]

Far from the battle of senior executives in the ABC TV corporation another story unfolds.

Susan worked as an assistant manager in a local downtown department store. Catherine was another assistant manager who worked for the same manager, Rosabeth Brown. Susan felt that although she worked hard and completed her assignments efficiently, Catherine got the most interesting projects and seemed to be a favorite with Rosabeth. In Susan's opinion, Catherine was a less conscientious worker and a real " brown-noser." Whenever there was an important or an urgent job to do, Rosabeth chose Catherine to do the work. No matter how hard Susan worked, she never seemed to make much of an impression on her boss. Rumor had it that Catherine would get Rosabeth's recommendation for an upcoming management vacancy in the furniture department. Susan was becoming frustrated and disillusioned. What was the point of coming to the store on time, taking administrative work home, and getting it all done correctly if it didn't get her anywhere? She was beginning to think, " Maybe it is time to quit and look for another job!"

Let's shift back to another major corporation now, the 3M company in St. Paul, Minnesota.

Art Fry has figured out a use for an adhesive that his friend, chemist Spence Silver, has developed. It is a temporary stickable glue that no one in 3M seems particularly interested in. (After all, 3M glue products — for example, cellophane tape — are supposed to be permanently stickable.) Fry and Spence collaborate to produce samples of this product and think it will be a useful stationery product; but unless they can get support from key senior managers and the interest of 3M's marketing department, it will go nowhere. Enter Geoffrey Nicholson, Art and Spence's boss. He champions the idea and develops a strategy that includes getting the little yellow sticky note pads into the offices of top managers and other key influencers in the 3M corporation (using their secretaries as " agents" to gain entry). All orders go through Geoff's secretary, Rose, but eventually, she gets so many requests that she cannot get any other work done. " That's it," said Geoff Nicholson, " from now on, redirect all orders to the marketing department, we are going to get their attention!" And they did. The rest, as they say, is history. Eventually, the new product, the Post-It note pad, found its way into the offices and homes across the United States, making many persons' administrative chores a little easier while making 3M a very substantial profit!

Finally, here is what Ralph Stayer, chief executive officer of family-owned Johnsonville Foods, a rapidly growing specialty foods and sausage making company in Sheboygan, Wisconsin, has to say about power in organizations. He was speaking about the use of power when the shape of the organization is flattened, creating fewer levels of management and larger numbers of people reporting to each manager.

> Flattening pyramids doesn't work if you don't transfer the power too. Before, I didn't have power because I had people wandering about not giving a damn. Real power is getting people committed. Real power comes from giving it up to others who are in a better position to do things than you are. Control is an illusion. The only control you can possibly have comes when people are controlling themselves.[2]

1. J. B. Kotter, *Power & Influence* (New York: The Free Press, 1985), pp. 15-16.
2. Thomas A. Stewart, "New Ways to Exercise Power," *Fortune* (Nov. 6, 1989), p. 53-54.

These examples give us some insights into how power and politics play out in organizational life. One way to understand how organizations work is to think about them as places where individuals and groups of individuals with different values, self-interests, preferences and perspectives on life come together to get work done. Members of an organization must, therefore, work through and with each other, they are dependent on one another to get things done or they wouldn't be in an organization. Often there are conflicts and disagreements over who gets what resources to do the work of the organization, about what the actual work of the organization should be, and how it should be done. Often, there are disagreements about what constitutes good work when it is done.

As a result of these clashes of interests, values and ways of seeing the world, it is often a struggle to figure out who and what is right, especially regarding management tasks in which the nature and outcome of the work involve some degree of ambiguity and uncertainty. This is especially true when the organization is experiencing uncertainty and change. The greater these ambiguities and uncertainties, the more subjective and personal will be the organization's management decisions and employee evaluations. In other words, people making judgments on other people's work (and on their own work, of course) will base their evaluations, to some extent, on the way they *feel* about what has been done. Thus, managers will often judge the performance of others based on what they, the managers, consider important and valuable — on what they believe to be the mandate and goals of the organization. Given that managers typically are not in an organizational world for altruistic purposes but want to meet their own self-interests while helping the company succeed, the activities and results that others provide will be judged in part on how these activities and results help managers get their work done and have their contributions recognized. When the path to success is unclear, or controversial, subjective factors often affect the judging process.

To understand the implications of this phenomenon on you as an employee, consider that your manager (or supervisor) typically looks at your work in terms of how it helps him or her get the department's job done. In some cases, however, a manager will allow you to help evaluate your own performance, so you can show that what you do and the way you do it is valuable. Typically, the manager will evaluate your work based on his or her interpretation of what you do. Such evaluations can help the manager understand the context of your contributions, so that you do not end up feeling — as did Susan, the assistant manager in the department store example — undervalued and underappreciated.

Organizations provide not only a means of accomplishing work, but also an arena for personal accomplishment and growth. Within organizations, people can get recognition from others and can earn promotions through the ranks of the company's management. The opportunities for advancement diminish, however, as people climb higher up the corporate ladder. As a result, the competition for high level positions can become fierce as the contenders focus on the prized positions at and near the top of the organization. To be sure, not everyone in an organization wants to be the chief executive officer, but whether we choose to climb and compete or simply want to get resources for our work and recognition for our contributions, we are still involved in the use (and sometimes abuse) of power. We are all a part of and involved in the political process of organizational life.

Name _____

ID# _____

Section _____

What is Power?

Before you read very far into your text and our "Textbook Tie-In" on this topic, we would like you to reflect on your own ideas and feelings about power. It is an important concept, one that has real impact on our lives. It is something most people have strong feelings about. So take some time alone and answer these questions from your perspective.

1. What is " power" to you? Write a brief description.

2. What one primary image represents power to your? Write a phrase, find a picture or draw an image that represents power to you.

3. Write a phrase, find a picture or draw an image that represents the kind of power you are afraid of or feel most threatened by.

4. Create a symbol that represents the kind of power you would most like to project or communicate. Draw it here.

Let's go back to the examples at the start of the chapter to get a sense of what we mean by organizational power and politics. Many textbooks have a definition of power as a potential, a capacity. You have power if you have the capacity to get others to do what they might not want to do. You also have power if you have the capacity to resist doing what others want you to do. Your textbook likely gives several bases for such power. (Legitimate authority, expertise, ability to reward or punish ideas or actions and personal attractiveness are commonly discussed bases). Another way of looking at power is as a capacity to create opportunities for others to do what they would like to do. We call this empowerment. Interestingly enough, empowering others is sometimes difficult especially in organizations where people are accustomed to being controlled by others. Ralph Stayer of Johnsonville Foods said that when he tried to empower others, " I had to work my fanny off to get people to want to have power...you have got to take your goal and break it down so that each person is accountable for his part of it."[3] In this statement, Stayer put his finger on an important point about power. It is a potential and for it to be realized, at least in the day-to-day life of organizations, takes a will to use power and a skill in applying it.

Using power means thinking about power in action — what we call **organizational politics.** Politics in organizations is action toward the accomplishment of some goal that, first of all, furthers the self-interests of the person who is being political and secondly, might be resisted by others having different self-interests if they recognized or detected what was going on. The best examples from those at the start of this chapter are the actions of Roone Arledge at ABC and of Geoffrey Nicholson and his team at 3M. Arledge hid his self-interested, political intentions (to wound his competitor for the ABC chairmanship, Elton Rule) behind a supposedly objective, rational release of information about the Charlie's Angels scandal. His ambitions were not apparent to those who viewed the news story.

Geoffrey Nicholson developed a strategy to force the 3M marketing department to take Post-It Notes seriously by getting the top managers on his side. The normal rules of 3M Company would be to have the marketing department measure interest in a proposed product. However, given the Post-It Notes did not stick like other 3M products, marketing was not very supportive. If Nicholson had told marketing how he proposed to interest others in his product, the marketing staff likely would have resisted the idea.

The Role of Politics in Organizations

Both these examples are about organizational politics. Is organizational politics good or bad? We would argue that it simply *is*. It is an inevitable part of the way organizations function. One can assess its outcomes to judge whether a given action is " good" or " bad." (Of course, to some extent we call it good or bad depending on whether we win or lose in a particular political encounter.) One way to examine this issue is to see who benefits from a particular political action. Remember, we have argued that all organizational politics is self-serving. It served Roone Arledge to expose his rival; it served Geoffrey Nicholson to get the marketing department's support of his product. It also served Ralph Stayer of Johnsonville Foods to empower his employees to do a better job for the company. However, one can ask the question: " Who else benefits?" It is not clear whether anyone in ABC other than Roone Arledge benefitted from exposing his rival. (If the charge against Elton Rule was correct, then certainly the company and the public was better off. However, it is not clear whether this was the case.) It is much easier to argue that Nicholson's political actions benefitted many others, including the marketing group and 3M as a whole, because the product made millions of dollars for 3M. In fact, 3M's culture and its systems encourage managers to bend the rules to get things done (see Chapter 3, "Organizational Culture"). Ralph Stayer's actions (it is likely

3. Thomas A. Stewart, "New Ways to Exercise Power,"*Fortune* (Nov. 6, 1989), p. 53.

that he had to keep some of his cards hidden as he tried to get his empowerment message across to his employees) were likely to be political at least in part. The employees were not all that excited about being powerful to start with. The point is that it becomes political because Stayer set the agenda — it was his self-interest that triggered the actions and spurred him to overcome the employees' resistance so they could grow and take on more responsibility.

In summary, organizational power can be thought of as potential, as a capacity to get things done through others; and organizational politics as power in action, as power we use to get what we want done by working around the resistances of others. Politics is inevitable in organizations. Deciding on politics' value is itself a value judgment and we need to know something about the intentions of political actors. To begin to make our call on whether it is good or bad, we need to know their personal agendas and whether they intend to benefit others.

Sources of Power in Organizations

Where does power come from in organizations? As we mentioned earlier, it can come from the position we hold, from the controls we exercise (to reward or punish), from our expertise or from how other people perceive us personally. Your textbook will likely expand on these and other issues around power. However, we think it important to discuss the source of power a little further here so that we can note some of the links between power and politics.

A number of writers on power make the point that a major source of power comes from the ability of a person or a department to resolve (or to be perceived as resolving) important uncertainties and complexities for others in the organization. It comes also from being perceived by others in the organization as playing a central and irreplaceable role in the organization. (For example, " This place couldn't function if our maintenance workers refused to work or were all sick at the same time!" or " I don't know what I would do if Catherine were not here to handle these matters.")

Being central, irreplaceable and capable of solving or removing major uncertainties for the organization and, very importantly, being *seen* to be this way confers power on an individual or a department. We do not really know all the factors and perceptions in the department store that Susan worked in. However, we can anticipate one possible scenario to explain Susan's lack of success in influencing her boss, Rosabeth Brown. If Rosabeth finds or sees that Catherine can deal successfully with crises and important projects, then it is not surprising that Catherine has more clout than Susan and will more quickly climb the ladder than will Susan. Even if Susan is just as good at her work as Catherine, if Rosabeth doesn't see her contribution as equal and if Susan cannot make her see it that way (or doesn't realize that she cannot simply assume that Rosabeth appreciates the value of her work) then Susan will not fare as well as Catherine. Now, the fact may be that Catherine's contributions are more valuable than Susan's. In that case, Catherine probably will have more power, and will do better than Susan. However, often in organizational life, especially when positions involved are apparently equal, perception is more important than fact. Rosabeth may see Catherine and Susan differently, which may, in turn, affect their respective power. This does not necessarily mean that Rosabeth is a poor manager. Managers are people with busy agendas. Catherine may be better at communicating the worth of her work than is Susan. Susan, like many of us, may assume that simply doing a good job should earn her a positive evaluation. In some circumstances it will — especially when there are clear technical specifications for a job and no ambiguity about how it contributes to the organization's success. However, in many jobs the contribution of the work to the organization and the manager's agenda is less clear. Susan needs to have the will and skill to show Rosabeth the value of her work to both the department and the organization. If Susan doesn't do this, or if Rosabeth doesn't give her a way to demonstrate her contribution, it is probable that Rosabeth will draw only on her own way of seeing and valuing work and Susan may lose out. It should be noted that this is only one scenario for understanding Susan's plight. However, it is an important one. It highlights the way power and policies affect many aspects of organizational life, including the perceived contributions of various assistant managers at local department stores.

You will find as you learn more about power and politics that it provides a useful way to understand and appreciate many situations in organizational life.

It is rare that people feel indifferent about the word " power." Some people seek it, others resist it, still others see themselves as on the receiving end of someone else's power. Why people feel and act the way they do about power is a complex issue and not one we will ask you to deal with directly. However, we think you will find it useful to reflect on your own feelings and thoughts about some types of power that are commonly found in organizations. These types are typically referred to in textbooks as bases of power. How power influences you can be classified into three different outcomes: commitment, compliance and resistance.

One expert on leadership and power describes each of these outcomes to the use of power as:

• Commitment, wherein the person is enthusiastic about carrying out the request and makes a maximum of effort.

•'Compliance, wherein the person is apathetic about carrying out the request and makes only a minimal effort.

• Resistance, wherein the person is opposed to carrying out the request and tries to avoid doing it.[4]

In the table below, we would like you to look at the kinds of power a person (for example, a manager or supervisor) can exert in an organization. In each case:

1. Try to recall at least one instance when you have experienced this kind of influence attempt from someone in an organization (for example, your supervisor or one of your university instructors).

2. Note, on a sheet of paper, the essential points of that situation.

3. Now look at the three categories of outcome: commitment, compliance and resistance. Which was your reaction in that instance? Note your answer in the appropriate section.

4. Then, reflect on why this was your response. Was this a typical response you make to this kind of influence attempt? Was there something particular to this occasion or set of circumstances that prompted you to respond in this way? Why did you choose to respond as you did? Write down one or two phrases or sentences to capture your answer.

5. Finally, note how you feel about your answer. Make a note of what, if any, behavior on the part of the other person would have led you to respond differently. Note also what, if any, behavior on your part would have changed the way you responded.

4. Gary Yukl, *Skills for Managers and Leaders* (Englewood Cliffs, N. J.: Prentice Hall, 1990), p. 59.

6. Please use this process to analyze your reactions to each type of influence attempt.

When a Leader Used This Type of Influence Attempt:	I Responded With:		
	Commitment	Compliance	Resistance
Use Of Power: *Legitimate/Position Power* Power that stems from a formal management position in an organization and the authority granted to it			
Reward Power Power that results from authority to reward others			
Coercive Power Power that stems from authority to punish or recommend punishment of others			
Expert Power Power that stems from special knowledge or from skill in the tasks performed			
Referent Power Power that results from characteristics of the leader/manager that results in others' respect, admiration, identification with and desire to be like the manager			

When a Leader Used This Type of Influence Attempt:	(Continued from page 77) I Did So Because:	I Would Respond Differently If…
Use Of Power: *Legitimate/Position Power* Power that stems from a formal management position in an organization and the authority granted to it		
Reward Power Power that results from authority to reward others		
Coercive Power Power that stems from authority to punish or recommend punishment of others		
Expert Power Power that stems from special knowledge or from skill in the tasks performed		
Referent Power Power that results from characteristics of the leader/manager that results in others' respect, admiration, identification with and desire to be like the manager		

As you look over your answers to these questions, reflect on these questions:

1. What patterns do you see in your response to power?

2. Are there some types of power that you are more comfortable with than others?

3. Do some forms of influence attempts make you more uncomfortable than others?

4. What types of influence attempts (if any) will produce commitment in you?

Use the space below to record any lessons for yourself about your reactions to the use of power toward you by others. What have you learned about yourself?

Lights

The video clip you will soon see is taken from the film *One Flew Over the Cuckoo's Nest* which is based on the 1962 novel of this name written by Ken Kesey. The background for the video clip is as follows:

R.P. McMurphy (played by Jack Nicholson) is serving time at a penal farm. He pretends to be insane so that he can be transferred to a mental institution where he believes life will be easier. He is assigned to a ward supervised by Nurse Ratched, "Big Nurse" (played by Louise Fletcher). Life on this ward is far from easy. Nurse Ratched uses tight discipline, a tough group of orderlies and a stern and unyielding exercise of authority to eliminate any resistance or rebellion from her patients. Most of the patients are there "voluntarily" and make no effort to assert themselves...until McMurphy arrives on the scene. The struggle between Big Nurse, a symbol of the establishment, and McMurphy, a symbol of the oppressed, is the central theme of the movie and the book.

Camera

The scenes you are about to see capture graphically and, at times, with strong language the way Nurse Ratched and McMurphy each use political actions to try to establish whose wishes will be adhered to. (You will see two actors playing ward patients who became well known movie stars in the 1980s.)

The first scene takes place at a daily therapy session for nine patients on the ward. McMurphy requests that evening work detail be rearranged so that patients can watch the 1963 World Series. Watch how Nurse Ratched deals with this request. Pay attention not just to the words in this scene but also the body language of the group members. The second scene shows McMurphy later that day betting the other patients that he can lift the water faucet control panel off the ground and use it to help him get out of the ward for the evening so he can watch the World Series game anyway. Watch how he works the group to build a coalition of supporters for his struggles with Nurse Ratched.

The final scene begins with the group therapy session on the following day. One of the patients, Billy, is being questioned by Nurse Ratched. Cheswick interrupts to ask whether the group can watch that evening's World Series game. Observe how this new request to Nurse Ratched plays out, particularly in terms of the way power and politics are used by the two protagonists. Once again, watch the body language. The acting in this movie is outstanding. Enjoy a powerful story well portrayed in these video clips.

The characters in the scenes are:

Nurse Ratched*	Chief Bromden*	Martini	Billy
McMurphy*	Sefelt	Frederickson	Bert
Cheswick*	Scanlon	Harding*	

*These patients play significant roles in these scenes.

Action

Now that you have seen the scenes, answer the following questions.

1. What base(s) of power is/are used by:

a. Nurse Ratched

Base _____   Example _____

" _____   " _____

" _____   " _____

b. McMurphy

    Base _____   Example _____

    " _____   " _____

    " _____   " _____

2. Give one example of successful political behavior by:

a. Nurse Ratched

_____

_____   Why is it effective? _____

_____

b. McMurphy

_____

_____   Why is it effective? _____

_____

3. Is McMurphy more successful in making his challenge to change the rules during the second therapy meeting? If yes, why so?

4. What is the significance of McMurphy's World Series skit at the end of Scene 3?

5. Why does Nurse Ratched get so angry when McMurphy does this skit?

6. This example of power and politics is set in a mental ward. What parallels can you draw between the actions and attitudes of Nurse Ratched, R.P. McMurphy and the other patients and life in other kinds of organizations?

MAKING CONNECTIONS: IN-CLASS INTERACTIONS

5. R. Fields et. al., eds., *Chop Wood, Carry Water* (Los Angeles: J.P. Tarcher, Inc., 1984), p. 264.
6. Fiona Crofton, 1990. We are grateful to Fiona Crofton for permission to use this exercise, developed by her for this book.

In India, Shiva is also called Nataraja, the King of Dancers, and is said to have danced the world into creation. Perhaps more than any other art form, we can say that dance joins us to creation. When we dance in a circle...we dance with the earth around the sun. We dance for joy, to reenact myths, to welcome the God in our bodies, to worship, to woo, to gather power and courage for the hunt.[5]

If dance is seen as a metaphor for the activities engaged in by organizations and for relationships between people, what are the " dances" performed in organizations? Most of us will remember particular people (whether we knew them well or not) who represent these characters on the dance floor. Who are their reflections in organizations? Reflect for a few minutes on the organization your instructor assigns you to focus on. (It may be the organization and characters in *One Flew Over the Cuckoo's Nest.*) Provide answers for as many of these questions as you can.[6]

1. Who are the musicians?

2. Who are the wallflowers?

3. Who has center floor?

4. Who can clear a space and build an audience?

5. Who moves at the edge, tentative and uncertain?

6. Who is clearly partnered with one person and rarely (if ever) dances with another?

7. Who changes partners frequently moving through the crowd and participating with many?

8. Who, in the midst of a dance, is spending more time seeking the next partner than attending to the one they're with?

Play with the metaphor of the dance. Together with others in your class, discuss other ways in which we might use the idea of dance to represent different kinds of power and political action in organizations. (You might want to think about different kinds of dances or dance songs or musicals.)

COMING TO OUR SENSES: MAKING A DIFFERENCE

 When we started this module on power and organizational politics, we asked you to think about power in your " Ready for Class" exercise. Without going back to your notes, we'd like you to revisit these concepts. Find a quiet place. Take a few moments to gather your thoughts. On a sheet or two of paper, write down your answers to the following:

1. Think. What is power to you, now? Write a brief description.

2. Feel. What makes you feel most powerful? Represent it by a phrase. What makes you feel most powerless? Represent this by means of an image or a symbol.

3. Sound. Think of power as a force. What sounds does it make when it is used? Why does it sound like this?

4. Create a symbol or a slogan that represents the kind of power you most like to communicate. Draw it here.

5. What do you need to do next to increase your ability and will to deal with power tactics in organizations?

Managers will always encounter politics within their organization. The two articles in this section provide interesting views on organizational power and politics. The first, "New Ways to Exercise Power" from *Fortune Magazine* applies our knowledge about bases of power to action in existing corporations. The second, "Women Managers Experience Special Power Failures" is an excerpt from a 1979 *Harvard Business Review* article titled "Power Failure in Management Circuits." The article points out the difficulties women managers face when they try to get things accomplished in an organization. It is hoped that the future generation of managers will make real progress in this arena.

Reading 5.1

NEW WAYS TO EXERCISE POWER[7]

by Thomas A. Stewart

Listen to the new gospel of executive power: "The more you have, the less you should use," says Reuben Mark, CEO of Colgate-Palmolive. "You consolidate and build power by empowering others." Mark expresses an increasingly common view. Virtually all the chief executives polled by *Fortune* say they share power more than they did five years ago, and more than the CEO before them. "My predecessor was more imperial, and I tend to be more collegial," says USX's Charles Corry. Down the street at PPG Industries, "We are now more team-oriented," says Vincent A. Sarni. The word "participatory" crops up again and again as the leaders of corporate America discuss power.

Not that they relish the discussion. "I don't like to talk about power," says Mark. "I prefer to think about it as responsibility and authority." Chief executives observe that major changes are under way in how power is deployed in U.S. corporations. Management experts — business school professors, consultants — agree. You can't manage today's work force like yesterday's, they say. The military command-and-control model went out with red meat. Your job is to set a strategic direction, get your people to agree, give them money and authority, and leave them alone.

This sounds good but raises a few large questions. Most people agree on what power is: the ability to get things done, to get people to do what you want, to make the final decision. If the boss exercises power less directly these days, how does he make sure that things get done, and done right? Where does power accumulate when hierarchies are flattened or when an organization is decentralized? The tyrannical CEO may be on the way out; the new boss is a nicer guy. But is he any less powerful?

Professor John Kotter, who devised the Harvard business school course Power and Influence, says that power comes in several forms "lined up on a shelf" for a leader to choose from. The experts list five basic kinds.

The first is the power to reward — to give someone a promotion, a raise, or a pat on the back. Its twin is the power to punish: to fire someone, to send him to Fargo, North Dakota, or to put her in charge of "special projects." Third is the power that experts call authority. Authority can be specific, and specifically granted — the right to sign $100,000 contracts or to approve a package design. Or it can be the office equivalent of "because-I'm-the-Mommy" power: "Package color may be my job, but the boss wants blue." The fourth kind of power derives from expertise: "I

know the market research better than anyone, and the research says red will sell better than blue." Finally, psychologists speak of "referent power," which attaches to a leader because people admire him, want to be like him, or are wowed by his integrity, charisma, or charm.

Jane Halpert, a professor of industrial and organizational psychology at Chicago's DePaul University, points out that the first three — reward, punishment, and authority — come with the office. The higher your rank, the more you usually have. But expertise and referent power inhere in the person. They can exist anywhere in an organization — in a crackerjack CAD/CAM engineer or a secretary who's the only one who really understands the files.

The better the leader, argues Halpert, the more likely he is to rely on the personal sources of power. In particular, the power to punish "would be the last one I'd use. You get back a lot of anger. Really effective leaders almost never have to put the screws on someone."

This — away from power based on position, toward the personal kinds — seems to be the direction corporate America is heading. The power to reward appears increasingly circumscribed by obligations like affirmative action, by formalized compensation systems, and by the fact that you have fewer promotions to hand out after you eliminate two layers of superfluous vice presidents. Punishment can't be used promiscuously on a mobile work force. Says Raymond E. Miles, dean of the University of California business school: "The raw use of power doesn't have the acceptance it did 25 years ago. People aren't willing to put up with it."

Power is also changing within companies because the nature of their organization is changing. New Age gurus hawk "pyramid power," but management gurus see the death of the pyramidal organization. In *The New Realities,* Peter Drucker predicts that in so-called knowledge-based companies, hierarchies will give way to something resembling a symphony orchestra, with dozens or even hundreds of specialists reporting directly to the conductor/CEO. Corning Chairman James R. Houghton says flatly, "The age of the hierarchy is over."

One company that has taken the new view of power to heart is Johnsonville Foods, a relatively small (1988 sales: $100 million) but rapidly growing specialty foods and sausage maker in Sheboygan, Wisconsin. Says Ralph Stayer, 46, CEO of the family-owned business since 1978: "Flattening pyramids doesn't work if you don't transfer the power too. Before, I didn't have power because I had people wandering around not giving a damn. Real power is getting people committed. Real power comes from giving it up to others who are in a better position to do things than you are. Control is an illusion. The only control you can possibly have comes when people are controlling themselves."

Stayer discovered, as Mikhail Gorbachev has, that perestroika isn't easy. "I had to work my fanny off to get people to want to take power," he says. "You've got to take your goal and break it down so that each person is accountable for his part of it." Stayer stopped rewarding people for length of service. Now, "No one

gets a raise unless he takes on more responsibility."

Gone, too, is Johnsonville's personnel department. As part of the effort to empower employees, it has become the Personal Development Lifelong Learning Department. Workers meet with a counselor who helps them articulate their goals and dreams — be they becoming a senior vice president, putting kids through college, or learning to grow roses. Each receives a small allowance — $100 a year — to spend on a personal-growth project. Some apply to college or graduate school, others join a cooking class — Stayer doesn't care. For big expenses like education, employees also may get scholarships.

What does Johnsonville get? A lot, insists Stayer. "Our people are an appreciating asset, not a depreciating one. They're more willing to change, to question. When they see that they can change something in their personal lives, they bring that attitude to work."

Since 1985 volunteers from the shop floor have written the manufacturing budget. At first a financial man walked them through the process, but now he just kibitzes. Last year, when the sales department aimed at upping volume 40%, the manufacturing group set — and achieved — a goal of providing the additional output while holding cost increases to 20%. Another group of workers designs the manufacturing line. If the workers want new equipment, they themselves do the discounted cash flow analysis to back up the request for it. Stayer wants goals to be set as far down in the company as possible, saving top managers' time for choosing which goals should have first claim on the company's capital. If all this makes you think he has spent too much time in a hot tub, note that in the last six years Johnsonville has doubled its return on assets, and that sales, rising more than 15% a year, have grown twice as fast as the payroll.

Why give up on centralized control now, after hundreds, maybe thousands of years? In a sense, the cause of the change is change itself. In an environment rapidly altering due to intensified global competition and new technology, CEOs need to promote speed, flexibility, and decisiveness. When every customer demands special service, every sales rep has to have the power to offer it. He can't do that in what Miles calls "the multi-multi-level organizations, which like great big thunderstorms suck everything up to the top."

In a rapid-change world, leaders have to be free to think strategically, which often entails delegating operating authority. John Nevin, who retired this year as CEO of Firestone Tire & Rubber, which is being combined with the other North American operations of its parent, Japan's Bridgestone, has twice confronted massive change. He was president and then chairman of Zenith from 1971 to 1979, when the Japanese moved into consumer electronics, and then head of Firestone when the tire industry continued to struggle through the blowout caused by the advent of radial tires. In a stable world, says Nevin, "the CEO was really the chief operating officer. Ford made cars, U.S. Steel made steel, Motorola made car radios, and the role of the CEO was to improve their design, manufacturing, and marketing." Set the world spinning faster, however, and Ford's Donald Petersen began to get a third of his profits from the finance business; USX's David Roderick became an oilman; and Motorola's Robert Galvin Jr. learned to slice silicon wafers every which way. The result: "You change what you're managing." While the CEO and his new best friends — the strategic planners, consultants, and outside directors — explore new possibilities, "somebody's got to keep the business running during alterations."

But how is the CEO to confer the necessary power on subordinates without abdicating his responsibility for the organization's performance? Here three things help the most, say the experts and the CEOs: unambiguous and loudly public delegation of authority, a rigorous planning process, and strong communication.

Clear delegation is crucial because the CEO who vests power in his subordinates for all to see is, in effect, cloning himself. It's not just title inflation that explains why so many second-tier executives are coming to be called presidents or CEOs of their divisions. By involving them as a team in key corporate decisions, the top boss ensures that these surrogates share his goals. Then he can send the mini-CEOs back into the company, making it clear that their use of power is not to be second-guessed.

Headquarters staff are typically the first victims of such decentralization. Staff are second-guessers by nature. Says Harvard's Kotter: "Staff make it very, very difficult to nurture leadership. The emerging leader will run into 16 staff guys, these checkers. They eat leaders."

More CEOs are coming to understand this. Reginald Jones ran General Electric using a strong staff system that his successor, Jack Welch, has dismantled. Five years ago at Owens-Illinois, says CEO Robert Lanigan, "There was a lot of time spent in exercising the power of this office through the corporate staff." Staff has been dramatically reduced, and line managers' salaries pegged higher than those of staffers. The result, according to Lanigan: "The staff are there as consultants, as advisers to me and to other line people."

At Heinz, Chairman Anthony J.F. O'Reilly has cut the staff out of the loop completely. "There is no interface between staff and the presidents of the affiliates," says O'Reilly. "No ambassadors, no courtiers, no fonctionnaires. It's me and the president of an affiliate, one

on one." Out of a worldwide work force of 50,000, only 150 are on the corporate staff.

The staff-like units that remain are located deeper in the Heinz organization, and their relationship to operating units has changed. Mary Ann McCollough runs one such unit. As general manager of marketing services for Heinz USA, she provides consumer research, promotion and advertising support, and test-kitchen services principally to the four divisions of Heinz USA, including Weight Watchers. She has no direct reporting relationship with her clients. And "clients" is the word: McCollough bills the line businesses for her unit's services. Market dynamics, not a hierarchy, determine what her unit does. Its day-to-day work is more likely to be critiqued — pro or con — by the units she serves than by the VP to whom she reports.

Using market forces to contain staff power is a growing trend. At Colgate, advisory groups in marketing and technology bill operating units for their help. Westinghouse's telecommunications staff has taken the process to its logical end: It now sells its information-services expertise outside the company under the name Wescor.

Somewhat ironically, decentralization of power has also brought with it a renewed emphasis on formal planning. Says J. Carter Fox, CEO of Chesapeake Corp., a $600 million paper and forest-products manufacturer: "We control the operating units through a system of profit plans and strategic plans." They're rigorously debated and analyzed, and "once we have an approved strategy and a profit plan, I want that person to take the initiative and let me know what he's done later."

Managing the boundaries for such initiative can be tricky. Once, in an emergency, a general manager ordered a $1.5 million piece of

machinery to replace one that had suddenly gone kaflooey. He didn't tell Fox beforehand, although the expenditure exceeded the limits even of what the CEO was allowed to spend without prior board approval. "I wouldn't want that to happen often," says Fox, who with his board approved the purchase retroactively.

Variations on the old philosophies of management by objectives and management by exception flourish under the new regime. At Heinz, says senior vice president David Sculley, 43, who oversees Weight Watchers, "We manage by exception generally" — using variances from projections to provide clues that something is going awry. "There's a goal post that is clear for every manager in the company — yearly and quarterly. Responsible managers won't make decisions inconsistent with those goals. And secrets are not well kept in our company. When we see a problem developing, we jump on it."

Communication is the most important source of personal power. You don't have to make everyone march in lock step if you're sure each is heading in the right direction. Says Heinz's O'Reilly: "It is the responsibility of the leader to provide inspiration, in any style with which he is comfortable. It can be the low-key dedication to frugality that was the hallmark of my predecessor, or a high-style, exhortative devotion to rhetoric, which is more my own." To get the word out to its employees, Colgate sends around videotapes the way the government sends around forms — "More than any company in the country," Reuben Mark guesses. Employees watch taped quarterly financial and technology reports, along with special videotapes on issues like corporate policy toward South Africa and the rights of women. Says John Bryan of Sara Lee: "When you get large, you have to go to the pulpit."

You also have to mingle at the coffee hour. The toughest challenge for an executive who gives up operating authority is to obtain firsthand information on how the business is running. Power in a old-style hierarchy may have "an abstract quality, with a lot of process and not much content," says John Rosenblum, University of Virginia business school dean. But power in a flat company can get remote too, as the span of control broadens. Without a big staff receiving hundreds of reports, how do you keep track of it all? The peripatetic CEO, forever flying off to a distant outpost of his far-flung empire, is compensating for the remoteness he may have created by delegating authority.

Smart CEOs of decentralized companies realize that they have to actively encourage communication among the different parts of the organization. Chesapeake's Carter Fox, for example, requires his division heads to take turns making presentations to the board about the entire company. Heinz promotes communication across the company through interdepartmental task forces, some short-lived and some continuing, that share knowledge and make policy on subjects such as purchasing and media buying. The advisory groups at Colgate serve as channels of communication as well as sources of specialized expertise.

The CEO must also take pains to see that all those independent operators running the company's different businesses have a care for the welfare of the whole. O'Reilly does this with money and charisma. Heinz executives enjoy lavish stock options and other incentives such as bonuses for short- and long-term performance. In O'Reilly's decade as CEO, employee ownership of Heinz stock has jumped from 4% of the total to 16%. All employees at the same level receive the same incentives based on the company's overall results, so their personal fortunes are tied to the success of the

whole, not of their particular operation. Thus, while vesting great autonomy in his managers, "I have banished the notion of territorial privilege," O'Reilly says.

He devotes much energy to building up camaraderie with weekend house parties at his Irish estate, Castlemartin, or working retreats — "Rolling Rock sessions," in company parlance, after the Pittsburgh country club where many take place. These gatherings hammer out policy and hammer in the company culture. One result, according to O'Reilly: When senior executives come in from the volleyball court to divvy up the marketing budget or capital funds, "our decisions are virtually always unanimous."

Fortune 500 CEOs may delegate and share more than before, but only a few say they have less power. The paradox of the new style in power is that to delegate it, and shake things up, itself requires a forceful use of power. Wrote Machiavelli, still one of the reigning experts on the subject: "There is nothing more difficult to carry out, nor more doubtful of success, nor more dangerous to handle, than to initiate a new order of things."

If power is to be given to a new breed of mini-CEOs throughout the company, they must be trained and chosen more carefully than ever. They may even have to be men and women new to the organization. Says Reuben Mark of his effort to push power down at Colgate: "I originally thought I could do it with the same people." He discovered instead — as did almost every other CEO whom FORTUNE talked with — that he had to clean house, that is, to wield the oldest, crudest form of power. Ralph Stayer had to fire a key sales executive: "One day I conferred this blessing on him, `From now on you'll make your own decisions.' The poor guy couldn't deal with it. I'd trained him extremely well in not taking responsibility."

But when the empowering of subordinates works, the total power in the organization available to the CEO may well increase. More people find ways to use the personal kinds of power latent within them. Harvard's John Kotter explains: "When you decentralize in a management sense, it does take power away from the corner office. But decentralizing leadership is different. The more power in the whole organization, the more you can influence and change." Management is an essentially conservative act; it helps you do better with the resources you have. But leadership can help you create new resources — "new products, new labor relations, new energy that, in turn, produce more power."

Take something as seemingly straightforward as spending authority. Surely if the CEO raises the limits on what a manager can sign off on from $50,000 to $100,000, the CEO has lost some of his power to the manager? Not so, argues consultant Allan Kennedy, co-author of Corporate Cultures. The key question about that new sign-off authority, he says, is "Subject to what? Subject to keeping within the budget, subject to the goals established for the division, subject to your annual review . . ." The fact is, says Kennedy, "You don't give away power — you barter with it." The boss who gives away power will extract a price for it.

What he should receive, at the very least, is a sharpened sense on the part of his subordinate of just what he or she is responsible for. The idea behind sharing power more broadly is to move decisions and resources as close as possible to where action can be taken — not to spread power around, but to pinpoint it. The decisions that result are faster and cleaner, so more decisions can be made, more work done. To Heinz's O'Reilly, there's a big difference between power that is decentralized and power that is diffused, as in "a local planning commission, where many people can say no but it's unclear who can say yes."

This is why the most radical visions of power sharing won't work. These tell tomorrow's managers to be prepared to shoulder responsibility without authority, to learn to get things done by discussion, encouragement, and faith in everyone's expertise — the hope that reason will reveal the best course of action, which the organization will automatically adopt as it becomes apparent. Like Communism, it looks better on paper than in practice. As Firestone's John Nevin points out, "If you want to drive a person crazy, the easiest way to do it is to give him a deep sense of responsibility and no authority. And the definition of terror is to give someone authority and no responsibility."

What will remain true in the best organizations, whatever else changes, is that power ultimately derives from performance. You can almost feel it flow to an executive who consistently performs well. Says Sara Lee's Bryan: "You see it in his ability to take on and argue with his superiors. He directs his managers with more authority and resists staff people more easily. He becomes a star, and over time comes to seem indispensable."

What's true for the individual is also true for the organization, or the unit of the organization. The decentralization of Heinz had its origins in this principle: 25 years ago the company's U.K. subsidiary brought in 85% of its worldwide profits. As a result, says O'Reilly, who joined the British team in 1969, "the authority that flows from performance — which is real power — vested itself automatically in the English company." Now, with 60% of profits coming from the U.S. and only 13% from Britain, American managers exercise more power than before.

Share power, and if profits go up everyone will praise the brilliant way you unleashed the latent energy of your people. But if profits go down, everyone will condemn the sloppy way you lost control of the company. Professor Robert Bies of Northwestern's Kellogg business school observes that the business reality these days is that "it's a tougher world, a leaner world, a meaner world." In this world, all that you can do by way of empowerment, teamwork and participation can't change one central fact: When it comes to power, the bottom line is the bottom line.

Reading 5.2

WOMEN MANAGERS EXPERIENCE SPECIAL POWER FAILURES[8]

by Rosabeth Moss Kanter

The traditional problems of women in management are illustrative of how formal and informal practices can combine to engender powerlessness. Historically, women in management have found their opportunities in more routine, low-profile jobs. In staff positions, where they serve in support capacities to line managers but have no line responsibilities of their own, or in supervisory jobs managing "stuck" subordinates, they are not in a position either to take the kinds of risks that build credibility or to develop their own team by pushing bright subordinates.

Such jobs, which have few favors to trade, tend to keep women out of the mainstream of the organization. This lack of clout, coupled with the greater difficulty anyone who is "different" has in getting into the information and support networks, has meant that merely by organizational situation women in management have been more likely than men to be rendered structurally powerless. This is one reason those women who have achieved power have often had family connections that put them in the mainstream of the organization's social circles.

A disproportionate number of women managers are found among first-line supervisors or staff professionals; and they, like men in those circumstances, are likely to be organizationally powerless. But the behavior of other managers can contribute to the powerlessness of women in management in a number of less obvious ways.

One way other managers can make a woman powerless is by patronizingly overprotecting her: putting her in "a safe job," not giving her enough to do to prove herself, and not suggesting her for high-risk, visible assignments. This protectiveness is sometimes born of "good" intentions to give her every chance to succeed (why stack the deck against her?). Out of managerial concerns, out of awareness that a woman may be up against situations that men simply do not have to face, some very well-meaning managers protect their female managers ("It's a jungle, so why send her into it?").

Overprotectiveness can also mask a manager's fear of association with a woman should she fail. One senior bank official at a level below vice president told me about his concerns with respect to a high-performing, financially experienced woman report to him. Despite *his* overwhelmingly positive work experiences with her, he was still afraid to recommend her for other assignments because he felt it was a personal risk. "What if other mangers are not as accepting of women as I am?" he asked. "I know I'd be sticking my neck out; they would take her more because of my endorsement than her qualifications. And what if she doesn't make it? My judgment will be on the line."

Overprotection is relatively benign compared with rendering a person powerless by providing obvious signs of lack of managerial support. For example, allowing someone supposedly in authority to be bypassed easily means that no one else has to take him or her seriously. If a woman's immediate supervisor or other managers listen willingly to criticism of her and show they are concerned every time a negative comment comes up and that they assume she must be at fault, then they are helping to undercut her. If managers let other people know that they have concerns abut this person or that they are testing her to see how she does, then they are inviting other people to look for signs of inadequacy or failure.

Furthermore, people assume they can afford to bypass women because they "must be uninformed" or "don't know the ropes." Even though women may be respected for their competence or expertise, they are not necessarily seen as being informed beyond the technical requirements of the job. There may be a grain of historical truth in this. Many women come to senior management positions as "outsiders" rather than up through the usual channels.

Also, because until very recently men have not felt comfortable seeing women as businesspeople (business clubs have traditionally excluded women), they have tended to seek each other out for informal socializing. Anyone, male or female, seen as organizationally naive and lacking sources of "inside dope" will find his or her own lines of information limited.

Finally, even when women are able to achieve some power on their own, they have not necessarily been able to translate such personal credibility into an organizational power base. To create a network of supporters out of individual clout requires that a person pass on and share power, that subordinates and peers be empowered by virtue of their connection with the person. Traditionally, neither men nor women have seen women as capable of sponsoring others, even though they may be capable of achieving and succeeding on their own. Women have been viewed as the *recipients* of sponsorship rather than as the sponsors themselves.

(As more women prove themselves in organizations and think more self-consciously about bringing along young people, this situation may change. However, I still hear many more questions from women managers about how they can benefit from mentors, sponsors, or peer networks than about how they themselves can start to pass on favors and make use of their own resources to benefit others.)

Viewing managers in terms of power and powerlessness helps explain two familiar stereotypes about women and leadership in organizations: that no one wants a woman boss (although studies show that anyone who has ever had a woman boss is likely to have had a positive experience), and that the reason no one wants a woman boss is that women are "too controlling, rules-minded, and petty."

The first stereotype simply makes clear that power is important to leadership. Underneath the preference for men is the assumption that, given the current distribution of people in organizational leadership positions, men are more likely than women to be in positions to achieve power and, therefore, to share their power with others. Similarly, the "bossy woman boss" stereotype is a perfect picture of powerlessness. All of those traits are just as characteristic of men who are powerless, but women are slightly more likely, because of circumstances I have mentioned, to find themselves powerless than are men. Women with power in the organization are just as effective — and preferred — as men.

Recent interviews conducted with about 600 bank managers show that, when a woman exhibits the petty traits of powerlessness, people assume that she does so "because she is a woman." A striking difference is that, when a man engages in the same behavior, people assume the behavior is a matter of his own individual style and characteristics and do not conclude that it reflects on the suitability of men for management.

Chapter 6

Leadership

What will twenty-first century leaders look like? What will be the prototype of our political, business and educational leaders? Are there certain qualities and characteristics that are classic, for all time? As you look around your classroom, are there certain students that you just know will be leading teams or projects or even organizations? Will you be one of these leaders? Many questions, few definitive answers. One thing is for certain, however. Leadership will be of critical importance in helping organizations handle the challenges to be faced in the twenty-first century.

Many of you probably have a gut sense about what a leader does. A leader is someone who is strong, directive, demanding, powerful and unafraid; someone who tells people what's wanted and gets it; someone who takes charge and inspires; someone who is knowledgeable about a group or organization; someone who can structure a task in an organized way; someone who sits atop the organizational hierarchy. These seem to be the undeniable qualities of leadership, or are they?

Wait a minute. There's another brand of leadership that some are saying will be the prototype for the twenty-first century. It's someone who empowers others, who orchestrates rather than directs, who asks people what's needed and provides the requested resources; who enlists the help of others; who recognizes that expertise resides with the "troops"; who behaves as if he or she reports to his or her own subordinates; who acts as coach, facilitator and informal guide. What a marked difference from the traditional leader!

People have struggled with the topic of leadership for centuries. After all, it is basic to any collective task. There is always the challenge of directing behavior towards some purpose and harnessing the horsepower necessary to accomplish a task. In business, this quality of leadership has become a type of "X" factor. It often seems to spell the difference in success for companies and teams. Someone seems to have "led" the group towards its desired outcome. Someone seems to have done more than "manage" the administrative and operational issues. And someone seems to stand out from the other with qualities that lead others to respond in ways they wouldn't have on their own.

And yet... we don't know as much about leadership as we would like. For example, is there a surefire way for selecting a "leader" type from a pool of job applicants? Are leaders born or made? That is, can people develop leadership qualities or are they inherent? Why is it that some leaders are effective for only a short period of time? For example, many sports team managers are heralded as "true leaders"... for only as long as the team is winning. When the team starts to lose, they suddenly lose their ability, it seems, and are fired! Maybe leaders are only as good as their "followers."

Indeed, is leadership always valuable or can it get in the way? Some groups say that they would be better off if left alone. With the cry for more leaders, is it possible to have too many, or to have leaders who can be destructive rather than constructive? Indeed, some leaders such as Hitler or Jim Jones have used their leadership skills to cause tremendous harm.

We want you to struggle with all these difficult questions so that you can have better understanding of what it takes to be an effective, humane leader- -and one who is right for the twenty- first century.

There have been many efforts to theorize about leadership over the last 50 years of behavioral science research. The various leadership theories will be discussed in detail in your textbook. To give you a flavor, though, essentially the focus has shifted from studying the traits of successful leaders, to looking at leadership styles, to focussing on contingency models of style and situation, and finally to differentiating leadership from management.

The earliest theories sought to identify the origins of leadership in genetic terms. Great leaders, they sought to prove, were born and not made and were great in all leadership situations and, presumably, throughout their lifetimes. Research, though, was unable to substantiate any genetic linkage and any sustainable impact through all times and situations.

Others favored the belief that leaders were made, rather than born, and that some universal traits were the bases of effective leadership. The search for these traits however did not produce a single best personality for leaders to possess or develop. Although one could point to some fairly universal traits, they were not exhibited in the same behaviors or styles. Studies of single best behaviors or styles were similarly unsuccessful in predicting leadership effectiveness across multiple situations. Thus arose a school of thought that underscored the contingent nature of leadership.

Focussing on situational leadership, Hersey and Blanchard defined leadership as an influence process, as any time you try to influence the behavior of another person.[1] Leadership style is the pattern of behaviors you use in the process of influencing another, as perceived by the other person(s). Initially, researchers characterized two broad types of styles, autocratic and democratic, or people-oriented and task-oriented.[2] Hersey and Blanchard, in their situational theory of leadership expanded this to four styles: delegating, supporting, coaching and directing — depending on the developmental level of the follower (that is, their commitment and competence).

For many today, these characteristics of leadership are still too internally focussed and too much based on hierarchy. Instead, a recent school of thought has emphasized the distinction between management and leadership. According to this thinking, the new corporate leader must demonstrate, for example, transformational skills (such as helping to fundamentally transform the organizational direction and processes in response to external conditions), skills of visionary foresight and a skill for developing and guiding beliefs.

Kotter argues that leadership, in this sense, complements management rather than replaces it.[3] In his study, he found that leadership is not fundamentally grounded in some special magic or exotic personality traits. He differentiates management from leadership as follows:

Management	Leadership
Planning and budgeting (near-term)	Setting a direction (long-term)
Organizing and staffing	Aligning people to the vision
Controlling and problem solving	Motivating and inspiring

Both sets of approaches are needed to make an organization effective but they are fundamentally oriented in different, yet complementary, directions. Kotter and others have tried to demystify leadership and yet clearly give it a domain that must be developed and nurtured in people.

1. P. Hersey and Kenneth Blanchard, *Organizational Behavior* , (New York: Prentice Hall, 1988).

2. R. R. Blake and J. S. Mouton, *The New Managerial Grid* , (Houston: Gulf, 1978).

3. J. P. Kotter, "What Leaders Really Do," *Harvard Business Review*, (May-June 1990), pp. 103-111.

In underscoring these special qualities of leadership, it has become virtually synonymous with leading change in organizations. Effective leadership helps to direct attention to new vistas and opportunities, to exemplify and model key behaviors for the future and to motivate others to new behaviors and attitudes. These all serve to enable an organization to change. Leaders thus play a role that some people call "visionary." According to one study, a successful visionary CEO behaves as follows:[4]

- Searches for ideas, concepts and ways of thinking until a clear vision crystallizes.

- Articulates the vision into an easy-to-grasp philosophy that integrates strategic direction and cultural values.

- Motivates company employees to embrace the vision through constant persuasion and setting an example of hard work.

- Makes contact with employees at all levels in the organization, attempting to understand their concerns and the impact the vision has on them.

- Acts in a warm, supportive, expressive way, always communicating that, "We're all in this together, like a family."

- Translates the vision into a reason for being for each employee by continually relating the vision to individual cares, concerns and work.

- Concentrates on the major strengths within the organization that will ensure the success of the vision.

- Remains at the center of the action, positioned as prime shaper of the vision.

- Looks for ways to improve, augment or further develop the vision by carefully observing changes inside and outside the organization.

- Measures the ultimate success of the organization in terms of its ability to fulfill the vision.

But leadership has one other dimension that is crucial. A leader must appreciate his or her role as a "leader of leaders." That is, organizations today are keenly aware that no one person can take on all the leadership required to respond to the fast emerging changes — threats and opportunities — to be faced in the years ahead.

Motorola is perhaps the best example of an organization that is dedicated to creating leadership capability throughout the company. It is not just the CEO and not just the management and not just those at headquarters, but rather a wide cadre of people who must exhibit these leadership qualities. Organizations like Motorola and General Electric are investing heavily in training and development to help people gain the confidence and skills to assume a more proactive, longer-term oriented, empowering style.

Before we conclude this brief review of thinking about leadership, consider, however, a devil's advocate position about leadership. Perhaps we have inflated the import and impact that leaders may have. Indeed, one author summarized some studies that would suggest the following conclusions:[5]

- Leaders really make far less difference than we give them credit for (not much more than 10 percent of the difference).

- A leader is only as good as the situation he or she finds himself or herself in.

- Leaders manipulate people.

4. Warren Bennis study cited in C. Hickman and M. A. Silva, *Creating Excellence*, (New York: New American Library, 1984), pp. 160-161.

5. W. Kiechel, "The Case Against Leaders," *Fortune*, (Nov. 21, 1988), pp. 217-219.

- Unchecked leaders can run off the rails, taking the organizations with them.

- Leaders don't inspire baby-boomers.

- Even if we do want leaders, we don't know how to produce them.

- As management becomes more participatory, leaders are increasingly unnecessary.

These provocative propositions raise some tough issues for us to consider in our discussions about leadership. They force us to consider the importance of the followers, the situation and the role of leadership as we enter the twenty-first century. These will be part of our discussions in the remainder of this chapter.

Name _____

ID# _____

Section _____

Sam Bond, a computer applications specialist with ABC Software, was asked to give an early morning presentation to a prospective client in a distant city. At the last minute, Bond decided to travel a day early so that he could spend an evening with the client as well. Bond's meetings went very well, and he garnered a substantial contract for his company.[6]

When he returned from his trip, he submitted his expense account—including a $182 hotel bill for the night prior to his client meeting. Company policy was that any lodging expense above $100 must be approved beforehand by a supervisor.

Three supervisors were asked how they would respond:

Supervisor A: "I would reluctantly approve the expense in full after discussing the situation with Bond and noting the special circumstances. I would make sure he submitted a supplemental memo explaining the details."

Supervisor B: "I would double-check the policy, and if so, I would approve only $100 for the hotel room—despite Bond's contention that the hotel was the only one with vacancies in the area and that his staying there helped him to land the account."

6. Case adapted from Dale McConkey, *Business Horizons*, as cited in Claire McIntosh, *Working Woman*, (February, 1990), p. 26.

Supervisor C: "I would view the policy as a general guide only. I would be more interested in what Bond accomplished during his trip. I would gladly approve the entire amount and commend Bond for his initiative."

1. Which supervisor's approach would you endorse and why?

2. Is this a situation in which you think "leadership" actions are appropriate? Why or why not?

3. Would you characterize your preferred approach as "leadership?"

LIGHTS, CAMERA, ACTION: MANAGEMENT LIVE!

Lights

On August 28, 1963, on the steps of the Lincoln Memorial in Washington, D.C., before an enthusiastic crowd of 250,000, Martin Luther King, Jr. proclaimed his dream to the world. This speech captured the imagination of a nation. It has remained a source of inspiration for all who aspire to a better world.

In addition, this speech was a hallmark of Dr. King's leadership and an interesting example of charisma for anyone watching it.

Camera: Martin Luther King's "I Have a Dream" Speech

Today you will have a chance to see this most important address to the American people.

Action

While you are listening and observing, please consider the following questions:

1. How did you feel as you were listening?

2. How would the audience have felt that day at the steps of the Lincoln Memorial?

3. What were the key messages of the speech?

4. What techniques did Dr. King use? Note all of his key phrases and rhetorical devices. Why was the message so powerful?

5. What contemporary leaders have you seen that have similar impact? Do they use the same techniques as Dr. King?

6. What would prevent you from using similar techniques in leading groups and projects with which you are involved?

Leadership and followership must be very closely linked. The roles and responsibilities of each must be clearly understood. For example, in the Martin Luther King speech, it is clear that the "followers" and the leader are in synch with each other. But what will be the actual follow-up after the speech? Will it be apathy, passivity and cynicism—or will the "followers" be action-takers and risk-takers? To better understand how we must not only develop effective leaders but also effective followers, we will examine each below:

Step 1: Each of you will be in a group that is divided in half. Each half must come to some agreement on the following questions:

Leadership Team

1. What would you as a leader want from your followers?

2. What qualities or attitudes would be unacceptable to you?

3. How might demographic differences between leaders and followers affect working relationships (for example, men leading women, women leading men, blacks leading whites, or whites leading blacks)?

FollowershipTeam

1. What would you as a follower want from your leader?

2. What qualities or attitudes would be unacceptable?

3. How might demographics between leaders and followers affect working relationships (for example, men leading women, women leading men, blacks leading whites, or whites leading blacks)?

Step 2. The two teams should compare their conclusions on each of the questions and then comment on the following:

1. What do you agree is crucial for leaders and followers to successfully work with each other?

2. On what issues do you disagree?

3. What would be the best indicators that leaders and followers were working well together if you were to be an observer?

MIRROR TALK: FOCUSSING ON ME

A natural place to look for examining the characteristics and situations of leadership is your own experience.

1. List the characteristics of people you consider leaders. With what kinds of projects or events do you associate them?

2. Consider a leader who has influenced or motivated you and describe the techniques that were used to engage you as a follower.

3. Think of a situation where a so-called "leader" disappointed you. What did he or she do, or not do?

4. Think of a situation when you or someone you know well was at their personal best. To what extent did someone's leadership play a part in stimulating this high performance?

Leadership is a very personal experience. Each and every one of us has been impacted by leadership and has impacted others. It is something that has the potential for doing tremendous good or harm. Think back on all that we have seen and discussed in this area and reflect on what it might mean to you and your future.

1. What's so gratifying to me about the prospect of becoming a more effective leader?

2. What do I need to work on to develop my own leadership skills?

3. What are the ethical responsibilities and burdens that I must be prepared to accept if I am to assume a leadership capacity?

4. What are the joys and rewards I might feel as an effective follower?

5. If there was one quality of leadership that I really wish I had, it would be:

    Explain why:

6. As I think back on the Martin Luther King video clip, I really came to appreciate a lot of things that I never realized before—

    About me:

    About my fellow students:

    About the United States of America:

We are still searching for better ways of exercising leadership. As times change, and as the needs and skills of "followers" change, new models are quickly emerging. They are being tested in this last decade of the twentieth century. They tend to be less hierarchical and less authoritarian. They tend to be based more on merit and skill than on position and formal power. Some say it is a more "feminine" method of managing that will emerge as the dominant mode.

The task of leadership is unquestionably becoming more complicated. You will be more and more dependent on people that are distant in location and culture; that are hooked up with each other and with you in electronic ways that we've never had before; that are much more intimately interconnected with constituencies that are not in the formal hierarchy but that exert a lot of demands (such as customers and regulators); and where collaboration and consistency will be critical skills.

In the article below, "The New Breed of Leaders," some of these emergent leadership models are exemplified. The authors argue that the era of the "bad bosses" is ending, replaced by leaders who are ethical, open, empowering and inspiring. Are these models too optimistic or simplistic? Can we find new leadership answers to the complicated human and organizational demands of the twenty-first century? Can we develop leaders who won't be overwhelmed by the changes they must help to drive? The answers to these questions are, in large measure, up to you.

Reading 6.1

THE NEW BREED OF LEADERS[7]

By Michele Morris

For many employees of the '80s will be remembered as the decade of the big bad boss. To stay competitive with businesses down the street — or factories around the world — American companies were forced to get lean and mean. Cost cutting became the rallying cry, and downsizing and restructuring a way of life. It took a tough boss to lay off fleets of workers and close the doors on scores of factories.

Too often, though, economic realities led to a harsh, survival-of-the-fittest management style. Some tough guys finished first-like Harold Geneen, the now retired CEO of ITT, who became notorious for "getting incredibly high goals driving his managers to meet them and humiliating those who failed," according to *Fortune* magazine. Like Hugh L. McColl, Jr., chairman of the North Carolina-based NCNB Corp, who kept a dummy hand

7. *Working Woman*, (March 1990), p. 73.

grenade on his desk; once, during a meeting, he pulled the pin to see who would flinch. Like Texas Air's widely despised Frank Lorenzo. And like Helmsley Hotels' president, Leona Helmsley, the tabloids' "Queen of Mean," who went through six hotels managers in one year.

We all know what happened to Leona. But other corporate heads are also finding out — albeit in less dramatic ways — that tough-guy tactics won't necessarily work in the '90s. Today the men and women who inhabit the executive suite understand that people are a company's greatest resource. And good people are getting harder to find: US business is facing its first labor shortage in 20 years. "The shrinking labor pool means managers will have to put a higher premium on employees," says Mary Anne Devanna, research director of Columbia University's Management Institute. And after the tough job of cutting costs, closing money-losing divisions and getting rid of the

deadwood is finished, business leaders have to win the heart's — not just the minds — of their employees. "Instead of emulating the autocratic, invincible models of the past, successful managers must lead by inspiring individuals," says John Sculley, chairman and CEO of Apple Computer. Caring about people is essential to good leadership, adds management consultant Jack Carew, whose clients include Coca-Cola and AT&T; he likes to talk about "managing people from the neck down." More and more companies send their managers to sensitivity seminars; the NTL Institute in Alexandria, VA, conducts more than 100 such workshops each year for executives from Fortune 500 companies and government agencies.

In the '90s, great leaders will be tough competitors but not harsh with their own people. One tough guy who's found a new religion is Jack Welch, CEO of General Electric and a member of *Fortune* magazine's 1984 roster of the toughest bosses in America. After taking over, Welch announced the closing of dozens of plants. Employees dubbed him Neutron Jack — after he visited a factory, they joked, the building was left standing but a lot of people were dead. As Welch pursues phase two of his long-term plan to make GE a global powerhouse, he's preaching a different message: "It has nothing to do with whips and chains and taking heads out," he told *Fortune* in 1989. "We're trying to unleash people to be self-confident and so to take on more responsibility."

Other top dogs share Welch's philosophy. Wayne Calloway, CEO of Pepsi Co., is a formidable competitor, but ask him the secret to his company's marketing prowess and he'll answer, "The three Ps: people, people, people." Liz Claiborne, Inc., one of the most admired companies in America, is known for its esprit de corps; the in-house directory even lists employees alphabetically by first name. And Max De Pree, chairman of Herman Miller Inc., the office-furniture maker, credits much of his company's fast track success to treating workers well — through its profit-sharing plan and employee-incentive programs. "If every company in America were managed like Herman Miller, we would not be concerned about the Japanese right now," says James O'Toole, author of *Vanguard Management*.

Voluntary effort is what ignites productivity. Maybe somebody should tell that to Margaret Thatcher. The Iron Lady may have been just what the doctor ordered to bring the British economy back to health in the '80s, but as the economy stagnates, social problems fester and cold war thaws, she is beginning to seem out of date and out of touch. She inspires parody, not productivity.

The problems facing us in the '90s require a new kind of leadership, a quality that's part inspiration, part gentle persuasion. Tomorrow's leaders must win converts and persuade them to share their visions. Donna R. Ecton, senior VP of franchising at Nutri/System, Inc., calls her leadership style "a cross between a cheerleader and an evangelist." It's a sentiment typical of the new breed, who believe that, in the words of John P. Kotter, author of *The Leadership Factor,* leadership is "the process of moving people in some direction mostly through noncoercive means." Today even GE's Jack Welch insists on calling his people leaders instead of managers. His reasoning: "Call people managers and they are going to start managing things, getting in the way. The job of a leader," he says, "is to take the available resources — human and financial — and allocate them, not to spread them out evenly like butter on bread. That's what bureaucrats do."

In their new book, *Megatrends 2000,* John Naisbitt and Patricia Aburdene call the '90s the "decade of women in leadership." And, they write, "Leaders recognize that people make or break a company. To harness their power, leaders inspire commitment and empower people by sharing authority. Responding to labor shortages with flexibility, they enable their firms to attract, reward and motivate the best."

The people who will lead companies as well as countries in the '90s will win commitment by setting an example of excellence — ethical, open, empowering and inspiring. And yes, George, kinder and gentler. But that doesn't mean wimpy. When change is in the wind, great leaders can be found with their followers in the thick of it, not on the sidelines. Great leaders are those women and men who see the future and seize the moment.

Reading 6.2
HOW TO BE THE LEADER THEY'LL FOLLOW[8]

By Warren Bennis

What is it that makes a person a leader? Some would say that it's charisma and you either have it or you don't. There are many leaders, however, who couldn't be described as particularly charismatic but who nevertheless manage to inspire an enviable trust and loyalty among their followers. Through their abilities to get people on their side, they are able to effect changes in the culture of their organizations and make their visions of the future real.

How do they do it? Ask them and they'll talk to you about human values: empathy, trust, mutual respect — and courage.

To Know Them
Is To Lead Them

Empathy, like charisma, may be a quality that people either have or don't have. Walt Disney producer Marty Kaplan says, "I've known leaders who have had none of it and nevertheless were leaders, but those who have had that quality have moved and inspired me more."

Former CBS executive Barbara Corday sees empathy as a special skill among women leaders. "I think women see power in a different way from men. I want to have the kind of power that is my company working well, my staff working well... As moms and wives and daughters, we've been caretakers, and we continue in caretaking roles even as we get successful in business. I'm very proud of the fact that I not only know all the people who work for me but I know their husbands' and wives' names, and I know their children's names... People appreciate that, and they're loyal and care about what they're doing.

8. *Working Woman*, (March 1990), p. 75. Excerpted from "On Becoming a Leader," by Warren Bennis. Copyright 1989 by Warren Bennis.

There are plenty of male leaders who prize empathy, too. Retired Lucky Stores CEO Don Ritchey says, "I think people are turned on when their bosses not only know they're there but know intimately what they're doing — that it's a partnership. You're trying to run this thing well together, and if something goes wrong our goal is to fix it, not see who we can nail."

Of course, empathy isn't the only factor in getting people on your side. Roger Gould, founder and president of Interactive Health Systems, a computer-assisted therapy program, explains how he took charge without taking control: "I've always been kind of a lone wolf, but when I was head of outpatient services at UCLA Medical Center, I developed a kind of consensus leadership. The fact that I was the boss didn't mean that I would or could take sole responsibility. Everyone was living with the same complexity, so we had to deal with it as a group."

Sydney Pollack, director of such popular films as *Tootsie* and *Out of Africa,* describes the leader's need to have people on his side this way: "Up to a point I think you can lead out of fear, intimidation, as awful as that sounds. But the problem is that you're creating obedience with a residue of resentment. If you want to make a physics analogy, you'd be moving through the medium but you'd be creating a lot of drag, a lot of backwash.

"There are two other qualities that I think are more positive reasons to follow someone. One is an honest belief in the person you're following. The other is selfish: The person following has to believe that following is the best thing to do at the time. You don't want people to follow you just because that's what they're paid for. You try to make

everyone feel they have a stake in it, that they'll learn something."

How To Be Trusted, Not Feared

Gloria Steinem, journalist and feminist leader, feels the strategy of getting people on your side makes the difference between what she calls "movement" and "corporate" leadership. "Movement leadership requires persuasion, not giving orders. There is no position to lead from; it doesn't exist. What makes you successful is that you can phrase things in a way that is inspirational, that makes coalition possible."

Betty Friedan, co-founder of the National Organization for Women, also endorses the idea of leading through persuasion rather than position. "I've never fought for organizational power," she says. "I have a great deal of influence just by my voice. I don't have to be president. I recently gave a speech at a university where only two percent of the faculty is women. I told the crowd, 'I must be in a place that is for some reason an anachronism.' I read the figures to them. I said, 'I'm surprised that you have not had a major class-action suit.' You could see the tension in the room. I said, 'You are really in a vulnerable position, since over 50 percent of your financing is federal funding. Just as a warning. Watch it.' Then I went on with my lecture. And something happened in that room. The last ten years I haven't been the head of any organization, but I don't need to be."

The basis of leading with your voice is trust. You generate and sustain trust by exemplifying:

• **Constancy** Whatever surprises leaders themselves may face, they shouldn't create any for the group. Leaders stay the course.

• **Congruity** Leaders walk their talk. There should be no gap between the theories they espouse and the ones they practice.

• **Reliability** Leaders are there when it counts; they are ready to support their co-workers in the moments that matter.

• **Integrity** Leaders honor their commitments and promises.

Frances Hesselbein, executive director of the Girl Scouts, says, "We're not managing for the sake of being great managers: we're managing for the mission. I don't believe in a star system. I believe in helping people identify what they can do well and releasing them to do it." Like Friedan, Hesselbein leads with her voice. She has learned the lesson of taking charge without taking control, that she must inspire her organization's employees and volunteers, not order them.

In *Leadership Is an Art,* Max De Pree, chairman of Herman Miller, argues that this is the way to treat everyone: "The best people working for organizations are like volunteers. Since they could probably find good jobs in any number of groups, they choose to work somewhere for reasons less tangible than salary or position... (such as) shared commitment to ideas, to issues, to values, to goals and to management process. Words such as love, warmth, personal chemistry, are certainly pertinent.''

The Need for Mutual Respect

Corporate leaders must have mastered their vocation or profession — they do whatever they do very well — but they also should be able to establish and maintain positive relationships with their subordinates inside the organization. A leader's ability to galvanize her co-workers resides in her understanding not only of herself but also of her co-workers' needs and wants, along with an understanding of what can be called their mission.

"They (your co-workers) have to believe that you know what you're doing," says Ritchey. "You have to believe that they know what they're doing, too, and let them know that you trust them."

A major challenge that all leaders are facing now is an epidemic of corporate malfeasance. And if there is anything that undermines subordinates' trust, it is the feeling that the people at the top lack integrity, are without a solid sense of ethics.

In today's volatile business climate, leaders must steer a clear and consistent course. "I start with the presumption that most people want to be ethical," says Ritchey. "It's sort of a golden-rule philosophy. So if you set up a climate where you not only say it but where people see that you mean it, and it works, then nobody has to make expedient choices because somebody was leaning on him, telling him on the one hand to be ethical and on the other hand to make the numbers even if he has to be cute about it. The fact that you are very hard-nosed about weeding out unethical behavior helps. Ethics is not Pollyanna stuff. It works better."

The Courage To Pioneer

Leading through voice, inspiring through trust and empathy, can help create a corporate climate that gives people elbowroom to do the right things and to grow. Successful leaders believe in change — in both people and organizations. They equate it with growth and progress. (Change in the world at large can be an obstacle, too.) "Circumstances beyond our control" was the operative phrase all too often in the 1980s.

A leader may discover that the culture of her own corporation is an obstacle to the changes she wants to introduce because, as currently constituted, it's devoted more to preserving itself than to meeting new challenges.

"My former boss at Pepsico and the current head of IBM were both World War II fighter pilots," says Apple's John Sculley. "The fighter pilot is no longer going to be our paradigm for leaders. The new generation of leaders is going to be more intellectually aware. Beyond the ways we have to change as leaders and managers within the context of our enterprise, the world itself is changing, becoming more idea-intensive, more information-intensive; so the people who will rise to the top are going to be people who are comfortable with and excited by ideas and information."

The best leaders deal with this mercurial world by anticipating, looking not just down the road but around the corner; by seeing change as an opportunity rather than an obstacle; and by accepting it rather than resisting it. One of the hardest lessons any novice skier has to learn is that she must lean away from the hill and not into it. The natural inclination is to stay as close to the slope as possible because it feels safer. But only when you lean out can you begin to control your own movements and not be controlled by the slope. The organizational novice does the same thing; leans close to the company's slope, submerging her own identity in that of the corporation. The leader stands tall and leans out, taking charge of her own course, with a clear view of where she's going.

Warren Bennis is a professor of business administration at the University of Southern California.

The One-Minute Motivator

By Lorraine Calvacca

"It only takes a few minutes to do small things that will keep employees motivated and caring about the company," says Marilynn Davis, vice president of the risk-financing division at American Express. Simple acts of recognition, says Davis, accomplish more than the crack of a whip any day.

Davis, 37, shows her concern through inquiries about employees' families and acknowledgments of watersheds such as weddings and graduations. When Davis took over the group two years ago, she started a tradition of "cake and bull" sessions for employees' birthdays. "People are your biggest component," says Davis, whose eight-person team helps American Express prepare for risks that include theft and property damage. "You can't expect them to be machines."

Mike Rubenstein, the director of risk finance, says Davis's empathic nature inspires employees' loyalty and trust. He recalls how last year he and Davis had to choose a mutually acceptable date for a major presentation to a corporate financial officer, who had given October 31 as one option. Although that day was fine for Davis, she ruled it out. "Marilynn knew I had a young son and that it was important to me to see him in his dinosaur Halloween costume."

"I have learned from Marilynn," Rubenstein adds, "that it's possible to strike a true balance during business hours between work and personal concerns. And it makes life much more interesting and fun." BOSS STYLE: Davis builds team spirit and morale by tempering business with pleasure.

The Determined Delegator

By Laurel Touby

Sheri Poe runs her Weymouth, MA-based athletic-footwear company, Ryka, Inc., like a good captain runs the ship: with a handpicked, highly skilled crew. Poe, 37, lets each staffer manager her post as she sees fit, without excessive input from the captain.

Poe didn't always employ such a progressive style of leadership. But Ryka's rapid growth — sales have climbed from zero to $16 million in less than two years — forced her to start delegating. "I just couldn't do everything myself. I knew that if I didn't delegate, some area in my company would suffer," says Poe.

The turning point came in 1988 at Ryka's second Sporting Goods Manufacturing Association trade show in Atlanta. Poe was torn between handling they myriad details of the show and managing the equally important task of doing interviews with retailers. "It was a big move for me to give up responsibility for the trade show," she says. But Poe's worries were for naught. Public-relations manager Lauri Ruddy did the event's planning, and "orders exceeded our expectations," Poe says.

Today Poe keeps tabs on operations through weekly checkup meetings with the head of each department. "Good employees just need guidance and freedom to do their jobs right," she says. BOSS STYLE: Sheri Poe doesn't overmanage. She gives managers strategic input — then lets them do the job.

The Team Builder

By Pamela Kruger

When Dee Joyner, the chief of staff to the St. Louis County government's executive, talks about her work, she almost never starts a sentence with "I." By using "we" instead, the 42-year-old Joyner isn't merely being modest' she genuinely see herself as part of a team.

Rather than dictate her wishes to her staff, Joyner shows them the importance of a project, why their involvement is critical and how they will benefit from the project's success. Because she is personable, unpretentious and sincere, her approach usually succeeds, say those who have worked with her. "With some managers, you might question their motives and wonder what they're getting out of it. Not with Dee," says Alan Richter, chairman of the board of the St. Louis County Economic Council.

From 1985 through 1989, Joyner was executive director of the Economic Council, which develops programs to attract and retain businesses in the county. Her first task as executive director was to merge five independent agencies into one central organization. By holding regular meetings with the staffs and managers of the various agencies, she was able to accomplish just that — without losing a single worker in the process. And under Joyner's direction, the agency helped make St. Louis County one of the country's fastest growing in the area of new employment. "If people are part of the process," Joyner says, "they become invested in the outcome, and they will try to achieve the organization's goals. And that's what it's all about." BOSS STYLE: When Dee Joyner gives directions, her staff goes into action — but not because they're afraid of her. As an involved leader herself, she sets the tone for the team.

The Democratic Dictator

By Pamela Kruger

Caroline Hirsch, owner of New York's hottest comedy club, Caroline's, trusts her own funny bone when it comes to business decisions. But she won't say no to her staff's suggestions — even if she doesn't like an idea initially. "She'll say, 'Convince me,'" says Joe Falzarano, her talent director, who also is in charge of television development.

When Falzarano suggested including comedy vignettes — little skits and gags — in Hirsch's new TV series, Caroline's *Comedy Hour,* the 39-year-old Hirsch was skeptical. The Arts & Entertainment Network already had nixed the first pilot show, so this effort was her second — and last — chance. A pragmatic businesswoman who opened her first small comedy club in 1981, Hirsch worried that the vignettes would cost too much and might "bring down" the weekly show, which features stand-up comedians at Caroline's.

But Falzarano was excited about his idea. After reviewing sample scripts, Hirsch agreed to shoot a few of the vignettes. As it turned out, Hirsch liked the finished product and included the skits in her first six shows, which debuted in January. The network's response was enthusiastic.

Should the vignettes not continue to meet her standards, though, Hirsch will drop them. She achieved her success by trusting her taste and showcasing comedians like Pee Wee Herman, Sandra Bernhardt and Jay Leno — before they were household names. "In a creative business, you have to be open," Hirsch says, adding that she has rejected comics and then booked them once their agents showed her some new work. BOSS STYLE: Part democrat, part dictator, Hirsch is open to new ideas but ultimately trusts her own opinions.

The Charismatic Crusader

By Lorraine Calvacca

"Leadership has a harder job to do than just choose sides. It must bring sides together," the Reverend Jesse Jackson once remarked. And one surefire way to do that, says National Black Women's Health Project (NBWHP) founder Byllye Avery, is to listen to different people's views — and show them respect.

But Avery, 51, is no armchair philosopher. By practicing what she preaches, the former special-education teacher has built a national health network that focuses on improving black women's health through education. Since 1984 the grass-roots project has grown from two volunteers and a handful of self-help groups to 19 full-time staffers and almost 150 self-help chapters in 24 states. Last August Avery received a $310,000 MacArthur Foundation fellowship to further her work.

For ACLU lawyer and NBWHP advisory-board member Lynn Paltrow, Avery's skill in bringing together disparate groups crystallized last April during a two-day reproductive-rights conference. "We had over 150 activists there with divergent views and priorities about a very emotional issue," Paltrow remembers. Confronted with a potentially divisive situation, Avery asked each group to choose one member to light a candle and make a statement about her or his cultural group. Says Paltrow, "It was because of Byllye that we were able to stay together in that room." BOSS STYLE: Avery is accessible to people of many different levels; she is both a strategist and a humanist.

Reading 6.3

THE END OF THE BIG BAD BOSS[9]

By Anne M. Russell

Welcome to the age of enlightenment, bosswise. We all know, too well, what a Big Bad Boss is (and yes, we may even have been one ourselves). Nor do we lack words to describe the Bad Boss and his or her character flaws.

But take heart. The era of the Good Boss has arrived. So here are a few things you won't need in order to excel as an executive in the '90s:

Military Lingo Business may be hell at times, but it isn't war. The boot-camp paradigm of unquestioning submission to a supreme authority — the Boss — is falling by the wayside as organizations recognize that good ideas and initiative come from all levels of the hierarchy. OK, you dogfaces, let's find some new analogies to replace the tired old blood-and-guts babble. Remember, Jack Tramiel (chairman of the board of Atari) may still tell the troops, "Business is war," but then again, lots of his lieutenants go AWOL.

Deniability Know-nothing leadership, so well exemplified by our former commander-in-chief Ronald Reagan, is out. Don't expect stockholders, federal judges or colleagues to excuse the exec who denies knowing that his or her manufacturing plant leaks toxins in the local aquifer. Ditto for Dr. Jekyll/Mr. "Hide" who makes feel-good promises and then takes cover, leaving subordinates to take the heat when fairy tales don't come true. (If the pew fits, sit in it, Jim Bakker.) To close the trust gap, leaders have to scrape off that Teflon coating.

The Golden Rule Forget about "Do unto others…"? No, that one still holds. We're talking about the other golden rule: He who has the gold makes the rules. Obscene displays of perks and privilege won't win workers' loyalty. (Nor will the wielding of patronage, as former New York City Commissioner of Cultural Affairs Bess Myerson learned from phone-tap-happy staffer Sukhreet Gabel.)

After all, what made the population of the Philippines revolt against longtime dictator Ferdinand Marcos? Injustice, oppression, a police state? Yes, but in the end, Imelda's shoe closet became the most public symbol of a boss gone really bad. Just because you have 1,000 pairs of shoes (or, like Mike Milken, an annual salary of $500 million) doesn't mean you're a leader.

Narcissism Sure there's something appealing about the idea of playing God and composing a staff in one's own image. (Just think of IBM founder Thomas J. Watson's legions of blue-suited sales clones of the '50s.) But that kind of egotism just won't cut it in the coming decade. Outside of totalitarian societies — like Helmsley Palace under Mean Queen Leona — there's not much quarter left for autocrats. In the 1990s workplace, wise is the manager who gives everyone a chance to shine.

An Iron Fist In other words, an abusive, humiliating and belittling interpersonal style. That's the way many Bad Bosses still dole out criticism — and it's usually done in public. Take Dawn Steel (the recently departed head of Columbia Pictures), notorious in Hollywood for her callousness toward subordinates. Steel's habit of excoriating secretaries with sexist expletives kept the exit doors at Columbia swinging.

Reign by terror is, sadly, a still widespread management style. Consider, for example, this statement by Robert Malott, chairman of FMC Corporation: "Leadership is demonstrated when the ability to inflict pain is confirmed." Ever try to do any productive work while in pain? It's not easy.

But salt-in-the-wounds managers have begun to pay the price for their love of the whip in high attrition and nonexistent employee loyalty.

Malott could stand to take a lesson from Good Boss Max De Pree, chairman of Herman Miller, who reminds us: "Leaders don't inflict pain; they bear pain."

9. *Working Woman*, (March 1990), p. 75.

Chapter ■7

Decision Making

Erica Jennings could feel the tension building. Six years of hard work and excellent results were in the balance. Her superiors were deciding her fate with the company. By the end of the afternoon she would know whether her efforts had been appreciated. A decision to promote her meant that she would join the inner circle of executives who would lead the company into the future. A choice of one of her co-workers meant more waiting and more than likely a signal for her to move to another firm. This meant starting anew, building a network of colleagues who would respect her work and enjoy her presence.

She wondered how the decision was being made. On paper her performance was exceptional, ranking at or near the top of productivity, interpersonal relations and loyalty to the firm. But how was the decision really going to be made? There were personalities to consider, allegiances to weigh. There was only one woman executive. Would gender be a factor? Could they welcome her openly to the "inner circle"? Would her boss make the decision alone? Whose input would be most valued?

Much of her tension existed because the decision seemed out of her control. She was reminded of her applications, a few years ago, to the most prestigious MBA programs. They were judged by a faceless group of decision makers, using criteria that were hidden from her. One by one the envelopes arrived, all praising her qualifications. Then each, using their own carefully crafted phrase, had said *no*. All except one that is, which began, "We are delighted to inform you..." It happened to be from one of her top choices. At that school the decision had gone her way. She recognized the stress of not knowing what was going to happen. Getting an answer allowed her to resume her normal life.

As she awaited the present big decision, Erica Jennings vowed to change the way that decisions were made. If she received the promotion, she would do her best to open up the decision-making process at work. She sensed that her superiors knew that about her and perhaps their choice would be influenced by this factor.

The decision-making process involves choosing a course of action from two or more alternatives. That seems quite straightforward. But *how* the choice is made is far more complicated. As individuals we make choices every day regarding what to eat, wear, do, buy — and when to do these activities. Marketing professionals engage in careful research trying to understand why we decide on one product over another.

Some of our decisions have a powerful and lasting impact on our lives. We usually choose a college, a career or a partner after we have given serious thought to the available alternatives. For most of us these personal decisions involve a combination of rational data and a feeling or hunch about what would be right for us. We often choose a college starting with numerical data about entrance requirements and geographical preference, but make a final selection based on our feelings during a campus visit. Choosing a roommate, lover or spouse usually combines some rational compatibility in values and interests and an emotional attraction that we call friendship or love. It is often hard to know whether the decision we have made will be lasting for us. Will we still love our chosen partner as we both grow older and change? Will our career choice stand the test of time in a changing world? Your ability to make good decisions increases the chances that your life will proceed in the direction of your goals and in accordance with your values. But whatever the outcomes of these individual decisions, their impact is primarily felt by a small group of people in our network of family and friends.

A managerial decision has an impact beyond its affect on the individuals involved. A decision to promote Erica Jennings will affect not only her. It will change the makeup of the executive group and impact policy decisions that will be felt throughout the company. A "correct" decision can yield tremendous benefit to the organization. An "incorrect" decision can hurt the effectiveness of the executive group and potentially diminish morale and productivity.

We expect managers to make decisions. Former President Harry Truman's famous statement, "The buck stops here," epitomizes that attitude. Taking responsibility is what managers are paid for. Truman had to make the final decision about whether to drop the first atom bomb during World War II. While he had many advisors, it was his responsibility as president and commander and chief to make this weighty decision.

1. Henry Mintzberg, *The Nature of Managerial Work* (New York: Harper and Row, 1973).
2. Robert E. Quinn, *Beyond Rational Management: Mastering the Paradoxes and Competing Demands of High Performance* (San Francisco: Jossey Bass, 1988).

Indeed, researchers who observe practicing managers have identified a number of choices that managers must make in the course of their jobs.[1] Applying these observations to the eight managerial roles described by Quinn[2] in Chapter 2, "What Do Managers Do," it is clear that each role requires the manager to make important decisions. The roles and corresponding decisions are shown in Table 7.1.

TABLE 7.1

Management Roles and Decisions

Role	Decision
Innovator	What changes to initiate and when to initiate them
Broker	How to negotiate toward agreements outside the unit
Producer	How to optimize motivation
Director	How to set goals and initiate action
Coordinator	How to maintain the structure and flow of the system
Monitor	How to collect and evaluate information about the unit's performance
Facilitator	How to build cohesive work teams and manage conflict
Mentor	How to develop subordinates and understand yourself.

It is apparent that a significant part of the manager's job involves making decisions. As a twenty-first century manager your success may be largely determined by your ability to understand the decision-making process. This doesn't mean that all of your decisions must be correct. It does mean that you understand the nature of the managerial decision process and what important questions must be answered before you decide how a decision should be made.

Managerial decision making usually begins when managers must choose from alternative courses of action to solve a problem or seize an opportunity.[3] A problem occurs when accomplishments fall short of established objectives. Opportunities exist when accomplishments can be enhanced to exceed current objectives.

Astute managers are highly attuned to the world around them and scan the work environment seeking problems and opportunities to be managed. The best managers have a highly trained network of peers and subordinates whose observations contribute to this scanning process. Failure to head off problems early or create opportunities can greatly diminish a manager's effectiveness. Once a manager becomes aware of a problem or opportunity, a series of steps that comprise the decision-making process follow.

Decision-making Steps

Using the example of Erica Jennings, who awaits word on her promotion, we can summarize the steps associated with effective decision making.[4] The steps are as follows:

1. Define the problem

2. Set objectives and criteria

3. Generate alternatives

4. Analyze alternatives and select one

5. Implement and evaluate decision

Erica Jennings's company might implement this decision-making process in the following way:

Define the problem Erica Jennings's company has the opportunity to bring fresh ideas to the executive group by promoting one of several promising employees. In this case the problem or opportunity is not simply to choose a replacement for a slot on the executive group, but rather to choose a person who will best adapt to changes and maintain a value system congruent with a work force of the twenty-first century. By specifically defining the decision to be made, managers can avoid solving the wrong problem.

Set objectives and criteria Once the problem has been defined, clear objectives that state what is to be accomplished within a given period of time are essential. Criteria for achieving these objectives will include both objective and impressionistic data. Erica Jennings's superiors have decided on the three sets of objectives and criteria shown in Table 7.2.

3. R. L. Daft, *Management* (Chicago, IL: Dryden Press, 1988), p. 172.

4. R. N. Lussier, *Human Relations in Organizations: A Skill Building Approach*, (Homewood, IL: Irwin, 1990), p. 278-280.

TABLE 7.2 Guidelines for promotion to executive group

Objective 1: Improving the executive committee's committed ability to make group decisions is important.

Criteria: The new executive should have evidence of good listening and negotiating skills as reported by participants in meetings she chaired or was a participant.

Objective 2: The executive that is chosen should be trusted by subordinates so that employee concerns can be accurately heard by the executive group.

Criteria: Positive ratings from peers and subordinates. Evidence of having raised employee issues with superiors and evidence of creative approaches to enhancing employee performance.

Objective 3: The executive that is chosen should be someone who will challenge the status quo, will take political risks to be innovative.

Criteria: Evidence of assertiveness with peers and superiors. Has championed unpopular ideas and followed them through to a successful result.

Generating alternatives Alternative solutions must be generated to achieve the objectives. Erica Jennings and two high performing colleagues are among the alternatives. Hiring outside the company is another.

Other alternatives could include restructuring the executive group or dropping the position entirely. The quality of the available alternatives is important. Yet realistically, managers must make a decision based on what information can be obtained in the time available to them. This is called bounded rationality.[5] Managers are willing to give up the perfect solution if its pursuit results in diminishing returns on the time invested. They seek a "satisficing" or satisfactory solution rather than maximizing or best possible solutions.

The selection group will have to decide whether the internal candidates meet their criteria or whether alternative approaches are necessary.

Analyze alternatives and select one Once the alternatives have been generated, they must be prioritized and a decision must be made. Under conditions of low uncertainty, data is often available to aid in this selection process. Many decisions are based on soft impressionistic data, and carry a higher risk. Analyzing the costs and benefits of each candidate can help to select the one with the greatest likelihood of achieving the stated objectives.

Implementation and evaluation Once the decision about who will be promoted is made, the new executive must be trained and oriented to their new job. Those not chosen must receive appropriate support and guidance. Finally, the performance of the new executive must be evaluated according to the stated objectives to see if the decision needs review.

5. H. A. Simon, *Models of Man: Social and Relational* (New York: Willey, 1957).

These are the basic steps of managerial decision making.

Categories of Decisions

Managerial decisions fall into two categories: programmed and non-programmed.

Programmed decisions are made in predictable, repetitive situations. Personnel policies typically include a number of programmed decisions. Failure to show up for work may require an automatic written warning and lead to further programmed actions. Students whose grades fall below a certain level will be put on probation, while those at the upper end are chosen through programmed decisions for the dean's list.

Non-programmed decisions are usually made in unique circumstances. When situations are poorly defined or have never occurred before, non-programmed decisions with their accompanying risk and uncertainty are required. It is these kinds of decisions that require managerial initiative. There was no computer program to tell President Harry Truman whether to drop the atomic bomb in 1945, nor to tell Ray Kroc that MacDonald's would expand to worldwide domination of the fast food industry, nor to tell Erica Jennings's bosses who would be the best addition to the executive team.

It is in the best interests of the manager to make programmed decisions on routine matters rather than having to make a unique decision about such issues as everyone's pay or benefits. Conversely, if unique decisions are treated with inflexible rules, inequities can occur. An astute manager should be able to distinguish between programmed and non-programmed decisions and handle them differently.

Group or Individual Decision Making

Perhaps the most critical question a manager must ask before making a decision is, "Do I make it myself or do I involve others in the decision-making process?"

There is no easy answer to this question, but there are guidelines to suggest when two heads are better than one, or when too many cooks might spoil the broth.

Conditions when individual decision making is most appropriate include:[6]

1. When the problem is routine and programmed and the manager has all the data.

2. When time is of the essence and key employees are not available.

Conditions where group decision making is most appropriate include:

1. Complex problems, where more diverse knowledge and alternatives are available from group members. Creativity is enhanced and better solutions result.

2. When acceptance of the decision by employees is important. When employees participate in solving problems and making decisions, they are more likely to understand the decision and "own" the solution. This increases their commitment to implement it.

There are several techniques that have been developed to facilitate group decision making.

Brainstorming is a technique in which group members suggest alternatives in an atmosphere free from criticism.[7] All ideas are listed no matter how extreme, so that ideas can build on one another. Only after all ideas are listed are they critiqued and prioritized.

The nominal group technique insures equal input in the decision-making process and evaluation of ideas through a ballot at the end.[8] Employees generate ideas in writing followed by presentation, discussion, elimination of weak alternatives and final vote.

The Delphi technique is a group decision format that does not bring individuals together to solve problems.[9] Rather, experts send written responses to the group leader which are then collated and distributed to all participants. After several rounds a consensus is usually reached.

6. Adapted from R. L. Daft, *Management* (Chicago, IL: Dryden, 1988), p. 186.

7. A. F. Osborn, *Applied Imagination*, 3rd Ed. (New York: Scribner's, 1963), p. 154 -163.

8. A. Delbecq et al., *Group Techniques for Program Planning* (Glenview, IL: Scott Foresman, 1975).

9. J. T. Preble, "The Selection of Delphi Panels for Strategic Planning Purposes," *Strategic Management Journal*. 5, (1984), p. 157-170.

As a twenty-first century manager you should know steps of the decision making process, when to make decisions yourself and when to involve others, and how to use groups to develop creative solutions to problems.

With all this information at your disposal, you are now ready to make a managerial decision.

In the "Ready for Class" activity that follows, you will be asked to make a decision in the face of considerable uncertainty and a pressing deadline, circumstances not uncommon for practicing managers.

The information you will receive is based on an actual case study. Thus you will be able to compare your own decision with that of the "real decision makers" and discover what actually took place.

Introduction

You are John or Joanne Carter, one of the owners of Carter Racing. Your cars have raced well so far this season but now the future of your firm is on the line. Carter Racing has tentatively arranged a major source of advertising support for the following season, but this support hinges on how well your team does in the big race, the Pocono, to be run today on national television. If your car does well, support is assured. Based on your team's overall performance the prospects look good. But on the down side there have been occasional engine blowouts. If this should happen in today's highly visible race, it would ruin your chances with a big advertiser. There is some disagreement on your team about the cause of the engine problems. But you are well aware that automobile racing is an inherently risky business.

Information about Carter Racing is presented in the following case study. To help you make your decision, the case includes information about team members, cost of entering the race and replacing the engine, prize money, sponsorship royalties and special repair problems and track conditions.

Case Study

"What should we do?"

John Carter was not sure, but his brother and partner, Fred Carter, was on the phone and needed a decision. Should they run in the race or not? It had been a successful season so far, but the Pocono race was important because of the prize money and TV exposure it promised. This first year had been hard because the team was trying to make a name for itself. They had run a lot of small races to get this shot at the big time. A successful outing could mean more sponsors, a chance to start making some profits for a change and the luxury of racing only the major events. But if they suffered another engine failure on national television...

Just thinking about the team's engine problems make John wince. They had blown an engine seven times in 24 outings this season with various degrees of damage to the engine and car. No one could figure out why. It took a lot of sponsor money to replace a $20,000 racing engine, and the wasted entry fees were no small matter either. John and Fred had everything they owned riding on Carter Racing. This season had to be a success.

Paul Edwards, the engine mechanic, was guessing the engine problem was related to ambient air temperature. He argued that when it was cold the different expansion rates for the head and block were damaging the head gasket and causing the engine failures. It was below freezing last night, which meant a cold morning for starting the race.

10. Adapted from J. Brittain, and S. B. Sitkin, "Facts, Figures, and Organizational Decisions. Carter Racing and Quantitative Analysis in the Organizational Behavior Classroom," *Organizational Behavior Teaching Review,* (1990), p. 62-81.

Tom Burns, the chief mechanic, did not agree with Paul's "gut feeling" and had data to support his position (see Figure 7.1). He pointed out that gasket failures had occurred at all temperatures, which meant temperature was not the issue. Tom had raced for 20 years and believed that luck was an import element in success. He had argued this view when he and John discussed the problem last week: "In racing, you are pushing the limits of what is known. You cannot expect to have everything under control. If you want to win, you have to take risks. Everybody in racing knows it. The drivers have their lives on the line, I have a career that hangs on every race, and you guys have got every dime tied up in the business. That's the

Figure 7.1 Note from Tom Burke

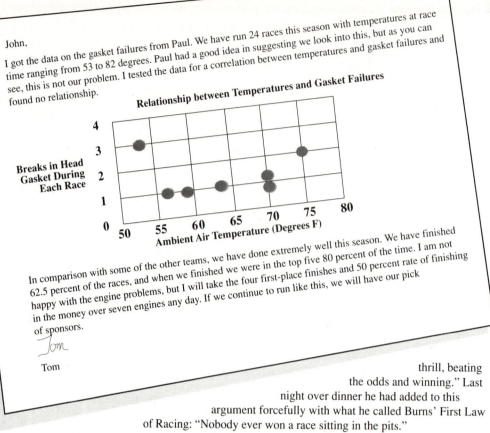

John,

I got the data on the gasket failures from Paul. We have run 24 races this season with temperatures at race time ranging from 53 to 82 degrees. Paul had a good idea in suggesting we look into this, but as you can see, this is not our problem. I tested the data for a correlation between temperatures and gasket failures and found no relationship.

Relationship between Temperatures and Gasket Failures

Breaks in Head Gasket During Each Race

Ambient Air Temperature (Degrees F)

In comparison with some of the other teams, we have done extremely well this season. We have finished 62.5 percent of the races, and when we finished we were in the top five 80 percent of the time. I am not happy with the engine problems, but I will take the four first-place finishes and 50 percent rate of finishing in the money over seven engines any day. If we continue to run like this, we will have our pick of sponsors.

Tom

Tom

thrill, beating the odds and winning." Last night over dinner he had added to this argument forcefully with what he called Burns' First Law of Racing: "Nobody ever won a race sitting in the pits."

John, Fred and Tom had discussed Carter Racing's situation the previous evening. The first season was a success from a racing standpoint, with the team's car finishing in the top five in 12 of the 15 races it completed. As a result, the sponsorship offers critical to the team's business success were starting to come in. A big break had come two weeks ago after the Dunham race, where the team scored its fourth first-place finish. Goodstone Tire had finally decided Carter Racing deserved its sponsorship at Pocono — worth a much needed $40,000 — and was considering a full season contract for next year if the team's car finished in the top five in this race. The Goodstone sponsorship was for a million a year, plus incentives. John and Fred had gotten a favorable response from Goodstone's racing program director last week when they presented their plans for next season, but it was clear that the director's support depended on the visibility they generated in this race.

"John, we only have another hour to decide," Fred said over the phone. "If we withdraw now, we can get back half the $15,000 entry and try to recoup some of our losses next season. We will lose Goodstone; they'll want $25,000 of their money back, and we end up the season $50,000 in the hole. If we run and finish in the top five, we have Goodstone in our pocket and can add another car next season. You know as well as I do, however, that if we run and lose another engine, we are back at square one next season. We will lose the tire sponsorship and a blown engine is going to lose us the oil contract. No oil company wants a national TV audience to see a smoker being dragged off the track with their name plastered all over it. The oil sponsorship is $500,000 that we cannot live without. Think about it — call Paul and Tom if you want — but I need a decision in an hour."

John hung up the phone and looked out the window at the crisp, fall sky. The temperature sign across the street flashed: "40 DEGREES at 9:23 A.M."

Name _____

ID# _____

Section _____

Decision

After reading the Carter Racing case:

1) Record your decision whether to race or not race in the box below by putting a check in the appropriate box below.

Race [   ]   **Not Race** [   ]

2) Describe the reasons for your choice.

3) Was there any information that was particularly influential in helping you make your decision?

Part A

1. Form groups of three.

2. List each individual's decision to race or not to race as chosen on your "Ready For Class" exercise.

Individual Decisions:

Check the appropriate boxes below:

Person 1	**Race** ☐	**Not Race** ☐
Person 2	**Race** ☐	**Not Race** ☐
Person 3	**Race** ☐	**Not Race** ☐

Part B

1. Discuss the reasons for your individual decisions, and arrive at a group decision about whether to race the car.

2. Choose a spokesperson who will report your group's reasoning and its decision to the larger group.

Group Decision:

Check the appropriate box below:

Race ☐   **Not Race** ☐

Reasons for Group Decision:

Part C

Large Group Discussion

Lights

The video segment you are about to see demonstrates how important it is to understand the managerial decision-making process. The managers in this video segment make an important decision. The consequences of that decision are enormous.

For students of management, there are powerful lessons to be learned by evaluating the decision-making process used here. In the chaotic world of work, decisions are often made too quickly and with too little data. They are influenced by forces of culture and history and forces of personal preference and style of the decision maker.

Camera

As you watch this video segment identify why the managers made the decision they did.

1. Why was the decision made?

2. How could those opposed to the decision have been more effective in making their point?

3. What was the "real" cause of the problem as you see it?

Action

What were the primary causes identified in class for the decision made in this video segment?

1.

2.

3.

4.

How did the decision process observed in this segment resemble the decision process you used in the Carter Racing Case?

How did the decision process observed here differ from your experience in the Carter Racing Case?

MIRROR TALK: FOCUSSING ON ME

Using groups to aid decision making can often improve the quality of a decision and increase employee acceptance of the decision. On the other hand, individual decision making may be most effective when managers face time pressures or when the decision requires little new information.

As a twenty-first century manager it is important to diagnose your own preferred style for making decisions. Managerial decisions are typically made in four different ways. These range from **autocratic** where the manager makes the decision without consulting the work group, to **laissez faire** where the work group makes the decision and the manager supports it. In between are the **consultative** style where the manager gathers information from group members and then decides, and the **participation** style where the manager asks for group input but may exercise veto power on the decision. The four decision making styles are described bellow.[11]

Autocratic. The supervisor makes the decision alone and announces it after the fact. An explanation of the rationale for the decision may be given.

Consultative. The supervisor consults the group for information, then makes the decision. Before implementing the decision, the supervisor explains the rationale for the decision and sells the benefits to the employees. The supervisor may invite questions and have a discussion.

Participative. The supervisor may present a tentative decision to the group and ask for its input. The supervisor may change the decision if the input warrants a change. Or the supervisor presents the problem to the group for suggestions. Based on employee participation, the supervisor makes the decision and explains its rationale.

Laissez-faire. The supervisor presents the situation to the group and describes limitations to the decision. The group makes the decision. The supervisor may be a group member.

Now assume you are in the decision making role in the following eight situations. Read each example and circle the letter on the right that describes how *you* would be most likely to make the decision.[12]

11. R. N. Lussier, Human Relations in Organizations: A Skill Building Approach (Homewood, IL: Irwin, 1990), p. 284.

12. Adapted from R. N. Lussier, op. cit. pp. 295-96.

Decision style questionnaire

(A=Autocratic; C=Consultative; P=Participative; L=Laissez Faire)

1. You have developed a new work procedure that will increase productivity. Your boss likes the idea and wants you to try it within a few weeks. You view your employees as fairly capable and believe that they will be receptive to the change.　　　A　　C　　P　　L

2. Your department has been facing a problem for several months. Many solutions have been tried, but all have failed. You have finally thought of a solution, but you're not sure of the possible consequences of the change required or the acceptance of the highly capable employees.　　　A　　C　　P　　L

3. Flextime has become popular in your organization. Some departments let each employee start and end work when they choose. However, because of the cooperative effort of your employees, they must all work the same eight hours. You're not sure of the level of interest in changing the hours. Your employees are a very capable group and like to make decisions.　　　A　　C　　P　　L

4. The technology in your industry is changing so fast that the members of your organization cannot keep up. Top management hired a consultant who has made recommendations. You have two weeks to decide what to do. Your employees are normally capable, and they enjoy participating in the decision-making process.

      A   C   P   L

5. A change has been handed down from top management. How you implement it is your decision. The change takes effect in one month. It will personally affect everyone in your department. Their acceptance is critical to the success of the change. Your employees are usually not too interested in being involved in making decisions.

      A   C   P   L

6. Your boss called you on the telephone to tell you that someone has requested an order for your department's product with a very short delivery date. She asked you to call her back with the decision about taking the order in 15 minutes. Looking over the work schedule, you realize that it will be very difficult to deliver the order on time. Your employees will have to push hard to make it. They are cooperative, capable and enjoy being involved in decision making.

      A   C   P   L

7. Top management has decided to make a change that will affect all of your employees. You know that they will be upset because it will cause them hardship. One or two may even quit. The change goes into effect in 30 days. Your employees are very capable.

      A   C   P   L

8. A customer has offered you a contract for your product with a quick delivery date. The offer is open for two days. Meeting the contract deadline would require employees to work nights and weekends for six weeks. You cannot require them to work overtime. Filling this profitable contract could help get you the raise you want and feel you deserve. However, if you take the contract and don't deliver on time, it will hurt your chances of getting a big raise. Your employees are very capable.

      A   C   P   L

Total of each letter circled   _____A _____C _____P _____L

Decision Style Scoring Instructions

1. Add up the number of circles on each column and put that number in the bottom row called *Total of each letter circled*.

The sum of the four totals should be eight.

2. The column with the highest total is your *predominant* decision making style. Circle below your predominant style.

    Autocratic   **Consultative**   **Participative**   **Laissez faire**

3. The column with the least number of circles is your *underused* style. Circle the style you use least frequently.

    Autocratic   **Consultative**   **Participative**   **Laissez faire**

4. A total of two in each column represents a balanced approach to decision making, that is, equal use of all four styles.

If you have four or more circles in any one column you may be overusing that approach. A zero score suggests underuse.

Overusing the autocratic style may signal your need to be in control and you may notice a lack of employee enthusiasm and support for your decisions. Underuse indicates a reluctance to act without input from others.

Overuse of the laissez faire style may indicate a lack of decisiveness when group input is not required and too much time spent in decision making. Underuse indicates a reluctance to trust others to make effective decisions without your control present.

Similarly, overuse of consultative and participative styles suggests a reluctance to be decisive in a crisis situation or a reluctance to delegate authority to capable employees, preferring rather to always confer on problems or maintain veto power over the decision, even when it is unnecessary. Underuse suggests difficulty with collaborative decision making.

Your score on this brief decision-making test should be considered only a very general estimate of your true decision-making activity, and raises important questions that will help you identify your preferred decision style with greater accuracy.

Your awareness of preferred and difficult decision styles and your ability to develop flexibility that allows you to adjust to the situation will be an important asset to your managerial effectiveness.

A Model for Selecting the Appropriate Decision-Making Style

Now that you have identified a predominant and underused decision-making style, you may be asking what is the right decision-making style for managerial decisions.

The answer to that question is, it depends on the situation. Research by Vroom and Yetton[13] and adapted by Lussier[14] has identified four factors in the situation to help you diagnose which decision style is most appropriate for a specific situation.

The four factors are:

1. Time   2. Information   3. Acceptance   4. Capability

Time When available, time allows for adequate discussion and debate. The participative and laissez faire style are indicated when there is time to include employee input in the decision. When time is short, the consultative style may be preferable. When there is no time to include employees in the decision the autocratic style is necessary.

Information If the manager has all the information necessary to make a high quality decision alone, the autocratic style is appropriate. Some information suggests a consultative approach. Little or no information available to the manager requires the participative or laissez faire approaches.

Acceptance The manager must understand whether the group is likely to enthusiastically implement the decision if the supervisor makes it alone. If so, the autocratic style would be appropriate. A reluctant group requires consultative or participative decision. If the group is likely to reject the decision without input, the laissez faire or participative style is required.

Capability The manager must diagnose the group's ability and willingness to become involved in problem solving. If the group's ability is low the autocratic style should be considered. Moderate capability suggest the consultative style. Strong and expert abilities warrant the participative and laissez faire styles.

13. V. Vroom, and P. Yetton, *Leadership and Decision Making* (Pittsburgh: University of Pittsburgh Press, 1973).

14. Lussier, *op. cit.*, p. 283.

When the manager has the time to use any style, acceptance takes precedence over information. In an emergency, an autocratic response is often called for. When information is lacking an autocratic style is usually ruled out. When employees do not share the organizational goals of the manager, the laissez faire style would not be effective.

Reanalysis of Decision Style Questionnaire Using the Decision Style Model

Let us try to apply these four factors to the eight situations that you explored when you completed the Decision Style Questionnaire. As you revisit each situation indicate the answer you selected before you knew about the four factors. Put that answer at the left of the situation number. Then answer each of the four questions that the decision style model suggests. Is time plentiful, moderate, or scarce? Does the manager have enough information to make a high quality decision alone or is more information required? Will the work group accept the manager's decision alone or is their input essential? Does the group have high, moderate or low ability to make this decision?

Diagnose the level of each factor for each of the eight situations and indicate what answer the model would recommend in the space that says *Model Recommends*. Then compare your original choice with the answer that the model would suggest.

The correct answers for each situation are listed in Appendix B.

Let us begin by using Situation One as an example.

Your Original Answer _____

1. You have developed a new work procedure that will increase productivity. Your boss likes the idea and wants you to try it within a few weeks. You view your employees as fairly capable and believe that they will be receptive to the change.

TIME: There is a moderate amount of time to make a decision. It is not an emergency or an open-ended time frame. Consultation or participation is appropriate.

INFORMATION: You have most of the information necessary to put this new procedure into place, but some input from employees would help refine it. The autocratic or consultative style is best used here.

ACCEPTANCE: The employees have been supportive of previous ideas so acceptance should not be a problem. However some consultation should iron out any areas of conflict. Use the consultative style.

CAPABILITY: Because employees are fairly capable, the consultative or participative style are likely to be most appropriate.

THE MODEL RECOMMENDS: *Consultative.* Laissez faire would not be very useful unless you wished to train team members to make such decisions. The autocratic style doesn't allow for enough input, and the participative style may involve more discussion on an already acceptable plan than is warranted.

Now try this analysis out on the other seven situations. Please realize that this model should be used to eliminate ineffective decision styles, and help you avoid making decisions that your employees will not be committed to and overusing discussion and input when a decision does not warrant them.

Your Original Answer

2. Your department has been facing a problem for several months. Many solutions have been tried, but all have failed. You have finally thought of a solution, but you're not sure of the possible consequences of the change required or the acceptance of the highly capable employees.

TIME:

INFORMATION:

ACCEPTANCE:

CAPABILITY:

THE MODEL RECOMMENDS:

Your Original Answer

3. Flextime has become popular in your organization. Some departments let each employee start and end work when they choose. However, because of the cooperative effort of your employees, they must all work the same eight hours. You're not sure of the level of interest in changing the hours. Your employees are a very capable group and like to make decisions.

TIME:

INFORMATION:

ACCEPTANCE:

CAPABILITY:

THE MODEL RECOMMENDS:

Your Original Answer

4. The technology in your industry is changing so fast that the members of your organization cannot keep up. Top management hired a consultant who has made recommendations. You have two weeks to decide what to do. Your employees are normally capable, and they enjoy participating in the decision-making process.

TIME:

INFORMATION:

ACCEPTANCE:

CAPABILITY:

THE MODEL RECOMMENDS:

**Your
Original
Answer**

5. A change has been handed down from top management. How you implement it is your decision. The change takes effect in one month. It will personally affect everyone in your department. Their acceptance is critical to the success of the change. Your employees are usually not too interested in being involved in making decisions.

TIME:

INFORMATION:

ACCEPTANCE:

CAPABILITY:

THE MODEL RECOMMENDS:

**Your
Original
Answer**

6. Your boss called you on the telephone to tell you that someone has requested an order for your department's product with a very short delivery date. She asked you to call her back with the decision about taking the order in 15 minutes. Looking over the work schedule, you realize that it will be very difficult to deliver the order on time. Your employees will have to push hard to make it. They are cooperative, capable and enjoy being involved in decision making.

TIME:

INFORMATION:

ACCEPTANCE:

CAPABILITY:

THE MODEL RECOMMENDS:

**Your
Original
Answer**

7. Top management has decided to make a change that will affect all your employees. You know that they will be upset because it will cause them hardship. One or two may even quit. The changes goes into effect in 30 days. Your employees are very capable.

TIME:

INFORMATION:

ACCEPTANCE:

CAPABILITY:

THE MODEL RECOMMENDS:

Your Original Answer

8. A customer has offered you a contract for your product with a quick delivery date. The offer is open for two days. Meeting the contract deadline would require employees to work nights and weekends for six weeks. You cannot require them to work overtime. Filling this profitable contract could help get you the raise you want and feel you deserve. However, if you take the contract and don't deliver on time, it will hurt your chances of getting a big raise. Your employees are very capable.

TIME:

INFORMATION:

ACCEPTANCE:

CAPABILITY:

THE MODEL RECOMMENDS:

COMING TO OUR SENSES: MAKING A DIFFERENCE

Managers must not only make decisions, they must *decide how to decide*. When a manager decides on too many important issues alone employees may feel left out of the process, feel unmotivated and lack creativity. When a manager always delegates decision making to others, leadership may suffer. Where is the balance for you? What have you learned about your own decision-making style from the "Decision Style Questionnaire," from the "Carter Racing Case," from the video segment and from your experiences outside this course. As you move toward becoming a twenty-first century manager, how can you make decisions that will make a difference?

• What have I seen?

• What did I hear?

• What did I feel?

• What did I think?

• And now, what will I do to make a difference?

For much of the twentieth century our study of managerial decision making has emphasized how American men solved problems. The twenty-first century managers must expand their horizons dramatically. With more women in decision making capacities, decision styles may be changing. The first reading, "Why There Aren't More Women in this Magazine," looks at how men and women view decision making from different perspectives.

The global business environment of the twenty-first century will require effective managers to be versatile enough to work easily with their counterparts in other countries. The second reading, "Continuum of International Decision-Making Styles," offers some insights into cultural differences in decision making. In the third and fourth readings we will observe how the results of faulty decision making can help an organization dramatically revise its structure to provide a better fit for a changed organization. Organizational change occurs at many levels. So, when a new organization with a great deal of informal communication grows, the decision-making system may isolate top management from the technical personnel who are closest to the vital information.

We have all experienced the emotions felt by Erica Jennings, waiting for an important decision from an employer, a university, a customer. We hope for a decision favorable to us, and wonder how the decision is being made. Are we being judged primarily on our quantitative record or primarily on an impression we have made? Are the decision makers aware of their biases and eager to balance them? As you emerge as a twenty-first century manager, you will find yourself increasingly in the decision-making role, responsible for important organizational decisions that will affect your company's future and impact the lives of your employees. The twenty-first century will not experience any letup in the number of decisions to be made but they will probably be made differently. There will still be a balance between fact and intuition. We will develop better technologies for gathering relevant facts. But the unknowns of whether a certain product or service will be appealing and the lack of certainty about how an individual will behave in a new position will always be present. The modern work force of the twenty-first century will have expectations that their knowledge and experience will be tapped to achieve organizational goals. For these employees, thinking creatively about their jobs will be an important way to gain personal fulfillment through work. The way you handle decisions will affect your success as a twenty-first century manager. And yes, Erica Jennings did get the job.

Reading 7.1

WOMEN IN BUSINESS MAKE DECISIONS DIFFERENTLY THAN MEN[15]

by Ellen Wojahn

Obviously, not all business-women are deaf to the old siren song of growth and expansion, wealth and power. But there is powerful evidence that women go into business for different reasons than men. And different motivations lead to a different set of measurements by which they judge success.

Women watch their profits (who doesn't), but they also evaluate their performances in terms of opportunities well met, creative urges satisfied, employees that are challenged and fulfilled. By and large, they place a higher value on respect from peers, satisfaction from customers, and good marriages that produce kids whose heads are screwed on straight.

Oh sure, men may claim to embrace some of the same ideals. But let's face it: these are not the hallmarks of male business culture. There aren't many men who stay up nights worrying about how to adapt their businesses to more human values.

From different motives and different goals come different ways of managing a business. Study after study show that women do a better job of encouraging and rewarding employees, of soliciting information and input, of seeking consensus. Men fight things on; women work things out.

15. Ellen Wojahn, ``Why There Aren't More Women in This Magazine.'' Reprinted by permission of *Inc.*. magazine, July 1986, pp. 45-48. Copyright © 1984 by Goldhirsch Group, Inc., 38 Commercial Wharf, Boston, MA 02110.

Reading 7.2

CONTINUUM OF INTERNATIONAL DECISION-MAKING STYLES[16]

Americans pride themselves on their ability to delegate effectively. Authority and responsibility are dispersed throughout the average U.S. organization. Moreover, delegation allows for flexibility. If an issue does not fall in a specific, prescribed area, some department will eventually take responsibility, even if only after some shuffling.

16. From L. Copeland and L. Griggs, *Going International*. Appearing in Pearce and Robinson, *Management*, (New York: McGraw-Hill, Inc., 1989), p. 67. Reproduced with permission of McGraw-Hill, Inc.

Actually, Americans seem to be about in the middle on a continuum of decision making/delegation styles, from totally authoritarian and centralized patterns on one extreme to the very participatory style of the Japanese on the other. In the center with us appear to be many Scandinavian and Australian concerns-in both countries, distance between those with authority and their subordinates is small. Nevertheless, American managers in those countries often find unexpected

differences. For example, as far as Americans are concerned, Swedes violate the corporate chain of command. When Swedes need information, they'll go directly to the source, even if this means bypassing their immediate bosses. Managers in Sweden are much more conductors, planners or diplomats than their American counterparts. When managing Swedes, you need not feel threatened when an employee goes over your head.

Chapter 8

Teams and Groups

A student was accepted at two graduate schools of business. Although University A was famous for its high-powered faculty, the student felt drawn toward the lower profile University B. Unsure as to which would be the better choice, he consulted a professor friend. "University A has a stronger set of individual superstars," the professor agreed. "But the program there as a whole is less than the sum of its parts. The professors don't talk to each other, and the school lacks a central core to tie the different disciplines together.

"University B, on the other hand," he continued, "doesn't have the big-name professors, but it's still a better program. The faculty works together, has real spirit and knows what the school stands for. The whole adds up to more than the sum of its parts." After considering the professor's words, the student chose to attend University B.

The professor's advice was apt: Whether talking about a university, a sports team or a company, what adds up to a winning combination is not just having an abundance of superstar performers, but bringing the "players" together in a working unit that can achieve more than the sum of each individual's contributions. The organization that can routinely create and sustain such high-performing teams has an enormous competitive advantage.

In fact, teams have become one of the latest "hot" topics in the business world as recognition of the importance of such group synergy has grown. Whereas 20 years ago, the interest in organizational teams focussed primarily on ad hoc task forces, or on T-groups and similar efforts aimed at improving worker interactions, today's teams usually have a more practical, long-term corporate focus: designing or manufacturing a product, developing a strategy or even running a company.

Top-selling management books stress a broad range of benefits that the astute organization can derive from teamwork. As one author wrote:

> From the executive suite to the front office to the shop floor, teams are becoming the competitive building blocks of choice. Companies are using teams to break down barriers between departments, bring products to market faster, solve and prevent quality problems, and produce better products and services. Managers, employees, and even unions are buying into the new philosophy.[1]

With such promising payoffs, it is no wonder that many companies are rushing to reorganize their work forces and to restructure tasks into a team format. Unfortunately, just putting five people in a room together does not create an effective team. All too often, despite outstanding individual talents, the collective effort is unfocussed and unproductive.

Every one of us has had the experience of sitting for hours in a meeting whose sole end product was boredom and frustration. Not only do the various participants leave with different understandings of what took place, there is often no effective follow-up to make certain that the meeting's discussions result in some action. After this kind of experience, many managers become convinced that they will achieve better results by working alone.

Unfortunately, long-term practically oriented team efforts can result in the same kinds of frustrations: a manufacturing group intended to increase flexibility by teaching employees how to rotate jobs falls short of expectations when the workers gravitate back to their old positions; or a cross-functional planning team is unable to resolve complex issues because each functional group is too protective of its own turf; or a team effort to determine the strategic challenges facing a corporation produces only platitudes because the participants are too concerned about pleasing the CEO. All of these are examples of teams that never reached their potential.

What, then, does it take for a group to click? What are the differences between "good" teams and "bad" teams? And do teams entail any hidden risks that employees should be aware of — forcing a "herd" mentality, for example, or snuffing out individual rights?

Answering these and other questions is an important task facing organizations today. Indeed, becoming a good team player is going to be a challenge for many managers brought up in cultures that place a high value on individual achievement. To work in teams, they must learn more about team dynamics, about how to be contributing members of a team, about how to lead and facilitate an effective team process and about how to manage the risks and difficulties involved.

1. Carla O'Dell, "Team Play, Team Pay — New Ways of Keeping Score," *Across the Board*, (November 1989).

In many ways, teamwork seems a natural and obvious approach for getting things done in an organization. In fact, as we head into the 1990s, the expression "Two heads are better than one" has become more and more appropriate. The complexity of running a company in this global era often calls for a range of skills that one person alone cannot provide. Bringing together teams that pool the skills, resources and ideas of all participants can help companies respond more effectively and nimbly to the broader range of issues they now face.

Nevertheless, successful and productive teams — let alone "superteams" that perform well above expectations — are hardly the norm. To better understand this phenomenon, we will examine a few of the issues affecting organizational teams — such as some barriers to teamwork, what can happen when a team goes awry and some of the challenges involved in building an effective team — as well as look at a few organizations where teams have flourished.

Groups often underperform for a variety of reasons, ranging from the personal to the cultural. Participants in a team, for example, may be too caught up in their own dreams of personal glory to work effectively with others. This "Superstar" mentality is likely to be especially pronounced in companies that reward and recognize standout individual achievements rather than group accomplishments.

In addition, employees and middle managers frequently have no "teamwork role model" to emulate within their own organizations: Management may claim to be one hundred percent behind teamwork, but if the top executives themselves are unable to function in this kind of cooperative environment, that message will spread quickly through the ranks. "Many (top executives) lack the skills to be objective participants in high-level team sessions," wrote Bandrowski.[2] "They attack group members, don't listen to the positions of others, and take sides. Worse still, they spread their lack of team building skills down the ladder."

Even if top management has a good understanding of the demands of effective group interactions, these can be difficult skills to relay. What many organizations are just beginning to understand is that team-building — like participative management and other organizational strategies — does not come without effort. And for some organizations, the "work" part of "teamwork" might not appear to be worth the payoff.

Those managers who hurriedly assemble teams without preparation, and then expect impressive results, are likely to be disappointed. Among the negative consequences that can result from a disjointed team are the following:

1. Low productivity level.

2. Arguments over trivial and irrelevant points.

3. Postponed or inept decision making.

4. Lack of commitment to decisions and resultant lack of implementation.

5. Limited range of ideas and information in the group.

6. Acting out of hidden agendas.

7. Little tolerance for conflicting ideas.

8. Limited cohesiveness and pride in the group.

9. Tension, anxiety, and a low level of conformity.

10. Little sharing of leadership.

11. Lack of member responsibility for task achievement and maintenance of the group.

2. J. F. Bandrowski, *Corporate Imagination Plus: Five Steps to Translating Innovative Strategies into Action,* (New York/London: Free Press, 1980), p. 100.

In other words, an organization that brings together a group like this has not only failed to form a superteam, it has created an organizational monster — capable of lowering the morale of all those involved and of eating up a great deal of energy that could have gone into making the company better and stronger.

But fortunately, as the potential value of teams has become more generally recognized, organizations are beginning to appreciate the time and effort that it takes to create and maintain an effective team. Many corporate leaders, in recognition of this fact, have begun to ask either key managers, or even their entire work forces, to attend special classes on team-building skills before attempting to move their organizations toward this more participatory structure. By employing specific tactics and team-building techniques, they hope to create groups that won't become bogged down in unproductive and unfocussed interactions.

Although the advice given at such classes varies, depending, in part, on what work a team will do, some common themes typically emerge:

• Effective teams allow members the freedom to air divergent viewpoints;

• They give all participants meaningful roles in the process;

• They establish mechanisms for resolving problems and disagreements;

• They establish a common understanding of the team's goals and purposes within the organization.

Even with such a preparation, however, companies that embrace the team concept can expect a substantial transition period as workers, managers, and leaders all test the limits and power of the group structure. One expert on team building has outlined a predictable four-step progression that almost any group will go through in the process of becoming an effective unit: The first stage is a period of questioning; the second is a struggle for control; the third is characterized by a growing sense of unity; and the fourth and final stage occurs when team members have finally grown comfortable in their roles and are ready to take on their appointed tasks. Table 8.1 shows these stages, along with the concerns and behaviors that typically accompany them:

Not surprisingly, not every team makes it to the fourth stage. Without proper guidance and support, a team can become bogged down at any stage in the process. But companies that are able to create fertile environments for group interactions, and join people together effectively — whether to build cars, design products or determine strategies — may find they have created a "Superteam," a potent competitive force, indeed.

What, then, are the characteristics of a so-called "Superteam"? The authors of a book devoted to the subject, *The Superteam Solution,* list 20 qualities that describe their vision of a high-performing group. Following are just a few of the features they identified that may characterize such a team:

TABLE 8.1 Stages of the Team Development Model

	Member Behaviors	Member Concerns	Leader Behaviors
Stage 1: Orientation to group and task	Almost all comments directed to the leader Direction and clarification sought Status accorded to group members based on their roles outside the group Members fail to listen, resulting in *non sequitur* statements Issues are discussed superficially, with much ambiguity	Who am I in this group? Who are the others? Will I be accepted? What is my role? What tasks will I have? Will I be capable? Who is the leader? Will he or she value me? Is the leader competent?	Provide structure by holding regular meetings and assisting in task and role clarification Encourage participation by all, domination by none Facilitate learning about one another's areas of expertise and preferred working modes Share all relevant information Encourage members to ask questions of you and one another
Stage II: Conflict over control among the group's members and with the leader	Attempts made to gain influence, suggestions, proposals Subgroups and coalitions form, with possible conflict among them The leader is tested and challenged (possibly covertly) Members judge and evaluate one another and the leader, resulting in ideas being shot down Task avoidance	How much autonomy will I have? Will I have influence over others? What is my place in the pecking order? Personal level: Who do I like? Who likes me? Issues level: Do I have some support in here?	Engage in joint problem solving: have members give reasons why idea is useful and how to improve it Establish a norm supporting the expression of different viewpoints Discuss the group's decision-making process and share decision making responsibility appropriately Encourage members to state how they feel as well as what they think when they obviously have feelings about an issue Provide group members with the resources needed to do their jobs, to the extent possible (when this is not possible, explain why)
Stage III: Group formation and solidarity	Members, with one another's support, can disagree with the leader The group laughs together; members have fun; some jokes made at the leader's expense A sense of "we-ness" and attention to group norms is present The group feels superior to other groups in the organization Members do not challenge one another as much as the leader would like	How close should I be to the group members? Can we accomplish our tasks successfully? How do we compare to other groups? What is my relationship to the leader?	Talk openly about your own issues and concerns Have group members manage agenda items, particularly those in which you have a high stake Give and request both positive and constructive negative feedback in the group Assign challenging problems for consensus decisions (e.g. budget allocations) Delegate as much as the members are capable of handling: help them as necessary

TABLE 8.1 Stages of the Team Development Model (continued)

	Member Behaviors	Member Concerns	Leader Behaviors
Stage IV: Differentiation and productivity	Roles are clear and each person's contribution is distinctive Members take the initiative and accept one another's initiatives Open discussion and acceptance of differences among members in their backgrounds and modes of operation Challenging one another leads to creative problem solving Members seek feedback from one another and from the leader to improve their performances	(Concerns of earlier stages have been resolved)	Jointly set goals that are challenging Look for new opportunities to increase the group's scope Question assumptions and traditional ways of behaving Develop mechanisms for ongoing self-assessment by the group Appreciate each member's contribution Develop members to their fullest potential through task assignments and feedback

Reprinted with permission from NTL Institute, "Developing a Productivity Team: Making Groups at Work Work," by Jane Moosbruker, pp. 90-91 in *Team Building: Blueprints for Productivity and Satisfaction*, edited by W. Brendon Reddy with Kaleel Jamison, (Alexandria, VA: NTL Publications, 1988).

Superteams are persistent and obsessive in the pursuit of their goals, but creatively flexible in their strategies for getting there. They are continuously returning to the question, "What are we trying to achieve?"

Superteams confront people or situations that lie in their path. They are tenacious and inventive in their efforts to remove all obstacles.

Superteams are committed to quality in performance and all aspects of teamworking. They have very high expectations of themselves and of others.

Superteams display significant understanding of the strategy and philosophy of their parent organization or that part of it which is important to their success.

Superteams are inspired by a vision of what they are trying to achieve. This provides a strong sense of purpose and direction. They also have a realistic strategy for turning the vision into reality.

Superteams are driven by success. They exude the energy, excitement and commitment that being successful releases. They also thrive on the recognition that success brings.[3]

Although the authors of this list were very clear about what a superteam *should* be like, they also hastened to add that they had yet to see or work with a group that had achieved this ideal. Instead, they offered these qualities as a model to which any team could aspire. But although the ideal may be unrealistic, a number of companies are succeeding with their own versions of superteams, drawing on the combined talents of a group of workers to solve a particular problem or accomplish a particular task within the organization.

3. Colin Hastings, Peter Bixby, and Rani Chaudhry-Lawton, *The Superteam Solution*, (San Diego: University Associates, 1987).

Hewlett-Packard, for example, at its Greeley, CO site has created cross-functional committees called "boards of directors" to plan and oversee new projects in such product areas as computer tape drives, optical disks and desk top publishing options.[4] Such a board rarely includes managers or top executives. Instead, it might be made up of lab engineers, technical writers, marketing representatives, manufacturing people and even legal staff. Those front-line workers not only make key design decisions, they even handle such details as product packaging, sales projections and customer support plans.

The boards have had their drawbacks: Under extremely tight time constraints, the company has occasionally had to bypass the committees' consensus process in order to meet deadlines. And some board members have complained about spending too much time in meetings. Nevertheless, from the company's standpoint, the divergent viewpoints brought to bear on each project have more than made up for any inconveniences inherent in the process.

RCA is another company that has made innovative use of teams. In 1985, the company's Indianapolis-based Consumer Electronics Division launched an ambitious effort to develop a self-contained computer for its color television sets to improve both picture resolution and sound, and to offer remote control of all functions.[5] Not only was the planned product sophisticated and complex, RCA intended to cut its typical four-year development time down to a record 30 months.

To achieve this feat, RCA realized it had to move away from its traditional reliance on the design engineering function as the focal point for all new product development. Instead, the company adopted a team format, creating Natural Work Teams — groups of individuals from different functional units who could address every aspect of the product development process.

Because the work force at the Consumer Electronics Division had always been structured according to functions, rather than around products, management realized that this kind of restructuring would take work. With the help of an outside consultant, RCA offered classes in areas such as problem solving, developing design and performance reviews and conducting effective meetings. The training paid off: With the teams in place, RCA cut its traditional product development cycle in half, and delivered the end product at less cost and with better quality than ever before.

As these examples illustrate, teams can be a potent organizational tool. Under the right conditions, and with the proper support and preparation, they can boost productivity, increase responsiveness and improve morale. Moreover, those teams that bring together differing views, functions and roles within the organization can create a broad-based perspective that is ideal for problem solving and decision making in today's complex business world.

4. Christine Ferguson, "Hewlett-Packard's Other Board," *The Wall Street Journal*, (February 26, 1990).
5. Daniel Valentino and Bill Christ, "Teaming Up For Market: Cheaper, Better, Faster," *Management*, (November 1989).

MIRROR TALK: FOCUSSING ON ME

All of us have had some sort of team experience, whether it be a class-related study circle, a community action group or some kind of committee involvement. Choose a team you were recently — or still are — a member of and answer the following questions:[6]

1. To what extent do I feel a real part of the team?

1	2	3	4	5
Completely a part all the time	A part most of the time	On the edge, sometimes in, sometimes out	Generally outside, except for one or two short periods	On the outside, not really a part of the team

2. How safe is it in this team to be at ease, relaxed and myself?

1	2	3	4	5
I feel perfectly safe to be myself, they won't hold mistakes against me.	I feel most people would accept me if I were completely myself, but there are some I am not sure about.	Generally, you have to be careful what you say or do in this team.	I am quite fearful about being completely myself in this team.	A person would be a fool to be himself in this team.

3. To what extent do I feel "under wraps," that is, have private thoughts, unspoken reservations or unexpressed feelings and opinions that I have not felt comfortable bringing out into the open?

1	2	3	4	5
Almost completely under wraps	Under wraps many times	Slightly more free and expressive than under wraps	Quite free and expressive much of the time	Almost completely free and expressive

4. How effective are we, in our team, in getting out and using the ideas, opinions and information of all team members in making decisions?

1	2	3	4	5
We don't really encourage anyone to share their ideas, opinions and information with the team in making decisions.	Only the ideas, opinions and information of a few members are really known and used in making decisions.	Sometimes we hear the views of most members before making decisions and sometimes we disregard most members.	A few are sometimes hesitant about sharing their opinions, but we generally have good participation in making decisions.	Everyone feels his or her ideas, opinions and information are given a fair hearing before decisions are made.

5. To what extent are the goals the team is working toward understood and to what extent do they have meaning for you?

1	2	3	4	5
I feel extremely good about the goals of our team.	I feel fairly good, but some things are not too clear or meaningful.	A few things we are doing are clear and meaningful.	Much of the activity is not clear or meaningful to me.	I really do not understand or feel involved in the goals of the team.

6. How well does the team work at its tasks?

1	2	3	4	5
Coasts, loafs, makes no progress	Makes a little progress, most members loaf	Progress is slow, spurts of effective work	Above average in progress and pace of work	Works well, achieves definite progress

7. Our planning and the way we operate as a team is largely influenced by:

1	2	3	4	5
One or two team members	A clique	Shifts from one person or clique to another	Shared by most of the members, some left out	Shared by all members of the team

8. What is the level of responsibility for work in our team?

1	2	3	4	5
Each person assumes personal responsibility for getting work done.	A majority of the members assume responsibility for getting work done.	About half assume responsibility, about half do not.	Only a few assume responsibility for getting work done.	Nobody (except perhaps one) really assumes responsibility for getting work done.

9. How are differences or conflicts handled in our team?

1	2	3	4	5
Differences or conflicts are denied, suppressed or avoided at all cost.	Differences or conflicts are recognized, but remain unresolved mostly.	Differences or conflicts are recognized and some attempts are made to work them through by some members, often outside the team meetings.	Differences or conflicts are recognized and some attempts are made to deal with them in our team.	Differences or conflicts are recognized and the team usually is working them through satisfactorily.

10. How do people relate to the team leader, chairman or "boss"?

1	2	3	4	5
The leader dominates the team and people are often fearful and passive.	The leader tends to control the team, although people generally agree with the leader's direction.	There is some give and take between the leader and the team members.	Team members relate easily to the leader and usually are able to influence leader decisions.	Team members respect the leader, but they work together as a unified team with everyone participating and no one dominant.

11. What suggestions do you have for improving our team functioning?

Before going on to the next section, think about these additional questions:

1. What was my role in the team's success or failure?

2. Could I have done better in a different sort of team?

3. Am I the kind of person who adapts easily to this type of collaborative venture? If not, how might I change this?

6. William G. Dyer, *Team Building: Issues and Alternatives*, (Reading, MA: Addison-Wesley, 1977), p.68-70.

Name _____

ID# _____

Section _____

The following articles express two opposing viewpoints on the impact teams have on blue-collar work forces. The first argues that workers have little to gain from teams and a great deal to lose, particularly in terms of control over their own environments and working conditions. The second insists that while there are some exceptions, most companies that have incorporated teams into the work place have created a better world for their workers. Read the pieces and then write a one-page reaction summarizing your own beliefs on the pros and cons of organizational teams. In writing, you might want to consider the following questions:

1. Are teams more appropriate in certain kinds of organizations than in others — for example, in a research facility versus an auto manufacturing plant?

2. What steps can employees take to ensure that teams will *not* become a management tool for breaking union work practices and forcing longer — or more intense — workdays?

3. How might management prove its good faith when installing a team system?

Reading 8.1

WORK TEAMS MUFFLE LABOR'S VOICE[7]

By Eric Mann

Eric Mann worked on assembly lines at the Ford Motor Company and the General Motors Corporation. He is the author of "Taking On General Motors: A Case Study of the U.A.W. Campaign to Keep G.M. Van Nuys Open."

The United Auto Workers convention, which opens next week in Anaheim, Calif., will mark the most fundamental debate in recent years about labor strategy. The debate is between those advocating non-adversarial labor-management relations and those advocating and adversarial approach. The former position is backed by Owen Bieber, president of the U.A.W., and the latter by the New Directions movement, led by Jerry Tucker and Donny Douglas.

The debate focuses on the team concept — a Japanese-style management system, which top management and U.A.W. officials claim fosters worker participation, greater productivity and cooperation. New Directions members, however, charge that it fosters what has been called management by stress, speeded-up assembly lines and the ideological manipulation of the workers. I agree with the New Directions Strategy.

But in the broader sense, the team concept has become a metaphor for the union's philosophy that says we are moving toward a classless society in which the interests of the working class and those of big business are becoming similar.

On another level, the team concept is seen by the union as an antidote to the destructive view of class struggle, where the workers' interests are pitted against the interests of the owners of corporate America. Unfortunately, the union's view of cooperation does

not extend to those union dissidents who disagree with the team strategy. For the dissidents, the team concept has meant a suppression of dissent.

On the shop floor the team concept is increasingly enforced by what is called the joint-activities staff, which some workers refer to as the "thought police." The workers' joint-activities staff members are paid both from union and management funds. They patrol the assembly lines, spread the propaganda of cooperation, single our opponents of union-management togetherness and interfere in union elections.

In the political arena, the team concept means that the U.A.W. administration has become an aggressive lobbying arm of the automobile and aerospace interests while standing virtually mute as corporations tyrannize local communities through threats of plant closings, refusing to pay fair taxes or to abide by environmental, health and safety regulations.

While the team subjects the workers to increasing personal insecurity and threatens the very existence of the union as an independent institution to promote working class interests, the present union leadership, under greater pressure from the workers, have become increasingly dependent upon top management for its power and prerogatives.

Thus, when reformers like Mr. Tucker and Mr. Douglas recently ran in insurgent U.A.W. union elections for regional directorships in St. Louis and Detroit, the U.A.W. leadership assessed every paid union staff member $500 to amass a $400,000 war chest against these insurgents. The union administration then orchestrated a huge shop floor staff campaign against the New Directions candidates with the full

cooperation of corporate management.

At one Chrysler truck plant, management prevented Mr. Douglas from campaigning and then gave his opponent full run of the plant. In another plant, management stopped the assembly line for 45 minutes to allow Mr. Bieber to campaign for his pre-team surrogate, Bob Lent. In the General Motors plant at Arlington, Tex., management held classes for employees that made it clear that a vote for Mr. Tucker could lead to a closing of the plant.

While the specific charges regarding these campaign irregularities are now being brought to the Department of Labor, the general pattern indicates how the team can become a dictatorial coalition of management and one-party union administration to prevent any shop floor or union democracy.

The strength of Mr. Tucker's and Mr. Douglas's candidacies, and the surprising New Directions victories in union elections at the G.M. Van Nuys, Calif., plant and the Mazda Motors Corporation plant in Detroit — both of which have team-management systems in place — indicates that there will be a second party in the U.A.W. that will have a chance to become a serious, long-term challenger for power.

But to succeed, New Directions will not have to re-invent the class struggle — for it has never gone away. Under the team concept, only one side — the corporation — has been allowed to aggressively pursue its interests, while it has been the workers who have been forced to cooperate. Now, New Directions, through the reassertion of adversarialism, provides the workers with a vehicle to once again make the battle with the corporation a fair fight.

---

7. *The New York Times*, (June 11, 1989). Copyright © 1989 The New York Times Company.

Reading 8.2

IS TEAMWORK A MANAGEMENT PLOT? MOSTLY NOT[8]

By John Hoerr

After 75 years of battling the mind-numbing drudgery of assembly-line jobs, auto workers might be excused for not recognizing management as an ally. Yet Detroit's current push to reorganize assembly workers into self-managed, multiskilled teams can produce better jobs, as well as boost quality and efficiency. Most workers seem to agree. But a militant minority is waging a publicity-wise but ultimately self-defeating campaign against the team concept.

True, the critics of teamwork are raising important questions about the pace of work, stress and the role of unions in work places where teams are operating. But critics such as Mike Parker and Jane Slaughter, former auto workers and authors of the 1988 book *Choosing Sides: Unions and the Team Concept,* also muddy the water by declaring that work teams are inevitably used by management as union-busting devices and, therefore, are no good for workers anytime or anywhere. The evidence doesn't support such a sweeping indictment. More often than not, workers who are part of teams find their jobs more rewarding and stimulating than fragmented, production-line work.

The teamwork critics are beginning to have an impact. *Choosing Sides* has received wide attention in union circles, and op-ed pieces by Parker and Slaughter recently have appeared in dozens of newspapers. Dissidents in the United Auto Workers are voicing protests against work teams in regional and local meetings, demanding the ouster of top UAW leaders who support the concept. And the clamor will get louder: Opponents intend to make a big issue of work teams at the UAW's convention in June.

8. *Business Week,* (February 20, 1989).

Big Three Key

The debate could be important for the future of the auto industry. Studies indicate that workteams, systems that allow workers real participation in decision-making — and not all do — can produce better quality cars more efficiently than do auto plants with traditional work organizations. For this reason, the Big Three auto makers, especially General Motors and Chrysler, see teamwork as a key to their competitiveness and are rushing to install the concept in many plants. But they need the cooperation of UAW locals.

The work-team concept has spread well beyond autos, into food processing, electronics, paper, oil refining, steelmaking and electrical products. The idea is now jumping from manufacturing into financial services and insurance. Actually, British, American and Scandinavian behavioral experts have been experimenting with teamwork for 40 years, hoping to reduce worker alienation in highly regimented work settings. There, employees are confined to a narrow set of minutely described tasks and watched over closely by a supervisor. Teams, on the other hand, typically consist of 5 to 12 workers who are given responsibility for producing an entire product or service, or a significant part of it.

The goal is for workers to learn all tasks performed by their team, rotate from job to job and assume most of the management functions of the old foreman. Critics say the gain in power for workers is illusory, and in some cases it is. But by no means always. At an LTV Steel Co. plant in Cleveland, for example, teams of highly trained technicians manage a huge electrogalvanizing line practically by themselves and participate in decisions on hiring, scheduling of work and hours and operations planning.

Power Loss?

Militants also object to the compression of job classifications that almost always accompanies teamwork. A team couldn't function if workers were forbidden to cross job boundaries. In auto plants, teams usually work with one production classification, down from hundreds in some cases. This means management can shift people much more easily, and workers don't have a wide choice of jobs to bid on. This is an ideological issue for Parker, who insists that dismantling the classification system essentially guts union power on the shop floor. He and other critics also contend that where work teams are combined with Japanese management, such as keeping parts inventories at a low level with a just-in-time system, employees usually are overworked. Parker and Slaughter call it "management-by-stress."

Yet, says Sidney P. Rubinstein, a consultant who works with unions and companies in setting up work teams, there is an easy solution for these problems: the union. "That's what the union is for, to prevent management from speeding up the line," he says, adding: "There's nothing inherent in work-team systems that says they have to be stressful."

Instead of fighting teams, says Harry C. Katz, an expert on auto labor relations at Cornell University, unions should "accept teamwork and come up with sensible plans to protect workers' interests. To just say no to teams, that's a British mineworkers' solution, going down with the ship, heads held high." Moreover, returning to the old way, as some team critics advocate, would mean giving up the drive for better-quality cars and more rewarding work.

Lights: Israeli Air Force

Today you are going to view a segment taken from a CBS *60 Minutes* news program about an unusually cohesive team. This group is not a commercial organization, but one that has been frequently described as an outstanding performer — the Israeli Air Force. In presenting this, we are not attempting to judge moral and political issues. Rather, we are using this segment to help illustrate one kind of high-performing superteam.

Action

As you watch this video, keep track of the special characteristics that give this team its "competitive advantage." In the left-hand column, write down the organization-wide enablers and supports that encourage the success of this team. In the right-hand column, note the personal attributes, attitudes and behaviors of the air force members that contribute to this high-performing system.

ORGANIZATION-WIDE CHARACTERISTICS	PERSONAL CHARACTERISTICS
1.	1.
2.	2.
3.	3.
4.	4.
5.	5.
6.	6.

MAKING CONNECTIONS: IN-CLASS INTERACTIONS

1. Break into small groups, and share your one-page reactions to the articles arguing the merits and drawbacks of work teams.

2. Come to a consensus within your group as to whether the potential benefits outweigh the dangers of such organizational restructuring.

If, as a group, you decide that teams pose too many risks, prepare a list of reasons justifying your decision, as well as a description of a preferable way of organizing a company's work force.

If, as a group, you support the team concept, prepare a list of precautions that could be taken to make certain the team does not become a mechanism for taking excess control over workers' lives.

3. Choose one person to report your findings to the class.

4. After all the presentations have been made, decide — as a class — on whether you would support organizational work teams.

COMING TO OUR SENSES: MAKING A DIFFERENCE

For many of us, it is not easy to give up personal preferences and freedoms on behalf of a larger goal. Being part of a team not only requires letting go of complete control, it also requires the ability to compromise, to negotiate and to stay open to new ideas and perspectives. This chapter has presented some guidelines for creating a superteam. Take stock now of your own willingness and ability to be part of a high-performing team:

1. Would you characterize yourself as a team player?

2. In what ways have you personally contributed to building a team/ organization that excelled in some significant way?

3. What are your concerns about being part of a high-performing system?

4. What strategies would you use in building a team that you had not considered before reading this chapter?

5. What key personal characteristics would you work on in yourself in order to become a better team player?

Can workers really function without a boss? The following article "Who Needs A Boss?" describes several companies that have already made major changes in the division of labor between managers and workers. By creating powerful and cohesive teams, these companies have given employees responsibilities and decision-making powers that formerly lay in the hands of their bosses.

The companies described here are at the leading edge of the move toward superteams. But judging from their success, many more companies are likely to be following in their footsteps. As you read this article, think back over what you have learned in this chapter, and imagine how you could apply these lessons to your next team experience.

Reading 8.3

WHO NEEDS A BOSS?[9]

By Brian Dumaine

Many American companies are discovering what may be the productivity breakthrough of the 1990s. Call the still-controversial innovation a self-managed team, a cross-functional team, a high-performance team, or, to coin a phrase, a superteam. Says Texas Instruments CEO Jerry Junkins: "No matter what your business, these teams are the wave of the future." Corning CEO Jamie Houghton, whose company has 3,000 teams, echoes the sentiment: "If you really believe in quality, when you cut through everything, it's empowering your people, and it's empowering your people that leads to teams."

We're not talking here about the teamwork that's been praised at Rotary Club luncheons since time immemorial, or the quality circles so popular in the 1980s, where workers gathered once a week to save paper clips or bitch about the fluorescent lights. What makes superteams so controversial is that they ultimately force managers to do what they had only imagined in their most

Boschian nightmares: give up control. Because if superteams are working right, *mirabile dictu,* they manage themselves. No boss required. A superteam arranges schedules, sets profit targets and — gulp — may even know everyone's salary. It has a say in hiring and firing team members as well as managers. It orders materials and equipment. It strokes customers, improves quality and in some cases, devises strategy.

Superteams typically consist of between three and 30 workers — sometimes blue collar, sometimes white collar, sometimes both. In a few cases, they have become a permanent part of the work force. In others, management assembles the team for a few months or years to develop a new product or solve a particular problem. Companies that use them — and they work as well in service or finance businesses as they do in manufacturing — usually see productivity rise dramatically. That's because teams composed of people with different skills, from different parts of the company, can swoop through walls separating different functions to get the job done.

Ten years ago there were practically no superteams. Only a handful of companies — Proctor & Gamble, Digital Equipment, TRW — were experimenting with them. But a recent survey of 476 *Fortune* 1,000 companies, published by the American Productivity & Quality Center in Houston, shows that while only 7 percent of the work force is organized in self-managed teams, half the companies questioned say they will be relying significantly more on them in the years ahead. Those who have already taken the plunge have seen impressive results:

At a General Mills cereal plant in Lodi, California, teams schedule, operate and maintain machinery so effectively that the factory runs with no managers present during the night shift.

At a weekly meeting, a team of Federal Express clerks spotted — and eventually solved — a billing problem that was costing the company $2.1 million a year.

A team of Chaparral Steel millworkers traveled the world to evaluate new production machinery. The machines they selected and installed have helped make their mill one of the world's most efficient.

9. Brian Dumain, *Fortune,* (May 7, 1990), p. 52. Copyright © The Time Inc. Magazine Company. All rights reserved.

Teams and Groups   147

3M turned around one division by creating cross-functional teams that tripled the number of new products.

After organizing its home office operations into superteams, Aetna Life & Casualty reduced the ratio of middle managers to workers — from 1 to 7 down to 1 to 30 — all the while improving customer service.

Teams of blue-collar workers at Johnsonville Foods of Sheboygan, Wisconsin, helped CEO Ralph Stayer make the decision to proceed with a major plant expansion. The workers told Stayer they could produce more sausage, faster then he would have ever dared to ask. Since 1986, productivity has risen at least 50%.

Like latter-day Laocoöns, the companies using superteams must struggle with serpentine problems. How do you keep a team from veering off track? How should it be rewarded for inventing new products or for saving money? How much spending authority should a team have? What happens to the opportunity for team members to advance as the corporate hierarchy flattens? How should disputes among its members be resolved? Answers vary from company to company. Read on to see how some organizations are coping.

Superteams aren't for everyone. They make sense only if a job entails a high level of dependency among three or more people. Complex manufacturing processes common in the auto, chemical, paper and high-tech industries can benefit from teams. So can complicated service jobs in insurance, banking and telecommunications. But if the work consists of simple assembly line activity like stuffing pimentos into olives, teams probably don't make sense. Says Edward Lawler, a management professor at the University of Southern California: "You have to ask, 'How complex is the work?' The more complex, the more suited it is for teams."

Lawler is getting at the heart of what makes superteams tick: cross-functionalism, as the experts inelegantly put it. The superteam draws together people with different jobs or functions — marketing, manufacturing, finance and so on. The theory is that by putting their heads together, people with different perspectives on the business can solve a problem quickly and effectively.

Contrast that to the Rube Goldberg approach a hierarchical organization would usually take. A person with a problem in one function might have to shoot it up two or three layers by memo to a vice president who tosses it laterally to a vice president of another function who then kicks it down to the person in his area who knows the answer. Then it's back up and down the ladder again. Whew.

Federal Express has been particularly successful using superteams in its back-office operations in Memphis. Two years ago, as part of a company-wide push to convert to teams, Fedex organized its 1,000 clerical workers into superteams of five to ten people, and gave them the training and authority to manage themselves. With the help of its teams, the company cut service glitches, such as incorrect bills and lost packages, by 13 percent in 1989.

At lunch with one team, this reporter sat impressed as entry-level workers, most with only high school educations, ate their chicken and dropped sophisticated management terms like *kaizen*, the Japanese art of continuous improvement, and *pareto,* a form of problem solving that requires workers to take a logical step-by-step approach. The team described how one day during a weekly meeting, a clerk from quality control pointed out a billing problem. The bigger a package, he explained, the more Fedex charges to deliver it. But the company's wildly busy delivery people some-

times forgot to check whether customers had properly marked the weight of packages on the air bill. That meant that Fedex, whose policy in such cases is to charge customers the lowest rate, was losing money.

The team switched on its turbo-chargers. An employee in billing services found out which field offices in Fedex's labyrinthine 30,000-person courier network were forgetting to check the packages, and then explained the problem to the delivery people. Another worker in billing set up a system to examine the invoices and make sure the solution was working. Last year alone the team's ideas saved the company $2.1 million.

In 1987, Rubbermaid began to develop a so-called auto office, a plastic, portable device that straps onto a car seat; it holds files, pens and other articles and provides a writing surface. The company assembled a cross-functional team composed of, among others, engineers, designers, and marketers, who together went into the field to ask customers what features they wanted. Says Rubbermaid vice president Lud Huck: "A designer, an engineer and a marketer all approach research from a different point of view."

Huck explains that while a marketer might ask potential customers about price, he'd never think to ask important design questions. With contributions from several different functions, Rubbermaid brought the new product to market last year. Sales are running 50 percent above projections.

Companies making the move to superteams often discover middle managers who feel threatened, and refuse — even for a millisecond — to think outside their narrow functional specialties, or chimneys, as they're labeled at some companies. Understandable, since the managers probably made it to where they are by being marketing whizzes or masters of the bean-counting universe. Why help some poor slob in engineering? For superteams to work, functional chimneys must be broken down and middle managers persuaded to lend their time, people and resources to other functions for the good of the entire corporation.

Robert Hershock, a group vice president at 3M, is an expert chimney breaker. In 1985 he introduced teams to his division, which makes respirators and industrial safety equipment, because it was desperately in need of new products. The old boss had simply told his underlings what to develop. R&D would sketch it up and deliver the concept to sales for comment, leaving manufacturing and marketing scrambling to figure out how to make or position the new offering. Says Hershock: "Every function acted as if it didn't need anyone else."

He formed an operating team made up of himself and six top managers, each from a different function. With suggestions from all interested parties, he hoped to chart new-product strategies that everyone could get behind. Under the operating team he established ten self-managed "action teams," each with eight to ten people, again from different functions. They were responsible for the day-to-day development of new products.

It wasn't all sweetness and light. Hershock says one manager on the operating team dragged his feet all the way. "He'd say he wasn't in favor of this or that," recalls Hershock. "He'd say to his people, 'Meet with the action teams because Hershock said so, but don't commit to anything. Just report back to me what was said.'" Hershock worked to convince the man of the benefits of the team approach, but to no avail. Eventually the manager went to Hershock and said, "I didn't sleep all weekend. I'm upset." The manager found a good job in another division. "You need to have a sense of who's not buying in and let the teams kick people off who aren't carrying their weight," Hershock concludes. Today his division is one of 3M's most innovative and fastest growing.

It's easier to build superteams into a new office or factory than to convert an old one to them. When an operation is just starting up, a company can screen people carefully for educational skills and the capacity to work on a team, and can train them without worrying about bad old work habits like the "it's not my problem" syndrome. Nevertheless, General Mills is organizing superteams in all its existing factories. Randy Darcy, director of manufacturing, says transforming an old plant can take several years, vs. only a year to 18 months for a new plant. Says Darcy: "It costs you up front, but you have to look at it as a capital project. If you consider the productivity gains, you can justify it on ROE."

Can you ever. General Mills says productivity in its plants that use self-managed teams is as much as 40 percent higher than at its traditional factories. One reason is that the plants need fewer middle managers. At one of General Mills' cereal plants in Lodi, workers on the night shift take care of everything from scheduling to maintenance. The company has also found that

superteams sometimes set higher productivity goals than management does. At its Carlisle, PA, plant, which makes Squeezit juice, superteams changed some equipment and squeezed out a 5 percent production increase in a plant management thought was already running at full capacity.

But you will never get large productivity gains unless you give your teams real authority to act. This is a theme that Johnsonville's Stayer, who teaches a case on teams at the Harvard Business school, preaches with messianic zeal. "The strategic decision," he explains, "is who makes the decision. There's a lot of talk about teamwork in this country, but we're not set up to generate it. Most quality circles don't give workers responsibility. They even make things worse. People in circles point out problems, and it's someone else's problem to fix."

In 1986 a major food company asked Johnsonville to manufacture sausage under a private label. Stayer's initial reaction was to say no, because he thought the additional volume would overload his plant and force his people to work grueling hours. But before declining, he assembled his 200 production workers, who are organized in teams of five to 20, and asked them to decide whether *they* wanted to take on the heavier workload. Stayer discussed the pros: Through economies of scale, the extra business would lower costs and thus boost profits; since everyone's bonus was based on profitability, everyone would make more money. And the cons: long hours, strained machinery, and the possibility of declining quality.

After the teams deliberated for ten days, they came back with an answer: "We can do it. We'll have to work seven days a week at first, but then the work will level off." The teams decided how much new machinery they would need and how many new people; they also made a schedule of how much to produce per day. Since Johnsonville took on the new project, productivity has risen over 50 percent in the factory. Says Stayer: "If I had tried to implement it from above, we would have lost the whole business."

Some large organizations still feel a need to exercise oversight of superteams' activities. What to do with a team that louses up quality or orders the wrong machinery? James Watson, a vice president of Texas Instruments' semiconductor group, may have the answer. At one of TI's clip factories in Texas, Watson helped create a hierarchy of teams that, like a shadow government, works within the existing hierarchy.

On top is a steering team consisting of the plant manager and his heads of manufacturing, finance, engineering, and human resources. They set strategy and approve large projects. Beneath the steering team, TI has three other teams: corrective-action teams, quality-improvement teams, and effectiveness teams. The first two are cross-functional and consist mainly of middle managers and professionals like engineers and accountants. Corrective-action teams form to tackle short-lived problems and then disband. They're great for those times when, as the technophantasmic novelist Thomas Pynchon writes, there's fecoventilatory collision: the s— hits the fan.

By contrast, TI's quality-improvement teams work on long-term projects, such as streamlining the manufacturing process. The corrective-action and quality-improvement teams guide and check effectiveness teams, which consist of blue-collar employees who do day-to-day production work, and professional workers.

What's to keep this arrangement from becoming just another hierarchy? "You have to keep changing and be flexible as business conditions dictate," says Watson. He contends that one of the steering team's most important responsibilities is to show a keen interest in the teams beneath it. "The worst thing you can do to a team is to leave it alone in the dark. I guarantee that if you come across someone who says teams didn't work at his company, it's because management didn't take interest in them." Watson suggests that the steering team periodically review everyone's work, and adds, "It doesn't have to be a big dog-and-pony show. Just walk around and ask, 'How are you doing?'"

Last spring a group of executives from a *Fortune* 500 manufacturer traveled to Midlothian, TX, to learn how Chaparral Steel managed its teams. Efficient superteams have helped make Chaparral one of the world's most productive steel companies. During the tour, one executive asked a Chaparral manager, "How do you schedule coffee breaks in the plant?"

"The workers decide when they want a cup of coffee," came the reply.

"Yes, but who tells them when it's okay to leave the machines?" the executive persisted.

Looking back on the exchange, the Chaparral manager reflects, "The guy left and still didn't get it."

Why do Chaparral workers know when to take a coffee break? Because they're trained to understand how the whole business operates. Earl Engelhardt, who runs the company's educational program, teaches mill hands "The Chaparral Process," a course that not only describes what happens to a piece of steel as it moves through the company, but also covers the roles of finance, accounting and sales. Once trained, a worker understands how his job relates to the welfare of the entire organization. At team meetings, many of which are held in the company's modest boardroom, talk is of backlogs and man-hours per ton. Financial statements are posted monthly in the mill, including a chart tracking operating profits before taxes — the key measure for profit sharing.

In the early 1980s the company sent a team leader and three millworkers, all of whom had been through "The Chaparral Process," to Europe, Asia and South America to evaluate new mill stands. These large, expensive pieces of equipment flatten and shape hot steel as it passes through the mill, much as the rollers on old washing machines used to wring clothes. After team members returned from their first trip, they discussed the advantages and disadvantages of various mill stands with other workers and with top management. Then they narrowed the field and flew off again. Eventually the team agreed on the best mill stand — in this case a West German model — and top management gave its blessing.

The team then ordered the mill stands and oversaw their installation, even down to negotiating the contracts for the work involved. At other companies it can take as long as several years to buy and install such a complicated piece of equipment. The Chaparral team got the job done in a year. Perhaps even more amazing, the mill stands — notoriously finicky pieces of machinery — worked as soon as they were turned on.

There remains considerable debate among employees, managers and consultants over the best way to compensate team members. Most companies pay a flat salary. And instead of handing out automatic annual raises, they often use a pay-for-skill system that bases any increase not on seniority but on what an employee has learned. If, say, a steelworker learns how to run a new piece of equipment, he might get a 5 percent raise.

While the young and eager tend to do well with pay-for-skills, some old-school blue-collar workers like Chaparral Steel's Neil Parker criticize aspects of the system. Says he: "New guys come in who are aggressive, take all the courses, and get promoted ahead of guys who have been here years longer and who showed up for overtime when the company really needed us. It's not fair." As Parker suggests, pay-for-skills does set up a somewhat Darwinian environment at the mill, but that's just the way Chaparral's management likes it.

When teams develop a hot new product, like Rubbermaid's auto office, or save money, like the Federal Express team that caught $2.1 million in billing errors, you would think they would clamor for rewards. Not necessarily. In many cases, surprisingly, a little recognition is reward enough. The Fedex team members seem perfectly content with a gold quality award pin and their picture in the company newsletter. Says one: "We learn more in teams, and it's more fun to work in teams. It's a good feeling to know someone is using your ideas."

In his book *Managing New Products,* Thomas Kuczmarski, a consultant to many of the *Fortune* 500 industrials, argues that recognition isn't enough. "In most companies multidisciplinary teams are just lip service because companies don't provide the right motivation and incentive. Most top managers think people should just find 20 percent more time to work on a new team project. It's a very naive and narrow-minded approach." His modest proposals: If a new product generates $1 million in profits, give each of the five team members $100,000 the first year. Or have each member write a check for $10,000 in return for 2 percent of the equity in the new product. If it flies they're rich; if it flops they lose their money.

Kuczmarski admits that no major corporation has adopted his provocative system, although he says a few are on the verge of doing so. One objection: Jack Okey, a Honeywell team manager, flatly states that it would be bad for morale to have, say, a junior engineer making more than a division vice president. "If you want to be an entrepreneur, there are plenty of entrepreneurial opportunities outside the company. You can have entrepreneurial spirit without entrepreneurial pay."

Perhaps. Awards dinners and plaques for jobs well done are common in the world of teams, but Texas Instruments vice president Jamie Watson thinks more can be done. He cites the example from Japan, where there is a nationwide competition among manufacturers' teams. Sponsored by the Union of Japanese Scientists and Engineers, the competition pits teams selected by their companies against one another. Once a year the teams travel to Tokyo to make presentations before judges, who decide which performs best at everything from solving quality problems to continuously improving a manufacturing process. The winners get showered with prizes and media coverage.

Sometimes, despite everyone's best efforts, teams get hung up. Leonard Greenhalgh, a professor of management at Dartmouth's Tuck School, says the most common problem is the failure by team members to understand the feelings and needs of their co-workers. At GTE's training center in Connecticut, Greenhalgh had middle managers do role-playing to bring out how such problems can creep up. In a fictionalized case, a team of six pretended they were Porsche managers who had to set next year's production schedule. Each was given a different function and agenda. The Porsche sales manager, for instance, wanted to manufacture more of the popular Carrera convertibles, but the general counsel thought it a bad idea because of the liability problems generally associated with convertibles.

The GTE managers spent several hours arriving at a consensus. Says Greenhalgh: "Typically, a team lacks skills to build a strong consensus. One coalition tries to outvote the other or browbeat the dissenters." To make sure everyone is on board, says Greenhalgh, it's important that each team member feel comfortable airing his opinions. But that can take some training for all group members in how to respond. For instance, the GTE managers learned it's better not to blurt out an intimidating, "I disagree," but rather, "That's an interesting way to look at it; what about this?"

Companies using teams sometimes run into another problem: With fewer middle-manager positions around there's less opportunity for advancement. The experts say they need to emphasize that because team members have more responsibility, their work is more rewarding and challenging. Harvard business school professor Anne Donnellon, who is doing a major new study of teams, sees this approach already working at some *Fortune* 500 companies: "People are adjusting to career-ladder shortening. If a team is operating well, I hear less talk about no opportunity for promotion and more about the product and the competition. They're focussing on getting the work done. After all, people want rewarding work."

If you've done all you can think of, and your team is still running on only three cylinders, you might consider something as prosaic as changing the office furniture. Aetna Life recently reorganized its home office operations into self-managed teams — combining clerks, technical writers, underwriters, and financial analysts — to handle customer requests and complaints. To facilitate teamwork, Aetna is using a new line of "team" furniture designed by Steelcase.

The furniture establishes small areas that the folks at Steelcase call neighborhoods. A central work area with a table lets teams meet when they need to, while nearby desks provide privacy. Says William Watson, an Aetna senior vice president: "I can't tell you how great it is. Everyone sits together, and the person responsible for accounting knows who prepares the bills and who puts the policy information in the computers to pay the claims. You don't need to run around the building to get something done."

The most important thing to remember about teams is that organizing them is a long, hard process, not a quick fix that can change your company in a few weeks. Says Johnsonville's Stayer: "When I started this business of teams, I was anxious to get it done and get back to my real job. Then I realized that, hey, this *is* my real job" — letting the teams loose. For those up to the challenge, there will be real results as well.

Chapter 9

Communication in Organizations

Cruising at 37,000 feet near the southern New Jersey coast, neither the crew of Avianca Flight 52 nor its passengers had any apparent reason at 7:40 p.m. on Jan. 25 to worry about reaching their destination safely.

The passengers had just watched Sean Connery in The Presidio. They had finished dinner: chicken and rice in the main cabin, trout in first-class. "It was a delightful flight, everything was pleasant, "said Jorge Lozano, an executive of Cargill Inc. who was the only passenger in first class to survive the jetliner's crash on Long Island.

From the crew's vantage point, too, the flight probably appeared to be running smoothly. The plane had burned almost precisely the amount of fuel called for at that point in the flight plan. It still had about 17,000 pounds of fuel — more than 2,500 gallons.

But the flight was at the very moment entering its hours of danger. In just under two hours it would burn almost every gallon of fuel in its tanks before its four engines died in rapid succession and it crashed at 9:34 p.m., killing 73 of the 158 people on board.''[1]

So far, the investigation assembled the following chronology of the delays and documented the crew's mounting concern about the fuel supplies during the final hour and a half of the flight.

1. John Cushman, "Avianca Flight 52: The Delays that Ended in Disaster,"New York Times, (February 5, 1990), p. B-1. Copyright © 1990 by the New York Times Company. Reprinted by permission.

At 8 p.m., a surviving passenger has told investigators, the pilots told passengers that they would be delayed for 20 minutes. The passenger said she was certain of the time, because she was constantly checking her watch during the flight.

At about 8:45 to 8:50, said air traffic controllers who have been interviewed by the safety board, the crew expressed concern to the controllers about the amount of fuel left. The investigators have been able to confirm this conversation by listening to Federal Aviation Administration recordings of the conversation.

A few minutes later, at about 9:05 to 9:10, the plane's crew members, speaking among themselves, again mentioned their worry about the dwindling fuel supplies. This conversation was not broadcast to the controllers on the ground, but it was recorded by devices on board the plane that taped all the sounds in the cockpit during the final half hour of the flight.

The pilots first attempted to land the plane at 9:24 but came in too low and in such poor visibility that they elected to abort that attempt. They had been informed of wind shear, or turbulence, at the airport.

When controllers gave them instructions for a flight path for a second attempt at landing, the pilots twice told the controllers that they were running low on fuel. This message was recorded both on the cockpit tape recorder and on recorders in the tower at Kennedy airport. But the pilots told controllers that the newly assigned flight path was "O.K."

At 9:32, just minutes before the crash, the pilots reported that they had lost power in two engines and were running out of fuel. That was their last report to the tower.[2]

The investigation into the crash of Avianca Airlines Flight 52 points up the critical role played by communications between airline crews and air-traffic controllers, as well as among the controllers themselves, in guiding jetliners to safe landings.

For example, the captain of the Avianca Flight 52 told controllers that he was concerned about his dwindling fuel supply as the jetliner circled in holding patterns that totaled nearly 90 minutes. But he never uttered the words "fuel emergency" — words that would have obligated controllers to direct the jet ahead of others and clear it to land as soon as possible.

"The pilot has to tell us whether he's low on fuel or we'll hold him until the airport opens up," said Robert Clacomazzo, a controller at the air traffic control center at Islip, NY, who, was not on duty that Thursday night. "If he declares an emergency, all rules go out the window and we get the guy to the airport as quickly as possible."

Mr. Clacomazzo said it is fairly common for pilots to advise controllers that they are running low on fuel but rare for a pilot to declare a formal fuel emergency.

"The controller has to assume that everyone has a fuel problem, because everyone is delayed," said one pilot. With its large share of long-distance flights, Kennedy International Airport has more planes arriving with potential fuel problems than airports that handle mainly domestic flights.

A former controller, who is now an official with the F.A.A., said he was trained to pick up subtle tones in a pilot's voice in such situations. "Sometimes you can sense when a guy is in trouble even when he doesn't say it," he said.

Pilots may be reluctant to formally declare an emergency, both out of a sense of pride and because of the paperwork that follows. If the pilot is found to be negligent in calculating how much fuel was needed for the flight, the F.A.A. can suspend his license.[3]

Thus, in Avianca Flight 52's final moments, "the crew told controllers that they were running low on fuel. But they did not declare an emergency, nor did they object to their newly assigned route, which although it was a tighter circle than the first approach, still took them out over the Long Island Sound."

2. Eric Weiner, "Right Word is Crucial in Air Control," *New York Times,* (January 29, 1990), p. B-5. Copyright © 1990 by The New York Times Company. Reprinted by permission.

3. Weiner, loc. cit., p. B-5. Copyright © 1990 by The New York Times Company. Reprinted by permission.

"Did you tell them we have an emergency?" the pilot asked his co-pilot, who was handling communications with the controllers.

"I told them we're low on fuel," he answered. A source who was not identified, recounted the exchange to The Associated Press.[4]

Poor weather conditions along the Eastern seaboard pressed an already fragile system of overcrowded airports, overworked air-traffic controllers, and overaged aircraft to their limits. But the crash of Avianca Flight 52 on January 25, 1990, was caused by a communication breakdown between the pilots of the aircraft and the air-traffic controllers. A closer look at the events of that evening help to explain why a simple message was neither clearly transmitted nor adequately received:

1. Pilots had asked for priority clearance to land but the information was not passed on to local controllers who guided the plane's final descent.

2. The words "priority"' or "running low on fuel" were used by pilots but never the word "emergency," which triggers an immediate right of way for the distressed aircraft.

3. The vocal tone of the pilot did not convey the severity of the fuel problem to the air-traffic controllers.

4. The culture and traditions of pilots and air-traffic controllers may have made the pilot reluctant to declare a final emergency and kept the harried air-traffic controller from asking about the precise level of the fuel supply.

The loss of life in the Avianca crash dramatically illustrates the potential consequences of flawed communications. Although less dramatic, poor communications in the work place can also be devastating. Anyone who has worked with confusing directions, unfair criticism, inadequate praise or very little communications of any kind has felt losses of productivity, creativity, motivation and trust. While these outcomes do not usually have life-threatening consequences, they do threaten our professional lives. Many firings and business failures have been traced back to technically excellent managers and companies with superb products that failed to understand the importance of high quality communication.

There are many theories of communication in organizations, but the key points are quite simple:

1. We can never *assume* that people understand what we mean — two-way communication is essential. For example, "Here is my communication! Now, tell me back what you thought I meant.

2. Much of what is communicated takes place non-verbally — communicating by memo often provides less information than meeting face to face.

3. Effective listening skills are the basis of clear communication. Managers must develop skills such as observing nonverbal cues, asking questions and acknowledging feelings of others before they can thoroughly understand their employees. If we feel listened to and understood, we are more willing to do the same for others.

4. Cushman, op. cit. p. B-6. Copyright © 1990 by The New York Times Company. Reprinted by permission.

5. A. R. Weitzel and P. C. Gaske, "An Appraisal of Communication Career-Related Research" *Communication Educations*, 33, (1984), pp. 181-194.

Studies have shown that both managers and subordinates place a high value on communication skills, but also that they disagree about how well they communicate with one another.[5] An impressive 95 percent of high ranking managers believed they had a good understanding of their employees' problems, while only 30 percent of subordinates perceived that their bosses understood their concerns. This 65 percent perceptual difference forms the basis of a serious misunderstanding about whether employees are understood.

Name _____

ID# _____

Section _____

Communication Interpretations

Please look at the cartoon on the previous page and write out your interpretation of its meaning.

My interpretation of the cartoon:

1.

2.

3.

4.

Group members' interpretation:

1.

2.

3.

Communication is "a process whereby symbols generated by people are received and responded to by other people."[6] For managers, "Communication is the process of exchanging information in a way that achieves mutual understanding between two or more people about work related issues."[7] The intent of communication is reflected in its Latin origin, *communicare*, to make common.[8]

When mutual understanding takes place, people attribute the same meaning to information. Misunderstandings at work cause confusion, delay, emotional distress and accidents. Efforts to improve communication can improve both productivity and morale.

In its most basic form, the communication process includes a **sender** who conveys a **message** to a **receiver.** So far only one-way communication has taken place. The sender has encoded a message such as the Avianca pilot's communication, "We are low on fuel." In this example, the receiver decoded the message to mean "We are low on fuel and need to land in the next half hour," rather than "We're almost on empty; you've got to get us down immediately." Without a common understanding, the communication is not complete. To complete the full cycle, feedback is required. The controller could have said, "The way I read your situation, it seems like you have half an hour of fuel left." The pilot could have responded, "No, we only have four minutes left; we must land immediately." The worst assumption you can make about a message that you send or receive is that it was received as intended. When it comes to communication, "Don't assume because *assuming* can make an *ass* out of *you* and *me* (ass-u-me)."[9]

Communicating may seem to be a fairly simple activity, but it can become a very complicated process for managers. Communication occurs between people, groups and across the entire organization. It takes place verbally and nonverbally, intentionally and unintentionally; it travels up, down and across organizational levels.

It can be helpful for managers to view the communications process from several perspectives as shown in Table 9.1.

Table 9.1

The Communication Process

1. Channels of communication
   a. Oral
   b. Written
   c. Nonverbal

2. Direction of communication
   a. Downward
   b. Upward
   c. Horizontal

3. Formality of communication
   a. Formal
   b. Informal

4. Unit of communication
   a. Individual
   b. Group
   c.. Organizational

---

6. S. W. King, "The Nature of Communication," in R. S. Cathcart and L. A. Samovar, eds., *Small Group Communications.* (Dubuque, Iowa: Wm C. Brown, 1988).

7. D. H. Holt, *Management, Principles and Practices,* 2nd ed. (Englewood Cliffs, NJ: Prentice Hall, 1990), p. 480.

8. Ibid.

9. R. N. Lussier, *Human Relations in Organizations: A Skill Building Approach* (Homewood, IL: Irwin, 1990), p. 180.

Channels of Communication

Channels of communication include oral, written and nonverbal communication.

Oral communication This type of communication occurs through telephone calls, personal contacts and presentations. It allows for interaction feedback but can take time and leaves no formal record.

Written communication This includes letters, memos and manuals. It can be widely distributed and leaves a formal record. It requires writing skills and offers little opportunity for feedback.

Nonverbal communication Nonverbal communication includes eye contact, facial gestures and office layout. It can enhance and support spoken statements but may give off incongruent messages.

In general, written channels provide an economical way to dispense information while oral communication is best used when dealing with feelings and conflict, because it allows two-way communication. Nonverbal reactions of others should be carefully observed and treated as important data.[10] Thus, routine simple messages are better communicated through leaner written channels while ambiguous non-routine messages usually require richer channels of face-to-face communication.

Direction of Communication

Downward communication "Downward" typically describes information sent from top management to layers of subordinates below through speeches, bulletins and other means. The information might include new company goals, job instructions, procedures and feedback. A major problem with downward communication is that it is estimated that only 20 percent of the intended message is intact by the time it reaches the entry level employee.[11] "Managing by walking around" can improve this problem.

Upward communication Messages flowing from the lower levels of the hierarchy to the top decision makers are upward communications. Upward communication helps managers know employees' accomplishments, problems and attitudes, and allows employees to make suggestions and feel part of the decision-making process. It also encourages ongoing two-way communications. Suggestion boxes, employee surveys and open door policies are often used.

Horizontal communications This type of communication helps peers keep informed within and across the departments. Coordinating efforts and sharing skills and information often requires meetings or task forces that cut across functional areas.

Formality of Communication

Formal communication Official episodes of information transmission such as prearranged meetings, written memos and official performance reviews are examples of formal communication.

Informal communication Channels for informal communication include the grapevine where "unofficial" information, rumors and truths about the organization not available in official documents and meetings are shared. The informal channels of communication may be less official but are no less important for understanding the organization. Informal networks cut across formal boundaries because people may share such activities as churchgoing, commuting to work or engaging in similar sports or hobbies.

10 J. R. Schermerhorn, *Management for Productivity*, 3rd ed. (New York: Wiley, 1989), p. 331.

11. T. S. Bateman and C. P. Zeitham, *Management, Function and Strategy;* (Homewood, IL: Irwin, 1990), p. 566.

Unit of Communication

Communication can take place at the individual, group and organizational level.[12]

Individual level of communication The impact one makes in face-to-face communication is the test of communication on an individual level. An effective communicator must be aware of how others perceive verbal and nonverbal behavior and be able to develop listening and influencing skills to communicate with people of any status or culture in the organization.

Group level of communication This category of communication emphasizes the special problems and opportunities that exist when more than two people work together and influence one another. Typically, groups are formed at work to solve problems or make decisions. Informal groups develop around common interests or physical proximity. Research has shown that the optimal size for problem-solving groups where two-way interaction takes place is five to seven people.[13] Communication networks in groups describe how information flows. For simple problems a wheel-shaped network with a central monitor reduces error. For complex problems , decentralized networks — in which group members can communicate directly with other group members — usually results in greater group satisfaction. Decisions that require the combined expertise of several people and where commitment to the decision is important are best made in groups.

Organizational communication This includes communication that is the sum of face-to-face individual communications, intra-group communications and inter-group communications. Managers must know how to communicate through formal and informal channels, upward, downward and horizontally, using oral, written and nonverbal methods.

People communicate all the time, whether they are aware of it or not. Even the manager who is physically unavailable is communicating a powerful message to others.

The Importance of Communication Skills

Observations of high ranking managers by Mintzberg[14] suggest that the manager who sequesters herself for hours on end to study reports or contemplate future directions for the firm is the rare exception.

Mintzberg observed the effective manager as a nerve center in an information processing network, with success resting on the ability to collect and send off information while fulfilling many different managerial roles and functions. The group of executives Mintzberg observed spent up to 80 percent of their time in oral communication, including 69 percent in scheduled and unscheduled meetings, six percent in telephone conversations, and 3 percent walking around talking and listening to employees. What this means to us is that managers get things done by talking to people and listening to them. While memos, reports and rules are part of the manager's job, the interpersonal relationship developed with colleagues is at the core of the different roles managers play.

Strong communication skills appear to be especially important for anyone aspiring to reach the top of an organization. A study[15] compared a group of executives who became chief executive officers with an equivalent group of derailed executives, those who were forced to plateau, resign or retire early. Both groups were highly intelligent, excellent in technical area and hard working. Of the CEO-bound executives, 75 percent possessed strong people skills. They could handle stress, laugh at themselves, confront problems without offending people and take blame for mistakes. These people were chosen to lead their organizations.

12. C. T. Lewis et al., *Managerial Skills in Organizations* (Boston: Allyn & Bacon, 1990), p. 13-44.

13. R. F. Bales and E. F. Borgatta, "Size of Group as a Factor in the Interaction Profile," in A. P. Hare et al., *Small Groups* (New York: Knopf, 1956).

14. T. R. Mintzberg, *The Nature of Managerial Work* (New York: Harper and Row, 1973).

15. Jr. M. McCall and M. M. W. Lombardo, "Off the Track: Why and How Successful Executives Get Derailed," *Technical Report #2*. Center for Creative Leadership (Greensboro, NC: January, 1983).

The "derailed group" had only 25 percent of their number rated as having strong people skills. They were generally seen as aloof, abrasive and arrogant. Despite their technical expertise and hard work ethic, they were forced to the sidelines early while the best communicators became the chosen leaders. Communication skills, alone, do not guarantee corporate success, but without them reaching the highest levels of the organization may be difficult.

The importance of strong communication skills will be even greater for twenty-first century managers who will function in a workplace that is multinational and multicultural. Furthermore, the increasing dominance of service industries requires more contact between people. Employees will require greater input into decisions, which demands that managers listen carefully to their ideas.

Developing self-awareness about communication

Textbook concepts help us to raise important questions that managers must answer about organizational communication. But having knowledge about communication is only a beginning. Self awareness and skill mastery are also essential. Our scientifically oriented educational system does little to teach students how to communicate effectively or how to judge one's own impact on others. Thus, we often communicate based on how some significant others have communicated with us.

One way to develop our communication skills is to follow the example of the Japanese Samurai Swordsman. These legendary warriors break their complex martial art into single skills that can be practiced until mastery is achieved.[16] They then retreat to a mountaintop for meditation and return with their individual skills integrated into flowing movements.

The road to mastery begins with awareness of your impact on others. One way to understand how we influence others is to understand how they influence us. When we first encounter someone, many things occur simultaneously. We see, hear or in some other way sense their presence and arrive at a first impression that can determine the future of that relationship. Our experience with people helps us to "read" their eyes, gestures, vocal tone and posture. Our perceptions are often clouded by stereotypes based on gender, race, age or other physical features. An important reason why managers spend up to 80 percent of their time engaged in interpersonal communication is because such communication offers them effective channels of information. For example, managers who are excellent communicators may notice discrepancies between an employee's verbal statements that support an idea and the absence of vocal enthusiasm or facial and bodily gestures to back up this attitude. The manager may then conclude that the employee felt it politically necessary to claim support for the idea, but held personal reservations nonetheless. The manager might never have sensed the employee's ambivalence had they communicated via memos or on the telephone.

At the same time that we are busily consolidating our first impressions of others, they are judging us. We walk into a room or we initiate a telephone conversation. Sometimes we are being observed from across the room; someone may be trying to fathom who we are. Time is of the essence and the data we display is sparse. Research has shown that the first two to four minutes are when first impressions become solidified.[17] Think of it. In a job interview, you have hardly begun to enlighten the interviewer about what an intelligent, hard working, ethical and pleasant person you are and the decision about you has virtually been made.

When the impression you make in these first few minutes is positive, you are likely to be granted greater credibility than someone who makes a weak first impression. Furthermore, quickly changing a negative first impression has been shown to be very difficult.[18]

16. A. E. Ivey, *Managing Face to Face Communication: Survival Tactics for People and Products in the 90s* (Lund, Sweden: Student litterative, 1988).

17. A. Mehrabian, *Tactics of Social Influence* (Englewood Cliffs, NJ: Prentice Hall, 1972).

18. D. Marcic, *Organizational Behavior: Experiences and Cases,* 2nd ed. (St. Paul, MN: West Publishing, 1989), p. 89.

Mehrabian[19] identified three dimensions of face-to-face communication: verbal, what we say; vocal, how we sound; and nonverbal, our look, gestures and eye contact.

If these three dimensions make up 100 percent of your first impression, can you guess what percent each one contributes to the total perception. Place your numbers in the three spaces below. They must total 100.

_____ %   Verbal: what you say

_____ %   Vocal: the way you sound

_____ %   Nonverbal: body, eyes, face, gestures, etc.

Total: _____

The answer to this question may surprise you. Mehrabian obtained the following results:

55%   Nonverbal

38%   Vocal

7%   Verbal

These results support the notion that "It's not what you say, but how you say it that counts."[20]

Upon first meeting someone, over half your impact comes from your facial expressions, gestures, eye contact, gender, age and other physical aspects. Whether we like it or not, whether it is accurate or not, people do make decisions about us from these nonverbal characteristics. Before we even begin to speak, people are deciding whether to hire us, buy our product, engage us socially or vote for us.[21] Your eye contact, appearance, the way you move and your facial expression all provide an enormous amount of information to people you meet.

The second most important medium to convey information about yourself is your voice. The way that you sound — excluding the actual content of your words — conveys 38 percent of your initial impact to others. The loudness, pitch, speed, power, hesitancies and variability of your voice leave strong impressions. We expect voices to convey meaning. The tone used by a boss, parent or teacher can convey support or criticism far more powerfully than the actual words spoken.

Finally, the words and what they mean comprise the final 7 percent of your impression during the first minutes of an interaction. Thus, the accuracy or usefulness of your statement may be ignored if the 93 percent of impact based on how you come across nonverbally and vocally gets in the way.[22] Sales people are particularly aware of the impact that the nonverbal and vocal impression can have. Most of us have been persuaded to purchase items we might not have really needed. Why? Possibly because of the power of a salesperson's nonverbal and vocal skills, which, after all, make up 93 percent of our first impression.

19. A. Mehrabian, op. cit.
20. Lussier, op. cit. p. 185.
21. Marcic, op. cit. p. 88.
22. Ibid.

Let us begin to look at the impact of nonverbal and vocal behavior on our impressions of people by first listening to how others sound and providing feedback to them.

Vocal Impact — Instructor Feedback

Your instructor communicates with you through such things as words, sounds, gestures and eye contact. In this class exercise, you are asked to listen to the vocal impact of your instructor. This is best done by not looking at your instructor so you do not receive nonverbal messages. Close you eyes and listen to how your instructor sounds.

1. Emotional impact.

a. This voice sounds: (for example, angry, fearful, bored, controlled, excited, sad, etc.)

b. It sounds that way because: (for example, the rhythm of its delivery is unchanging and it feels very calm, hypnotic.)

2. Vocal factors. Circle the most appropriate description in each row and put a check next to the factor (amplitude, pitch, etc.) that made the greatest impact.

_____	a) Amplitude	Loud	Med	Soft
_____	b) Pitch	High	Med	Low
_____	c) Speed	Fast	Med	Slow
_____	d) Hesitancy	Many	Med	Few
_____	e) Power	Tentative	Med	Forceful
_____	f) Variability	Constant	Med	Changing

3. In what situation (other than teaching) would this voice work most naturally? (Example: giving directions, because the voice seems very precise and exact.)

4. In what situation would this voice likely be misunderstood? (Example: in an emergency, because this voice seems very calm and could not cause me to move quickly out of harm's way but it may help me avoid panic.)

5. What motive might this voice most closely represent?

Power	Achievement	Affiliation
(control)	(accomplishment)	(friendship)

6. Why?

Now that you have practiced on your instructor, it is time to learn about the impact of your own voice on others. Like the Samurai warrior, try to be aware of a single component of your impact by isolating how you sound from how you look, move and think. Since many of our first impressions occur in busy place and, by definition, with people we do not know, the class environment offers a perfect environment to give and receive feedback on one's initial vocal impact. Read the following directions before you begin this exercise.

MAKING CONNECTIONS: IN-CLASS INTERACTION

Name _____

ID# _____

Partner's Name _____

Section _____

Vocal Impact — Partner Feedback

1. Choose a partner you do not know.

2. Face your partner and stand or sit close enough so that you can hear each other.

3. When told to begin, you and your partner will converse about whatever topic you choose, such as your five-year professional goals, how you got interested in your present course of study, how you feel about your present job or two-career couples.

4. Listen to each other's voices carefully. You will be simultaneously talking about yourself and listening to characteristics of your partner's voice.

5. During this conversation: Follow three rules

   a. Do not discuss voices themselves;

   b. Keep your eyes closed so you do not confuse physical gestures with the impact of the voice;

   c. Pay attention to the *sound* behind your partner's voice rather than the content of the words. If your partner's voice were a song, emphasize the music, not the lyrics.

6. Look over the "Class Interaction" worksheet. After your conversation, provide feedback for your partner and give your partner the worksheet to read and keep.

Worksheet

1. Emotional Impact — My partner's voice felt: (for example relaxed, precise, angry, fearful, controlled, joyful, bored, tired; avoid vague descriptions like pleasant, interesting, nice).

2. What vocal factors made the voice have the emotional impact that I felt. Circle the most appropriate description in each row and put a check next to the one factor in the left column that had the greatest impact.

_____	a) Loudness	Loud	Med	Soft
_____	b) Pitch	High	Med	Low
_____	c) Speed	Fast	Med	Slow
_____	d) Fluency	Smooth	Med	Hesitancy
_____	e) Power	Forceful	Med	Tentative
_____	f) Variability	Consistent	Med	Changing

3. In what situation would this voice work most naturally?

4. In what situation could this voice be understood?

5. What motive might this voice most closely represent

Power   Achievement   Affiliation
(control)   (accomplishment)   (friendship)

6. Why?

The single focus on vocal tone is only a beginning, but an important one. Feedback that we sound bossy or unsure of ourselves, joyful or disinterested can help us to understand how others perceive us. One of the authors has been told by his class that he sounded calm and supportive, but he looked serious and sometimes angry. He was able to control his initial impact by speaking soon after meeting a new person, when the calming voice was useful. He was also told by class members that his tests were more difficult than they expected. This happened even when he gave clear instructions about what was to be covered on the test. After several similar experiences, one student finally solved the confusion by explaining that the instructor did not "sound" like someone who would give a difficult exam. What you convey with your voice and how others perceive you may not always be congruent with your thoughts and feelings. Nevertheless, people do respond to you initially based on what they perceive. You should be aware of what their perceptions may be.

MIRROR TALK: FOCUSSING ON ME

If you found it difficult to listen to the emotional messages conveyed by your partner and to offer useful feedback, you are not alone. A study of business school curricula[23] has suggested that business education emphasizes the technical, analytical aspect of business while interpersonal skill components are neglected. Without training and practice in listening and communication skills, you may feel uncomfortable evaluating the messages conveyed by voices. What is needed in business education is a balance between technical and people skills. Business people need both knowledge of important information and procedures and the ability to get through to people.

How do your business skills balance out? Do you find the technical issues easier to master than "getting through" to others? Or might communicating with others be your greater strength? A brief illustration of how this balance operates in the work place can help you to assess your own situation.

You have just returned from the computer center where the person on duty was teaching you a new word processing program. She was very knowledgeable about the computer technology but did not seem to understand why you would have to repeat several questions that she said she had already answered. After a while, you thanked her politely and left, feeling somewhat defeated by your lack of ability but frustrated by her lack of empathy for your confusion.

The next time you visited the computer center you were greeted by someone who asked you several questions about your experience with computers and who acknowledged that word processing programs can be hard to master. You felt listened to and relaxed as your trial-and-error learning was warmly supported. After learning some basic commands, however, you were forced to wait while your instructor referred to the manual to figure out how to do the more complex tasks that you were ready to tackle.

Effective managing requires a balance of technical and interpersonal expertise. In this example the first instructor excelled technically but could not communicate with you effectively. The second instructor communicated well but lacked the adequate technical expertise. In each case you were somewhat frustrated and your learning was limited.

Assessing your Communication Balance

Because communicating is so involved, it is very difficult to evaluate how you actually are perceived to others. Yet it is essential to identify how well you convey both information and also empathy and understanding.

This "Mirror Talk" exercise provides three approaches to identifying your approach to communication. The first portion asks you to choose three anchor points: (1) a person who you would definitely identify as having strong technical communicators, but weak interpersonal communicators: (2) a person who is strong at interpersonal communication but lacks technical knowledge, and (3) someone who has a balance of each.

23. L. W. Porter and L. E. McKibbin, *Management Education and Development: Drift or Thrust Into the 21st Century?* (New York: McGraw-Hill, 1988).

1. Identify one person as representative of each of the three categories below:

a. Strong technical skills, but could benefit from interpersonal skill training.

Name:

b. Strong interpersonal skills, but could benefit from technical skill training.

Name:

c. Strong technical and interpersonal communication skills. A balanced communicator.

Name:

d. Which of these three individuals are your most similar to?

Name:

e. Which one do you work best with?

Name:

2. Using these three persons as anchor points, how would you predict that others who know you well will predict your balance of technical and interpersonal communication skills? If you were instructing someone on a topic that required both technical expertise and interpersonal sensitivity how would others rate you?

Scoring System

A simple way to evaluate how someone else would evaluate your balance of technical and people skills is to imagine a scale and basket of 100 weights. If you predict that you would be perceived as having a perfect balance of skills then 50 weights would be placed on each side of the scale. Or, if you were very technically oriented then the scale might have 80 weights on the technical side and 20 on the interpersonal side. Generally, a 70/30 measureindicates a strong preference for one style over another, a 60/40 measure a moderate preference and a 55/45 measure a small preference. In the space below, distribute the 100 weights in the way you believe someone else would evaluate your communication style. Please do not use the 50/50 balance.

Predicted score of others:

	Technical		Interpersonal	
	_____	+	_____	= 100

Using the same scoring system how would you rate your own communication skill balance?

	Technical		Interpersonal	
	_____	+	_____	= 100

The final step in assessing your communication skill balance is to ask others how they would evaluate your communication style. Have someone who you know well complete the following "Communication Style Assessment Form" based on how they perceive your communication skills.

Communication Style Assessment Form

Please consider your experiences with the person who has asked for your assessment. Your goal is to judge how well they balance the technical and interpersonal aspects of communication.

For example, if you have tried to learn a new word processing program on a computer, a technically oriented instructor might emphasize the mechanics of the program, sometimes at the expense of listening to the basis for your confusion. On the other hand, the instructor who is oriented toward interpersonal issues might emphasize your experiences in the learning process, but may be less able to explain technical details.

Please evaluate this person's skills by dividing an imaginary 100 weights on a scale between the technical and interpersonal sides of communication.

80 weights/20 weights:: Would be an extreme emphasis on one over the other.

70 weights/30 weights: A strong preference for one over another.

60/40: A moderate preference for one over another.

55/45: A small preference for one over another.

Avoid using 50/50: An equal balance.

How would you distribute the 100 weights on this scale? (The sum of the numbers should be 100.)

Technical   Interpersonal

_____   +   _____   = 100

A Final Look

1. Did you find agreement among your self-assessment, your prediction of how someone else would judge you and the actual judgment of an acquaintance?

2. What feedback have you received from other sources to support or refute these perceptions?

3. Do you work better with technical or communications oriented persons?

Active Listening

Communicating face to face begins with awareness of our nonverbal impact on others, but it includes an extensive set of skills that help excellent communicators move a discussion or interview toward a productive outcome. Professor Allen Ivey[24] of the University of Massachusetts has identified a group of active listening skills that can help managers understand their superiors, subordinates and peers. The most important listening skills include:

1. Attending skills: the nonverbal side of listening — eye contact, vocal tone, gestures.

2. Questioning: using questions to elicit data and zero in on solutions.

3. Paraphrasing: rephrasing for the other person the essence of what they have said to ensure you have heard them accurately.

4. Reflecting feelings: acknowledging the emotional content of a communication.

5. Summary: summarizing the main ideas of an interview or meeting.

Each of these skills can be used to manage the flow and direction of communications. Most beginning communications training in corporations begins with a video analysis of your attending skills. What do you look and sound like? What gestures interfere with your ability to communicate?

Asking Questions — A Basic Active Listening Skill

An essential active listening skill is asking questions to gather information about a person or a problem.

According to Ivey's single skills model, there are two basic types of questions: closed or focused questions, and open or expanding questions.

Closed questions are those that can be answered with short answers. *Did you turn in that report today?* This closed question does not ask for elaborations or explanations. It simply asks a yes or no question to focus on a solution.

Open or expanding questions seek to encourage the other person to talk, elaborate and to state thoughts and feelings in their own words. A manager might ask her subordinate, "How do you think we might approach this problem?" This question moves beyond from the narrow yes or no response desired in the focussed question and allows the subordinate to direct the interaction for the duration of her response.

In their simplest form closed or focused questions begin with words such as *did you, is it, are you.* Because the respondent is likely to answer *yes* or *no,* the questioner does most of the talking and controls the agenda. Too many closed or focused questions may feel like an interrogation and important input of the subordinate may be ignored by the narrow focus.

Open questions typically begin with what are you, how can we, could you tell me. Expanding questions used by the manager turn the spotlight on the employee. Too many open questions, however, may lead to a discussion that is too unfocussed and lengthy.

Most communications are a mixture of open and closed questions. Usually at the beginning of an interaction, open questions help explore the issue. For example, a job interview might begin with the question, How do you feel you can contribute to our company? Later more focussed questions can pinpoint details and clarify ambiguities. An important focussed question might be, Are you willing to relocate?

Most important is the manager's sense of control and skill at directing the communication to an outcome that satisfies both the manager and interviewee. The ability to intentionally use open and closed questions to guide the communication is a basic active listening skill.

24. Ivey, op. cit.

Lights

Some of the best examples of intentional questioning are in TV interviews. Interviewers have the difficult task of eliciting entertaining, newsworthy or revealing comments from sometimes famous, sometimes camera-shy interviewees. Their task is made more difficult because they must try to keep their subjects on the topic and complete the interviews within minutes. Some of the best of the current interviewers are Ted Koppel, Barbara Walters, Diane Sawyer and Mike Wallace.

Camera

In the following clip from Diane Sawyer's *60 Minutes* interview with Hyman Rickover already viewed in Chapter 2, let us examine how she is able to combine open and closed questions to move the discussion along.

Action

Your task will be to identify open and closed questions and observe how Rickover responds to them.

As Ms. Sawyer asks each question of Hyman Rickover, note on the following form whether the questions are open or closed. The Question Identification portion of the exercise begins in Part II.

60 Minutes interview of Hyman Rickover, by Diane Sawyer

Part I

RICKOVER.
No — I never have thought I was smart. I thought the people I dealt with was dumb, including you.

SAWYER.
I'll tell you, to be called dumb by you is to be in very good company. Edward R. Murrow for one. I think you said he asked you stupid questions.

RICKOVER.
Oh yeah, well I told him the same thing. I told him he was asking stupid questions and he agreed. He said, "well, what questions should I ask?" and I told him.

* * *

RICKOVER.
You're looking for easy solutions. The trouble with you is you want easy answers but you don't know the proper questions.

EDWARD R. MURROW.
Alright you go ahead and phrase the question and then phrase the answer.

RICKOVER.
Perhaps the question should be, What should be the role of educated or intellectual people in the United States? Now does that sound like a better question?

EDWARD R. MURROW.
That's a fine question.

What did Sawyer and Murrow do in Part I of this interview to handle Rickover?

Part II

SAWYER.

And you just thought that the rules of the Navy were silly.

RICKOVER.

I don't know about...I never read the rules. I prohibited it and never had a book of Navy regulations in my office. I prohibited it. One time some guy brought it in. I told him to get the hell out and burn it.

SAWYER.

Because you wanted them to think.

RICKOVER.

I wanted them to think. If they knew what their job was they didn't need a book of regulations.

SAWYER.

How can you run the Navy if everyone in it acts like you do?

Question 1: _____ **Open** _____ **Closed**

RICKOVER.

Well, I don't- I- I never told the others how to act. I acted my own way, my own genius.

SAWYER.

But you know, they said you were unaccountable.

RICKOVER.

I was 100 percent accountable. If anything had ever gone wrong with a nuclear ship to whom would they have pointed the finger at. What they mean is I would not do all the things they asked me to. I did the things I thought was right.

SAWYER.

But that's not working within the system. Isn't that what the military is about?

Question 2: _____ **Open** _____ **Closed**

RICKOVER.

My job wasn't to work within the system. My job was not to work within the system. My job was to get things done and make this country strong.

Part III

DIANE SAWYER.

What drove you down into the body of the ship to learn about why the cranks cranked and the ....

Question 3: _____ **Open** _____ **Closed**

RICKOVER.

Well for Christ's sake, what the hell is there about standing up and saluting and dressing up in uniform? You can put dummies to do that job.

SAWYER.

That's why you became an engineer?

> Question 4: _____ Open _____ Closed

RICKOVER.
Well I was in the Navy and I could do more and I could learn more. I couldn't see myself standing officer of the deck watches and saluting and all that nonsense.

SAWYER.
But why did you work so hard?

> Question 5: _____ Open _____ Closed

RICKOVER.
I was getting paid for it.

SAWYER.
No, why did you work...?

> Question 6: _____ Open _____ Closed

RICKOVER.
I would have worked hard at any job. No job that I ever undertook that I didn't work hard at.

SAWYER.
Why, why did it all matter to you?

> Question 7: _____ Open _____ Closed

RICKOVER.
Because that's what being a human being is. To do the best you can under any circumstances.

SAWYER.
What is the heart of leadership?

> Question 8: _____ Open _____ Closed

Is it in personality, charisma?

> Question 9: _____ Open _____ Closed

RICKOVER.
No, for example I have the charisma of a chipmunk. So what the hell differences does that make?

Looking at communication is truly coming to our senses. The Avianca case, interpreting a cartoon, listening to voices and watching a professional interviewer may have triggered some awareness of how you communicate.

Changing Communication Patterns

The most difficult part of the sequence for most people is how to change communication patterns, so that they can get the maximum impact during interactions. The following case study shows how one manager experienced the change process.[25]

Tom Haymond, manager of the research and development department of the chemicals division of a large manufacturing company, had just returned from a management training program. It had been an intensive five days and he had heard some things about his own management style and strategy that bothered him. Tom knew things were not going all that well in his department. Because of that, he had contacted the training office and asked them to recommend a good management development course — maybe he could get some new ideas that would be helpful. The training office had directed him to a well known program that had a strong laboratory-training group focus and Tom made arrangements to attend.

The week's activity had been a real eye-opener for Tom. The seven other people in his group had given him a lot of feedback about the way he tried to handle things in the group, and there were a lot of comments when he described how he ran his department back home. Tom knew he was a hard-driving, results- oriented person; he couldn't stand to see anyone or anything just sitting around. The group members at the conference told him that his insistence that the group get organized and moving had really antagonized them, and some had deliberately tried to block his efforts. One member commented that she would certainly not like to work under Tom, if Tom were the same way back home as he was when the group started. Tom was quite sure he was the same way back home. That's what bothered him.

Tom had talked with his group facilitator before he left and got an agreement that if Tom wanted to do something in his own department, the facilitator would be available to help as an outside resource person.

After returning home from the conference, Tom spent part of several days planning a strategy. Finally he was ready to take action. He called an extended staff meeting for all of the section heads and project directors who reported to him — a group of ten people. At the staff meeting, Tom laid out a series of issues and concerns:

1. He described the conditions in the department that had led him to attend the training course — the number of new developments was down, some key people had recently quit or asked for transfers, in one exit interview the terminating person had placed the reason for leaving on Tom's ineffective management behavior and the attendance and participation at staff meetings was low.

2. Tom summarized the feedback given him at the management program. He pointed out his concern about the feedback and his fear that his behavior at work was similar to that displayed during the conference. He felt that if he were to get feedback from the work group, it would be similar.

3. Tom pointed out the dilemma for him. On the one hand he wanted to improve performance level of the R & D department, but, on the other hand, he had some information that indicated he himself might be a contributing factor to low performance. Without clear feedback both from them to him and from him to them, they might not get the basic problems. A plan of action for improving the situation was badly needed.

25. William G. Dyner, *Team Building*. © 1987, by Addison-Wesley Publishing Company, Inc., Reading, MA, pp. 29-31. Reprinted with permission of the publisher.

4. Tom asked for their suggestions. "What can I do and what can you do to help us all work on the problems that I have identified?" There was a long silence. One project head said, "I don't think things are as bad as you paint them Tom. In my book, you're a pretty good manager," (There were nods of agreement and someone said, "Right on!")

Tom replied, "I appreciate your support, but I think we would all have to agree that this department has not been as effective recently as it was two years ago. Something has happened and I'd like to find out what it is and remedy it."

"I would like to make a suggestion, I propose that we spend two or three days away from the office looking intensively at the issues I have raised today. Each person would then come prepared to give his or her own information — what basic problems affect each of us personally on the job, what causes these problems, and what we might do about them. If we put all of our information together, we might come up with some interesting new solutions.

"Also, I would like to recommend bringing in an outside resource person to help us during the two- to three-day meeting. This person could watch us work and see if anything in my actions or the way we work together might need improving. What do you think?"

The staff began to discuss the proposal at length and, after an intensive wrestling with the issues presented, the group agreed both to go ahead with the meeting (it would start Wednesday evening and finish Friday afternoon) and bring in an outside resource person.[26]

Changing behavior, say Bolman and Deal, creates incompetence and neediness.[27] Without the skills and the confidence to venture into new territory, we will likely stay with old patterns even if they have failed to work well for us. Many people will remain in jobs or relationships that are unfulfilling primarily because they fear the unknown.

Tom Haymond's willingness to risk hearing critical feedback about his supervisory style and his communication skills was a momentous change from his previous way of managing. To acknowledge that he, as the manager, might be contributing to low team performance is a substantial shift in the direction of communication. Tom Haymond is beginning to balance his communication style by listening to the input of others, "hearing" what they are saying to him, and taking steps to behave differently. We have already seen how the proud Avianca pilots were unable to convey clearly their desperate fuel problem. Tom Haymond can take pride in directly seeking help. The respect and appreciation of his employees is likely to reinforce further his willingness to learn and change. What have you learned from Tom Haymond's case? How many of us are able to take such powerful steps to hear what others have to say about us?

Now it is your turn. It is easy to identify how others ought to change. What actions can you take that are similar to Tom Haymond's? Your senses can help you become aware of what works well in your communication interactions and what could work better.

What have I seen?

What did I hear?

What did I feel?

What did I think?

And now, what will I do?

26. Dyer, loc. cit., pp. 29-31. Copyright © 1987, by Addison-Wesley Publishing Company Inc., Reading, MA . Reprinted with permission of the publisher.
27. L. G. Bolman and T. E. Deal, *Reframing Organizations,: Artistry, Choice, and Leadership* (San Francisco: Jossey-Bass, 1991), p. 377-78

Do you hope to be a successful manager who gets promoted quickly? Or would you prefer to be an effective manager who has satisfied, committed subordinates and high performance work units? Your answer will probably be both. The intriguing finding of the study that follows is that successful and effective managers behave differently on the job, especially the ways they communicate.[28] As you contemplate the task of communicating with the twenty-first century work force, can you become effective *and* successful? Your decision will be critical to your career and to the ability of organizations in the United States to be creative and competitive.

Communication is at the core of effective management. It is as simple and basic as listening carefully to others and checking whether you have understood their message. It is as complex as trying to collectively reach a huge number of organization members, each with their own perceptions and biases that will affix different meanings to anything that is said. Yet each of us can identify great communicators we have known. These individuals usually maintained an attitude toward us of wanting to understand what we meant. When they taught us it was less to inform us than to transform us.[29] That is, they did not just communicate information but they helped us discover ourselves in a new way. Usually we realized increased capabilities, greater awareness and, most important, a desire to help others discover these qualities in themselves.

These great communicators did not rely on clever techniques to reach us, but practiced listening so their responses were based on our mutual realities not only theirs. Despite the rapid social and technological changes that the twenty-first century will bring, excellent communication will still be based on a simple desire to understand and empower people by first understanding them.

28. F. Luthans "Successful vs. Effective Real Managers," *Academy of Management Executive*, Vol. II. No. 2 (1988), pp. 127 -132.

29. R. E. Quinn, et al., *Becoming a Master Manager: A Competency Framework* (New York: John Wiley & Sons, 1990), p. vi.

Reading 9.1

SUCCESSFUL VS. EFFECTIVE REAL MANAGERS

by Fred Luthans, University of Nebraska, Lincoln

What do *successful* managers — those who have been promoted relatively quickly — have in common with *effective* managers — those who have satisfied, committed subordinates and high performing units? Surprisingly, the answer seems to be that they have little in common. Successful managers in what we define as "real organizations" — large and small mainstream organizations, mostly in the mushrooming service industry in middle America — are not engaged in the same day -to-day activities as effective managers in these organizations. This is probably the most important, and certainly the most intriguing, finding of a comprehensive four-year observational study of managerial work that is reported in a recent book by myself and two colleagues, titled *Real Managers*.[30]

The startling finding that there is a difference between successful and effective managers may merely confirm for many cynics and "passed over" managers something they have suspected for years. They believe that although managers who are successful (that is rapidly promoted) may be astute politicians, they are not necessarily effective. Indeed, the so-called successful managers may be the ones who do not in fact take care of people and get high performance from their units.

Could this finding explain some of the performance problems facing American organizations today? Could it be that the successful managers, the politically savvy ones who are being rapidly promoted into responsible positions, may not be the effective mangers, the ones with satisfied, committed subordinates turning out quantity and quality performance in their units?

This article explores the heretofore assumed equivalence of "successful managers" and "effective managers." Instead of looking for sophisticated technical or governmental approaches to the performance problems facing today's organizations, the solution may be as simple as promoting effective mangers and learning how they carry out their jobs. Maybe it is time to turn to the real managers themselves for some answers.

30. The full reference for the book is Fred Luthans, Richard M. Hodgetts, and Stuart Rosenkrantz: *Real Managers*. Cambridge, MA Ballinger, 1988. Some of the preliminary material from the real managers study was also included in the presidential speech given by Fred Luthans at the 1986 Academy of Management meeting. Appreciation is extended to the coauthors of the book, Stu Rosenkrantz and Dick Hodgetts, to Diane Lee Lockwood on the first phase of the study, and to Avis Johnson, Hank Hennessey and Lew Taylor on later phases. These individuals, especially Stu Rosenkrantz, contributed ideas and work on the backup for this article.

And who are these managers? They are found at all levels and in all types of organizations with titles such as department head, general manager, store manager, marketing manager, office manager, agency chief or district manager. In other words, maybe the answers to the performance problems facing organizations today can be found in their own backyards, in the managers themselves in their day-to-day activities.

The Current View of Managerial Work

Through the years management has been defined as the famous French administrator and writer Henri Fayol said, by the functions of planning, organizing, commanding, coordinating, and controlling. Only recently has this classical view of managers been challenged.[31] Starting with the landmark work of Henry Mintzberg, observational studies of managerial work have found that the normative functions do not hold up. Mintzberg charged that Fayol and others' classical view of what managers do was merely "folklore."[32]

On the basis of his observations of five CEO and their mail, Mintzberg concluded that the manager's job consisted of many brief and disjointed episodes with people inside and outside the organization. He discounted notions such as reflective planning. Instead of the five Fayolian functions of management, Mintzberg portrayed managers in terms of a typology of roles. He formulated three interpersonal roles (figurehead, leader and liaison); three informational roles (monitor or nerve center, disseminator and spokesman), and four decision-making roles (entrepreneur, disturbance handler, resource allocator and negotiator).Although Mintzberg based this view of managers on only the five managers he observed and his search of the literature, he did ask, and at least gave the beginning of an answer to, the question of what managers really do.

The best known other modern view of managerial work is provided by John Kotter. His description of managers is based on his study of 15 successful general managers. Like Mintzberg, Kotter challenged the traditional view by concluding that managers do not so simply perform the Fayolian functions, but rather spend most of their time interacting with others. In particular, he found his general managers spend considerable time in meetings getting and giving information. Kotter refers to these get-togethers as "network building." Networking accomplishes what Kotter calls a manager's "agenda" — the loosely connected goals and plans addressing the manager's responsibilities. By obtaining relevant and needed information from his or her networks, the effective general manager is able to

implement his or her agenda. Like Mintzberg, Kotter's conclusions are based on managerial work from a small sample of elite managers. Nevertheless, his work represents a progressive step in answering the question of what managers do.

Determining What Real Managers Do

The next step in discovering the true nature of managerial work called for a larger sample that would allow more meaningful generalizations. With a grant from the Office of Naval Research, we embarked on such an effort.[33] We used trained observers to freely observe and record in detail the behaviors and activities of 44 "real" managers.[34] Unlike Mintzberg's and Kotter's managers, these managers came from all levels and many types of organizations (mostly in the service sector — such as retail stores, hospitals, corporate headquarters, a railroad, government agencies, insurance companies, a newspaper office, financial institutions and a few manufacturing companies).

We reduced the voluminous data gathered from the free observation logs into managerial activity categories using the Delphi technique. Delphi was developed and used during the heyday of Rand Corporation's "Think Tank." The panel offers independent input and then the panel members are given composite feedback. After several iterations of the process, the data were reduced into the 12 descriptive behavioral categories shown in Exhibit 1. These empirically derived behavioral descriptors were then conceptually collapsed into the four managerial activities of real managers.

31. The two most widely recognized challenges to the traditional view of management have come from Henry Mintzberg, *The Nature of Managerial Work*, New York: Harper & Row, 1973: and John Kotter, *The General Managers*, New York: Free Press, 1982. In addition, two recent comprehensive reviews of the nature of managerial work can be found in the following references: Colin P. Hales, "What Do Managers Do? A Critical Review of the Evidence," *Journal of Management Studies*. 1986. 23, pp. 88- 115; and Stephen J. Carroll and Dennis J. Gillen, "Are the Classical Management Functions Useful in Describing Managerial Work?" *Academy of Management Review*. 1987, 12, pp. 38- 51.

32. See Henry Mintzberg's article, "The Manager's Job: Folklore and Fact," *Harvard Business Review*, July-August 1975, 53, pp. 49-61.

33. For those interested in the specific details of the background study, see Luthans, Hodgetts and Rosenkrantz (Footnote 30 above).

34. The source that details the derivation, training of observers, procedures, and reliability and validity analysis of the observation system used in the real managers study is Fred Luthans and Diane L. Lockwood's "Toward an Observation System for Measuring Leader Behavior in Natural Settings." in J. Hunt, D. Hosking, C. Schriesheim, and R. Stewart (Eds.) *Leaders and Managers: International Perspectives of Managerial Behavior and Leadership*, New York: Pergamon Press, 1984, pp. 117-141.

Exhibit 1: The Activities of Real Managers

Descriptive Categories Derived from Free Observation	Real Managers' Activities
Exchanging Information Paperwork	Communication
Planning Decision Making Controlling	Traditional Management
Interacting with Outsiders Socializing/Politicking	Networking
Motivating/Reinforcing Disciplining/Punishing Managing Conflict Staffing Training/Developing	Human Resource Management

1. Communication. This activity consists of exchanging routine information and processing paperwork. Its observed behaviors include answering procedural questions, receiving and disseminating requested information, conveying the results of meetings, giving or receiving routine information over the phone, processing mail, reading reports, writing reports/memos/letters, routine financial reporting and bookkeeping and general desk work.

2. Traditional Management. This activity consists of planning, decision making and controlling. Its observed behaviors include setting goals and objectives, defining tasks needed to accomplish goals, scheduling employees, assigning tasks, providing routine instructions, defining problems, developing new procedures, inspecting work, walking around inspecting the work, monitoring performance data and doing preventive maintenance.

3. Human Resource Management. This activity contains the most behavioral categories: motivating/reinforcing, disciplining/punishing, managing conflict, staffing and training developing. The disciplining/punishing category was subsequently dropped from the analysis because it was not generally permitted to be observed. The observed behaviors for this activity include allocating formal rewards, asking for input, conveying appreciation, giving credit where due, listening to suggestions, giving positive feedback, group support, resolving conflict between subordinates, appealing to higher authorities or third parties to resolve a dispute, developing job descriptions, reviewing applications, interviewing applicants, filling in where needed, orienting employees, arranging for training, clarifying roles, coaching, mentoring and walking subordinates through a task.

4. Networking. This activity consists of socializing/politicking and interacting with outsiders. The observed behaviors associated with this activity include non-work-related "chit chat"; informal joking around; discussing rumors, hearsay and the grapevine; complaining, griping and putting others down; politicking and gamesmanship; dealing with customers, suppliers, and vendors; attending external meetings; and doing/attending community service events.

These four activities are what real managers do. They include some of the classic notions of Fayol (the traditional management activities) as well as the more recent views of Mintzberg (the communication activities) and Kotter (the networking activities). As a whole, however, especially with the inclusion of human resource management activities, this view of real managers' activities is more comprehensive than previous sets of managerial work.

After the nature of managerial activity was determined through the free observation of 44 managers, the next phase of the study was to document the relative frequency of these activities. Data on another set of 248 real managers (not the 44 used in the initial portion of this study) were gathered. Trained participation observers filled out a checklist based on the managerial activities at a random time once every hour over a two-week period. We found that the real managers spend not quite a third of their time and effort in communication activities, about a third in traditional management activities, a fifth in human resource management activities, and about a fifth in networking activities. This relative frequency analysis based on observational data of a large sample provides a more definitive answer to the question of what real managers do than the normative classical functions and the limited sample of elite managers used by Mintzberg and Kotter.

How the Difference Between Successful and Effective Real Managers was Determined

Discovering the true nature of managerial work by exploding some of the myths of the past and extending the work of Mintzberg and Kotter undoubtedly contributes to our knowledge of management. However, of more critical importance in trying to understand and find solutions to our current performance problems is singling out successful and effective managers to see what they really do in their day-to-day activities. The successful-versus-effective phase of our real managers study consisted of analyzing the existing data based on the frequencies of the observed activities of the real managers. We did not start off with any preconceived notions or hypotheses concerning the relationships between successful and effective managers. In fact, making such a distinction seemed like "splitting hairs" because the two words are so often used interchangeably. Nevertheless, we decided to define success operationally in terms of the speed of promotion within an organization. We determined a success index on a sample of the real managers in our study. It was calculated by dividing a manager's level in his or her organization by his or her tenure (length of service) there.[35] Thus, a manager at the fourth level of management, who has been with his or her organization for five years, would be rated more successful than a manager at the third level who has been there for 25 years. Obviously, there are some potential problems with such a measure of success, but for our large sample of managers this was an objective measure that could be obtained.

The definition and measurement of effectiveness is even more elusive. The vast literature on managerial effectiveness offered little agreement on criteria or measures. To overcome as many of the obstacles and disagreements as possible, we used a combined effectiveness index for a sample of real managers in our study that represented the two major — and generally agreed upon — criteria of both management theory/research and practice: (1) getting the job done through high quantity and quality standards of performance, and (2) getting the job done through *people*, which requires their satisfaction and commitment.[36]

We obviously would have liked to use "hard measures" of effectiveness such as profits and quantity/quality of output or service, but again, because we were working with large samples of real managers from widely diverse jobs and organizations, this was not possible.

What Do Successful Real Managers Do?

To answer the question of what successful real managers do, we conducted several types of analyses — statistical (using multiple regression techniques), simple descriptive comparisons (for example, top third of managers as measured by the success index vs. bottom third), and relative strength of correlational relationships.[37] In all of these analyses, the importance that networking played in real manager success was very apparent. Of the four real manager activities, only networking had a statistically significant relationship with success. In the comparative analysis we found that the most successful (top third) real managers were doing considerably more networking and slightly more routine communication than their least successful (bottom third) counterparts. From the relative strength of relationship analysis we found that networking makes the biggest relative contribution to manager success and, importantly, human resource management activities makes the least relative contribution.

What does this mean? It means that in this study of real managers, using speed of promotion as the measure of success, it was found that successful real managers spent relatively more time and effort socializing, politicking and interacting with outsiders than did their less successful counterparts. Perhaps equally important, the successful managers did not give much time or attention to the traditional management activities of planning, decision making and controlling, or to human resource management activities of motivating/reinforcing, staffing, training/developing and managing conflict. A representative example of this profile would be the following manager's prescription for success:

35. For more background on the success portion of the study and the formula used to calculate the success index see Fred Luthans, Stuart Rosenkrantz, and Harry Hennessey, "What So Successful Managers Really Do? An Observational Study of Managerial Activities", *Journal of Applied Behavioral Science*, 1985, 21, pp. 255-270.

36. The questionnaire used to measure the real managers' unit quantity and quality of performance was drawn from Paul E. Mott's *The Characteristics of Effective Organizations*, New York: Harper & Row, 1972. Subordinate satisfaction was measured by the job Diagnostic Index found in P. C. Smith, L. M. Kendall, and C. L. Hulin's *The Measurement of Satisfaction in Work and Retirement*, Chicago: Rand-McNally, 1969. Subordinate commitment is measured by the questionnaire in Richard T. Mowday, L. W. Porter, and Richard M. Steers' *Employee-Organizational Linkages: The Psychology of Commitment, Absenteeism, and Turnover*, New York: Academic Press, 1982. These three standardized questionnaires are widely used research instruments with considerable psychometric back-up and high reliability in the sample used in our study.

37. For the details of the multiple regression analysis and simple descriptive comparisons of successful versus unsuccessful managers, see footnote 35 above. To determine the relative contribution the activities identified in Exhibit I made to success, we calculated the mean of the squared correlations (to approximate variance explained) between the observed activities of the real managers and the success index calculated for each target manager. These correlation squared means were then rank ordered to obtain the relative strengths of the managerial activities' contribution to success.

38. The calculation for the relative contribution the activities made to effectiveness was done as described for success in Footnote 37. The statistical and top third-bottom third comparison that was done in the success analysis was not done in the effectiveness analysis. For comparison of successful managers and effective managers, the relative strength of relationship was used; see *Real Managers* (Footnote 30 above) for details.

"I find that the way to get ahead around here is to be friendly with the right people, both inside and outside the firm. They get tired of always talking shop, so I find a common interest — with some it's sports, with others it's our kids — and interact with them on that level. The other formal stuff around the office is important but I really work at this informal side and have found it pays off when promotion time rolls around."

In other words, for this manager and for a significant number of those real managers we studied, networking seems to be the key to success.

What Do Effective Real Managers Do?

Once we answered the question of what successful managers do, we turned to the even more important question of what effective managers do. It should be emphasized once again that, in gathering our observational data for the study, we made no assumptions that the successful real managers were (or were not) the effective managers. our participant observers were blind to the research questions and we had no hypothesis concerning the relationship between successful and effective managers.

We used the relative strength of correlational relationship between the real managers' effectiveness index and their directly observed day-to-day activities and found that communication and human resource management activities made by far the largest relative contribution to real managers' effectiveness and that traditional management and — especially — networking made by far the least relative contribution.[38]

These results mean that if effectiveness is defined as the perceived quantity and quality of the performance of a manager's unit and his or her subordinates' satisfaction and commitment, then the biggest relative contribution to real manager effectiveness comes from the human oriented activities — communication and human resource management. A representative example of this effectiveness profile is found in the following manager's comments:

Both how much and how well things get done around here, as well as keeping my people loyal and happy, has to do with keeping them informed and involved. If I make a change in procedure or the guys upstairs give us a new process or piece of equipment to work with, I get my people's input and give them the full story before I lay it on them. Then I make sure they have the proper training and give them feedback on how they are doing. When they screw up, I let them know it, but when they do a good job, I let them know about that too.

This manager, like our study of real managers in general found that the biggest contribution to effectiveness came from communication and human resource management activities.

Equally important, however, was the finding that the least relative contribution to real managers' effectiveness came from the networking activity. This, of course, is in stark contrast to our results of the successful real manager analysis. Networking activity had by far the strongest relative relationship to success, but the weakest with effectiveness. On the other hand, human resource management activity had a strong relationship to effectiveness (second only to communication activity), but had the

weakest relative relationship to success. In other words, the successful real managers do not do the same activities as the effective real managers (in fact, they do almost the opposite). These contrasting profiles may have significant implications for understanding the current performance problems facing American organizations. However, before we look at these implications and suggest some solutions, let's take a look at those real managers who are both successful and effective.

What do managers who are both successful and effective do?

The most obvious concluding question is what those who found to be both successful and effective really do. This "combination" real manager, of course, is the ideal and has been assumed to exist in American management over the years.

Since there was such a difference between successful and effective managers in our study, we naturally found relatively few (less than 10 percent of our sample) that were both among the top third of successful managers and the top third of effective managers. Not surprisingly, upon examining this special group, we found that their activities were very similar to real managers as a whole. They were not like either the successful or effective real managers. Rather, it seems that real managers who are both successful and effective use a fairly balanced approach in terms of their activities. In other words, real managers who can strike the delicate balance between all four managerial activities may be able to get ahead as well as get the job done.

Important is the fact that we found so few real managers that were both successful and effective. This supports our findings on the difference between successful and effective real managers, but limits any generalizations that can be made about successful and effective managers. It seems that more important in explaining our organizations' present performance problems, and what to do about them, are the implications of the wide disparity between successful and effective real managers.

Implications of the Successful Versus Effective Real Managers Findings

If, as our study indicates, there is indeed a difference between successful and effective real managers what does it mean and what should we do about it? First of all, we need to pay more attention to formal reward systems to ensure that effective managers are promoted. Second, we must learn how effective managers do their day-to-day jobs.

The traditional assumption holds that promotions are based on performance. This is what the formal personnel policies say, this is what new management trainees are told and this is what every management textbook states *should* happen. On the other hand, more "hardened" (or perhaps more realistic) members and observers of *real* organizations (not textbook organizations or those featured in the latest best sellers or videotapes) have long suspected that social and political skills are the real key to getting ahead, to being *successful*. Our study lends support to the latter view.

The solution is obvious, but may be virtually impossible to implement, at least in the short run. Tying formal rewards — and especially promotions — to performance is a must if organizations are going to move ahead and become more productive. At a minimum, and most pragmatically in the short run, organizations must move to a performance-based appraisal system. Managers that are *effective* should be *promoted.* In the long run organizations must develop cultural values that support and reward effective performance, not just successful socializing and politicking. This goes hand-in-hand with the current attention given to corporate culture and how to change it. An appropriate goal for cultural change in today's organizations might simply be to make effective managers successful.

Besides the implications for performance-based appraisals and organizational culture that came out of the findings of our study is a lesson that we can learn from the effective real managers themselves. This lesson is the importance they give and effort they devote to the human-oriented activities of communicating and human resource management. How human resources are managed — keeping them informed, communicating with them, paying attention to them, reinforcing them, resolving their conflicts, training/developing them — all contribute directly to managerial effectiveness.

The disparity our study found between successful and effective real managers has important implications for the performance problems facing today's organizations. While we must move ahead on all fronts in our search for solutions to these problems, we believe the activities basic to the effective real managers in our study — communication and human resource management — deserve special attention.

Chapter 10

Managing Information Systems

Have you recently bought a bag of Frito-Lay "Lite" potato chips? If you perhaps do not exactly recall when or where you did, Frito-Lay probably knows for sure. The company has developed a revolutionary tracking system that enables it to have a wide array of information in "nanoseconds." For example, when Frito-Lay launched a new line of "light" snack foods, managers wanted to know if the new products were cannibalizing other Frito-Lay brands and if they were outselling competitors. In a matter of days, managers could determine supermarket sales from the previous week, supermarket sales versus smaller accounts, average sales on a particular route and the success of their promotions.[1]

1. Robert Beeby, "How to Crunch a Bunch of Numbers," *Wall Street Journal*, June 11, 1990.

How did they get this information? Managers received detailed sales and inventory information derived from a decision support system used by 10,000 route salespeople equipped with hand-held computers. With this system, salespeople can walk around a store and enter information into their computers about such things as sales and prices. There is virtually no more paperwork for these salespeople. And the reports get transmitted in seconds to headquarters. In short, this system helps in tracking new products, facilitates faster and more accurate decisions and provides instantaneous feedback to store managers.

The challenge for management is to get needed information as quickly as possible, information that can be used for competitive advantage. It is both a matter of new management systems and new technological tools. Of course, there are many challenges associated with advancement and progress. People still have to select the right type of information to collect, people still have to be comfortable with the technology that allows for this collection and people have to interpret and act upon the information effectively.

This chapter will give us some hints about the explosion and impact of new information systems and new modes of information exchange. It will profoundly impact all of the management processes, and our lives, as we head for the twenty-first century.

We see the signs of things to come: mobile phones, fax machines, interactive computers, business centers in every airport (and soon on every plane), computer-aided meetings and CNN in every hotel room in major cities around the world. These are only what we have already begun to see. Given the pace of these break-throughs, and the quantum leaps they have generated, one can only speculate on the changes yet to come.

The field of management information systems has many different aspects to it. We will use the term MIS as defined by Stoner: "A formal method of making available to management the accurate and timely information necessary to facilitate the decision-making process and enable the organization's planning, control and operation functions to be carried out effectively."[2]

This field continues to grow in importance as information-processing requirements have grown, as the widespread use and application of computers has become a fact of doing business and as the impact on how managers manage and control has been increasingly recognized.

Peter Drucker, a leading management expert, argued that there is an important distinction between data and information. We can get swamped in data. We can have the same kind of data, only get it faster. But information connotes the transformation of data into something that ultimately affects decision processes, management structure and the way work will get done.[3]

The information-based organization, according to another expert, Shoshana Zuboff, will harness information technology towards three interdependent goals:

1. To increase continuity (functional integration, enhanced automaticity, rapid response)

2. To increase control (precision, accuracy, predictability, consistency and certainty)

3. To increase comprehensibility of productive functions (visibility, analysis and synthesis)[4]

As with any tool, MIS is only as useful as its design and implementation. The problems and challenges of using MIS are summarized in Table 10.1. They may derive from the economics, the technology and the management of the MIS.

2. James Stoner, *Management*, (Englewood Cliffs, NJ: Prentice Hall, 1982).

3. Peter Drucker, "The Coming of the New Organization," *Harvard Business Review*, (Jan-Feb, 1988), pp. 45-53.

4. Shoshana Zuboff, "Automate/ Informate: The Two Faces of Intelligent Technology," *Organizational Dynamics*, (1985).

Table 10.1 Recent Changes and Their Impact on MIS

Factors	Changes	Impact on MIS
Economic	Global business systems Worldwide inflation Sudden energy crises Growing shortages of many vital national resources Control of key resources by new third-world countries Taxation inhibiting capital formation in basic U.S. industries High interest rates Unfunded pension plans growing beyond control Declining growth in productivity	Increased monitoring and prompt reporting of worldwide events Need for rapid reporting for rapid response to currency fluctuations Increasing need for forecasting resources and costs Better models of the firm in terms of plant locations to reduce taxes Better forecasts of interest rates for borrowing Use of MIS for controlling productivity

Factors	Changes	Impact on MIS
Technological	Tremendous increase in computer capabilities at rapidly decreasing cost for functions Radical changes in communications systems such as satellites Video word-processing developments Replacement of the U.S. Postal Service	Increased ability to model complex systems Ability to process masses of data, such as global currency transactions Expansion of real-time MIS Better management reports Growth of number of MIS workers
Social	Higher level of education Health care Reduced age and sex discrimination Pollution Computers in the home Privacy threats	Higher quality of personnel available over a longer life span Managers always available or "on call" day and night Legal challenges to information gathering and storage Obstacles to linking government and private data bases
Political-Legal	Government trend towards "Big Brother" as data bases grow Standards Privacy laws Liability laws	Concern for keeping corporate data bases inaccessible to governments Possible reduction of innovations but improved compatibility of hardware Increased liability hazards
Management and Organization	Increased importance of systems people relative to managers Development of organizational systems theory Greater reliance for decisions on individual workers rather than on managers	A larger role for MIS in decision assisting Better trade-offs in decision making Supplying of more information by MIS to lower-level managers and key specialists

Source: Adapted from R. G. Murdick, *MIS: Concepts and Design,* (Englewood Cliffs, N.J.: Prentice-Hall, 1980), p. 6. In Carl Anderson, *Management,* (Dubuque, IA: Wm Brown, 1984).

One of the management problems described in Table 10.1 is the classic problem of accepting technological change. The computer is often the center of new information systems. We marvel at its power and potential. We envy the wizards for whom the sky is the limit. We are bombarded by products that promise to ease our burdens and provide all sorts of services. But we also recognize that "all systems are not go" unless the "knowledge workers" use the new technology and are sold on it. In essence, this is a matter of how the change, that is, the new system, is used and managed.

There are a variety of common mistakes that managers make in trying to manage technological change:

1. Neglecting to warm up users to the idea of a new system.

2. Introducing the new system to the wrong people first.

3. Failing to pretest the system completely.

4. Pulling out the old system too quickly or too slowly.

5. Expecting too much too soon.

6. Providing training that has nothing to do with employees' real-life work.

7. Failing to offer sufficient follow-up after training.[5]

A new system requires a carefully considered and implemented introduction. Users need to participate in the process. At a minimum, the rationale for the new system must be explained, while ideally the users should be involved with the selection and design of the system and be sold on it. This should be targeted at the users as well as the "purchasers" and senior managers. Focus groups and or pilots should be set up to test the system.

The pace at which the old system is replaced is a very tricky problem. When Northwest Airlines merged with Republic Air, the companies operated with two different reservations systems from two different vendors. The merged company then decided to convert to a third system. How could the conversion be made while handling the day's business? After all, the company couldn't suspend reservations while the new system was being installed and the reservations agents were being retrained!

Although the company conducted trial runs and retrained supervisors initially, managers believed that the whole new system had to be turned on and the old system shut down "in one fell swoop." They found that training people off-line on the new system while then going back to operate the old system (until the new one was ready and the training completed) was not workable. The switch-over caused a multitude of problems and errors but probably could not have been done any other way.

The pace of a switch-over must be determined on a situation-by-situation basis. When you can run parallel systems it may allow for a smoother transition. But if you can't, it is often necessary to make the change and be prepared to deal with the post-change glitches.

5. Sharon Efroymson First, "All Systems Go: How to Manage Technological Change," *Working Woman*, (April 1990).

In any case, there is an expected learning curve that will involve some mistakes and inefficiencies until people get used to the new system. Training can help to accelerate this curve, obviously, as will ongoing help and support.

Name _____

ID# _____

Section _____

Please read the article by Peter Drucker, "The Coming of the New Organization," in which he tries to characterize the impact of information technology on business enterprises. How will life in organizations be transformed?

1. List five major differences between this new organization and what Drucker calls the "command and control" organizations we are accustomed to.

a.

b.

c.

d.

e.

2. What would be most exciting for you about working and managing in "the new organization"?

3. What would be most worrisome for you about managing in this new form of organization?

Reading 10.1

THE COMING OF THE NEW ORGANIZATION[6]

by Peter F. Drucker

The typical large business 20 years hence will have fewer than half the levels of management of its counterpart today, and no more than a third the managers. In its structure, and in its management problems and concerns, it will bear little resemblance to the typical manufacturing company, circa 1950, which our textbooks still consider the norm. Instead it is far more likely to resemble organizations that neither the practicing manager nor the management scholar pays much attention to today: the hospital, the university, the symphony orchestra. For like them, the typical business will be knowledge-based, an organization composed largely of specialists who direct and discipline their own performance through organized feedback from colleagues, customers and headquarters. For this reason, it will be what I call an information-based organization.

Businesses, especially large ones, have little choice but to become information-based. Demographics, for one, demands the shift. The center of gravity in employment is moving fast from manual and clerical workers to knowledge workers who resist the command-and-control model that business took from the military 100 years ago. Economics also dictates change, especially the need for large businesses to innovate and to be entrepreneurs. But above all, information technology demands the shift.

Advanced data-processing technology isn't necessary to create an information-based organization, of course. As we shall see, the British built just such an organization in India when "information technology" meant quill pen, and barefoot runners were the "telecommunications"

systems. But as advanced technology becomes more and more prevalent, we have to engage in analysis and diagnosis —that is, in "information" — even more intensively or risk being swamped by the data we generate.

So far most computer users still use the new technology only to do faster what they have always done before, crunch conventional numbers. But as soon as a company takes the first tentative steps from data to information, its decision processes, management structure, and even the way its work gets done begin to be transformed. In fact, this is already happening, quite fast, in a number of companies throughout the world.

We can readily see the first step in this transformation process when we consider the impact of computer technology on capital-investment decisions. We have known for a long time that there is no one right way to analyze a proposed capital investment. To understand it we need at least six analyses: the expected rate of return; the payout period and the investment's expected productive life; the discounted present value of all returns through the productive lifetime of the investment; the risk in not making the investment or deferring it; the cost and risk in case of failure; and finally, the opportunity cost. Every accounting student is taught these concepts. But before the advent of data-processing capacity, the actual analyses would have taken man-years of clerical toil to complete. Now anyone with a spreadsheet should be able to do them in a few hours.

The availability of this information transforms the capital-investment analysis from opinion into diagnosis, that is, into the rational weighing of alternative assumptions. Then the information transforms the capital-investment decision from an opportunistic, financial decision governed by the numbers into a business decision based on the probability of alternative strategic assumptions. So the decision both presupposes a business strategy and challenges that strategy and its assumptions. What was once a budget exercise becomes an analysis of policy.

The second area that is affected when a company focuses its data-processing capacity on producing information is its organization structure. Almost immediately, it becomes clear that both the number of management levels and the number of managers can be sharply cut. The reason is straightforward: It turns out that whole layers of management neither make decisions nor lead. Instead, their main, if not their only, function is to serve as "relays" — human boosters for the faint, unfocused signals that pass for communication in the traditional pre-information organization.

One of America's largest defense contractors made this discovery when it asked what information its top corporate and operating managers needed to do their jobs. Where did it come from? What form was it in? How did it flow? The search for answers soon revealed that whole layers of management — perhaps as many as six out of a total of 14 — existed only because these questions had not been asked before. The company had had data galore. But it had always used its copious data for control rather than for information.

6. *Harvard Business Review,* (January-February 1988), pp. 45-53. Reprinted by permission of *Harvard Business Review.*" Copyright ©1988 by the President and Fellows of Harvard College. All rights reserved.

Information is data endowed with relevance and purpose. Converting data into information thus requires knowledge. And knowledge, by definition, is specialized. (In fact, truly knowledgeable people tend toward overspecialization, whatever their field, precisely because there is always so much more to know.)

The information-based organization requires far more specialists overall than the command-and-control companies we are accustomed to. Moreover, the specialists are found in operations, not at corporate headquarters. Indeed, the operating organization tends to become an organization of specialists of all kinds.

Information-based organizations need central operating work such as legal counsel, public relations, and labor relations as much as ever. But the need for service staff — that is, for people without operating responsibilities who only advise, counsel, or coordinate— shrinks drastically. In its *central* management, the information-based organization needs few, if any, specialists.

Because of its flatter structure, the large, information-based organization will more closely resemble the businesses of a century ago than today's big companies. Back then, however, all the knowledge such as it was, lay with the very top people. The rest were helpers or hands, who mostly did the same work and did as they were told. In the information-based organization, the knowledge will be primarily at the bottom, in the minds of the specialists who do different work and direct themselves. So today's typical organization in which knowledge tends to be concentrated in service staff, perched rather insecurely between top management and the operating people, will likely be labeled a phase, an attempt to infuse knowledge from the top rather than obtain information from below.

Finally, a good deal of work will be done differently in the information-based organization. Traditional departments will serve as guardians of standards, as centers for training and the assignment of specialists; they won't be where the work gets done. That will happen largely in task-focused teams.

This change is already under way in what used to be the most clearly defined of all departments — research. In pharmaceuticals, in telecommunications, in papermaking, the traditional sequence of research, development, manufacturing and marketing is being replaced by *synchrony:* Specialists from all these functions work together as a team, from the inception of research to a product's establishment in the market.

How task forces will develop to tackle other business opportunities and problems remains to be seen. I suspect, however, that the need for a task force, its assignment, its composition and its leadership will have to be decided on case by case. So the organization that will be developed will go beyond matrix and may indeed be quite different from it. One thing is clear, though: It will require greater self-discipline and even greater emphasis on individual responsibility for relationships and for communications.

To say that information technology is transforming business enterprises is simple. What this transformation will require of companies and top managements is much harder to decipher. That is why I find it helpful to look for clues in other kinds of information-based organizations, such as the hospital, the symphony orchestra and the British administration in India.

A fair-sized hospital of about 400

beds will have a staff of several hundred physicians and 1,200 to 1,500 paramedics divided among some 60 medical and paramedical specialties. Each specialty has its own knowledge, its own training, its own language. In each specialty, especially the paramedical ones like the clinical lab and physical therapy, there is a head person who is a working specialist rather than a full-time manager. The head of each specialty reports directly to the top, and there is little middle management. A good deal of the work is done in ad hoc teams as required by an individual patient's diagnosis and condition.

A large symphony orchestra is even more instructive, since for some works there may be a few hundred musicians on stage playing together. According to organization theory then, there should be several group vice president conductors and perhaps a half-dozen division VP conductors. But that's not how it works. There is only the conductor — CEO — and every one of the musicians plays directly to that person without an intermediary. And each is a high-grade specialist, indeed an artist.

But the best example of a large and successful information-based organization, and one without any middle management at all, is the British civil administration in India.[7]

---

7. The standard account is Philip Woodruff, *The Men Who Ruled India,* especially the first volume, *The Founders of Modern India,* (New York: St. Martin's, 1954). How the system worked day by day is charmingly told in *Sowing,* (New York: Harcourt Brace Jovanovich, 1962), volume one of the autobiography of Leonard Woolf (Virginia Woolf's husband). — Peter Drucker.

The British ran the Indian subcontinent for 200 years, from the middle of the eighteenth century through World War II, without making any fundamental changes in organization structure or administrative policy. The Indian civil service never had more than 1,000 members to administer the vast densely populated subcontinent — a tiny fraction (at most 1 percent) of the legions of Confucian mandarins and palace eunuchs employed next door to administer a not-much-more populous China. Most of the Britishers were quite young; a 30-year-old was a survivor, especially in the early years. Most lived alone in isolated outposts with the nearest countryman a day or two of travel away, and for the first hundred years there was no telegraph or railroad.

The organization structure was totally flat. Each district officer reported directly to the "Coo," the provincial political secretary. And since there were nine provinces, each political secretary had at least 100 people reporting directly to him, many times what the doctrine of the span of control would allow. Nevertheless, the system worked remarkably well, in large part because it was designed to ensure that each of its members had the information he needed to do his job.

Each month the district officer spent a whole day writing a full report to the political secretary in the provincial capital. He discussed each of his principal tasks — there were only four, each clearly delineated. He put down in detail what he had expected would happen with respect to each of them, what actually did happen, and why, if there was a discrepancy, the two differed. Then he wrote down what he expected would happen in the ensuing month with respect to each key task and what he was going to do about it, asked questions about policy, and commented on long-term opportunities, threats and needs. In turn, the political secretary "minuted" every one of those reports — that is, he wrote back a full comment.

On the basis of these examples, what can we say about the requirements of the information-based organization? And what are its management problems likely to be? Let's look first at the requirements. Several hundred musicians and their CEO, the conductor, can play together because they all have the same score. It tells both flutist and timpanist what to play and when. And it tells the conductor what to expect from each and when. Similarly, all the specialists in the hospital share a common mission: the care and cure of the sick. The diagnosis is their "score"; it dictates specific action for the X- ray lab, the dietician, the physical therapist and the rest of the medical team.

Information-based organizations, in other words, require clear, simple, common objectives that translate into particular actions. At the same time, however, as these examples indicate, information-based organizations also need concentration on one objective or, at most, on a few.

Because the "players" in an information-based organization are specialists, they cannot be told how to do their work. There are probably few orchestra conductors who could coax even one note out of a French horn, let alone show the horn player how to do it. But the conductor can focus the horn player's skill and knowledge on the musicians' joint performance. And this focus is what the leaders of an information-based business must be able to achieve.

Yet a business has no "score" to play by except the score it writes as it plays. And whereas neither a first-rate performance of a symphony nor a miserable one will change what the composer wrote, the performance of a business continually creates new and different scores against which its performance is assessed. So an information-based business must be structured around goals that clearly state management's performance expectations for the enterprise and for each part and specialist and around organized feedback that compares results with these performance expectations so that every member can exercise self-control.

The other requirement of an information-based organization is that everyone take information responsibility. The bassoonist in the orchestra does so every time she plays a note. Doctors and paramedics work with an elaborate system of reports and an information center, the nurse's station on the patient's floor. The district officer in India acted on this responsibility every time he filed a report.

The key to such a system is that everyone asks: Who in this organization depends on me for what information? And on whom, in turn, do I depend? Each person's list will always include superiors and subordinates. But the most important names on it will be those of colleagues, people with whom one's primary relationship is coordination. The relationship of the internist, the surgeon and the anesthesiologist is one example. But the relationship of a biochemist, a pharmacologist, the medical director in charge of clinical testing and a marketing specialist in a pharmaceutical company is no different. It, too, requires each party to take the fullest information responsibility.

Information responsibility to others is increasingly understood, especially in middle-sized companies. But information responsibility to oneself is still largely neglected. That is, everyone in an organization should constantly be thinking through what information he or she needs to do the job and to make a contribution.

This may well be the most radical break with the way even the most highly computerized businesses are still being run today. There, people either assume the more data, the more information — which was a perfectly valid assumption yesterday when data were scarce, but leads to data overload and information blackout now that they are plentiful. Or they believe that information specialists know what data executives and professionals need in order to have information. But information specialists are tool makers. They can tell us what tool to use to hammer upholstery nails into a chair. We need to decide whether we should be upholstering a chair at all.

Executives and professional specialists need to think through what information is for them, what data they need: first, to know what they are doing; then, to be able to decide what they should be doing; and finally, to appraise how well they are doing. Until this happens MIS departments are likely to remain cost centers rather than become the result centers they could be.

Most large businesses have little in common with the examples we have been looking at. Yet to remain competitive — maybe even to survive — they will have to convert themselves into information-based organizations, and fairly quickly. They will have to change old habits and acquire new ones. And the more successful the company has been, the more difficult and painful this process is apt to be. It will threaten the jobs, status and opportunities of a good many people in the organization, especially the long-serving middle-aged people in middle management who tend to be the least mobile and to feel most secure in their work, their positions, their relationships and their behavior.

The information-based organization will also pose its own special management problems. I see as particularly critical:

1. Developing rewards, recognition and career opportunities for specialists.

2. Creating a unified vision in an organization of specialists.

3. Devising the management structure for an organization of task forces.

4. Ensuring the supply, preparation and testing of top management people.

Bassoonists presumably neither want nor expect to be anything but bassoonists. Their career opportunities consist of moving from second bassoon to first bassoon and perhaps of moving from a second-rank orchestra to a better, more prestigious one. Similarly, many medical technologists neither expect nor want to be anything but medical technologists. Their career opportunities consist of a fairly good chance of moving up to senior technician, and a very slim chance of becoming lab director. For those who make it to lab director, about 1 out of every 25 or 30 technicians, there is also the opportunity to move to a bigger, richer hospital. The district officer in India had practically no chance for professional growth except possibly to be relocated, after a three-year stint, to a bigger district.

Opportunities for specialists in an information-based organization should be more plentiful than they are in an orchestra or hospital, let alone in the Indian civil service. But as in these organizations, they will primarily be opportunities for advancement within the specialty, and for limited advancement at that. Advancement into "management" will be the exception, for the simple reason that there will be far fewer middle-management positions to move into. This contrasts sharply with the traditional organization where, except in the research lab, the main line of advancement in rank is out of the specialty and into general management.

More than 30 years ago General Electric tackled this problem by creating "parallel opportunities" for "individual professional contributors." Many companies have followed this example. But professional specialists themselves have largely rejected it as a solution. To them — and to their management colleagues — the only meaningful opportunities are promotions into management. And the prevailing compensation structure in practically all businesses reinforces this attitude because it is heavily biased towards managerial positions and titles.

There are no easy answers to this problem. Some help may come from looking at large law and consulting firms, where even the most senior partners tend to be specialists, and associates who will not make partner are outplaced fairly early on. But whatever scheme is eventually developed will work only if the values and compensation structure of business are drastically changed.

The second challenge that management faces is giving its organization of specialists a common vision, a view of the whole.

In the Indian civil service, the district officer was expected to see the "whole" of his district. But to enable him to concentrate on it, the government services that arose one after the other in the nineteenth century (forestry, irrigation, the archaeological survey, public health and sanitation, roads) were organized outside the administrative structure, and had virtually no contact with the district officer. This meant that the district officer became increasingly isolated from the activities that often had the greatest impact on — and the greatest importance for — his district. In the end, only the provincial government or the central government in Delhi had a view of the "whole," and it was an increasingly abstract one at that.

A business simply cannot function this way. It needs a view of the whole and a focus on the whole to be shared among a great many of its professional specialists, certainly among the senior ones. And yet it will have to accept, indeed will have to foster, the pride and professionalism of its specialists — if only because, in the absence of opportunities to move into middle management, their motivation must come from that pride and professionalism.

One way to foster professionalism, of course, is through assignments to task forces. And the information-based business will use more and more smaller self-governing units, assigning them tasks tidy enough for "a good man to get his arms around," as the old phrase has it. But to what extent should information-based businesses rotate performing specialists out of their specialties and into new ones? And to what extent will top management have to accept as its top priority making and maintaining a common vision across professional specialties?

Heavy reliance on task-force teams assuages one problem. But it aggravates another: the management structure of the information-based organization. Who will the business's managers be? Will they be task-force leaders? Or will there be a two-headed monster — a specialist structure, comparable, perhaps, to the way attending physicians function in a hospital, and an administrative structure of task-force leaders?

The decisions we face on the role and function of the task-force leaders are risky and controversial. Is theirs a permanent assignment, analogous to the job of the supervisory nurse in the hospital? Or is it a function of the task that changes as the task does? Is it an assignment or a position? Does it carry any rank at all? And if it does, will the task-force leader become in time what the product managers have been at Procter & Gamble: the basic units of management and the company's field officers? Might the task-force leaders eventually replace department heads and vice presidents?

Signs of every one of these developments exist, but there is neither a clear trend nor much understanding as to what each entails. Yet each would give rise to a different organizational structure from many we are familiar with.

Finally, the toughest problem will probably be to ensure the supply, preparation and testing of top management people. This is, of course, an old and central dilemma as well as a major reason for the general acceptance of decentralization in large businesses in the last 40 years. But the existing business organization has a great many middle-management positions that are supposed to prepare and test a person. As a result, there are usually a good many people to choose from when filling a senior management slot. With the number of middle-management positions sharply cut, where will the information-based organization's top executives come from? What will be their preparation? How will they have been tested?

Decentralization into autonomous units will surely be even more critical than it is now. Perhaps we will even copy the German *Gruppe* in which the decentralized units are set up as separate companies with their own top managements. The Germans use this model precisely because of their tradition of promoting people in their specialties, especially in research and engineering; if they did not have available commands in near-independent subsidiaries to put people in, they would have little opportunity to train and test their most promising professionals. These subsidiaries are thus somewhat like the farm teams of a major-league baseball club.

We may also find that more and more top management jobs in big companies are filled by hiring people away from smaller companies. This is the way that major orchestras get their conductors — a young conductor earns his or her spurs in a small orchestra or opera house, only to be hired away by a larger one. And the heads of a good many large hospitals have had similar careers.

Can business follow the example of the orchestra and hospital where top management has become a separate career? Conductors and hospital administrators come out of courses in conducting or schools of hospital administration respectively. We see something of this sort in France, where large companies are often run by men who have spent their entire previous careers in government service. But in most countries this would be unacceptable to the organization (only France has the *mystique* of the *grandes ecoles)*. And even in France, businesses, especially large ones, are becoming too demanding to be run by people without firsthand experience and a proven success record.

Thus the entire top management process — preparation, testing, succession — will become even more problematic than it already is. There will be a growing need for experienced business people to go back to school. And business schools will surely need to work out what successful professional specialists must know to prepare themselves for high-level positions as *business* executives and *business* leaders.

Since modern business enterprise first arose, after the Civil War in the United States and the Franco-Prussian War in Europe, there have been two major evolutions in the concept and structure of organizations. The first took place in the ten years between 1895 and 1905. It distinguished management from ownership and established management as work and task in its own right. This happened first in Germany, when Georg Siemens, the founder and head of Germany's premier bank, *Deutsche Bank,* saved the electrical apparatus company his cousin Werner had founded after Werner's sons and heirs had mismanaged it into near collapse. By threatening to cut off the bank's loans, he forced his cousins to turn the company's management over to professionals. A little later, J. P. Morgan, Andrew Carnegie and John D. Rockefeller, Sr. followed suit in their massive restructurings of U. S. railroads and industries.

The second evolutionary change took place 20 years later. The development of what we still see as the modern corporation began with Pierre S. du Pont's restructuring of his family company in the early twenties and continued with Alfred P. Sloan's redesign of General Motors a few years later. This introduced the command-and-control organization of today, with its emphasis on decentralization, central service staff, personnel management, the whole apparatus of budgets and controls and the important distinction between policy and operations. This stage culminated in the massive reorganization of General Electric in the early 1950s, an action that perfected the model most big businesses around the world (including Japanese organizations) still follow.[8]

Now we are entering a third period of change: the shift from the command-and-control organization, the organization of departments and divisions, to the information-based organization, the organization of knowledge specialists. We can perceive, though perhaps only dimly, what this organization will look like. We can identify some of its main characteristics and requirements. We can point to central problems of values, structure and behavior. But the job of actually building the information-based organization is still ahead of us — it is the managerial challenge of the future.

---

8. Alfred D. Chandler, Jr. has masterfully chronicled the process in his two books *Strategy and Structure,* (Cambridge: MIT Press, 1962) and *The Visible Hand,* (Cambridge: Harvard University Press, 1977) — surely the best studies of the administrative history of any major institution. The process itself and its results were presented and analyzed in two of my books: *The Concept of the Corporation,* (New York: John Day, 1946) and *The Practice of Management,* (New York: Harper Brothers, 1954) -- Peter Drucker.

Lights

Management information systems are created to generate, store, retrieve, compute and disseminate information to management. We will continue to be exposed to various kinds of technological advances that permit us to accomplish these ends more effectively. While no one can anticipate all the challenges and opportunities that lie ahead, Apple Computer is one company that has prided itself on its ability to be on the leading edge.

We will now see a video produced by Apple called, "The Knowledge Navigator." It is a view of the future and not a view of products under development. Thus, your attention should be focussed less on the wizardry of the technology than on the implications of the technology for your future world of work, and, for that matter, your home life.

Camera

The video shows a slice of life of a hard-working Professor Bradford, who is not like any professor you've seen before. He receives, retrieves and utilizes information quite differently. Take a look at a day in the life of this Professor Bradford, sometime in the not-too-distant future, perhaps. As you are watching, observe the following:

1. What's different about this professor's daily regimen?

2. How do you think his life is better and easier? More difficult?

3. Does anything about this new world of information access and knowledge bother you? Are you worried about "Big Brother" watching your problems?

4. How would your life as a student change if you had a professor like Bradford? How would your life change if you had the same kind of technology he has? How would education be different then?

Action

Discuss your observations and link these to management issues for the twenty-first century manager.

MAKING CONNECTIONS: IN-CLASS INTERACTIONS

Computer-aided meetings are now emerging that utilize an electronic medium for collecting and exchanging information. This represents an entirely new way of conducting meetings and communicating ideas and information. Read the short description of such meetings in the following article, "At These Shouting Matches, No One Says a Word," and discuss the article with your classmates.

1. What would an electronic meeting be like?

2. What are the advantages and benefits of such an approach?

3. What are the shortcomings and how could they be overcome, if at all?

4. When would you want to use the electronic format?

5. If time permits, try to simulate what such a meeting would be like and be prepared to show the class. Address the question, "Will new technologies such as portable phones, fax machines and computers improve or diminish our quality of life?"

Reading 10.2

AT THESE SHOUTING MATCHES, NO ONE SAYS A WORD[9]

by Jim Bartimo

There's a bloody meeting going on. "This company has no leader — and no vision," says one frustrated participant. "Why are you being so defensive?" asks another. Someone snaps: "I've had enough — I'm looking for another job." Rough stuff — if these people were talking face-to-face. But they're not. They're sitting side-by-side in silence in front of personal computers, typing anonymous messages that flash on a projection screen at the head of the room.

Electronic encounter groups like this could soon be the meeting place of Corporate America if some key high-tech companies and researchers have their way. Most enticing is what happens during so-called electronic meetings: People become brutally honest. The anonymity of talking through computers "turns even shy people powerful," says Alethea O. Caldwell, president of Ancilla Systems Inc., an Elk Grove, IL, health care company that used an electronic meeting to hammer out its five-year plan.

Timesaver

The delivery may be bruising, but the honest answers offer valuable, unfiltered information. Samuel L. Eichenfield, president of Greyhound Financial, a division of Greyhound Dial Corp., asked 20 staffers at a recent electronic meeting to rate their bosses. The results? "One manager enrolled in a management-improvement session, and another took a strategic-planning course," says Eichenfield.

Outwardly, electronic meetings are simple: Up to 50 people sit around a horseshoe-shaped table, empty except for a series of PCs. A complex local-area network tracks and sorts by topic and order of response every sentence typed in by participants. It then displays them on the projection screen. When attendees want to vote on an issue, the computers tally the results and display them. At the end of the meeting, everybody gets a printed synopsis.

IBM is one of the biggest boosters of electronic meetings. In 1986, it gave the University of Arizona $2 million to perfect the concept and since then has built 18 electronic-meeting rooms at IBM sites and plans 22 more. Eighty employees at IBM's Federal Sector Div. are pitching the concept to such customers as Proctor & Gamble Co. and General Motors Corp. and to other IBM units. So far, 7,000 IBMers, including Chairman John F. Akers, have taken part. These sessions, says IBM project manager Christopher J. McGoff, have "brought people together" who have traditionally skirmished, such as employees from product development and marketing.

Even managers who wince when electronic meetings make peers out of subordinates give the format high marks for efficiency. Chitchat is eliminated, and discussions don't digress. A study by IBM and the University of Arizona claims that electronic meetings are as much as 55 percent faster than traditional ones. Phelps Dodge Mining Co. in Phoenix has proof. Last year, it held its planning meeting electronically. Usually, says Robert E. Johnson, Phelps Dodge's director of research

and business development, this session takes days. This time, it lasted 12 hours. A big plus: "A lot of people were able to talk at once" without stepping on toes, he says.

IBM won't have the electronic-meeting market to itself for long. Andersen Consulting is building two electronic-meeting rooms that will accommodate long-distance sessions as well. And the University of Arizona has spawned a startup, Ventana Corp. Ventana plans to run electronic meetings for customers and sell a software package for those who want to lead their own sessions.

'It's Sad'

Electronic meetings attract diverse groups: Last year, Arizona's Democratic state legislators and Southwest Gas Corp. were among dozens of companies using them. But they do have some key drawbacks. While anonymity prevents bloody noses, it makes it impossible for people to get credit for a good idea, says Ventana CEO J. F. Nunamaker. Also, computer-shy participants may have trouble keeping up with those who can pound out messages rapidly. And even though a crude computer shorthand can mimic human touches such as some facial expressions, many participants find the process unnatural.

Critics say these problems prove there's no substitute for oral communication. Notes one participant in a recent electronic meeting: "It's sad that we can't talk without sitting at terminals." Maybe. But similar sentiments have been heard before. In the 1890s, people said the bane of human communications would be a new invention, the telephone.

---

9. *Business Week*, (June 11, 1990), p. 78.

MIRROR TALK: FOCUSSING ON ME

We are a society that is bombarded with data and information — through TV, radio, newspaper, mail, telephone, magazines, books, even computer services. As a manager, one of your tasks will be to decide what information you really need to function effectively, what information is available and what information you don't want. You can do a dry run of this exercise by examining your personal life in the same way.

1. What information do you now receive that you didn't five years ago?

2. Which information do you now receive more quickly than you did five years ago?

3. What information do you now have available that you don't need?

4. Do you generally feel yourself to be overloaded with information or undersupplied?

5. What other information would you want to have, or receive more quickly, to help you make personal decisions?

Many experts have argued that organizations and management will be revolutionized as information becomes more widely available and shared in a company. To the extent that information is a highly valued and scarce resource, it is a source of power and control. To the extent that it is diffused widely, power and authority will similarly be diffused. Thus, the implication is that as organizations involve more and more people in information gathering and utilization, the authority structure of an organization will change.

Middle managers in particular may be threatened by this. Indeed, some have projected that the middle manager role may become extinct, as you saw in the Drucker article. In his new book, *Powershift: Knowledge, Wealth and Violence at the Edge of the 21st Century,* Alvin Toffler, the futurologist, looks at business in the twenty-first century. He argues that there will be profound effects on the old hierarchical pyramid of companies:

> In the traditional pyramidal corporation...knowledge in the company is compartmentalized, and each of these compartments essentially operates as a small information monopoly. Information has to flow across departmental lines to a greater extent than ever before. It is no longer feasible to move information up and down the vertical channels. There's no time. Monopolies are breaking up...bypassing middle managers...The middle manager becomes obsolete to the extent that his other job was purely mechanical. To the degree that they brought some creativity to the job, or added value to the information, the job will remain vital.[10]

Many of you who aspire to become middle managers will be affected if this position is as radically affected as Toffler implies. Do you buy his argument? Do you need to rethink your own career paths? As information becomes so much more widely shared, how will managing in an organization at all levels be affected? How will you and the companies you will work for adapt to all the prospective changes? These are some of the crucial questions being posed now as we approach the twenty-first century.

10. Interview with Alvin Toffler, *Boston Globe,* (Nov. 11, 1990).

COMING TO OUR SENSES: MAKING A DIFFERENCE

You have been exposed here to a changing world of information: new access, new channels, new forms. Managing will require some very different skills in the future.

1. What skills will I need to be an effective manager of information?

2. What do I need to work on to prepare myself better for the technological challenges ahead?

3. How did I feel about all these "advancements" and changes? What am I excited about? What am I fearful about?

Chapter 11

Operations and Control

Every moment, lots and lots of things are happening down there. Practically everything I'm seeing is a variable. The complexity in this plant — in *any* manufacturing plant — is mind-boggling if you contemplate it. Situations on the floor are always changing. How can I possibly control what goes on? How the hell am I supposed to know if any action in the plant is productive or non-productive toward making money?[1]

If you have ever eaten or worked in a McDonald's restaurant, you have witnessed a company's "shop floor" operation. Staff members in the kitchen carry out their various tasks — one person lowering batches of french fries into the cooking oil, another putting burgers on the hot plates while someone else is packaging burgers. As a customer you see all these activities come together at the front desk as you pay for your hamburger and fries and pop.

1. Eliyahu M. Goldraft and Jeff Cox, *The Goal* (Croton-on-Hudson, New York: North Rivers Press, Inc., 1986), p. 43.

McDonald's is renowned for the simplified and standardized systems it has developed to control the production process from start to finish. Another, perhaps less enjoyable, system of operation is the one you go through when you register for classes each term, or the one you experience when you buy books at the start of the term. Registrar's offices and campus bookstores also involve systems of operation and control. Operations in organizations are managed by applying special tools and techniques to what is done in the organization so that the materials being worked on can be transformed into goods and services.

In McDonald's, the operations transform meat and potatoes into burgers and fries. In a university, operations transform professor's expertise and expectations, departmental rules and requirements and administration's plans into calendars, schedules, registration forms and so forth, which aid in the creation of each student's program of study. (On a larger scales, the operations of a university are designed to transform students from enthusiastic, reasonably knowledgeable individuals — a high school diploma does give you a start in the knowledge game— into well educated college graduates, ready, if they choose, for employment in the "real world")

For both manufacturing and service institutions, organizing is a complex and sometimes frustrating process. It requires understanding tools and people and the way they interact. An important and closely linked function to operations is that of control. Webster's dictionary defines the verb "control" as, "To have under command; to regulate; to check; to restrain; to direct."[2] Control often involves mechanistic approaches that have positive and negative impacts on the people in the system being controlled. The purpose of a control process is to signal whether a goal has been reached; it is a mechanism for providing feedback on performance of the tasks of an organization. We will explore these concepts in this chapter.

2. *Webster's Dictionary* (Larchmont, NY: Book Essentials Publications, 1981) p. 86.

Operations and operations management occur in all organizations. In manufacturing organizations, like General Motors Company, Coca Cola, or Panasonic, the primary products are physical goods. In service organizations, the product is a service, such as education, legal advice or entertainment. As author Richard Daft points out:

> Services differ from manufactured products in two ways. First the service customer is involved in the actual production process. The patient actually visits the doctor to receive the service…. The same is true for hospitals, restaurants and banks. Second, manufactured goods can be placed in inventory while service outputs, being intangible, cannot be stored. Manufactured products such as clothes, food, cars and VCRs can all be put in warehouses and sold at a later date. However, a beautician cannot wash, cut and set hair in advance and leave it on the shelf for the customer's arrival…. The service must be created and provided for the customer exactly when he or she wants it.[3]

Whether the organization produces goods or services, it must deal with several operational problems. The manager must first figure out where and how to obtain materials and supplies — for example meat, potatoes, tomatoes and cartons in the case of McDonald's, or students, instructors, texts and financial support in the case of universities. Second, the manager needs to schedule the operations of the firm. McDonald's does this very efficiently; university officials spend many hours working out class timetables, exam schedules, room allocations and other logistic details. Thirdly, managers in both manufacturing and service organizations are constantly struggling to make their operations more productive and to ensure that their goods or services are of high quality.

Manufacturing and service organizations share many operational problems. The tools for resolving these problems can be applied in both settings. Many organizations use computers to schedule work and to monitor productivity and quality.

To illustrate some issues and challenges of operations and control systems we will describe the experience of Randy and Debbie Fields, owners of Mrs. Fields Cookies, a company that in the late 1980s was projected to comprise close to 500 company-owned stores in 37 states and that annually sold more than $80 million in cookies.

The Fields chose not to franchise their organization. They run the empire with a head-office staff of only 115 people — approximately one corporate person per five stores, a lean operation by any standards. A computer is at the core of the operations and control systems. The telephone and the computer make Debbie in Park City, Utah, and her store managers, such as Richard Lui who runs Pier 39 Mrs. Fields in San Francisco, as close as if they were next door to each other. Here is a sample of operations and control systems in action:

> On a typical morning at Pier 39, Lui unlocks the store, calls up the Day Planner program on his Tandy Computer, plugs in today's sales projection (based on year-earlier sales adjusted for growth) and answers a couple of questions the program puts to him. What day of the week is it? What type of day: normal day, sale day, school day, holiday, other?

3. Richard L. Daft, *Management* (New York: The Dryden Press, 1988) pp. 627-28.

Say, for instance, it's Tuesday, a school day. The computer goes back to the Pier 39 store's hour-by-hour, product-by-product performance on the last three school-day Tuesdays. Based on what you did then, the Day Planner tells him, here's what you'll have to do today, hour by hour, product by product, to meet your sales projection. It tells him how many customers he'll need each hour and how much he'll have to sell them. It tells him how many batches of cookie dough he'll have to have and when to mix them to meet the demand and to minimize leftovers. He could make these estimates himself if he wanted to take the time. The computer makes them for him.

Each hour, as the day progresses, Lui keeps the computer informed of his progress. Currently he enters the numbers manually, but new cash registers that automatically feed hourly data to the computer, eliminating the manual update, are already in some stores. The computer in turn revises the hourly projections and makes suggestions. The customer count is OK, it might observe, but your average check is down. Are your crew members doing enough suggestive selling? If, on the other hand, the computer indicates that the customer count is down, that may suggest the manager will want to do some sampling — chum for customers up and down the pier with a tray of free cookie pieces or try something else, whatever he likes, to lure people into the store. Sometimes, if sales are just slightly down, the machine's revised projections will actually exceed the original on the assumption that greater selling effort will more than compensate for the small deficit. On the other hand, the program isn't blind to reality. It recognizes a bad day and diminishes its hourly sales projections and baking estimates accordingly.

Hourly sales goals?

Well, when Debbie was running *her* store, *she* set hourly sales goals. Her managers should, too, she thinks. Rather than enforce the practice through data, Randy has embedded the notion in the software that each store manager relies on. Do managers find the machine's suggestions intrusive? Not Lui. "It's a tool for me," he says.[4]

Lui noted several things the computer does for him:[5]

1. It helps him schedule his crew, in a fraction of the time it would take to do this manually.

2. It helps him to interview crew applicants. A selection test on the computer helps him screen individuals looking for a job.

3. It assists him with personnel administration by generating personnel folders and payroll entries.

4. It is an aid in maintenance. If a mixer isn't working, he punches in a repair program on the computer that asks him questions and guides his problem search.

The computer keeps Randy & Debbie in close contact with their managers. It also removes much of the paperwork so managers can focus on their stores and customers instead of on filling out forms for the head office. The system of operations created and implemented by Randy and Debbie adds up to control over their rapidly growing chain of stores and provides information that can lead to better decision making.

4. Tom Richman, ``Mrs. Field's Secret Ingredient," *Inc. Magazine* (October, 1987), pp. 68. Reprinted with permission, *Inc.* magazine. Copyright © 1987 by Goldhirsch Group, Inc., 38 Commercial Wharf, Boston MA 02110.

5. Ibid.

Several factors covered in your management texts are touched on in this case. Randy and Debbie recognized the importance of an operations strategy in their drive for growth and success. Part of that strategy involved a decision not to franchise. The other was to place the computer at the core of their strategies. (You will likely read about computer-aided design, CAD, and computer-aided manufacturing, CAM, in your text.) Facilities layout is an important decision in operations management. Common layers are based on process (similar machines grouped together as they do the same task), product (machines and tasks are set up so that there is a linear progression from beginning of the operation to the completion of the product), and fixed-position (the product stays in one position and tasks and equipment are brought to the product). The operations layouts for the cookie company can be identified by viewing the layout of the company as a whole — a process layout — or that used within each store — probably a product layout.

Other parts of a company's operations system include inventory management — how and where cookies are kept before the sales are made — and inventory control. Inventory control is commonly accomplished through materials requirement planning (MRP) — a system that schedules the exact amount of all materials required to support the desired end product. Given the precision of controls in Mrs. Fields Cookies, it is probable that this system or one like it (such as the Just-in-time inventory systems that ensure that suppliers deliver materials close in time to when they are needed) is a central feature of the company's operations.

We'll close this textbook tie-in with a comment from Randy Fields on operations and control. It is important, Randy says, to have a consistent vision of what you want to accomplish with technology. What functions do you want to control? What do you want your organizational chart to look like? "We image what it is we want," says Randy "We aren't constrained by the limits of what technology can do. We just say, 'What does your day look like? What would you *like* it to look like?'"[6] It is crucial then that managers think about what a particular operations and control system can do for their organization rather than implementing a system because it has been suggested to them or because it is what other companies use.

6. Richman, op. cit., p. 72.

Name _____

ID# _____

Section _____

It is important to have a plan of operation, to have some system that allows us to operate effectively, whatever the activity is. This is particularly true when the activity involves numerous people and many steps between the start and the completion of the activity. Choose an activity that you are familiar with that involves several steps and requires the inputs of several people. It can be a sport, an activity such as a dance group or a theater project, even a group project for a class. Once you have decided on the activity answer the following questions.

Brief description of activity (2-3 sentences):

How are resources acquired for the activity?

What are the main operations systems for completing the activity?

In what ways is the system controlled so that those who manage and those who are in the system know how they are doing?

What measures of productivity and quality are used in this system?

In what ways could the system of operation and control be improved? (Assume you can implement whatever ideas you come up with. Draw from what you are learning about systems in this segment of your course.)

MIRROR TALK: FOCUSSING ON ME

Operations and control is a somewhat abstract topic. The issues may seem to be of concern only to managers of large, complex manufacturing operations. What has this topic got to do with me, we might ask. Let's see how the idea of control might relate to our daily lives.[7]

Make a list of five to 10 areas in your life where you feel that you are in total control. Make a second list of five to 10 areas in which you feel somewhat in control. Finally, make a list of five to 10 areas where you feel you have no control.

Then respond to the following questions.

7. This exercise is adapted, with permission, from Robert E. Quinn, et al., *Becoming a Master Manager: A Competency Framework* (New York: John Wiley and Sons, Inc., 1990), p. 109.

1. How easy or difficult was it to identify areas in your life where you are in total control and somewhat in control? How do you know you are in control? What does control mean to you in these cases?

2. How easy or difficult was it for you to identify areas where you feel you have no control? What does control mean to you in these cases?

3. Why do you think it is important for individuals to feel in control?

4. Why do you think it is important for organizations to have controls?

5. What similarities and differences do you see in your answers to questions 3 and 4?

6 What steps might you take to increase your feeling of control in areas where you stated this was absent? Pick one or two areas to focus on.

Experts emphasize the importance of the production function in organizations and have criticized business schools for their lack of attention to this aspect of management and operation. We have focussed on operations and control as essential parts of the production function. Whether you ever work in a manufacturing plant or not, it is useful to understand the operations of such a plant. The exercise that follows allows you to do this.

A "balanced" plant is often described as one in which every resource is exactly equal in capacity to market demand. This might seem to imply that excess inventory would be a thing of the past and that shortages would disappear. However, are we making inappropriate assumptions when we think of a balanced plant in this way? The following exercise represents a model of a perfectly balanced manufacturing plant. Let's test our beliefs about balanced plants, inventory and shortages.[8]

1. Form a group of five people. You will need a bag of beans, a die, some bowls (or divide up your table into five boxes in a line) and the chart on the following page.

2. Each person is to sit behind one of the bowls. The idea is to move as many beans as possible from your bowl to the bowl on your right. The die will determine how many beans you can move at a time. You can move only as many beans as are in your bowl; if you roll a 5 and there are only two beans in your bowl, you can only move two beans.

This system is intended to "process" beans. It does this by moving a quantity of beans out of their bag at the beginning of the line and through each of the bowls in succession. The die determines how many beans can be moved from one bowl to the next. The die represents the capacity of each resource, each bowl. The set of bowls are dependent events, representing the stages of production. Each has the same capacity as the others, but its actual yield will fluctuate somewhat (from one to six depending on the role of the die). In effect, from the first bowl you can move to the next bowls in line any quantity of beans ranging from a minimum of one to a maximum of six.

"Throughput" will refer to the speed at which beans come out of the last bowl. Inventory consists of the total number of beans in all the bowls at any time. It is assumed that market demand is exactly equal to the average number of beans that the system can process. Since the maximum number of beans that can be moved at any time is six and the minimum is one, the average number moved is expected to be 3.5. Production capacity of each resource and market demand are perfectly in balance.

3. Each person, in turn, rolls the die and moves the beans accordingly. (Each person will have 10 turns.)

4. Record each of your rolls and the number of beans you could move on the chart provided.

5. Record "Inventory" for each turn. Your inventory will be the number of beans left in your bowl at the end of your turn.

6. For each point, graph your cumulative deviation from the expected average by circling the appropriate point on the chart provided.

Unless each of us can roll the same number every time, and, since the number of beans we move depends on both the roll and the number of beans that have been moved into our own bowl, we will not actually move the same number of beans each time. To account for the fluctuations and to determine how these fluctuations affect throughput, graph the deviations from the "systems average."

8. Adapted with permission from Eliyahu M. Goldratt and Jeff Cox, *The Goal: A Process of Ongoing Improvement* (Croton-on-Hudson, NY: North River Press, 1986), p. 103-111.

In a real plant, the deviations are cumulative. In this game they are, too. In theory, the average number of beans that can be moved are 3.5 (even though we can't actually move half a bean or half a 'part'). Any deviation from 3.5, therefore, represents a deviation from the average. For example, if you were able to move four beans, you will have deviated from the average by +.5 for that move. Let's say this was your first move. Since deviations are cumulative, you will be "ahead" +.5 when you begin your second move. Let's say that in your second move, you are only able to move two beans (deviation −1.5). Your cumulative deviation is then −1.0. You would graph the point −1 at the end of your second turn.

FIGURE 11.1

SYSTEM "OPERATIONS" CHART OF BEAN PROCESSING

Person:	First	Second	Third	Fourth	Fifth
Turn:	1234567890	1234567890	1234567890	1234567890	1234567890
Rolled:	_____	_____	_____	_____	_____
#Moved:	_____	_____	_____	_____	_____
Inventory:		_____	_____	_____	_____

Change +/-

	First	Second	Third	Fourth	Fifth
+2.5	....	....	....	....	....
+2	....	....	....	....	....
+1.5	....	....	....	....	....
+1	....	....	....	....	....
+0.5	....	....	....	....	....
0	....	....	....	....	....
−0.5	....	....	....	....	....
−1	....	....	....	....	....
−1.5	....	....	....	....	....
−2	....	....	....	....	....
−2.5	....	....	....	....	....
−3	....	....	....	....	....

7. Once each person has had 10 turns, discuss your observations. How did it feel to be at the beginning of the line? In the middle? At the end? How might these translate in an actual manufacturing plant?

Look at your chart. Since we assumed that any fluctuations would average out over time, we would expect that in 10 turns 35 beans should be at the end of the line, giving us our average throughput.

How many beans are at the end of your line? How do you account for the difference?

We often think of production and operations management as a matter of having the right nonhuman resources available and assembling them in the right order to produce quality products for sale. At times production and operations management seems to give more consideration to technical issues than to the people carrying out the tasks. In the film *Broadcast News,* news is the "product" and the technical issues take a back seat to the human element of production.[9]

Jane is a news producer and Aaron a news reporter. The two are highly educated, take their work very seriously and have a close and effective working relationship. They spend a lot of time talking about the ethics of news reporting; they believe news should be reported not staged, that news people must have the utmost integrity, that personal opinion should be distinguished from fact and that there is a difference between entertainment and news. Enter Tom, a former sports commentator who has been hired as the new news anchorman. Tom is attractive and very salable to the public but is uneducated, can't write and often doesn't know anything about the news he's reading. His lack of education and apparent lack of understanding is appalling to Jane and Aaron, and they are outraged that the station has hired a pretty face over others they consider more competent for the position.

Tom is anxious to learn the ropes and approaches both Jane and Aaron on different occasions to ask for their assistance; they are not very responsive to his initial requests. He is advised by another staff member to observe wherever he can and he begins by observing Jane's production of a news piece that has to air within 14 minutes. He is brusquely told to stay out of the way as Jane pushes everyone working with her to the limit in order to script a piece with the addition of another voice-over with only three minutes to go. Tension mounts as Aaron is called to record a reading from a Norman Rockwell book; the recording is rushed back to the production room to be spliced to the main piece and then the tape is rushed to the transmission center. Jane's desire for perfection increases the pressure of time constraints. Small things such as a dropped pencil, a slight hesitation in action and an open file cabinet drawer become crisis events in getting the piece to air on time. Without a second to spare, the clip does air on the heels of its announcement. Jane shifts from her production-centered behavior to warmly thank and congratulate everyone on a job well done. The "product" is well received.

The experience was exhilarating for Tom and his enthusiasm spills over into another request of Jane to help him; she informs him that it's not her job to teach remedial reporting and brushes him off. But unforeseen events quickly throw the two together. A news call comes in during a social gathering and the station president assigns responsibilities for immediate production of a special report: Jane as executive producer and Tom as anchor. The party disintegrates as everyone mobilizes to get the story. Jane is astounded that the president would assign Tom to the story when Aaron clearly has more background and experience. Believing it to be her responsibility to inform the president of the inadequacy of his choice, she seeks him out. The president does not agree and tells her she'd best be on her way.

9. The narrative for this segment was prepared by Fiona Crofton in discussion with Peter Frost. It is reprinted with permission from *Management Principles and Practices,* D. H. Holt, Prentice Hall, 1990.

Jane, with her desire for a high quality product, has now been handed the increased responsibility of an executive producer, and has to work with Tom whom she believes to be less than adequate for the job. Jane has to tie together reports from various locations and other resources and have them all filter through Tom as the public coordinator of the events; she can't rely on Tom for any interpretation or extension of the information received from various locales and must feed everything to him through his earpiece. Meanwhile, Aaron is at home drowning his feelings of rejection while listening to music, simultaneously singing and reading and watching the broadcast. Nonetheless, Aaron comes to Jane's aid as he phones in suggestions and information that Jane is able to use for the broadcast. Aaron is amazed at the results: "I say it here, it comes out there... What's next? Lip synching?"

In the end, the broadcast is a success and everyone is congratulatory. Tom is "juiced" from the experience and anxious to celebrate. Jane is somewhat confused by the experience of having been in Tom's head ("It was an unusual place to be"). Aaron sits on his front steps reflecting on his life and work. We are left wondering what will happen with the team members and how they will handle future production efforts.

Classroom Questions

1. What factors were involved in the production of the newscasts?

2. What controls were used to ensure success?

3. In what ways might these production and control factors be similar and be different from those in manufacturing plants?

The experiences of Randy and Debbie Fields provide one window onto the world of operations and control. The high-speed interactions of Jane, Aaron and Tom in *Broadcast News* provide another perspective on these systems and activities. Your own encounters with university registration systems and bookstores will have given you yet another picture of this aspect of organizations. As a way to tie some of this together, think about the interaction between humans and technology — something that is inevitable and important in each of our lives. The operation and control of an organization affect more than the organization's products, level of product quality and productivity, they also affect the experiences of people in the system of production.

As you understand and experience this system:

1. Where are the major stresses on humans when they are in the organizational trenches—that is where the day-to-day operations and controls are focussed?

2. What do you feel are the emotions (both positive and negative) people experience when they are in this system?

3. Given your answers to Question 2, outline three things you, as a future manager, need to keep in mind when you are implementing or designing an operations and control system.

What does the future hold for systems of operations and control? Certainly managers will try to refine these systems to minimize negative impacts on people and the environment. This is both socially responsible and good business practice. Damage to the environment creates major costs to society. Similarly, hurting people leads to social costs that will eventually cut into the profits of every firm. Human costs can include illness from stress on the job, loss of initiative of people who are over-controlled and loss of jobs as technology displaces individuals. Who pays these costs? Ultimately we all do.

The technological revolution will continue into the next century. If we use computers intelligently, as Randy and Debbie Fields appear to have done, we can make operations and control systems more efficient and humane, freeing people from mindless routines and allowing them to do more interesting and challenging work. (We will always have to deal with the displacement of workers when we do this, however. When Fields took over La Petite Boulangerie from Pepsi Co. in 1987 the size of the headquarters staff was reduced in four weeks from 53 people to three people.)

What will managers face in terms of technology and operational systems in the twenty-first century? It is always hazardous to predict the future, especially with today's rapid pace of change. Nevertheless, it is interesting to think what these changes might mean for operations and control in educational organizations, given that information and education have become the core resource of this age. Here is what Peter Drucker, whom some refer to as the grand old guru of management, has to say about this matter:

> Every major change in educational technology changes not only how we learn but also what we learn. Just as the printed book totally changed the curriculum of the schools, so are the computer and tape recorder and video. The printed book is primarily a tool for adults. The new tools are for children; they fit the way children learn best. We now know how to make the accumulated wisdom of the human race relevant again. We should know that the old approach to education is theoretical and unsound. We still believe that teaching and learning are two sides of the same coin, but we ought to realize that they are not: one learns a subject, and one teaches a person. The process is increasingly going to shift to self-teaching on the basis of new technology because we now have these self-teaching tools.[10]

If Drucker is correct, such changes will dramatically alter the look of education organizations and the way operations take place. If systems of operation and control can be successfully self-managed, will we need large classrooms? Will we need lecture halls and common finals? Will we need instructors?

10. Edward Reingold, "Facing the New and Dynamic," *Time*, Jan. 22, 1990), p. 42.

We are confident that in this era and in the next one, quality of product or service will remain important and its attainment will be a major goal of managers. The reading that follows, *Making it Right the First Time*, discusses this topic.

Reading 11.1

MAKING IT RIGHT THE FIRST TIME[11]

by Christopher Knowlton

In 1979, Tennant Co. received two pieces of life-threatening news. Word arrived at Minneapolis headquarters that a potentially fatal defect had appeared in the motorized factory floor sweepers that it was exporting to Japan. The sweepers were chronically dripping oil. The second piece of news was Toyota's announcement that it was bringing out a competing product. In an all-out effort to save its 40 percent North American market share, Tennant, the world's biggest manufacturer of floor maintenance equipment, embarked on an ambitious, by-the-book quality improvement program that over the next few years upgraded its sweepers and scrubbers from good to great. Today the company has 60 percent of the North American market and 40 percent of the world market; sales grew from $98 million in 1979 to $167 million last year.

President Roger Hale started the process of upgrading the company's goods by consulting the quality expert Philip Crosby. Arguing that the product had to be made right the first time, Crosby recommended that the company eliminate its rework area, where 18 of the most experienced mechanics fixed mistakes made during the assembly process.

The repercussions of Crosby's reform were enormous: Workers had to make fewer blunders and catch those they did make. In order to eliminate errors, management and workers, brainstorming in small groups, developed scores of new assembly procedures that changed the shape of assembly lines and rerouted the delivery of parts. Employees were taught statistical process control, a method of monitoring defects and setting goals to reduce them.

The group that looked into the oil leaks discovered that the company's engineers had ignored the latest hydraulics technology, and a number of the assembly workers had been improperly trained to put together the hose joints. Worse, 16 different suppliers were delivering fittings and hoses made to varying specifications. As a result, the parts didn't go together properly. Once the workers had been retrained and the number of suppliers reduced, leaks—which averaged two per machine in 1979 — occurred in fewer than one of every 18 machines by 1986. Says Roger Hale proudly: "The leadership on the quality program has come from the factory floor."

Tennant succeeded in protecting its leading marketing share and enhancing its reputation within the industry. Better yet, says Robert Maples, a security analyst with Piper Jaffray, "improved product quality is largely credited with forestalling Toyota's expansion into the U.S. market." Morale has soared. Murals of paddling loons, grouse and jumping bass adorn what were once bare factory walls. The floors shine, and the workers gladly show off their handiwork to visitors while chatting knowledgeably about quality control. Employees award each others teddy bears — known as Koala T. Bears — for taking the initiative in problem solving and achieving quality goals.

Every 18 months, to keep things in sharp focus, the company celebrates Zero Defect Day with a magic show and other live entertainment. At the end of the all-day fete, the workers renew their pledge to do their work correctly. "It sounds corny," says Maples, "but the corniness works."

11. Christopher Knowlton, *Fortune* (March 28, 1988), ©1988 The Time Inc. Magazine Company. All rights reserved.

Chapter 12

Human Resources Management

Ann's exceptional grades and test scores as an undergraduate premedical student had earned her acceptance at several of the nation's best medical schools including the highly respected program in her state. She had long dreamed of attending her state's medical school. But after interviewing with each of the schools, her plans changed dramatically.

At the state school, her interview consisted of a list of requirements that she would be expected to meet. She was informed of the specialties of the school's faculty and told how she might fit into their projects.

At another leading school thousands of miles away her interview had a completely different tone. The interviewers asked about her interests and were thrilled to hear of her undergraduate research on childhood AIDS. They told her that the school would work hard to support her interests in this emerging area of medicine, and mentioned several potential internships in which she could pursue her interests. Ann chose to attend medical school not at the long admired state university, but rather at the school thousands of miles away which she felt had values very close to her own.

* * *

After delaying their plans to raise a family becuase they wished to establish themselves professionally, Jane and Allen were disappointed to learn that they could not conceive children. While this caused considerable emotional turmoil to the couple they were eventually able to adopt a wonderful baby girl. Jane was amazed to learn that her company's "benefits" for adoptive parents allowed only four weeks away from work instead of the customary twelve weeks. "After all," the company stated, "you weren't actually pregnant." Jane knew that it was common practice in European companies to allow a full year for all new parents, male or female. Allen's company strongly supported flex-time work schedules, so that he could be home earlier to be with his daughter. The company also provided paid day-care at the at the corporate offices and generous leave policy when a baby joined the family, whether by birth or adoption, for both male and female employees. Allen's empoyers knew that valued employees are difficult to replace and that child-rearing patterns and expectations were changing as the twenty-first century approached. Allen was granted a six-month leave of absence to be at home with his daughter with the promise that he would be given his job back when he returned to work. On the other hand Jane felt guilty about having to leave her daughter after one month and resentful toward a company that made her choose between her career and family.

* * *

Phillip's performance appraisal was going well. Not that he was doing everything perfectly, but he felt that his manager was an advocate. She pointed out specific instances of excellent job-related performance and gave examples of work skills that could be improved. She asked him his response to these situations and his ideas about how he might make changes. The company had an excellent training and development program, and Phillip asked if he might attend the time management program to improve his daily organization. "Just what I had expected from you, Phillip. I'm giving you the highest rating on the eager-to-learn category. By working on a few of these problem areas, we should have you at the managerial level very soon. Let me know how I can help you along the way."

* * *

It is clear from the preceding episodes that the way people are treated by an organization can have a powerful impact on their productivity, creativity, loyalty and commitment to the job. Thus the recruiting strategy of the medical school chosen by Ann is likely to attract creative and assertive students. Companies that train and develop employees like Phil through effective performance appraisals will encourage employees to improve and will provide them with positive models to emulate when training their own subordinates. Organizations that anticipate demographic and social changes at work will provide more enlightened, flexible human resource practices. This will be essential for attracting a modern work force of two-career couples, many of whom have had children later in life and now seek to balance their commitment to family and career.

Lights

The movie *9 to 5*, a comedy about oppressed office workers dominated by a nasty, sexist boss, concludes with a video segment that depicts the latest in progressive human resource practices. After years of a sterile office environment, devoid of pictures, plants and humane policies, three female employees "kidnap" the boss, Mr. Hart, as part of an elaborate scheme and write memos in his absence that dramatically change office policies and working conditions. The three women have implemented several progressive HRM strategies that lead to an astounding 20 percent increase in office productivity, which has caught the attention of the chairman of the board. As the video segment begins, Mr. Hart has escaped from his kidnapping eager to revenge his captors, but just as he returns to work the company chairman arrives to commend him for his innovative management techniques. Since he knows nothing about these changes he must rely on his "captors" to explain to the chairman the nature of these innovative programs that led to the jump in productivity.

Camera

In this scene you will be introduced to several human resource management programs that are being used in some of the more progressive companies in the United States. Note each of the different programs on the list that follows by circling the number.

Action

Consider the following list of human resource practices. Choose three that would be at the top of your list to be included in the organization you might manage in the twenty-first century. You may list other practices not listed here if you wish.

1. Flexible work hours
2. Job sharing
3. Subsidized day-care
4. Profit sharing
5. Pleasant physical work environment
6. Job security — a no lay off policy
7. Excellent training and development programs
8. Health benefits — strong insurance coverage
9. Progressive leave policy — for having children or for subbatical
10. Employee fitness center, pool, tennis court
11. Team spirit, parties, recognition of accomplishments, other evidence the company cares
12. Travel and related perks
13. Employee assistance programs — alcohol and drug counseling

List the practices most important to you in the twenty-first century workplace.

1. _____ Why?

2. _____ Why?

3. _____ Why?

Human Resource Management (HRM) includes the sum of activities required to attract, develop and retain people with the knowledge and skills needed to achieve an organization's objectives.[1,2] Human resources professionals attract quality employees through effective recruiting and interviewing practices that select the right person for the job. Employee development is facilitated by a rich menu of training programs and well designed performance appraisals that help employees build skills. Human resource professionals retain quality employees by designing compensation packages that meet different employee needs. Organizational benefits that provide insurance, job flexibility, travel, professional growth, job security and a pleasant work environment can help retain quality employees. HRM activities are unique in that they are almost always shared with line managers.[3] For example, quality recruiting is one way to attract an effective work force. The HRM specialist is often the person who goes to college campuses to interview prospective applicants. It is the line manager who reviews this information and makes the final hiring decision. Similar sharing takes place when employees are developed through performance appraisal techniques. HRM professionals may develop performance appraisal forms and train managers to conduct a performance appraisal interview.[4] The line manager typically conducts the interview and gives feedback directly to the employee.

HRM professionals maintain an effective work force by developing a wage and salary structure that rewards activities related to high performance. They also develop benefit packages that are sensitive to changing employee lifestyles, the typical employee no longer being a married man with a dependent wife and two children who needs only life and health insurance.[5]

Indeed, fewer than 10 percent of American workers fit that description of the typical employee.[6] In response, HRM specialists have designed cafeteria-style benefit packages that allow employees to choose benefits most appropriate for their life situation.[7] Once again line managers share the human resources responsibilities with HRM professionals by contributing to decisions on how compensation and benefits will be awarded to employees.

HRM specialists also engage in human resource planning that helps organizatons prepare for future staffing needs. Many HRM specialists are interested in labor relations and the ways in which managers relate to labor unions. In industries where laborers have felt oppressed by management, labor unions have offered workers bargaining power on issues such as wages, benefits, working conditions and job security. HRM specialists may have a particular interest in union rules, grievance procedures and negotiations. These specialists can help companies stay competitive in the global economy of the twenty-first century. By improving labor -manage-ment collaboration, costs can be lowered while quality is increased.

HRM specialists are becoming increasingly involved in managing legal and ethical problems in the work place. Many laws passed over the last 30 years have at-tempted to protect the rights of employees regardless of race, religion, gender or age. Furthermore, affirmative action programs have tried to improve employment opportunities for women, minorities, the handicapped and other groups of employ-ees. Recently, HRM expertise has been required by firms to develop fair drug testing policies and to develop strategies to deal with the growing AIDS crisis in the work place.

1. D. H. Holt, *Management: Principles and Practices* (Englewood Cliffs, NJ: Prentice Hall, 1990), p. 384.

2. R. L. Daft, *Management* (Chicago: Dryden Press, 1988), p. 336.

3. Ibid.

4. Ibid.

5. "New Benefits for New Life Styles," *Business Week* (Feb. 11, 1980), pp. 111- 112.

6. J. H. Haslinger, "Flexible Compensation: Getting a Return on Benefit Dollars," *Personnel Administrator*. 224 (1985), pp. 39-46

7. Daft op. cit., p. 359.

Such work requires a strong commitment to work with people, from recruitment through retirement. HRM professionals must forecast human resource needs, appraise employee competencies, confront conflicts and grievances and interpret legislation. For many, the human resources side of management serves as a counterpoint to the financial side. The goal of human resource experts is to develop ways that a strong corporate commitment to the needs of employees pays off with a diverse, creative, motivated and productive work force.

Performance Appraisal

One of the most important and difficult tasks that managers and HRM specialists share is performance appraisal. Performance appraisal is the process "of observing and evaluating an employee's performance."[8] When handled properly, performance appraisals can improve morale, decrease absenteeism, decrease turnover and increase productivity.[9] On the other hand, inadequate performance appraisals can have the opposite effect, deflating morale and diminishing productivity.

Effective performance appraisals require a complex set of skills and attitudes that begin with a clear description of job responsibilities and performance standards. Then valid measurement tools are needed to accurately assess performance. Finally, communication skills and attitudes toward employees are critical. In the performance appraisal interview, employees must understand their evaluation, take pride in their strengths and feel motivated to improve behaviors needing further development. This requires that the employee trust that a manager is trying to coach rather than criticize, that the manager is an advocate rather than an adversary.

How does a manager come to be a supportive coach rather than a critical adversary? Part of the answer to this question may be based on the manager's own history with feedback. How did significant people in the manager's life provide feedback? In the following "Mirror Talk" exercise we will begin to explore your feedback history and examine how your history has shaped your present feedback patterns.

8. Daft op. cit., p. 350.
9. Lawrence Bonifant, "The 423 Minute Manager," *Personnel Administrator* (July, 1986), p. 25.

MIRROR TALK: FOCUSSING ON ME

The way we give and receive feedback is often learned from the key persons in our lives. It begins at a very early age as we get praised, reprimanded or ignored for our behaviors. Some people grow up receiving feedback frequently, while others rarely receive any. Moreover, some people have heard primarily criticisms, while others hear mostly praise. For some, feedback is usually delivered in a direct verbal fashion, while others have received feedback primarily through a smile, touch or a raised eyebrow.

If we are fortunate to have been taught the art of giving and receiving feedback well, we may be able to pass these skills on to others in our personal and professional lives. If effective feedback skills have not been modeled for us, we may fail to provide feedback that can motivate and improve others.

Instruction

In the following "Mirror Talk" exercise we would like you to examine your own feedback history. Specifically, what kind of feedback have you received from significant people in your life and how do you give feedback to others. Consider your father and mother, and a significant teacher, boss, or co-worker, friend and lover or spouse. In the event that any one of these individuals has not been a significant part of your feedback experience, substitute a similar individual. Concentrate on three feedback dimensions:

1. Frequency of feedback:

Very Frequently	Frequently	Moderate Amount	Infrequently	Very Infrequently

2. Type of feedback:

Almost All Negative	More Negative	About Equal	More Positive	Almost All Positive

3. Style of feedback:

Almost All Nonverbal	More Nonverbal	About Equal	More Verbal	Almost All Verbal

Feedback Past and Present

Receiving Feedback

Identify the following seven people who have played a significant role in your life (or those in a similar role if necessary). How frequently do you receive feedback from various significant people in your life? Does it tend to be positive (focusing on your strengths and successes) or negative (focussing on your weaknesses or failures)? Verbal or nonverbal? Complete the following by circling the appropriate indicator for each person.

Frequency:	Very Infrequently	Infrequently	Moderate Amount	Frequently	Very Frequently
Father	VI	I	M	F	VF
Mother	VI	I	M	F	VF
Teacher	VI	I	M	F	VF
Boss	VI	I	M	F	VF
Coworker/Employee	VI	I	M	F	VF
Friend	VI	I	M	F	VF
Lover/Spouse	VI	I	M	F	VF

Type:	Almost All Negative	More Negative	About Equal	More Positive	Almost All Positive
Father	NN	N	=	P	PP
Mother	NN	N	=	P	PP
Teacher	NN	N	=	P	PP
Boss	NN	N	=	P	PP
Coworker/Employee	NN	N	=	P	PP
Friend	NN	N	=	P	PP
Lover/Spouse	NN	N	=	P	PP

Style:	Almost All Nonverbal	More Nonverbal	About Equal	More Verbal	Almost All Verbal
Father	NV+	NV	=	V	V+
Mother	NV+	NV	=	V	V+
Teacher	NV+	NV	=	V	V+
Boss	NV+	NV	=	V	V+
Coworker/Employee	NV+	NV	=	V	V+
Friend	NV+	NV	=	V	V+
Lover/Spouse	NV+	NV	=	V	V+

Giving Feedback

How frequently do you give feedback to various significant people in your life? Does it tend to be positive (focussing on their strengths and successes), or negative (focussing on their weaknesses or failures)? Verbal or nonverbal? Complete the following by circling the appropriate indicator.

Frequency:	Very Infrequently	Infrequently	Moderate Amount	Frequently	Very Frequently
Father	VI	I	M	F	VF
Mother	VI	I	M	F	VF
Teacher	VI	I	M	F	VF
Boss	VI	I	M	F	VF
Coworker/Employee	VI	I	M	F	VF
Friend	VI	I	M	F	VF
Lover/Spouse	VI	I	M	F	VF

Type:	Almost All Negative	More Negative	About Equal	More Positive	Almost All Positive
Father	NN	N	=	P	PP
Mother	NN	N	=	P	PP
Teacher	NN	N	=	P	PP
Boss	NN	N	=	P	PP
Coworker/Employee	NN	N	=	P	PP
Friend	NN	N	=	P	PP
Lover/Spouse	NN	N	=	P	PP

Style:	Almost All Nonverbal	More Nonverbal	About Equal	More Verbal	Almost All Verbal
Father	NV+	NV	=	V	V+
Mother	NV+	NV	=	V	V+
Teacher	NV+	NV	=	V	V+
Boss	NV+	NV	=	V	V+
Coworker/Employee	NV+	NV	=	V	V+
Friend	NV+	NV	=	V	V+
Lover/Spouse	NV+	NV	=	V	V+

How would you judge your overall feedback giving style? Circle one for each factor:

FREQUENCY	Very Infrequently	Infrequently	Moderate	Frequently	Very Frequently
TYPE	Almost All Negative	More Negative	About Equal	More Positive	Almost All Positive
STYLE	Almost All Nonverbal	More Nonverbal	About Equal	More Verbal	Almost All Verbal

Self-assessment Questions

Review the responses you gave on the worksheets regarding giving and receiving feedback. Then complete the following:

1. I receive feedback most frequently from:

   I receive feedback least frequently from:

2. The person who gives me negative feedback most often is:

3. The person who gives me positive feedback most often is:

4. Overall, does the feedback you receive tend to be negative (focussing on weaknesses) or positive (focussing on strengths)?

   How much of the feedback that you receive is verbal and how much is nonverbal?

5. I give feedback most frequently to:

   I give feedback least frequently to:

6. I tend to give negative feedback most often to:

7. I tend to give positive feedback most often to:

Overall, the feedback I give tends to be _____ % positive _____ % negative

How much of the feedback you give is verbal and how much is nonverbal. How do you know? Check with friends and peers to see what they think about your nonverbal messages.

8. Which of the seven significant people that you rated does your style of giving feedback most resemble?

9. Do you give feedback differently to different people? How would you account for the differences?

10. Whose pattern of giving feedback to you (among the seven people) best fits your needs? Whose pattern does not fit your needs very well? In each case, have you given these individuals your feedback?

11. After assessing your feedback patterns, what is one behavior of yours that you would like to improve?

The answers to these questions begin to identify ways that people have taught you about feedback and how you are impacting others with the feedback you give. Even though we give and receive feedback every day, we rarely explore how it affects us and others whom we hope to affect.

When we are being evaluated, feelings of defensiveness or embarrassment can be easily aroused. Negative feedback is usually hard to absorb and there is a tendency to place blame elsewhere for the problem. Positive feedback also can be uncomfortable if delivered inappropriately. Effective managers must be able to give both positive and negative feedback in ways that will motivate employees to improve deficits and maintain strengths. In the "Ready for Class" exercise that follows we will examine what situations make it difficult or easy for you to deliver and receive feedback.

Name _____

ID# _____

Section _____

What makes feedback hard or easy to give and receive?[10]

What makes it hard or easy to give and receive feedback? Individuals differ in their responses to this question. For example, some say that it is easy to give feedback to people they know well, but difficult to deliver feedback to subordinates or colleagues at work. Others report that professional feedback is easy to give but that giving feedback to friends can become very touchy. Some individuals say that feedback is easy to receive if it is positive, while others find positive feedback embarrassing, especially when it is given in the presence of others.

Instructions

Think about situations where you have given or received feedback at work, school or in important interpersonal situations.

In the boxes below identify one factor that made it: (1) Easy for you to give feedback, (2) Hard for you to give feedback, (3) Easy for you to receive feedback, (4) Hard for you to receive feedback

10. Adapted from an exercise developed by Joseph Litterer, University of Massachusetts.

Be prepared to discuss your experiences with others in class.

1. What made it easy to give feedback?

2. What made it hard to give feedback?

3. What made it easy to receive feedback?

4. What made it hard to receive feedback?

Giving and Receiving Feedback

The purpose of this "In-Class Interaction" is to share individual reasons that make it easy or difficult for people to give and receive feedback. It is likely that the employees you will be managing will share many of these reasons. Awareness of individual differences around the ways people experience feedback will enhance your performance appraisal skills.

Instructions

1. Form groups of three.

2. Choose one of the four quadrants from the preceding "Ready for Class" exercise.

3. Share with the group your reasons why it was—for example—hard to give feedback. List each person's experience.

First person's experience:

Second person's experience:

Third person's experience:

4. As a group, choose the one individual response that you believe most important to share with the entire class. Circle that reason in Question 3 above.

5. Choose a spokesperson to share that reason with the large group.

Guidelines for Feedback Delivery

Now that we have explored your experiences and history with feedback, we can list some guidelines for feedback delivery.

1. Feedback should describe behavior, not evaluate it. "When you spoke to the customer you looked away from him" describes behavior and is easy to improve. In contrast, "Your eye contact with the customer was awful" can prompt an employee to be defensive.

2. Feedback must be specific. "I am pleased that four students who haven't previously participated have raised their hands to contribute to the discussion today" is specific. "I was very pleased with class today" is vague.

3. Useful feedback considers the needs of the receiver, rather than serving as a method for the manager to release frustrations. If the goal of feedback is to improve performance, employees should be asked to respond how they might improve an ineffective behavior, or a meeting can be arranged at a time when the employee is able to "hear" the feedback.

4. Feedback should occur in a timely fashion. In other words, feedback should be given as close as possible to the behavior, not months later at the annual review.

5. Feedback is most useful when it is asked for rather than imposed upon the employees. Effective managers encourage employees to ask for feedback, by rewarding such behavior and by creating an environment where asking for feedback frequently results in praise and improved performance.

6. Feedback should be largely positive. Research shows that positive feedback is more effective in improving performance than criticism. The balance of positive to negative feedback is important to monitor.

7. Feedback should be frequent. Employees should not be made to "walk on eggs." Most employees like to know how they are doing and to get supported for their strengths and coaching on their weaknesses.

All of these guidelines may seem reasonable in the calm of academia. But in the real world of work, you must be prepared for several realities.

1. Emotions can overrule logic. Managers must avoid criticizing employees when they are angry; rather they should teach employees the type of behavior necessary to do a job correctly.

2. Employees live in a political world. They may be afraid to ask questions for fear of appearing ignorant.[11]

3. Employees may not trust a manager's sincerity. This may be true especially if a manager's feedback is not reinforced by supporting behavior.

4. Employees have personality differences. Some will concentrate on only negative comments, even when an assessment includes positive comments as well. Managers must check that their entire message has been heard.

5. Mixed messages can confuse employees. When your nonverbal behavior is to look away from an individual while your verbal behavior states that you are extremely interested in the employee's professional growth, what do you think will be believed?

6. Are you open to employee feedback? Can you encourage and reward employees for letting you know how you're doing and then change behaviors that require it?

There are many volumes written about how to measure employee performance and conduct effective performance reviews. Thoroughly understanding the feedback process will help you not just evaluate employees but also to stimulate employee productivity.

11. R. N. Lussier, *Human Relations in Organizations: A Skill Building Approach* (Homewood, IL: Irwin, 1990), p. 189.

Human resource management has become critical to major corporations because corporate decisions can no longer be based strictly on economic factors.

A study comparing work values of employees who were over 40 years old indicated that younger employees did not trust authority as much as did their elder counterparts.[12] Younger employees felt work should be fun rather than be simply a vehicle for financial sustenance. The younger employees also believed in quick advancement, based primarily on competence rather than experience, and believed "fairness" at work meant supporting people's differences rather than treating everyone equally, as their elders believed. These differing attitudes will profoundly impact how work is carried out. Can organizations handle individual differences, support quick promotions, allow authority to be questioned and also make work "fun" in the twenty-first century?

The demographics of the work force is changing dramatically. Growth in the labor force will largely come from increasing numbers of women, minorities and immigrants, with only a small percentage of growth due to increased numbers of white males. What will these changes mean to the twenty-first century manager? Human resource management will likely play an increasingly important role in how organizations function. Our preview of tomorrow's work force begins with a 1988 *Business Week* article, "For American Business, A New World of Workers."

12. Work Attitudes: "Study Reveals Generation Gap." *Bulletins At Management* (Oct. 2, 1986), p. 326.

FOR AMERICAN BUSINESS, A NEW WORLD OF WORKERS[13]

By Elizabeth Ehrlich, with Susan B. Garland

Once upon a simpler time not so long ago, "work force" meant white men in ties or blue collars. The image was never quite exact. One generation back, as the nation settled into postwar prosperity, 30 percent of all women worked outside the home — even if *Leave It to Beaver* relected the cultural ideal of family life. "Negro," "Oriental," and "Spanish-American" workers always have helped to do America's work. But with a plentiful labor supply, few employers had to reach beyond the male Caucasian in his prime except for the least-wanted jobs. Indeed, by the late 1960s, as employers awarded self-winding watches to 65-year-olds, the first fresh-faced baby boomers were on their way to Personnel.

13. Reprinted from the September 19, 1988 issue of *Business Week* by special permission, copyright ©1988 by McGraw-Hill, Inc.

The last of that numerous cohort is now straggling into the world of paychecks and withholding taxes. The boss is losing that confident glow. The decline in birth rates after 1960 has slashed the numbers of young people available to fill jobs right up to the year 2010 and maybe beyond.

The years of picky hiring are over. Vicious competition for all sorts of workers — entry-level, skilled, seasoned — has begun. Employers must look to the nonmale, the nonwhite, the nonyoung. There may be a push for non-citizens as well: Over the next 10 years, predicts the Hudson Institute, an economic think tank, only 15 percent of work force entrants will be native-born white males.

Building a new, more diverse work force and making it tick will be one of Corporate America's biggest challenges in the decade ahead.

Mother, Daughter, Worker, Wife

In the past 15 years, as women ventured into the workplace in growing numbers, it has been widely expected that employers would take major steps to accommodate their special needs. So far, though, employers have been able to hire 52 percent of all women without doing much very differently. That's partly because in a world of stagnant real earnings, women and their families have needed the money more than companies needed the women. Feminism, higher education levels, and rising expectations pushed women into the work force, too.

But as employers fish in a shrinking pool for new workers and try to retain experienced ones, women will be in a position to make demands. Companies will be forced to make it easier for workers to balance work and family.

Three-quarters of working women are in their childbearing years; more than half of all mother work. Those with children younger than 6 make up the faster- growing segment of the work force. For many such women, as well as for their spouses, balancing work life with parenting at a distance presents logistical challenges worthy of an air-traffic controller.

It isn't only children. As the U.S. population becomes older — and by 2000, 51 percent will be between 35 and 54 — more people must take responsibility for their parents. Americans are living longer, thanks to better nutrition and medical breakthroughs, but those beyond the age of 75 are often ill or infirm. Services are expensive, so care usually falls to family members — many of whom work. About 40 percent of workers over age 40 already provide care to parents, according to Anthony Gajda of Mercer-Meidinger-Hansen, an employee-benefits firm. About 12 percent of women who care for aging parents must quit their jobs to do so.

A growing body of research links employees' concerns for the care of children or elderly relatives with productivity losses from increased absences, tardiness and stress on the job — and such time-wasters as excessive use of the phone. This holds for men in dual-career marriages as well as for single fathers and single sons. But it's particularly true for women. At Touche Ross & Co., Susan Schiffer Stautberg figures the average working woman spends 17 years raising kids and 19 years caring for aging relatives. Her grim joke: "Middle age is 15 minutes in between."

The productivity issues are greater than a workday lost when the babysitter walks out or Grandma breaks her hip. Family leaves, allowing parents time off to care for a new baby or deal with a family crisis, help retain women workers and boost morale and loyalty among others as well. A 1986 report by the General Accounting Office indicated that such policies don't cost much even though temporary workers may have to fill in or other staff may have to work overtime.

Care-Givers

There is widespread agreement that the federal government has some role to play, beyond the current $3.9 billion dependent-care tax credit, the $660 million spent on day care, and $1.5 billion for the Head Start early childhood program for disadvantaged kids. States, expanding their programs, are crying for more funding. California subsidizes day care for low-income toddlers. Texas school districts provide prekindergarten for 4-year-olds from poor families. Massachusetts is trying to increase the supply of child care with loans to build centers and grants to expand referral programs, train "care-givers," and pay them more.

The problem, however, is falling increasingly into the corporate lap. Boston University researchers Bradley K. Googins and Dianne S. Burden recently surveyed 1,500 workers in big corporations. Some 43 percent said employers and government should share responsibility for helping balance work and family life; 41 percent said companies should take the lead.

About 60 percent do offer some degree of work-schedule flexibility. But less than 5 percent of U. S. companies — a grand total of 3,300 — help with child care. Most of those either allow employees to save tax dollars by setting aside pretax income for day care in flexible benefit plans, or they provide information and referral advice. Only 250 or 300 companies have helped start child care centers.

It's likely that more women would enter the job market if they could find good child care. In the 1982 census, 26 percent of all nonworking mothers with preschoolers said they would look for work if "reasonably priced child care were available." An additional 13 percent said they would work more hours. If half the women claiming they are so constrained went to work in the 1990s, the labor force would gain 850,000 workers, notes Columbia University economist David E. Bloom.

A Benefit

Indeed, some companies are looking at child care as a recruiting device, especially in clerical, food services and hospital jobs, which depend on women workers. But the impetus is growing elswhere. Faced with a local labor shortage, Echo Bay Mines Ltd. at Round Mountain, NV, has enticed parents to hire on for swing shifts by keeping open its on-site day care center 24 hours a day, seven days a week.

Eastman Kodak Co. helps its American employees look for child care. In addition, the company is experimenting with job-sharing. Two Rochester (N.Y.) mothers with young children split the title "professional recruiter"; their 24-hour stints overlap on Wednesdays. Kodak allows up to 17 weeks of unpaid leave to care for a spouse, parent, sick child, or new baby, including adopted or foster children. "We have a lot of money invested in training. This is protecting our investment," declares Mary J. Harrington, Kodak's corporate employee relations director.

Corporate efforts to help workers cope with elderly parents are still primitive. Most women must find ad hoc solutions. A quarter of those responsible for aged parents take extended leaves or cut down their work hours. The challenge is to keep them on the job as much as possible by providing social supports for the parents. As the pressures of labor shortage build, companies will also have to see to it that employees don't forfeit seniority or status if they are forced to take time off for family reasons. "I really think demographics are destiny here," says Dana E. Friedman, work and family research direction at the Conference Board.

Young, Troubled, and in Demand

It has been a long time since America's population profile bore much resemblance to the party that landed at Plymouth Rock. Now this nation of ethnicity and social flux is changing anew. It is becoming less white and more Spanish-speaking. Birth rates among blacks exceed those of whites. Immigration, mainly from Latin America and Asia, has accounted for a fifth of America's population growth in the 1980s. Compared with the native-born, immigrants are younger and their families are larger. The youth cohort of the work force is shrinking, but more of its members will be black, Hispanic, or Asian.

These changes have significant implications for U. S. work force. A disproportionate number of these youths are growing up in families that are poor or headed by single parents. In minority communities, many of today's adults lack the skills to find decent employment. Their kids face worse prospects at a time of dramatic technological change. A disturbing new term, underclass, describes some who are from such disorganized backgrounds that — without intervention or a social miracle — they may never be employable....

Many young people — especially minorities — are caught in a vicious cycle. About a quarter of all kids are born out of wedlock to parents who "are poorly educated, frequently young, and unskilled," says George Washington University's Sar Levitan. In the U. S., about 44 percent of all marriages fail. Female-headed households are more than four times more likely to be poor than are two-parent families. A startling one in four members of the Class of 2000, now entering first grade, is living in proverty.

Part of the problem is child support. Fewer than half of fathers not living with their kids pay anything toward their keep. In 1985 more than half of all mothers with child-support orders received less than the full amount due. The average annual payment was $2,315. Another aspect of the poverty problem is women's pay. Women's earnings average $16,232, 70 percent of men's. Many mothers work part-time for less pay.

Harvard sociologist David Ellwood predicts that more than two-thirds of children who grow up in a single-parent household will spend at least some of their childhood in proverty. They are three times more likely than others to drop out of school, and they are more deficient in skills. Black and Hispanic children, while a minority of the poor, are nearly three times more likely to be poor than whites. A National Assessment of Educational Progress found that only 60 percent of white young adults could locate information in a news article or an almanac. The number was 25 percent for blacks and 40 percent for Hispanics.

Labor shortages in the future could present an unprecedented opportunity to improve the lot of the poor. "The new workers — although they are from groups disadvantaged

by discrimination, lack of education, and language barriers—will be in very great demand," says Labor Secretary Ann D. McLaughlin. Already employers are having to reach further and further along the labor queue. Where necessary, they are patching up the rag tag skills they find there, sometimes at huge expense.

Social thinkers say early intervention, with such proven child-development programs as Head Start — or even earlier with nutrition programs and parenting classes — is the real ticket to building a competent work force over time. Half of all teenage mothers eventually escape poverty through education, with measurable improvements in their kids' achievement and prospects, notes economist Andrew Summ of Northeastern University. "If minorities are to succeed, we have got to start educating children much younger and work through their parents," says Gloria G. Rodriguez, director of a support and training program for poor Hispanic families in San Antonio. Despite its track record, only 18 percent of eligible chidren are served by Head Start, due to inadequate funding.

The challenge is clear. If minority skills are not upgraded, they will deteriorate further. Companies will be forced to substitute capital for the unskilled labor. Technology, after all, has many faces. Given skilled workers, it can upgrade a job task and add value. Or, to cope with work-force shortcomings, it can be used to "de-skill." The classic example is McDonald's Corp. Dependent on young workers with poor skills, the hamburger chain has replaced words on the keys of its cash registers with pictures. That may work for McDonald's. But for society to take that path implies low wages and a declining standard of living.

Bringing the Retired Back from Retirement

In our time, the shrinking of the American manufacturing sector has written off a generation of middle-aged blue-collar workers caught between the foundry and the computer. And even as the economy faces labor shortages at all levels, the most striking employment trend in recent years has been a shift to early retirement. Only about 15 percent of men over age 65 are in the work force today, down from 25 percent in 1970. Only 68 percent of those age 55 to 64 still work, compared to 83 percent two decades ago.

Such trends were perhaps understandable as baby boomers crowded into the workplace and companies downsized. Today, though, it is waste on a vast scale. A typical American who has reached the age of 65 can expect to live an additional 17 years. By 2003 the U.S. National Center for Health Statistics predicts life expectancies at birth will be 84 years for women and 10 years less for men. Today the 58-year-old who takes early retirement is essentailly middle-aged, and retirement may last half as long as his or her work life did.

The good health, skills, and work histories of the "young old" can help the nation out of its demographic fix. "People should work longer and be productive longer. We should get away from the rigidities that go along with age 65," argues Alan Pifer, chairman of the Southport Institute for Policy Analysis.

Pifer, who directed the Carnegie Corporation's Project on Aging, advocates continual education and retraining throughout one's working life. The emphasis should be on that restless age around 50 when kids are gone and "you've gone about as high as you're going to go in the hierarchy. It would be nice if a lot of people could be 'repotted,'" he suggests. As a vision for the nation, that projects a huge agenda: reordering what is now an an hoc and haphazard retraining process. It also requires new benefits systems, such as portable pensions, to erase disincentives for middle-aged workers to move on.

Many over-60s, furthermore, don't want to be put out to pasture for 20 years. Smart companies are finding ways to retrain and employ them. In Florida, where 18 percent of its population is over 65, the future is now — fast-food chains recruit workers in retirement villages. Last year, Kelly Services Inc. in Troy, Mich., put out a call for workers over 55. Now they're 8 percent of the "temp" rolls. In Boston, one BayBanks Inc. unit has hired 45 retirees as clericals, tellers and clerks since last November.

Keeping older workers in the job market won't be easy. Says Census Bureau forecaster Cynthia M. Taueber: "They can afford to retire and will." The elderly have escaped Reagan-era spending cuts. Social Security, medicare and medicaid spending on nursing homes have eliminated most proverty among the old. Still, retirement can be boring. If business makes work attractive, the oldsters may come back in droves.

The U.S. Could Lower the Drawbridge… Again

Faced with labor shortages in earlier times, America has opened its borders. Immigration is still a policy option — the wild card in the labor-market outlook.

For Cornell University economist Vernon M. Briggs, unleashing even more immigration will stall efforts to integrate women, blacks, and other minorities into the economy. In a recent book, *Immigration Policy and the American Labor Force,* Briggs argues that minority youths could soon be competing with immigrants — legal and illegal — for entry-level jobs. Rand Corp. researchers say there's no evidence of this yet. But they warn the U. S. born Latinos must improve their skills to qualify for the high-tech jobs of the future or compete with new immigrants for low-paid jobs.

Today's immigrants, on average, are less skilled than the native-born. Most lack a high-school education. Only 20 percent are admitted because their skills are in great demand. But the criteria could change toward more preference for skills. this year, U. S. hospitals, to allay shortages, will hire 20,000 foreign nurses on five-year visas.

The idea of hospitals staffed by skilled foreign professionals and low-paid native-born janitors doesn't sit well with some like Pat Choate, TRW Inc.'s futurist. "Ultimately we have to have an economy that works — and do everything with our own people," he says. Yet, he adds, the U. S. should "use its incomparable advantages" to attract the world's talent. Foreigners here to study engineering, say, could be required to stay and work.

Unlike immigration policy, population trends hold few surprises. "We have a lot of control over how demography hits us. It's more of a glacier than a thunderbolt," reflects Jack A. Meyer, president of New Directions for Policy, a Washington think tank. "If we sit back, we're in for some problems." The danger is that the U. S. will fail to address its demographic challenges in time.

COMING TO OUR SENSES: MAKING A DIFFERENCE

Managing human resources is a shared responsibility in organizations. Organizational policies and traditions often convey an attitude toward people who work there. Some of the best companies to work for in the United Sates, according to a 1984 book on the topic, include Delta Airlines, Bell Labs and IBM.[14] All of these firms stand behind their slogans about the importance of their people by offering above average pay, benefits, job security, opportunities to advance and ambience. Sometimes their policies place the welfare of employees above profits. They take risks by trying innovative benefit programs or management styles unheard of in their industries.

What about your attitudes toward human resources management? While we might see ourselves as warm, people-oriented professionals, feedback from others can sometimes reveal that our motivation to work in the business world has more to do with creating new technology, working with numbers or the excitement of "the deal." What is important is the awareness of your own motives and how the human resources component fits into this mosaic. As you have observed the *9 to 5* movie clip, examined your history with feedback and showed how you presently use it, what have you learned? As a twenty-first century manager, will you be prepared for a changing work force driven by new attitudes toward work and different jobs to be done?

14. R. Levering, et al., *The 100 Best Companies to Work for in America* (Reading, MA: Addison-Wesley, 1984).

- What have I seen?

- What did I hear?

- What did I feel?

- What did I think?

- And now, what will I do to make a difference?

Human Resources Management   237

We are often affected by human resource management practices and values. For Ann, an arrogant interviewing policy at one school prompted her to choose another school that seemed interested in her needs. Archaic maternal leave policies cost Jane's firm her invaluable loyalty and commitment. Phillip, when given feedback in a supportive and skillful manner increased his motivation and productivity.

Treating people well on the job is at the core of human resource management. People are an investment for an organization. When recruiting, training and compensation issues are neglected in favor of financial and technical considerations, motivation and productivity can suffer. The twenty-first century manager will be faced with understanding the needs of a changing work force, a work force that is changing in its demographics and its values. In the long run, organizations that spend time to listen to employee needs and spend money to develop progressive benefits programs to meet those needs will retain a skilled and committed work force.

Figure 12.1 One Approach to Human Resource Management

The Beatings Will Continue Until Morale Improves!

—Management

Some companies try using humorous approaches to boost morale.

Chapter **13**

Motivation

You could feel the excitement at Valley Video. Most of the employees were high school seniors working after school and on weekends. For Jeremy, it was his first job and he loved it. Even though he had to miss a family ski weekend and cut back on other after-school activities, Jeremy was proud of his performance at Valley Video. The regular customers often asked him which tapes were entertaining. He even began reviewing tapes at home on his own time so he could give customers better advice. The store manager noticed these efforts and soon gave Jeremy a raise and had him training new part-time employees. Jeremy was just one of an enthusiastic group of Valley Video workers who agreed that, "When you go to work there you just feel motivated to do your best."

Just a few doors down from the enthusiasm of Valley Video was the Campus Cafe. Laura had taken a job there at the same time Jeremy had been hired at the video store. Unfortunately, her experience was quite different. Even though she worked about the same hours and for the same pay as her friend, her job at Campus Cafe was becoming a chore. While she enjoyed serving customers and learning other jobs in the restaurant, she noticed that other employees were quitting or not showing up for work. One busy weekend night, she had only two other people to help her out front, when five were supposed to be on duty. When she mentioned this to the owner, he said, "You know, it's hard to find motivated employees these days. But in a campus town like this I've got 50 applicants on file eager to replace you. Now stop your complaining and get back to work." Within a few weeks Laura had filled out a job application at Valley Video. Her enthusiasm for the Campus Cafe job had evaporated and she dreaded the thought of facing her disgruntled coworkers and frustrated customers.

Beginning with our first job and throughout our entire career, motivation is crucial to a successful, productive and satisfying experience at work. As with most questions about how people perform at work, the question of how to motivate them to work toward organizational goals is a difficult one to answer. We know that individuals differ in what it takes for them to do their best. On the other hand, there are many similarities that can be found in work situations that are either highly motivating or that are extremely unmotivating.

Name _____

ID# _____

Section _____

The first step toward understanding motivation is to identify what it means to you. In the "Ready for Class" exercise that follows, please think about a real job or project where you felt extremely motivated and productive. Describe the important details of this motivation and productivity. Then recall an extremely unmotivating job or a project in which you performed poorly. Describe the important details of this situation and identify the factor that accounted for your poor performance. As you describe your high and low motivation circumstances, please include how you felt in those situations.

High and Low Motivation at Work

1. High Motivation

Think about a job or project where you found yourself highly motivated and productive. What factors contributed to your high motivation?

Choose the one factor that was most important to your high level of motivation.

2. Low Motivation

Think about a job or project where you found yourself extremely unmotivated and unproductive. Describe important details of this situation. What factors contributed to your low motivation?

Choose the one factor that contributed most to your low level of motivation.

High and Low Motivation Work Situations

1. Join with two other students to form a group of three.

2. Share your high and low motivation work situations with each other. Identify the factor most responsible for your high or low performance. List these in the table below.

	High Motivation	Low Motivation
Person 1:		
Person 2:		
Person 3:		

3. Look at the list of factors. As a group, identify one high motivation factor and one low motivation factor that represents the factors your group considers particularly influential. The factors you identify may be a synthesis of those listed by individuals or may be another factor that becomes evident in your discussion.

	High Motivation	Low Motivation
Group Choice:		

4. Choose one person to report to the class.

5. Record the class list of factors (The "Score Video" column below will be used with the video segment that follows.)

Score Video		High Motivation	Low Motivation	Score Video
	1.			
	2.			
	3.			
	4.			
	5.			
	6.			

LIGHTS, CAMERA, ACTION: MANAGEMENT LIVE!

Lights

By identifying factors in work situations that contributed to your level of motivation you have begun to give the concept of motivation greater personal meaning. You have probably noticed differences between the factors you identified and those listed by classmates. This awareness is crucial, as it is likely to occur in the work place as well.

Camera

In this video segment, we take a second look at Pat Carrigan, the successful plant manager at the General Motors parts plant in Bay City, MI. In Chapter 2, we noted the management roles that Ms. Carrigan used most and least frequently.

Pat Carrigan is dealing here with a difficult motivational problem, how to keep employee productivity and morale high when work is dull and repetitive. As you watch this video segment again, you will sense something present in her that is creating and maintaining high motivation for employees and management alike.

Action

Take the roles of management consultant and evaluate Ms. Carrigan's motivational techniques. How do her strategies address the factors you have identified on your class's list? Are there some factors she seems to address that your class did not mention? Are some factors evident on your list that Pat Carrigan should be addressing? Are any of your low motivation factors evident in the video segment?

1. Refer to your class list of high and low motivational factors on the "Making Connections: In-Class Interaction" worksheet on the previous page.

2. Put a check in the column marked "Score Video" (Question 6) if the factor listed appears in the video.

Our own experiences in high and low motivation work settings offer clues about the nature of motivation. Yet, we may also have found ourselves in situations where our best efforts to motivate others did not work very well. As a twenty-first century manager it will be crucial to your success to be seen as a leader who can motivate people to perform beyond the requirements of their job. But what causes people to put forth strong effort and maintain their commitment to a job?

Unfortunately, the answer is not simple. The complexities of human behavior and organizational life make it difficult to motivate employees. Moreover there are differing views of the source of motivation. Is it within the person or does it reside in the organization? Or are both important? What steps can a manager take to assure a highly motivating work situation for all?

Questions about motivation have been with us ever since people have had needs to be satisfied. Our primeval ancestors were motivated to satisfy hunger, thirst and other survival needs by exploratory and hunting behavior. While our basic physiological needs are now routinely satisfied by opening the refrigerator or turning up the thermostat, modern organizational life has set before us many "higher order" needs to be satisfied. Employees want to receive fair compensation for their labor, they wish to be recognized for their accomplishments and many desire input into decisions that affect them.

Textbook definitions of motivation present a cycle of events that begin with human needs to be satisfied followed by the emergence of forces that prompt people to take action to satisfy these needs. If the action taken satisfy the needs, the actions are likely to be repeated. If ineffective, other behaviors must be tried. Those individuals who survived in prehistoric times were the ones who discovered what they needed to survive. Modern managers who survive and excel in organizational settings have found ways of satisfying their needs and those of their employees and maintaining high levels of motivation over time. Your textbook introduces several ways of thinking about motivation.

Each approach explains the nature of motivation somewhat differently. Each approach raises a different question that a manager must ask when trying to solve motivational problems at work. The following theories of motivation comprise the most respected ways of explaining how motivation works.

Content Theories of Motivation

Content theories of motivation state that people have underlying needs. The twenty-first century manager must be good at diagnosing how to tap these needs to satisfy both the individual and the organization. Three important theories of this type are Maslow's hierarchy of needs theory, Herzberg's two-factor theory and McClelland's acquired needs theory.

1. Maslow's hierarchy of needs theory states that underlying needs must be satisfied in a specific order but that once satisfied they no longer motivate.[1,2]

2. Herzberg's two-factor theory suggests that only underlying needs related to the nature of work — such as how interesting and meaningful it is — will yield employee motivation, while needs related to working conditions will not motivate employees.[3] When satisfied, these "hygiene factors" — those needs related to working conditions — only neutralized employee dissatisfaction and frustration.

1. A. F. Maslow, "A Theory of Human Motivation," *Psychological Review*, 50 (1943), pp. 379-396.
2. A. F. Maslow, *Motivation and Personality* (New York: Harper and Row, 1954).
3. F. Herzberg, "One More Time: How Do You Motivate Employees?" *Harvard Business Review*, (Jan.-Feb. 1968), pp. 53-62.

3. McClelland's Acquired Needs Theory indicates that people acquire needs through their life experiences.[4] The three most important, the need for achievement, affiliation and power, differ in potency among individuals. Thus managers must consider different ways of motivating each employee.

All content theories suggest that people are motivated by internal needs and that managers must learn to "read" them correctly. Managers must learn to structure work to fit the prevailing needs of individual employees.

Process Theories of Motivation

Process theories of motivation agree with content theories that the essence of motivation is within the individual, but their focus is on the person's perceptions and thought processes rather than underlying personality characteristics. People decide how hard they will work depending on how fairly they believe they are being treated and how much they expect their hard work to pay off. Important among process theories of motivation are the equity and expectancy theories.

1. Equity theory says that people expect to be treated fairly on the job.[5] The theory says they feel their motivation will suffer they feel they are not being rewarded in a way that is comparable to someone who they regard as similar to themselves professionally.

2. Expectancy theory predicts that employees must believe three things before they will work hard.[6] First, they must believe that working hard will result in improved performances. Second, that improved performance will pay off for them through job-related payoff. Third, that the payoff they receive is desirable to them.

The process theories of motivation thus emphasize an employee's perceptions and thoughts about work. When motivation problems occur, process theories would require managers to check whether inequities on the job or unavailability of positive work-related outcomes are at the root of the problem.

Reinforcement Theories of Motivation

Reinforcement theories of motivation shift emphasis from the employees' underlying needs and thinking processes to the rewards and punishment in the work environment.[7] Reinforcement theories emphasize the consequences of an individual's behavior. The key lesson of reinforcement theories is that managers should reward behaviors desirable to the organization. Managers must not allow excellent performance to be ignored or taken for granted. Behaviors that do not support organizational objectives should be systematically ignored, or punished only as a last report.

Studies have shown that consistent rewards for organizationally desirable behavior result in long-term positive performance. In contrast, punishment as a primary motivational tool contributes little to high motivation because employees learn to avoid the punisher and do not learn appropriate behaviors. Because what is rewarding and punishing for individuals differs, managers must carefully observe and manage the consequences of work-related behavior.

Each of these theories of motivation has some scientific support. Thus, managers must ultimately pay attention to needs, perceptions and consequences for behaviors if high motivation is to be maintained. The prudent manager should consider the primary question raised by each theory when attempting to resolve motivational problems or when trying to improve performance in the work place.

4. D. C. McClelland, *Human Motivation* (Glenview, IL: Scott Foresman, 1985).

5. J. S. Adams, "Injustice in Social Exchange," *Advances in Experimental Social Psychology*, 2nd ed., ed. L. Berkowitz (New York: Academic Press, 1965), and J. S. Adams, "Toward an Understanding of Inequity," *Journal of Abnormal and Social Psychology*, (November, 1964), pp. 422-436.

6. V. H. Vroom, *Work and Motivation* (New York: Wiley 1964).

7. B. F. Skinner, *Science and Human Behavior* (New York: Free Press, 1953).

Table 13.1 shows questions that can help managers focus on probable causes for work place motivation problems.

Table 13.1	**Motivation Questions for Managers to Ask**
Theory	**Question**
ContentTheories	Are the internal needs of employees satisfied?
Maslow Hierarchy of Needs Theory	What is the employee's lowest level of unsatisfied need?
Herzberg's Two-Factor Theory	Is the manager trying to motivate employees through meaningful work or pleasant working conditions?
McClelland's Acquired Needs Theory	What is the relative potency of acquired needs for each individual?
Process Theories of Motivation	How do employees think about work?
Equity Theory	Are employees treated fairly as compared to professional equals?
Expectancy Theory	Do employees expect their efforts to pay off in desirable work related outcomes?
Reinforcement Theories of Motivation	Are managers aware of the precise consequences for an employee behavior?
	Are desirable behaviors systematically rewarded and undesirable behaviors ignored or punished?

 Even with different theories in mind, the answers to motivational questions remain elusive. Managers often make the mistake of assuming that what motivates them will motivate their employees. Such simplistic notions of human behavior are likely to contribute to limited motivational strategies and unmotivated employees. In the following "Mirror Talk: Focussing on Me" exercise, you will be asked to complete a brief questionnaire that will help you assess which of your needs is primary and which ones have less importance for motivating your behavior. Using you questionnaire scores and your behavior observations you can roughly estimate your dominant and less influential motives, and can get ideas about managing employees with motive strengths that differ from yours.

Self Assessment Questionnaire

What Motivates You?[8]

1. Label each of the 15 statements according to how accurately it describes you. Place the appropriate number from the scale below on the line before each statement.

Like Me		Somewhat like me		Not like me
1	2	3	4	5

_____ 1. I enjoy working hard.

_____ 2. I enjoy competition and winning.

_____ 3. I want/have lots of friends.

_____ 4. I enjoy a difficult challenge.

_____ 5. I enjoy being in charge.

_____ 6. I want to be liked by others.

_____ 7. I want to know how I am progressing as I complete tasks.

_____ 8. I confront people who do things I disagree with.

_____ 9. I tend to build close relationships with co-workers.

_____ 10. I enjoy setting and achieving realistic goals.

_____ 11. I enjoy influencing other people to get my way.

_____ 12. I enjoy belonging to groups and organizations.

_____ 13. I enjoy the satisfaction of completing a difficult task.

_____ 14. In a leaderless situation I like to take charge.

_____ 15. I enjoy working with others more than working alone.

8. Adapted from Robert N. Lussier, *Human Relations in Organizations: A Skill Building Approach* (Homewood, IL: Irwin, 1990), p. 120.

2. Before scoring your answers, predict which of the following describes your most powerful motive by circling the appropriate description below.

a. I like to be accurate and effective at what I do. I seek challenging activities and want lots of feedback on my performance. (Need for achievement)

b. I like to be in control and have influence. I am willing to confront others. (Need for power)

c. I like close relationships with others. I enjoy working in groups and sharing ideas. (Need for affiliation)

3. Now that you have predicted your primary motive, compare your prediction to your score on the "Motivation Questionnaire" by completing the following scoring key.

To determine your primary need, place the number 1-5 that represents your score for each statement next to the number for the statement. Each statement represents a specific need—and each column represents a group of statements related to one of the three types of needs.

Achievement	Power	Affiliation
1. _____	2. _____	3. _____
4. _____	5. _____	6. _____
7. _____	8. _____	9. _____
10. _____	11. _____	12. _____
13. _____	14. _____	15. _____
Totals: _____	_____	_____

Add up the total of each column. The sum of numbers in each column should be between 5 and 25 points. The column with the highest score is your dominant or primary need.

4. Now compare your predicted primary motive with your actual primary motive. Place an X next to PREDICTED and ACTUAL highest scores

Predicted Highest Score

_____ A. Achievement

_____ B. Power

_____ C. Affiliation

Actual Highest Score

_____ A. Achievement

_____ B. Power

_____ C. Affiliation

5. Next, try to observe the presence of your primary motive in your behavior. It is often difficult to identify your highest strength motive by using a brief questionnaire. Another important clue to consider is your behavior in work situations.

Think back to the "Making Connections" exercise where you compared work situations that were either highly motivating or were unmotivating. Your primary motive may have been evident in the role you played in that class interaction.

If you scored high in the need for achievement you may have attempted to make sure everyone understood the task and that it was completed on time. You may have referred to the workbooks for clarification and felt disappointed if someone had not completed the exercise.

If you were high on power as a motive, you may have initiated the discussion of motivation in work situations by suggesting that you (or someone else) begin telling about their experiences. You may have influenced who became spokesperson for the group and your choice for group high and low factors may have been selected.

If you were high on affiliation as a motive, you may have desired to know the names of others in your group and perhaps gone beyond the assignment to learn about them. You may have helped resolve conflicts over which factors should be put on the group's list. Check which of the three descriptions came closest to describing your behavior in the small-group "Making Connections" exercise.

6. Your behavior during the exercise in class may have been consistent or different than your predicted and actual scores on the questionnaire titled "What Motivates You." Compare your primary motive scores on these three measures in the space below.

	Predicted Score on Motivation	Actual Score on Motivation	Behavior Description in high/low motivation exercise
1. Achievement			
2. Power			
3. Affiliation			

If all three checks are in the same row, it suggests that your behavior is consistently based on a set of needs that guide how you will manage others in the work place. You may be quite effective with those who have similar primary motives, but you must be cautious with others whose primary motive differs from yours.

On the other hand, if your scores on the three types of motives do not differ greatly it may suggest that your primary motive is not much stronger than the other two motives and that you can be flexible in dealing with employees who have a different primary motive than yours.

Whatever your scores on these three tests, we know that these three motives are present in everyone, but the order of their importance may differ depending on learning experiences, value systems and employment situations. Finally, it is crucial that this self evaluation serve only as a starting point for further self-examination—and not as a definitive measure of what motivates you.

The self assessment activities in "Mirror Talk: Focussing on You" have identified the relative potency of each of three needs: achievement, power, and affiliation. According to McClelland's theory, each of these needs leads to a corresponding motive. In the description that follows, characteristics of each need will be identified and the implications for how you might motivate employees with each primary motive will be discussed.[9]

9. Adapted from Lussier, loc.cit.

The Need for Achievement (n Ach)

People with a high need for achievement tend to be characterized as:

• Wanting to take personal responsibility for solving problems.
• Goal oriented; they seek moderate, realistic, attainable goals.
• Seeking a challenge, excellence and individuality.
• Taking calculated, moderate risks.
• Desiring concrete feedback on their performance.

People with a high need for achievement think about ways to do a better job, how to accomplish something unusual or important, and career progression. They perform well in nonroutine, challenging and competitive situations, while people low in need for achievement do not perform well in these situations.

McClelland's research shows that only about 10 percent of the U. S. population has a dominant need for achievement. There is evidence of a correlation between high achievement need and high performance. People with a high need for achievement tend to enjoy sales and entrepreneurial-type positions. Managers tend to have a high, but not a dominant need for achievement.

Managers can motivate employees with a high need for achievement by giving them nonroutine, challenging tasks in which there are clear attainable objectives. They should also be given prompt and frequent feedback on their performance. Continually giving them increased responsibility for doing new things contributes to high levels of motivation.

The Need for Power (n Pow)

People with a high need for power tend to be characterized as:

• Wanting to control situations.
• Wanting to influence or control others.
• Enjoying competition in which they can win; they do not like to lose.
• Willing to confront others.

People with a high need for power think about controlling a situation and others, while seeking positions of authority and status. People with high need for power tend to have a low need for affiliation.

Managers can motivate employees with a high need for power by letting them plan and control their jobs as much as possible. Managers can also try to include them in decision making, especially when they are affected by the decision. They also tend to perform best alone rather than as a team member so a manager should try to assign them to a whole task rather than just a part of a task.

The Need for Affiliation (n Aff)

People with a high need for affiliation tend to be characterized as:

• Seeking close relationships with others.
• Wanting to be liked by others.
• Enjoying lots of social activities.
• Seeking to belong; they join groups and organizations.

People with a high need for affiliation think about friends and relationships. They tend to enjoy developing, helping and teaching others. They tend to have a need for power. People with high need for affiliation seek jobs as teachers, in personnel and in other helping professions. They tend to avoid supervision because they like to be one of the group rather than a leader.

Managers can motivate employees who have a high need for affiliation by letting them work as part of a team. Typically, such employees will derive satisfaction from the people they work with rather than the task itself. Managers should also give them lots of praise and recognition and may be able to delegate responsibility for orienting and training new employees to them because they make great buddies and mentors.

There are many pieces to the puzzle of motivation. What motivates you? What motivates others? What have your experiences taught you? What did your observations of Pat Carrigan suggest? How is the changing world of work affecting what motivates people? What must you do to make a difference as a twenty-first century manager?

- What have I seen?

- What did I hear?

- What did I feel?

- What did I think?

- And now, what will I do to make a difference?

What motivated our parents and grandparents on the job seems quite different from what seems to motivate modern employees. The days when people were just thankful to have a job, any job, or when they maintained lifelong loyalty to a company because they knew the founder, seem gone forever. Motivated employees of tomorrow will expect to have input on decisions, challenging work, recognition by firm and a flexible work life that includes time for bearing and raising children and pursuing outside interests. They will seek opportunities to learn new job skills and to be part of a company whose values and culture are consistent with their own.

There is one company that has developed a unique approach to promoting employee motivation, including hiring a "Vice President of Fun." Ben and Jerry's Homemade Inc. is a company that is facing a crisis that may have been caused by paying attention to employee needs. That crisis is success! As the company grew, its original vision and style were threatened. All the ingredients of a highly motivational workplace — familiarity, loyalty, fun, communication — were threatened by growth. Ben and Jerry wanted to remain the leaders of a socially conscious, funky company in the midst of dramatic growth. Here is an update:

Reading 13.1

FOREVER YOUNG

Ben and Jerry's Quest to Keep Their Company's Spirit Alive as the Business Grows

by Erik Larson

Ben Cohen is confident that he, for one, is weird enough to carry on the funky good works of Ben & Jerry's Homemade Inc., the company he cofounded. There is evidence to support this. A year ago, for example, Ben stripped down and swathed himself sumo style, then marched out into the shipping-and-receiving bay at Ben & Jerry's headquarters in Waterbury, Vt. Rick Brown, the company's director of sales, came out dressed the same way. They squared off amid the cheers and blood-lust stomp of nearly all the company's employees, and did what any pair of normal American executives would do, what Lee Iacocca no doubt would do if he had to settle a debate of this magnitude. Ben and Rick puffed out their pale prodigious stomachs and bounced each other, a couple of human bumper cars trying to determine once and for all who had the baddest belly in the Ben & Jerry's empire.

10. *Inc..* (July 1988), p. 50. Copyright ©1988 by Erik Larson. Reprinted with the permission of Georges Borchardt, Inc., and the author.

But these days Ben is worried. What started out as a simple ice-cream parlor has now, almost in spite of itself, become a growth company, doubling in size each year through 1986, adding scores of new employees, reaching $31.8 million in sales last year. The company got to this point by breaking rules and taking chances, and by a lot of good luck. Its puckish marketing maneuvers and dense ice cream won it goodwill and sales; the sheer energy of its young, dedicated work force kept the company from stumbling, albeit sometimes just barely.

Once, Ben could be confident that everyone else at the company was just as weird as he, that everyone got off on the funk and adventure, and most importantly, that everyone bought into his philosophy of corporate responsibility — that Ben & Jerry's existed for one reason, to act as a force of social change. But lately, the company has gotten so businesslike, so corporate. Its explosive growth has stressed and eroded the Ben & Jerry's culture, diminished the fun, brought strangers into the happy family. There are controls, departments, memos.

Product introductions take so much more effort than they used to, require so many approvals. And now Ben finds he faces resistance from within to some of his favorite ideas and policies — even the company's five-to-one salary ratio, which limits the top salary to five times that of the lowest-paid employee. You can almost see the spore of change. Some of Ben & Jerry's managers actually wear ties from time to time; the top marketing man, Allan Kaufman, roves the halls dressed like Indiana Jones, in bush hat and jacket.

All this comes as Ben is trying to pull back from day-to-day management and as competition rises for dominance of the superpremium ice-cream market. Last year, wholesale factory shipments totaled $500 million, according to Find/SVP, a market-research firm. Ben & Jerry's, ranked third by Find/SVP, now faces the likes of Pillsbury, which owns Häagen-Dazs; Kraft, owner of Frusen Glädje; and Steve's Homemade Ice Cream, run by Richard Smith, an aggressive streetwise marketeer.

Ben's office shudders — this is no metaphor. His office takes up the hind end of a leased trailer, and it shakes when the wind gusts. Ben is wearing gray denim with a band of red showing at the neck. He's got an unruly beard and scraggly smoke-tipped hair, which wisps off his balding scalp. He looks like a chubby Central American guerrilla — Daniel Ortega Cohen. But Ben is a capitalist guerilla; that rim of Marxist red is the neckline of a Ben & Jerry's cow T-shirt. His company is 10 years old this year. "Now, we're at the stage of young adulthood," Ben says. "I'm kinda interested in kicking the kid out of the house, and the kid pretty much wants to split."

But does the kid still possess all the right values? Is the kid "weird" enough, a term Ben and Jerry use as shorthand to describe the things that make the company unique? Can funk survive the big bad world of business? "I know so many liberal, nonconforming parents who end up having conservative kids," Ben says. He quickly qualifies this — he doesn't really believe that's the case here. He just wants to be sure, and to feel secure that his company will continue stretching the boundaries of what a socially responsible business can be.

The events of the past year, however, have not brought him this security. A kind of cultural revolution has taken place at Ben & Jerry's. It began last February at the Hulbert Outdoor Center, in Fairlee, Vt., when 18 senior managers climbed ropes together, fell from ladders into one anothers' arms, trudged bound and blindfolded across a frozen field, and bared their souls in a tearful night of confession and self-critique.

The revolution at Ben & Jerry's is more than a simple internal struggle to come to terms with growth, change, and success. The company is an experiment. It is founded on principles alien to mainstream business. If Ben & Jerry's ever becomes just like any other corporation — Ben's great dread — the experiment will have failed. Ben says chief operating officer Fred Lager, "is looking to show other people that you can run a business differently from the way most businesses are run, that you can share your prosperity with your employees, rewrite the book on executive salaries, rewrite the book in terms of how a company interacts with the community — and you can still play the game according to the rules of Wall Street. You can still raise money, still go to the banks, still have shareholders who are getting a good return on their investment."

For Ben, the company is the message. But this message has at times been contradictory.

There is a saying at Ben & Jerry's that Ben is Ben. This is invoked, in-house, as a kind of verbal elixir, a spiritual hit of Anacin, to cope with some new change of course, some new idea, some new contradiction between what Ben says the company will do and what it actually does. The greatest contradiction involves growth, and it has marked the company's history ever since May 5, 1978, the day Ben Cohen and Jerry Greenfield opened an ice-cream parlor in a renovated Burlington, Vt., gas station. All along, Ben has questioned and feared growth, disputing the maxim that a business either grows, or it dies. From time to time he calls on the company to stop growing and look inward. But all along Ben & Jerry's grew — quickly. And Ben, with his maverick marketing ideas, has often been the cause.

He and Jerry, best friends since seventh grade, had no intention of doing more than starting an ice-cream parlor. Once the business got going, they planned to sell it and move on. Their ice cream, rich and packed with tasty shrapnel, sold well from the first day. Something always seemed to force them to grow, some new cost, some unexpected threat — the need, for example, to increase sales just to cover the repair bills of an ancient ice-cream truck, whose breakdowns were consuming all the company's cash flow.

Ben and Jerry's, uneasy with the cash-based morality of corporations, nonetheless found themselves and their company becoming far more businesslike. In 1982, they even hired a bona fide businessman, an M.B.A., no less — Fred Lager, known universally as "Chico." He had owned and operated and then sold a successful Burlington nightclub. As chief operating officer, he is now the company's fiscal soul, Ben's foil. Any measure to improve profits or control costs is known in-house as being "Fredlike." Employees who come up with money-saving ideas win the Fred-of-the-Month award, a Fred's Famous T-shirt — the Fredlike thing to do is nominate yourself for the award. Under Chico's direction, the company slashed costs, boosted production, and started making some real money.

For the founders, this was a moral and fiscal plateau. Success played to Jerry's qualms about business. Granted, ice cream is not napalm. But becoming a businessman — a successful businessman — was too much for his Aquarian psyche. He retired late in 1982 and moved to Arizona; he had no intention of coming back. (He returned in 1985.)

Ben, saddened, alone, sharing Jerry's fears, put the company on the block. "I had this horrible feeling come over me that I had become a businessman," Ben says. "Worse, that now I was just some kind of mindless cog in the overall economy, taking in money with one hand and paying it out with the other, adding nothing."

He did not sell, however. Another Vermont entrepreneur persuaded Ben to keep the company and find a way to run it that would ease his conscience. Ben decided he would make the company a force for social change and began to consider Ben & Jerry's as being held in trust for the community. This moreover, gave him a way — the only way, he believes — to justify further growth. The more the company grew, he reasoned, the more good works it could pursue. But to grow, it would need to build a new factory with greater capacity. To pay for the plant, Ben took the company public but offered the first shares only in Vermont, to Vermonters, thereby making the community the real, not just metaphoric, owner. He deliberately set the minimum-buy price low. "We want to make it available to all economic classes," says Ben. "We were seeking somewhat to redistribute wealth."

Now, Ben & Jerry's had stockholders to worry about — not just stockholders, but neighbors, friends. To be socially responsible meant the company *had* to grow.

The bigger the company got, the more heat it drew from competitors, in particular Richard Smith, of Steve's Homemade, who threatened a preemptive national blitz with look-alike ice cream. Instead of pursuing controlled growth — Ben's plan had been to enter one major market a year — he responded to the threat by entering eight new major markets over a nine-month period, including Atlanta and Los Angeles.

For a man who questions growth, Ben has come a long way. This year, the company's sales may surpass $45 million, up more than 40 percent, with profits sure to top last year's $1.4 million.

Ben could *say* stop, but he could not do it.

What he could control, or at least shape, was Ben & Jerry's mission. Throughout the company's growth, a culture evolved that emphasized fun, charity and goodwill toward fellow workers up and down the line. In September 1985, the company founded The Ben & Jerry's Foundation Inc., which receives 7.5 percent of the company's pretax income and spends it on a broad array of causes. Jeff Furman, vice-president and a director, came up with the five-to-one salary ratio. The company hires the handicapped, provides free therapy sessions — including anonymous drug and alcohol counseling — to any employee who needs it and takes workers on all-company outings to baseball and hockey games in Montreal. There is a changing table for babies in the men's room as well as in the women's room.

The best way to sample life at Ben & Jerry's is to sit in one of the company's staff meetings, held once a month in the receiving bay of the Waterbury plant. Production stops so every employee can attend.

Coffee. Cider doughnuts, freshly made. It's 8 a.m. on a Friday. Some 150 managers and line workers jam the bay, all sitting in folding chairs, knee to lumbar region, like passengers on a cut-rate flight to Shanghai. There are four neckties, three skirts; Allan Kaufman comes dressed to explore the Temple of Doom. Otherwise, the dress is basic woodchuck. Levis. Timberland boots. Nikes. Ben is absent, but Jerry is here, in weary slacks, a cow T-shirt, and a crumpled red flannel shirt, tails out, one button fastened.

The routine stuff comes first. Jerry reports on Ben's effort to open an ice-cream parlor in Moscow, with profits used solely to support East-West exchange programs. He updates the progress on another of Ben's ideas, the plan to refurbish and maintain a New York City subway station for one year, and explains how the idea is currently bogged down in bureaucracy and transit authority/union debate. The company, expecting the deal to fall through, ran an ad in *The New York Times* asking the public for other marketing ideas. One suggestion, now read out loud, calls for the company to produce large, collapsible cardboard boxes emblazoned with the Ben & Jerry's logo and cows — and distribute these to the homeless in New York as places to sleep.

Next, Jerry talks about joy. This is not something he takes lightly. Ever since his return to Ben & Jerry's, his role has been to serve as the embodiment of Ben & Jerry's spiritual soul: his is a clear blue space on the organizational chart. He proposes a "Joy Committee," charged with putting more joy into the workday. No one giggles.

"There was an incredible amount of discussion about this at the department-head meeting," he tells the crowd. "There were a lot of varied opinions, ranging from some people who felt it was too much fun at work already..."

He times this like a comedian. A wall of laughter cuts him off. "That was a minority opinion, by the way."

But this question of joy at work has lately become a serious issue. Jerry gets serious.

"There was pretty much an agreement that things at work are tough, and that with all the tasks we have to perform, and the stress people are under, it would be a good idea to try to infuse a little more joy." He asked if anyone's interested. Hands go up; the crowd applauds.

Chico now rises and announces the birthday of an employee. Someone shouts that Chico should sing a Frank Sinatra version of "Happy Birthday." The Sinatra part is a joke, because Chico is known to be tone-deaf and can barely sing any version of "Happy Birthday," let alone Sinatra's. Chico seems unwilling at first, but the applause is insistent. There are hoots, whistles. Slowly he rises, puts out one hand, palm up, the international symbol of crooners everywhere, and begins to sing. Everybody joins in, in a warm and slow and sweet rendition.

These meetings are fun. Joyful. This is not the spooky, overheated joy conjured up by get-rich preachers at tent revivals. These people like being here, they like one another.

For all the fun, however, the Ben & Jerry's Way has its stressful side — a pervasive sense of crisis that has always lingered within the company. No one has ever been entirely sure where Ben & Jerry's was headed, or where it ought to head. Ever now and then Ben would talk about slowing growth, maybe stopping altogether — $50 million once seemed a good number, and the company aimed at that. In lieu of planning, Ben & Jerry's relied on a small cadre of energetic, motivated staff, universalists who could drop everything when the alarm bells rang.

And the bells ring often at Ben & Jerry's. Milly Badger, controller since she joined the company in 1985, says she tells new hires to come to work in running shoes and be prepared to sprint from one task to another. "We don't have adequate staff to do the job," she says. "If you have any knowledge of anything, and people know it, they're going to come to you."

When the company was small, this was kind of fun. Everyone knew everyone else; employees were like family. But growth brought malaise. Departments began duplicating work. Communications broke down. Employees, for example, found out about the company's new Springfield, Vt., plant from newspaper accounts. And Badger recalls a meeting in which Jim Rowe, director of retail operations, announced his department's plan to add 50 new stores. She was shocked. That kind of expansion would require heavy support from her department, yet she knew nothing about it. Production was likewise in the dark. "I said, 'We can't do that,'" Badger recalls. "He said, "Well, it's done.'" And just who were all these new workers and managers roaming in the halls? Says Wendy Yoder, a shift supervisor and five-year employee: "It's hard to feel you're part of a big family if you don't know the brothers and sisters."

Within the context of ordinary corporate life, these sins are hardly lethal. But at Ben & Jerry's, they constituted violations of an unwritten agreement: give the company 110 percent, and you should get it right back — maybe not in cash, but certainly in joy. The forces that once held Ben & Jerry's together and made it lean and nimble had fallen out of alignment.

Says Ben, "Everybody was trying to do the right thing, everybody was putting out an incredible amount of effort." But even tasks as routine as preparing for a trade show became complicated. Product introductions were handled as if they were the first the company had ever made. "We didn't have good systems or standard operating systems. So every time we had to so something that was pretty much a repetitive process, it would get started from the beginning — instead of just pulling out the procedure and following it." Ben holds out his hands, flutters them, "I had this image of these molecules jiggling, going back and forth like this, instead of going in a straight line. Eventually we'd get the job done, but it looks a whole lot more energy."

Consider, for example, the crisis that took place in spring of 1987, one crisis too many for some of Ben & Jerry's faithful — the crisis, says plant manager Jim Miller, that "woke the sleeping giant."

The company, in keeping with Ben's quest to be first, wanted to become the first ice-cream maker to produce pints with tamper-evident seals, and ordered a new machine supposedly capable of doing the job. It bought another machine, too, this one to automate the process of filling pints, previously done by hand. The idea was to get both machines up and running before summer. What could possibly go wrong?

The machines came late, and when they did arrive, they proved cantankerous, difficult to master. Each alone was new technology. Together, they were confounding. Demand was up, the summer was approaching, but instead of making more ice cream, the plant was producing less. The company abandoned the tamper-evident seal machine and scrambled to get the other one working. "We realized how painfully clear it had all been and how foolish we were for trying to do two things at once," Chico says. The awareness came a bit late.

One Friday, Chico walked to the loading dock to see how things were going. To his horror, he discovered the company would be short that coming week by well over 300 pallets of ice cream. He sounded the alarm. He called for all hands to man the production line. He, Ben, Jerry and nearly everyone else did a stint, wiping containers, emptying the garbage. Jerry, as Undersecretary of Joy, hired a masseuse to give workers massages during their breaks. Some staffers cooked dinner for the crew. The company ordered in pizza. This was war.

There was a positive side to the struggle. Some employees felt it rekindled the spirit of the old days. "The drawback," Chico says, "was that once again we were running around like chickens with our heads cut off, scrambling, trying to put out a fire. People came through, people always come through. But I think every time you go through something like that you lose a little credibility, and it becomes a little harder to go to them the next time and say, well, guess what? Another fire."

The culture, the Ben & Jerry's Way, is clearly under pressure. Most symbolic is the debate over salary and the five-to-one ratio. Right now, based on that ration, the highest possible salary is $84,240. Jeff Furman says the ratio helps screen employees — new hires come already knowing they won't get rich and, presumably, having already accepted the company's broader mission. Ben feels the ratio helps the company more fully recognize the role of the workers who actually make the ice cream. If managers want more money, fine, but first raise the lowest salaries. He believes many companies pay their executives far too much money.

There is broad agreement at Ben & Jerry's with the underlying concept. But the ratio rankles some managers. Chico doesn't like it. He says it makes recruiting difficult. Allen Kaufman, for example, declined three job offers from the company, until his own financial condition improved enough to allow him to accept the salary Ben offered. Of the first salary offered — $50,000 — Kaufman says: "It was a joke." Rick Brown director of sales, figures he's making 60 percent to 70 percent of what he could make elsewhere.

Jim Rowe, director of retail operations, flat-out rejects the ratio. "I, for one — I'm materialistic. I realize other people aren't that way. I'm also a career person. I'm an expert at what I do. I've trained for years and years and years. I don't think a five-to-one ratio recognizes that." Meanwhile, some of the people to whom Rowe has sold franchises are making well over $100,000 a year.

Rowe questions, too, the need for everyone to be weird. "I don't claim to be that way," he says. "I claim to have a talent in a different area that's also needed by this company."

This is the kind of thing that worries Ben Cohen. He worries that his managers see the company's existing social programs — The Ben & Jerry's Foundation, for example — as fulfilling its mission and that no new programs are needed; that they've grown fearful of undertaking risky projects; that they see any project that does not optimize profits as being unworthy of pursuit. "Some people feel the company's first goal is to make as much money as possible, and then spend it in a socially responsible way," Ben says. He does not agree. "I see those values as influencing the way the company does business in all facets, and influencing how it makes all its decisions."

In the old days, Ben kept himself informed and in touch through the monthly staff meetings. Employees would break into small groups, mull over a specific problem, then return with solutions. This was genuine two-way communication. But over time the meetings had changed — "degenerated," Ben says. They became one-way affairs with him talking at the crowd. Last September, after the production crunch, Ben brought back the old format to ask a simple question: what are the most pressing problems confronting us?

David Barash, director of human resources and corporate communications, spent a night helping Ben categorize the responses. He recalls: "It was like having this eight-ton dump truck back up and dump its load over you."

Whereas once employees had been privy to every decision management made, now they felt left out. No one knew what anyone else was doing. And where, by the way, was Ben & Jerry's headed. The employees, says Barash, were asking, "What are we? What do we want to be? Where do we want to go?" They complained about getting mixed signals regarding growth, the great Benlike debate. If anything, growth was accelerating.

By some accounts, Ben was stunned. Ben, however, says "elation" better describes his reaction: "I felt that we were on the track. The first step in making anything better is to identify the problems. That's what we had done. And we were about to start working on those problems"

Hulbert Outdoor Center, Fairlee, Vt. One by one, each of 18 Ben & Jerry's managers, including Chico Lager, climbs a ladder, then falls backward into the arms of fellow employees. this teaches trust. They break into two groups, blindfold themselves, are roped together, and set off across a field, trying to locate three big rubber tubes. This teaches teamwork. They all spend a night doing mind maps — tracing their heads onto a large piece of paper, then dividing the silhouette into four parts, asking four questions: What do you want said about you when you leave Ben & Jerry's? What are the three things you hold most dear? Who are the three people who most influenced your life? The three events? Each of the group then bares his or her soul; the talk is wrenching, heartbreaking — divorce. Vietnam, death. This builds a bond.

The retreat, indirectly, was Ben's doing. But can he live with the results?

Well before the big production crisis, Ben had begun feeling a need to tinker with the company and its structure. The company, he felt, should shore itself internally and, to do so, should simply stop growing. "I felt if we did not take the time to create an excellent organization, soon we would no longer have an excellent product."

Ben himself wanted to put more power in the hands of lower management. He also wanted to make life at the company more enjoyable for the staff. "Everyone was paddling away madly, individually, trying to bodysurf on this big wave; and we were all trying to stay in front of this wave so we would keep on getting carried along by it. And we were all going crazy. And I said, maybe it's time for us to stop trying to keep up with the wave, and take our time and build a boat. Once we had that boat built we could go anywhere we wanted."

This rekindled the great debate. Many managers believe the company has no choice in the matter; it must grow, both to survive and to fulfill its obligations. Says Kaufman: "My feeling is, the day the company went public, it committed itself to growth. The day it sold its first franchise, it committed itself to growth — because you're tying someone's future to how you do."

The company needs to grow to retain its position on supermarket shelves as competition increases. Richard Smith, for one, has no intention of halting the growth of Steve's Homemade while Ben & Jerry's considers the meaning of life in the '80s. Moreover, the market for superpremium ice cream is maturing. Last year, the market grew only 15 percent; in the four prior years, it grew between 25 percent and 30 percent annually. And there are upstart companies out there using the same maverick marketing tactics Ben and Jerry's used, for example, The Great Midwestern Ice Cream Co., based in Fairfield, Iowa. Before the Iowa caucuses, the company won nationwide publicity with its line of Presidential flavors, including Bush's Preppie Mint, Kemp's Quarterback Crunch, and Dukakis Massachewy Chocolate.

"Growth can't be stopped," says Chico Lager. "You can't say you're going to grow to a certain level and that's it. It doesn't work that way, not in the real world." Growth by itself can't kill culture, he believes. "It's a convenient scapegoat. You can say we can't grow because we're not going to be the same company we used to be, and we're not going to be a family. I don't agree with that. I say you can be every bit as much the company you used to be as you grow, *if* — I underline the word *if* — you pay attention to those issues and deal with them."

The board struck a compromise. Ben & Jerry's would continue to grow, but would devote a lot more effort to developing its internal organization. For this, the board hired a consultant, Philip Mirvis, a research fellow at Boston University's Center for Applied Science — in effect, an organizational therapist. His mission was to improve communications, help the board hammer out a statement of mission, and build a strong, unified cadre of managers. "The management team was fragmented all over the place," says Mirvis. "Everyone had very different perceptions of what Ben & Jerry's was and should be."

The retreat got Mirvis's program off to an unexpectedly fast start. By the end of the three days, the managers had traded dark secrets, gnawed the bones of long-dead skeletons. They'd acted in skits, one parodying Ben and his corporate philosophies. Rick Brown, Ben's opponent in The Great Belly Bounce, played Ben while a Greek chorus chanted, "Social responsiblity."

By design, Ben and Jerry stayed away — after all, they wanted to ease out of daily management. This would give the managers some elbow room and underscore the new separation of power. Ben and Chico were now members of the board, and Jerry was an unofficial member. All the others were management. Ben and Jerry, however, were invited to speak on the last evening, to pass the pipe of the corporate culture — two plump shamans telling tribal tales to their adoring warriors.

Ben and Jerry sat back and told the usual stories: why Jerry had left the company. Ben's theories about corporate responsibility. It didn't sit right. This was not what the Hulbert group wanted to hear. Wedded by confession, they expected more of the same. Self-exploration. Honesty. Spilled tears might have been nice.

"We'd been incredibly honest with one another." says Brown. "When Ben and Jerry showed up, I guess we expected an openness with them that we'd had with one another." Instead, it seemed, Ben and Jerry were intruding. "For the hour or so we were listening, we couldn't keep the same emotion. It sort of broke the spell."

Director of sales and marketing Allan Kaufman spoke first. Even though the first day of the retreat had been his first day on the job, he already felt close to the other managers. If Ben & Jerry's is so socially responsible, he asked, why was this retreat forced on everybody — people worked hard enough without having to leave their families for three days. Chico remembers Kaufman's challenge of the company rhetoric: "Ben, you didn't invent charity."

Others jumped in, first about the family issue, then about other matters. The managers wanted something more than the same old stories; they felt good, empowered, and wanted a new business vision. "We couldn't just tra-la anymore," says Diane Cadieux, director of franchise marketing. "We could tra-la, but we had to do it with business in mind."

Ben told how he'd rather fail at something new than succeed at something old. Later, Chico rose and said — as Ben remembers it — "Ben, that statement scared the shit out of me."

Ben calls that night a positive experience. Nonetheless, it played on his fear about growth, the potential damage growth could do to the moral pilgrimage of Ben & Jerry's Homemade.

Back in Waterbury, the management group continued to coalesce rapidly. The board of directors planned meetings with all the departments, starting with the franchise department, to hammer out goals and disucss the strategic role of franchises. A snowstorm, however, led most of the board members to cancel. The franchise department went ahead and met anyway. Why not? The management group was supposed to be making decisions; holding the meeting without the board would underscore management's independence. For the first time, a department had settled down for some strategic planning, "It was a great meeting," says Chico. "Up until then, it was probably the best meeting I'd ever been to."

The management group spent two more months building goals for the other department clusters as well, the most concentrated planning the company had ever done. And the board had not been involved; Ben had not been involved. In April, the managers presented the board with working drafts of their plans, all so businesslike and attuned to the bottom line.

But where was the rakish funk of times gone by? The board — meaning primarily Ben, Jeff Furman, and Jerry, who holds a nonvoting membership — reacted in a way no one had expected. Afterward, the managers felt a keen personal hurt.

Chico brought the news. A director as well as the senior officer of the management group, Chico straddles the divide and is said to have a "pronoun problem." When to use "we," when to use "they"? His sympathies, however, lies with management. The board, Chico reported, was concerned that management had not fully bought into the social agenda; that the company was becoming less creative, less ready to move on new ideas. Jerry, moreover, had suggested that perhaps Ben ought to have a separate budget so he at least could keep coming up with ideas. There was talk, too, of giving Jeff Furman a job as a kind of new-ideas czar. What the board was asking, Chico reported, distilling the board's own words, was, "Are you weird enough?"

Oh, rip out our hearts and grind them in the dust!

But after the hurt came compassion. Controller Milly Badger says the board's reaction was not so surprising, if you put yourself in Ben's shoes: "You've brought the company to where it is, and all of a sudden we're saying OK, you've done your job, now we'll do ours. We don't need you anymore."

Is Ben & Jerry's weird enough? By circumstance and necessity, the company has grown more corporate. For example, when the company went public, it automatically enceased itself in new restrictions and requirements. Milly Badger worries about the balance between the corporate and the weird. She cites the passing of the Cowmobile, a motorhome painted Ben & Jerry's colors and decorated with cows. It made its last national scooping tour in September 1987. (A previous Cowmobile burst into flames and was destroyed just outside Cleveland in 1986.) Now, Badger says, with evident dismay, the Cowmobile is going to be a museum piece, set out in front of the Waterbury plant and used as an ice-cream kiosk.

"What made us is Ben and Jerry going out there, being funky, being different," she says. "If we don't continue to do the things that made Ben & Jerry's, we're going to lose something."

What the company needs is to find a new balance. Diane Cadieux believes more structure will enhance the company's creativity, rather than dampen it, by giving people a break from fighting fires. The board and the managment group just aren't that far apart, she says. "My feeling is we're all talking about the same stuff. I don't think we're spending enough time together. They're getting all this very cold paper laid out like a business plan, and they're not really getting the feeling behind it."

Jeff Furman, who shares Ben's concerns, says there is nothing to despair about. "This is living, it's an organic thing here. It's got a lot of fluidity. Right now, everybody's huddled in their corners. The organizational consultant [Phil Mirvis] wanted it that way. There's a 'we' and a 'they' because we haven't gotten together yet."

That process is underway now, with the management group and the board meeting and talking. It is clear, however, that Ben & Jerry's can't go home again, and that what will emerge, regardless of the weirdness of the next decade's ideas, will be a more mature business — the last thing in the world Ben and Jerry ever expected back in May 1978, the last thing, for that matter, they ever wanted.

Jerry has made his peace. He is sitting in a booth at the Waterbury Holiday Inn, half a mile from the plant. The music coming over a speaker is kind of sad, something from an old movie, Jerry smiles: "The idea, I think, is to maintain the values of your culture and yet bring it along with you. I mean, you don't want to stay stuck in the past. The gas station we started in was an amazing place, but it is there no longer. It's a parking lot. You can tell me wonderful stories about the place — but tell me the wonderful story about what happened at the plant last month. I think our company will be changed. I think there's no doubt about that. It will be changed. We just have to make it a good change."

For anyone who's looking, there are plenty of symbols, metaphors, and artifacts to describe the evolution of Ben & Jerry's. The Belly Bounce, for example — Ben the visionary versus Rick the salesman. The T-shirt, designed to commemorate the company's 10th anniversary — "Be 10 again!" it cries.

And then there are the one-year hats.

It's Friday again, toward the close of the staff meeting, time for Chico to hand out Ben & Jerry's baseball caps to honor new employees who've completed their first year of work. Ben is absent, on an ice-cream mission to Thailand, so Chico calls for nominations for Ben stand-ins. He gets three, including Jim Rowe, who is wearing a tie and a trenchcoat and does not even have a beard. All three line up at the front of the room to the right Jerry. Chico calls out the names of the one-year employees, and each comes forward to shake hands with Jerry and the stand-in Bens. The applause for each is loud, the cheers warm and joyous; one man curtsies to Jerry, bringing down the receiving bay with laughter. Then Chico calls out another name and scans the room; no one responds.

Now Chico is trying to make out what a few people are saying through the din. And in a sense they're telling him once again, as if he needed to hear it, how much times have changed, how large and unfamiliar his big family has become. One hundred and fifty people jam the floor in front of him; father Ben is off in Thailand; Jerry is smiling his benign, slightly lopsided grin.

Chico again calls the name of the honored employee. At last, someone shouts, "She quit." "Retired early," another says. And Chico did not know it.

In summary

What was happening at Valley Video and missing at Campus Cafe may seem a bit clearer to you now. But probably not as clear as you would like. The information available to us from our personal experiences, knowledge of theories and assessments of self and others will be helpful as we strive to motivate others toward successful performance on the job. Perhaps most important is the commitment we saw from Pat Carrigan to make the workplace a setting where people can do their best and feel appreciated for it. Motivating others during periods of rapid change will not be easy. Employees may resist new technology. The old guard may not understand the Young Turks. Managers may see labor as adversarial. Success may breed bureaucracy and systems, where cooperation once got the job done. The twenty-first century manager's job is to be prepared for these circumstances.

Chapter 14

Gender and Race in the Work Place

The words you were hoping for are still ringing in your ears. "We are very pleased to tell you that you are the top choice for our management trainee program. Your excellent university performance and your articulate and enthusiastic interviews have convinced us that you are the kind of person who will lead our firm into the twenty-first century." The fact that it was one of the company's top executives that called with this news added to your feelings of pride and relief. The salary was better than you had hoped. The company's location was perfect. The company was a leader in the industry and was expanding quickly. You could easily imagine professional growth coming along very quickly. At this special moment, the beginning of a professional career, your possibilities seemed limitless.

We begin our examination of gender and racial issues on the job by focussing on the balance you will choose between your personal and professional lives. How might marriage or children affect the unlimited possibilities you envision in your professional future? Will the twenty-first century work environment give you the flexibility to live your personal life according to your values without restricting your professional advancement? For some, the prospect of a fully engaging professional life that is minimally impacted by marriage or family commitments is ideal. For other, partnership, marriage, children and all the related activities are essential for achieving personal fulfillment.

The following "Ready for Class" exercise raises these questions for you and allows us to survey how you and your classmates are expecting to handle this important issue. It asks basic questions about marriage, work, two-career couples, parent care or day-care. Please answer the following questions based on honest expectations of what you would like to see happen in your work and family life, and have them "Ready For Class."

Name _____

ID# _____

Section _____

Family and career attitude survey

Every worker must make important decisions regarding the balance of careers and family life. Please answer the following questions about your expectations of work and family life.[1]

	Yes	No
1. Do you plan to work full time throughout your adult life?	_____	_____
2a. Are you already married, do you intend to marry, or do you expect to become involved in an ongoing relationship with a significant other in your adult life? (If you answer no to Question 2a, go to Question 6.)	_____	_____
2b. Do you expect that your spouse will work full time throughout his or her adult life?	_____	_____
3. Do you plan to have children?	_____	_____
4a. Do you plan to take time off from your career or job to care for your children?	_____	_____
4b. Do you expect your spouse to take time off from his or her job to care for your children?	_____	_____

Your sex: Female _____   Male _____

5. If you answered yes to Question 3 and thus as you anticipate having preschool children to care for, rank the following alternatives from 1 (most desirable) to 10 (least desirable).

_____ Care is given primarily by mother

_____ Care is given primarily by father

_____ Primarily mother during work hours; primarily father after work and weekends

_____ Primarily father during work hours; primarily mother after work and weekends

_____ On-site day-care (at work)

_____ Shared care by mother and father at all times

_____ Private day-care

_____ State day-care

_____ Private baby-sitter (at home)

_____ Care by relatives other than mother and father

6. (Answer only if you said no to 2a.) If you do not intend to marry or become involved in an ongoing relationship, what other activities or responsibilities do you expect will take enough time and commitment that you will need to make some decisions about how to balance them with your career goals?

1. Adapted from S. W. Jacobson, R. Jacques and S. Morse, "Prisoners of Gender: Individual and Institutional Attitudes adn Behaviors; Sex/Gender Exercises for the OB Classroom." Presented at the Organizational Behavior Teaching Conference, Columbia, MO, June, 1989.

This chapter is about fairness in the work place. If we work hard and succeed, we expect to receive rewards and promotions commensurate with our contributions. Yet studies have shown that the limitless career opportunities envisioned by the new management trainee described earlier may be severely curtailed for significant segments of the work force. For many women, the mere *possibility* that they may bear children, and thus be temporarily away from the job, has contributed to company policies and customs that have limited their career advancement. Similarly people of color have seen limited professional opportunities because of long-standing discriminatory attitudes, fueled by inadequate educational and training opportunities.

One of the most important challenges you will face as a twenty-first century manager is to work toward eliminating sexist and racist policies and customs from your work place. You can begin to do this best by being aware of your attitudes and behavior and by influencing others to do the same. If the United States is to prosper in the emerging global economy we cannot afford to have anyone, especially women and people of color, relegated to jobs well below their capabilities because of their gender of skin tone. Beyond any economic justification for treating people fairly on the job we must simply remind ourselves that it is a core value of American culture to maintain justice for all. And fairness in the work place is a critical prerequisite to economic opportunity and personal self-esteem.

It is not easy to explore attitudes toward racial and gender issues, especially in the classroom setting.[2] Feelings of discomfort, guilt, confusion and anger are not uncommon. But if we fail to address this issue head-on, we risk leaving you, the manager of the twenty-first century, unprepared to welcome the contributions of a work force that will be increasingly comprised of women, immigrants and people of color. Your understanding of these issues and the awareness of your behavior and attitudes toward a diverse work force will help you work toward the goal of a fair and nurturing work place.

2. E. L. Bell, "Racial and Ethnic Diversity in Organizational Behavior Courses," *The Organizational Behavior Teaching Review*, Vol. 13, Issue 4 (1988- 89), pp. 56-67.

It is generally thought that in the 1980s women and minorities have made substantial gains in their attempts to become managers and executives in our nation's important corporations. But the statistics tell a different story. As of 1988, only one black person headed a Fortune 1000 company[3] and only two of Business Week's 1,000 companies were headed by women.[4] For women and minorities the top rungs of the corporate ladder have been restricted territory. While estimates show that about one-third of managerial positions have been filled by women[5] and 9 percent by minorities,[6] most of these positions have less authority and lower pay than those managerial positions held by white males.

Legal avenues to modify these unfair labor practices have been initiated by state and federal laws protecting equal opportunity for members of minority groups, women, people over 40 and differently abled individuals.[7]

Examples of such equal opportunity legislation are shown in Table 14.1

3. C. Leinster, "Black Executives, How They're Doing," *Fortune,* (Jan. 18, 1988), pp. 109-120.

4. J. Byrne and R. Baum, "The Limits of Power." *Business Week,* (Oct. 23, 1987) , p. 35.

TABLE 14.1 Legislation Promoting Equal Opportunity in the Work Place

Legislation	Date	Requirements
Equal Pay Act	1963	Requires equal pay for men and women performing similar work
Title VII Civil Rights Act	1964	Prohibits discrimination in employment on the basis of race, religion, color, sex or national origin
Age Discrimination in Employment Act	1967	Prohibits discrimination against persons ages 40-70 and restricts mandatory retirement requirements
Vocational Rehabilitation	1973	Prohibits discrimination against handicapped individuals
Affirmative Action Amendment	1977	Requires firms doing business with the federal government to make special efforts to recruit, hire and promote women and members of minority groups
Pregnancy Discrimination Act	1978	Prohibits discrimination against women affected by pregnancy

5. A. M. Morrison and M. Von Glinow, "Women and Minorities in Management," *American Psychologist,* Vol. 45, No. 2 (1990), pp. 200-208.

6. J. A. Leavitt, *Woman in Administration: An Information Sourcebook* (New York: Orys Press, 1988).

7. J. A. Pierce II and R. B. Robinson, *Management* (New York: Random House, 1989), p. 416.

8. Morrison and Von Glinow, loc. cit.

9. W. B. Johnston and A. H. Packer, *Workforce 2000: Work and Workers for the 21st Century* (Indianapolis, IN: Hudson Institute, 1987).

10. B. Betters-Reed and L. L. Moore, "Managing Diversity in Organizations: Professional and Curricular Issues," *Organizational Behavior Teaching Review,* Vol. XIII, Issue 4 (1988-1989), pp. 24-32.

While laws designed to discourage discrimination in the work place have been in place for years, discrimination remains rampant. In a recent survey of 12,000 workers, over 66 percent "reported sex discrimination and 60 percent saw signs of racism."[8] If you are a working woman or person of color these statistics suggest that the chances are high that you have been discriminated against on the job and that your talents have been underutilized.

Unless remedial action is taken, discrimination in the work place will accelerate. While 46 percent of today's American work force are native-born white males, demographic studies predict that between 1990 and the year 2000 only 15 percent of new labor force entrants will be native-born white males. The remaining 85 percent will be women, people of color and new immigrants.[9][10] The resulting dramatic shift in the composition of the work force will require firms to recruit, train and promote large numbers of these employees to fill positions previously held by white males.

Thus far, we have reported only the startling statistics, but more important to understand are the hurt, anger and fear caused by sexism and racism in the work place. For women or member of a minority group who has been leered at, passed over for promotion, ignored or discriminated against in any other way, the feelings do not go away and if left to fester can result in a chronic state of anger, helplessness and diminished self-worth that pervades one's work and family life.

Discriminatory practices toward women and minorities can be quite overt. Consider the case of sexual harassment, where a woman may be made to feel her job is in jeopardy if she does not give in to sexual advances. A minority member may be denied a promotion while a less qualified colleague who goes to the same church as the manager is promoted. Such incidences of overt discrimination are outrageous violations of fairness at work. They are also illegal and should be prosecuted. More pervasive, however, are the subtle forms of job discrimination. When women managers are consistently asked to take notes at meetings attended by both male and female managers or when their recommendations are ignored in favor of nearly identical suggestions from male colleagues, frustration and anger are aroused. When a person of color is not invited by colleagues to informal business lunches or is relegated to deal with minority issues in the organization, the expectations of support and acceptance from the firm are undermined. Some acts of sexism or racism on the job are imbedded in long-standing policies about pregnancy leave, child care, working hours, compensation and promotion. Other discriminatory actions occur because of ignorance and insensitivity.

Some of you have grown up in highly segregated environments where your experiences with people from other racial or ethnic groups have been limited. Similarly, young men who grow up in a family setting where the female members play a subservient role may enter the work force with an unenlightened view of the roles that women play when they are seen as equal partners.

The stories of Larry and Cindi illustrate the impact of discrimination on the personal and professional lives of its victims.

Larry Taylor recalled the words that had influenced him to accept a job as a fast-track entry level manager at his company. "You will be treated fairly here. We will make every effort to help you reach your maximum potential. We need your help to teach us how to bring qualified minorities into our firm." After some time on the job, Larry realized that actions are often more difficult than words. The last four years had been a series of difficult learning experiences for Larry and his company. As a new MBA from a top business school Larry brought prestige to the firm, and as a minority, he helped his company project an image of social responsibility and enlightened management.

But the truth was that Larry's acceptance in the firm had come slowly. His assignments often had a racial emphasis, serving on task forces that dealt with recruitment of minorities. His marketing talents so highly regarded during his graduate work were often overlooked by colleagues who sought Larry's opinion on issues of race. "How would blacks respond to a direct mail campaign?" they would query him. His persistent efforts not to be treated as a resident black, but as a marketing expert, finally began to bear fruit. It required all the emotional maturity he could muster not to become angry at his co-workers; he truly felt that their narrow perception of him came from ignorance more than prejudice. He realized that his efforts had begun to take hold when the officers of the firm and his co-workers celebrated his recent promotion by holding a luncheon in his honor. They highlighted his marketing achievements and then handed him a plaque listing "The 10 dumbest comments your colleagues have made to you since you arrived..." Heading the list was, "Your name is the same as Lawrence Taylor, that black football player on the New York Giants. Do you like football, too?" His response to that had been, "No." His colleagues had come a long way since then. But they still had a long way to go.

About the time 11-month-old Christine began to take her first steps, Cindi, her mother was getting her legs knocked out from under her. "It's not fair," she said with a mixture of anger and sadness. "That promotion was promised to me based on my top performance in all categories. But as soon as I mentioned that Christine needed a little brother or sister to complete our family I feel like the firm began treating me like a part-time employee. In many subtle ways I am not included in key decisions even though my productivity continues to be very strong." "What makes it all the more unfair," replied Mark, her husband, "is that except for the normal recovery period after Christine was a newborn you haven't missed a day of work. We knew all along that my software development job offered me the flexible hours to be Christine's primary care giver while you were at work. I don't see how you can stay with a company that discriminates against women for having children."

Whether discriminatory actions such as those depicted in the stories of Larry and Cindi are deliberate or unintentional, overt or subtle, they are detrimental to the work environment and injurious to their victims. Unfortunately, women and minorities face social and cultural barriers every day on the job.

Minorities and women must struggle to fit into two distinct cultural worlds: their world as a female, a minority, or both; and the white male world of corporate America. This phenomenon is called biculturalism.[11] Research on bicultural conflict has described the tension that black woman feel as they move between the unfamiliar behavioral culture of the dominant work group and the familiar culture of their home lives.[12]

While the minority male is already conversant with the male aspect of the dominant culture and the white female is a product of the dominant Caucasian culture, black females face the added pressure of trying to overcome both racial and gender barriers. Because white males have historically been the decision makers in organizations, the corporate culture is an expression of their values and thus they are generally spared significant bicultural tension. There are plenty of role models, mentors and traditions that favor their easy socialization into the organization.

To appreciate the cultural barriers women and minorities face as they seek equal treatment in the work place, white males might imagine how confusing it can be conducting business in a foreign country, where the customs differ and small social errors can offend. In foreign settings, one is often not fluent in the subtleties of language and protocol. The resulting uncertainties can undermine the effectiveness of an otherwise competent professional.

Women and minorities face these barriers regularly on the job. But they are not temporary visitors to a foreign culture. They are simply trying to succeed in a business environment that historically has been structured around the language and needs of white males.

There is reason to be optimistic that racial and gender bias on the job can be attacked. In recent years, several large firms such as Digital Equipment Corp., Xerox and Proctor & Gamble have established significant programs to learn how to manage diversity. These and many other organizations are committed to a fair work place that encourages women and people of color to work in jobs that are commensurate with their qualifications. They have embraced a number of remedial actions to accelerate this process including the following:[13]

• Increased child care assistance for greater work flexibility. Only 5 percent of U.S. companies help their employees with child care.[14] Only 18 percent of survey mothers are pleased with their child care arrangements.[15]

• Education and training to help managers work together in a diverse work force.

• Conflict resolution training specifically for women and people of color.

11. D. A. Thomas and C. P. Alderfer, "The Influence of Race on Career Dynamics. Theory and research on minority career experiences." In M. Arthur et al., eds., *Handbook of Career Theory* (Cambridge, England: Cambridge University Press, 1989).

12. E. Bell, *The Bicultural Life Experience of Career Oriented Black Women*, unpublished manuscript, (1988).

13. Morrison and Von Gilnow, loc. cit.

14. "For American Business, A New World of Workers," *Business Week*, (Sept. 19, 1988).

15. "Their Child Care," *The Wall Street Journal*, (May 24, 1988), p. 1.

• Working alongside a woman or person of color to decrease discrimination.

• Bonuses and incentives to employees who effectively recruit and manage women and people of color.

• Career management strategies to eliminate the "glass ceiling" for women and people of color. Challenging assignments in the mainstream of the organization including careful support from superiors.

• Mentors and role models. Successful women and people of color teach new employees how to succeed in the firm.

• Affirmative action programs. Planned special efforts to recruit, hire and promote women and minority groups. Can help put women and people of color into jobs previously unattainable. However, if women or minorities are hired only to meet affirmative action guidelines without organizational support, harmful outcomes can result.

As a twenty-first century manager, you must be ready for a changing environment where men wish to play a more active role in parenting and women are more committed to their careers than their male colleagues.[16] You must be ready to challenge the threat of perpetuating the inequities of the current work environment and use your creative energies to seize the opportunity by "building a new and more diverse work force and making it tick."[17]

16. G. Powell, B. Posner, and W. Schmidt, "Women: The More Committed Managers," *Management Review*, (June, 1985), p. 45.

17. "From American Business: A New World of Workers," *Business Week*, (Sept. 19, 1988).

Lights

There are many ways that discrimination is felt in the work place. The following two segments explore only two of them. Each one raises important questions about equal employment opportunities.

Camera: Segment 1

In this segment about the "Mommy Track" you will observe what it is like for a woman to be forced to choose between fast-track professional growth and significant participation in the life of her children. The segment is from Ted Koppel's *Nightline*. It aired on March 16, 1989.

As you watch the "Mommy Track" video segment we will ask you to imagine that as a follow-up to the video, Ted Koppel will ask you to comment on what you have seen. Koppel often asks the opinions of several experts with different viewpoints on the evening's topic. Be prepared. The studio lights are on and the camera is waiting.

Please choose one of the following perspectives from which to comment on what you have observed.

1. You are a male and the chairman of an executive search firm that has focussed on successful careers for women. What is your position on the "Mommy Track" issue?

2. You are a female and a pioneer in the feminist movement. What is your position on the "Mommy Track" issue?

You may choose either role regardless of whether you are a male or female.

Prepare for this exercise by looking at the results of your "Ready for Class: Family and Career Attitude Survey." Then get into groups of four — preferably with two males and two females or at least one of each sex in the group.

As a group, identify the important findings that emerge from your class's data. List them in order of importance.

-

-

-

What can you do as a twenty-first century manager to address these issues?

Camera: Segment II

In this segment from *The Oprah Winfrey Show* you will examine what it feels like to be affected by an affirmative action decision.

We would like you to put yourself into the shoes of these real individuals. You will see three examples:

- John and Oleta, school teachers

- Paul and Robert, police officers

- Jose, who handles affirmative action in a different way

Action

As you watch each segment, remember that affirmative action programs are deliberate efforts to increase the proportion of women and minorities in organizations when they are significantly underrepresented compared to their availability in the recruitment area.

Notice what is happening to each of the winners and losers. What are the advantages and disadvantages of winning? How effective can affirmative action programs be for solving racial and gender imbalance in the work place? Are there any similarities in the reactions of affirmative action losers? What are your feelings about affirmative action programs?

MIRROR TALK: FOCUSSING ON ME

Much of this module has focussed on barriers that women and people of color must overcome to achieve fairness at work. But the goal to be achieved by twenty-first century managers is to move through these barriers and gain an appreciation of their own racial and ethnic groups so that they can engage in cross-cultural dialogues. Ella Bell of the University of Massachusetts has observed that white students, because they are members of a dominant group, are not forced to think about themselves as a racial group and thus have a less clearly defined sense of their own racial identity.[18] Students of color, who have experienced an ongoing struggle for equal opportunity, have greater identification with their racial identity.

Bell suggests that students can use self-reflection to explore their own cultural roots and understand the experiences of other racial and ethnic groups. Let us begin considering your racial-ethnic heritage by asking the following questions:[19]

18. E. L. Bell, "Racial and Ethnic Diversity: The Void in Organizational Behavior Courses," *The Organizational Behavior Teaching Review*, Vol. 13 (4), (1988-89), pp. 56-67.

19. Adapted from E. L. Bell, loc. cit.

1. What does it mean to be a member of your racial or ethnic group? (Examples of such groups include White-Anglo-Saxon, Protestant, German-American, Irish-Catholic-American, Italian-American, Jewish-American, Afro-American, Asian-American, Latin-American.

2. What are the strengths and important values of your racial-ethnic group?

3. What is the price of membership in your racial-ethnic group?

What are the sounds, visions and feelings that are bubbling within you from our exploration of race and gender at work? Perhaps as a woman, you recall the feelings of anger when your ideas were not given full credit or when an insensitive colleague asked you to be the "secretary" at a meeting. Perhaps as a person of color you have felt excluded from the inner circle that was led by a group of white employees. Perhaps as a white male you recall erroneous stereotypes such that when you observed a well-dressed man and women in conference, you assumed that the man was the superior, when the reverse was true. Perhaps you have enjoyed a superb relationship with members of other racial groups or the other gender and take pride in your ability to work toward changing behavior in your school or work environment.

Please list your own impressions below.

- What did I see?

- What did I hear?

- What did I feel?

- What did I think?

- What will I do to make a difference? What is the most effective action I can take to reduce racial and gender bias? Your actions may be as simple as asking for feedback from co-workers about your behavior. As a woman or person of color it may require giving feedback to a colleague or superior. It may require talking with, including supporting and mentoring, those who would benefit from your attention. What will it be for you?

Managing diversity will require twenty-first century managers to understand what the problems are. A recent *Wall Street Journal* article, "Minority Women Feel Racism, Sexism are Blocking the Path to Management" describes some of these problems. The second article, "The New Old Boy" illustrates how changing social mores have modified the way that sexism is expressed on the job and offers strategies for dealing with it. The third article — "The Best New Managers Will Listen, Motivate, Support. Isn't That Just Like a Woman?" — presents Tom Peters' view of the place of women in the modern corporation. Finally, a *Newsweek* article, "Post Tokenism," illustrates some of the approaches used by top companies to manage diversity in their organization.

Discrimination on the job goes well beyond the narrow focus of race and gender described here. It often affects those who are older, fired or prematurely forced into diminished roles. It affects the physically handicapped or differently abled employee whose physical difficulties may be irrelevant for many jobs. It affects individuals who are overweight and do not fit a corporate stereotype. It affects those of nonmajority religious beliefs, whose social customs differ from the majority. Discrimination, sometimes fueled by the fear of AIDS, can also affect homosexual employees.

It is very difficult to be completely free of prejudice. People tend to favor those who share their political beliefs, social activities, language of origin. It is not uncommon to be less comfortable with those who differ from us. Even an accent from a different region of the country can elicit harmful stereotypes that result in discrimination in hiring and promoting. Corporations are losers when such discrimination leads to the advancement of individuals who are less capable of doing the job and less able to contribute to the diversity of ideas and opinions that comprise a healthy organization.

It is very difficult to legislate fairness. We challenge you to become a manager who leads the way for others by challenging inequities and bias even when it puts you at risk. Treating people with fairness and decency will help everyone in the long run.

Reading 14.1

Minority Women Feel Racism, Sexism Are Blocking the Path to Management[20]

By Keith L. Alexander

Minority women, suffering discrimination on two fronts, are making little headway breaking into management ranks of corporate America.

While white women complain about the glass ceiling that keeps them from the very top ranks, women of color are hardly present in the management pipeline. Faced with both racism and sexism, they're still struggling to land middle-management jobs. And they've made few inroads in entrepreneurial jobs, the refuge for those shunned in the corporate world.

Black women made up just 2 percent of managers in companies with 100 or more employees in 1988, compared with black men who accounted for 3 percent of this group and white women who totaled 23 percent according to the latest data available from the Equal Employment Opportunity Commission. Not one black woman was among the top 25 black managers in corporate America when Black Enterprise Magazine ran an article naming them in 1988.

Women of color — who accounted for 10 percent of the work force in 1988 — complain they are bypassed for promotions and relegated to staff positions that aren't on the fast track and are vulnerable to corporate streamlining. Moreover, they suffer from isolation, lack of mentors and stereotyping. Personnel executives sometimes call them "twofers" because they fulfill two equal opportunity employment obligations, and that label undercuts their credibility on the job.

20. *The Wall Street Journal* (July 25, 1990). Reprinted by permission of *The Wall Street Journal*, ©1990 Dow Jones & Company, Inc. All rights reserved worldwide.

'Doesn't Move You Up'

Being a "twofer" helps some minority women get hired by a company. But "being a twofer doesn't give you legitimization, doesn't give you a voice or power and doesn't move you up," contends Ella Bell, a University of Massachusetts professor who is studying more than 100 black and white women managers in companies throughout the U.S. "You're a showpiece," she says, and that "won't get you to be a general manager."

Those who do land management jobs find themselves constantly trying to prove that they can perform. "They feel they have to be 20 steps ahead in terms of being the best," Ms. Bell says. "They feel they have to outperform, outshine and outthink."

Consider 40-year-old Charleyse Pratt, who recently left Hyatt Legal Services to form her own consulting company in Cleveland after working at a number of Fortune 500 companies. "I've never been embraced in corporate America with open arms," she says.

At corporate meetings in previous positions, Mrs. Pratt was often the only minority woman — and the victim of sexual as well as racial slurs. She says she learned early in her career to develop a tough skin.

As an assistant personnel director at a Midwest electronics company, she gave seminars to senior executives on sexual and racial harassment. One day, after a four-hour presentation to 20 white males senior managers, one of the men, whose last name was pronounced "coon," stood up and said, "Do you mean the coons can't stick together?" All the men, including her boss, broke into laughter.

"I was speechless," recalls Mrs. Pratt. "It was the first time I was ever referred to as that." She coolly ended her presentation — and later "cried all the way home." (She reported the incident to a vice president, who temporarily suspended the executive who made the remark.)

More recently, at a Midwestern manufacturer, she was told outright that she was hired to meet affirmative action goals. And not long ago, she found herself teaching her job to a white man who had been promoted over her. "He told me, 'You're going to have to learn to subordinate yourself to me,'" says Mrs. Pratt.

Companies may be forced to promote more minority women into management in coming years, however, as the composition of the work force changes drastically and more minority women enter the labor market. By the year 2000, the number of black women in the work force is expected to total 8.4 million, up from 6.5 million in 1987, while the number of Hispanic women is projected to increase to 5.8 million from 3.4 million, according to Harbridge House, a Chicago consulting company.

Some companies are already making efforts to promote minority women into management. Companies making strides in placing minority women in these jobs include Corning Inc., Xerox Corp., International Business Machines Corp. and Digital Equipment Corp.

Race as a Barrier

"Right now there's a tremendous effort in corporate America to look at multiculturalism," says Bea Young, vice president of Harbridge House. Yet, many companies resist promoting minority women to positions of authority, she says, "because of the myth that no one will work for them."

Marriam Gonzales, manager of ethnic marketing and advertising for Kraft General Foods Inc. in Chicago, believes race is a bigger barrier than sex is in business. She has little difficulty, she says, establishing a rapport with customers and clients on the telephone. The problems occurs when they meet her in person. "They become standoffish," she says.

"I think some white people find it easier to deal with light-skinned Hispanics than darker-skinned Hispanics like me. I just wish we could be judged by our work and not our skin color," she says.

One of the success stories, Dorothy Turrell started at Digital Equipment Corp. as a management development manager in the Westminster, MA, plant in 1976. Five years later, after holding several staff positions, she was promoted to a much more visible, senior job as plant manager at DEC's Boston plant.

"I wanted that job," says the 45-year-old Mrs. Turrell, who says she has learned the importance of "being upfront" about her ambitions. But some companies are also more receptive to advancing women of color than others, she notes. "I realize I could be at another company and not be where I am now," she says.

Getting promoted, however, is only a small part of the battle. As a new plant manager — and the only black female to hold that job at DEC — Mrs. Turrell had to work hard to gain the loyalty of subordinates. Among other things, she elicited workers' opinion and relied on team management "instead of having all the answers myself." She still had to contend with some employees who felt she should have an advanced technical degree — rather than her liberal arts diploma — along with "20 years experience."

But for the most part, she won their support and respect — and another promotion. She's currently plant manager at DEC's Cupertino, CA, computer plant, overseeing 800 workers.

As a black woman, she says, "It's inevitable that you're going to be challenged and observed. In some cases, it's going to feel like every time you walk through the door, you have to be on." but she says she attained enough inner confidence so "I don't have to be perfect all the time."

While Ms. Turrell has advanced steadily through the ranks of DEC, other minority women say the only way they've been able to get ahead is by zigzagging from company to company. Thirty-eight-year-old Jacquelyn Gates, a personnel executive, started her career at J.C. Penney and has since worked at such companies as PepsiCo, Paramount, Revlon and Time. she is now manager of employment for New York's Nynex Mobile Communications Co.

She admits to being a "twofer" and says when she began her career, she used that label to get her foot in the door. "I'm certain I've received extra consideration because I was a black female," she says.

Once in the door, however, Mrs. Gates found herself with only a handful of minority women peers — and no mentors. The dearth of top black managers — let alone female black managers — makes it nearly impossible to find a savvy ally who has both faced the difficulties and blazed a trail.

"White women have to worry about penetrating the male network in corporate America. Black women have to worry about that and the white network," says Mrs. Gates. As president of the National Association of Negro Business and Professional Women's Clubs Inc., based in Washington, she herself serves as a mentor to younger minority women as they enter management jobs.

Will the twofer ideology ever end? Only slowly, says Harbridge House's Ms. Young. "I still hear jokes about hiring the black women to get two points," she says. "That's so demeaning — to hire someone because of her race and gender and not her qualities."

Reading 14.2

THE NEW OLD BOY[21]

By Annetta Miller and Pamela Kruger

He's your colleague, your equal, a post-liberated man. But compete with him and you'll find that this new dog knows some very old tricks…

By now the classic corporate good old boy — the cigar-chomping, backslapping type who said, with no shame, that women belong in the kitchen — is a nearly extinct species. Changing social mores, not to mention antidiscrimination laws, have made his blatant brand of sexism unacceptable.

The rising young male executive these days is a more enlightened breed: He was educated in a good coed school and talks proudly about his wife, the corporate lawyer. Of course, he would say, women should have the same opportunities as men, and he would think himself quite sincere.

That's why it comes as something of a shock when this man — who could be your peer, your subordinate or your boss — shows signs of some distinctly archaic attitudes. In the daily department meetings, he directs his conversation only to the men. Or he makes "kidding" remarks about your wardrobe or love life in front of a (male) vice president. Sometimes he'll flash you a patronizing smirk after you've made an important point.

Hardly worthy of an EEOC investigation — but that's what makes his behavior so insidious and why, in many ways, the New Old Boy is a more formidable obstacle than the old-style sexist pig. You can go for months working very well with him — until he feels threatened. Then he will use any weapon in his arsenal to fight back. That includes finding ways to tap into a lingering sexism and using it against you. "His methods are so subtle that some women may wonder if the behavior is intentional or if they are being overly sensitive," says Joyce Russell, PhD, an associate professor of management at the University of Tennessee in Knoxville. In fact, many women executives won't give a name to the problem for fear of being thought petty or paranoid.

But the New Old Boy exists. As Jonathan Schmidt, a 31-year-old editor at Alfred A. Knopf, put it, "There are men who know that it isn't acceptable to be sexist but who have found subtle ways of perpetuating the old-boy network." Adds Lynn Laurenti, a Fort Lauderdale, Florida, public-relations executive, "The old-boy network has a new name. It's called male bonding."

Boy Talk

The favorite bonding activities are games and sports, and women definitely are not welcome. At a Fortune 500 company's New York office, a sign in one of the engineering departments announced the "men's golf league." When a women scribbled, "What about women?" someone scribbled back, "Start your own." Last year an officer at a large Chicago financial services firm — an experienced golfer — tried to enter the company's annual holiday golf tournament. She was treated as though she'd asked to join the PGA. "They said, 'You're not really serious about playing, are you?'" she recalls. A 32-year-old male manager at a Connecticut-based Fortune 500 company occasionally hosted poker games at his home and invited only men from the company. Soon the games became a weekly ritual and included department supervisors. "They began talking about games at work, and it was clear they were discussing work issues during the games," says a female executive.

Were any of these women's careers hurt by the exclusion from "leisure" activities? They knew it would be hard to prove, so they kept quiet and resigned themselves to losing the extra opportunity to entertain clients or make contacts.

But some New Old Boy tactics are harder to let slide. One political reporter was invited to have dinner with a small group of high-level politicians — standard press-politician schmoozing — but she endured weeks of ribbing about her "flirting" and her "date" from colleagues who'd have killed for the same invitation. A Washington, DC, economics analyst has had to develop strategies for maintaining control of her presentations; though she's the expert at the podium, members of her mostly male audiences address questions to other men in the audience. And another executive, who recently lost 25 pounds, recalls how her New Old Boy associate constantly made derisive "jokes" about her weight loss. When they were having lunch with a client and the client ordered a low-calorie meal, the associate said, "You know, Susan has been dieting lately. She used to be a real porker."

21. *Working Woman*, (April, 1990). Reprinted with permission from *Working Woman* magazine. Copyright ©1990 by NWT Partnership.

Lip Service, Gut Reactions

These moves obviously are meant to put women in their place. They are powerful and difficult to counter because they tap into widely shared, deeply held assumptions about female and male roles.

Although polls in the 1980s consistently reported that men have a positive attitude toward female professionals, a 1988 study suggests that men's unconscious attitudes toward women manager have changed little in the past 15 years. Madeline Heilman, PhD, of New York University and Caryn J. Block, PhD, of Columbia University surveyed 268 male insurance-company manager about how they perceive female and male managers; the results closely paralleled those of a similar 1973 study, which suggested that men considered women to have fewer of the qualities of successful managers. "Men, like women, have intellectually changed their views of what's appropriate in the workplace, but it's going to take some time before our emotions and behavior match what we want to believe," says Kathy E. Cram, PhD, an associate professor of organizational behavior at Boston University's School of Management.

The New Old Boy may receive from the old boys in upper management cues that he doesn't have to be completely fair to women in order to get ahead. A male financial analyst at a Fortune 500 computer manufacturer, for example, recalls a meeting during which the group needed copies of a particular document in a hurry. The highest-ranking executive there, a male, turned to the sole woman at the meeting and asked her to make the copies. She complied — and soon found that the other, younger men in the office began to burden her with similar requests.

The New Old Boy also may get tacit reinforcement for expressing stereotypical attitudes. The old boys who are still in the executive offices are quick to believe a New Old Boy when he says that a female colleague is indecisive or flirtatious — and young male colleagues may wonder whether there isn't some truth to the characterization.

How to Outwit Him

Smart female executives have developed their own strategies of outwitting the New Old Boy. Most agree that confronting him with his sexist behavior should be a last resort; you're almost certain to run into denial and perhaps also outrage.

What can you do? "You have to nip it in the bud," says the economics analyst. "If you don't set the rules from the beginning, you lose control." When she gives a presentation and a man in the audience addresses a question to another man, she waits courteously for the response. Then she takes control: "I say, 'What he just said is very interesting. But I actually have expertise in this area. And I know...'"

Mary Quinlan, an advertising sales manager, also advocates an active approach. "Just because some men act like their fathers, we don't have to act like our mother," Quinlan says. No New Old Boy can exclude Quinlan from sports talk; she's become a football fan for this very purpose. Once, she was having coffee with her male boss and a male client when the boss said to the client, "Oh, we haven't even talked about the 6 and 0 and 5 and 1. Sorry, Mary," he said, turning to Quinlan, "this is boy talk." Quinlan replied coolly, "Well, I know the 5 and 1 refers to the Jets. But both the Bears and the Giants are 6 and 0. Which one do you like?" she asked the client.

The boss never tried that ploy again.

And what about when the New Old Boy makes "innocent" jokes that actually are condescending remarks meant to put you in your place? Sometimes, women managers say, the best response is an icy comeback. After a consultant chastised her male subordinate for not producing work she wanted, he put his arm on her shoulder and said, "Those deadlines are crazy. After this is all over we'll get you a massage." She replied evenly, "I don't need a massage. What I need is for you to produce this work on time."

When all is said and done, you can outwit the New Old Boy, but can you change him? His female colleagues have their doubts. "If you said to an old boy that he was a sexist, he'd say, 'Damn straight.' But if you said that to one of these young guys, he'd just get defensive," says Quinlan. Perhaps, she adds, if you took him aside and had a talk with him he might glean a bit of insight into himself and be embarrassed.

But he'd probably forget it as soon as he had a beer with his buddies.

Still, there's hope: In the next decade the New Old Boys' base of support will erode rapidly. Their high-level conspirators — the men in the executive suite who are in their 50s and 60s — soon will retire. And two-thirds of new workers will be women. Ultimately demographics — with a help from smart women — will force the New Old Boy to grow up.

THE BEST NEW MANAGERS WILL LISTEN, MOTIVATE, SUPPORT. ISN'T THAT JUST LIKE A WOMAN?

By Tom Peters

Gone are the days of women succeeding by learning to play men's games. Instead the time has come for men on the move to learn to play women's games.

It's perfectly obvious that women should be better managers than men in today's topsy-turvy business environment. As we rush into the '90s, there is little disagreement about what businesses must become: less hierarchical, more flexible and team-oriented, faster and more fluid. In my opinion, one group of people has an enormous advantage in realizing this necessary new vision: women.

Hierarchy is out. The new organization will be a network of some sort: Spiderwebs and Calder mobiles are among the metaphors gaining widespread use. "Down with walls, up with relationships" is the wise firm's battle cry, from Detroit, Silicon Valley and Wall Street to Osaka and Dusseldorf.

The Firm is no longer the center of the universe. A company is conceived of only in relationship to outsiders of any size, from anywhere — customers, customers' customers, vendors, vendors' vendors, middlepersons.

The team always comes before the star. Work teams dot the office and factory floor. Ad hoc, cross-functional teams that completely disrespect all boundaries do almost all of an organization's day-to-day work. The Ford Motor Company has even gone as far as adopting the slogan "No More Heroes" to underscore its new, participative management style.

The new job is never done. Constant improvement and perpetual

22. ©1990 TPG Communications. First appeared in *Working Woman*, pp. 142-217, vol. 15, September 1990.

change are the winner's watch-words. "We eat change for breakfast," chortles Harry Quadracci, president of the stellar Wisconsin printer Quad/Graphics. "Our employees see change as survival."

Process is at least as important as result. Emphasis on the "lifetime value" of a customer, as superstar Connecticut grocer Stew Leonard calls it, replaces the focus on today's sale. This is also true for vendors: Relationship and partnership, not adversariness and nickel-and-diming, drive the most effective producer-supplier couplings.

Values dominate rules. In a fluid, hypercomplex, relationship-based environment, little can be specified ahead of time. Underscoring key values, constantly improving skills and learning to love changes (and a willingness to change the shape of the task or organization almost daily) mark the new-look winners. Long lists of rules and detailed procedural policies become counterproductive in such circumstances.

Voluntarism underpins the company's pact with every employee. In the new brain-based economy, "value added" comes from the head, or the collective head. Bricks, mortar, lumps in general and muscle are out. Brains are in. "All our assets walk out the door at 5 PM," more than one executive has sighed. Inducing workers to commit their heads to improvement every day — by definition a voluntary commitment — is the very essence of the new leadership task.

Employee empowerment determines managerial success. In a fluid world with little or no hierarchy, those closest to the action *must* have the technical and psycho-

logical support to get on with the job — unsupervised. Managers with a great need for control are tomorrow's dinosaurs. Trust, care and information sharing have swiftly become managerial survival requirements.

Teamwork leads to success. The value-adding project is the company's alpha and omega. Those with a talent for creating and participating in such team-based tasks — almost all of which will cross old organizational boundaries and demand the breaking of old rules — will be valued. Those with shortfalls in team-project skills are little use to _any firm in _any job.

Lovers of ambiguity shine. Forget yesterday's placid and predictable environment. Those who can cope with ambiguity — or, better yet, thrive on it — will make their mark. Those who can't face a rocky road.

On the one hand, this list hardly constitutes normal practice in most firms in this country. One the other hand, it is no fantasy. The best new firms, and numerous bits of old firms, already exhibit these traits. Moreover, almost all companies are at least attempting to move in this direction.

These new principles are the chief reason I'm so excited about the publication of Sally Helgesen's *The Female Advantage: Women's Ways of Leadership* (Doubleday). The women-in-management idea finally is moving from defense to offense (to use a tired male metaphor).

Helgesen was influenced greatly by the Canadian organization expert Henry Mintzberg. He set a century's worth of management thinking on its ear in 1973 with *The Nature of Managerial Work* (Harper & Row), by being the first researcher to pay

exclusive attention to what successful managers actually *do*. Their days
were punctuated not by "strategic
planning," "delegating" and "decision making." but by an endless,
framented stream of microevents
that the best of them stitched into a
meaningful tapestry.

Sally Helgesen chose to mimic
Mintzberg and examine the minute-
by-minute working lives of four
successful women executives:
former Girl Scout chief exective
Frances Hesselbein (management
guru Peter Drucker has called her
the best manager in America),
Denver contractor Barbara Grogan
(president of Western Industrial
Contractors), Ford Motor Company
exec Nancy Badore (an old friend of
mine, which made the book all the
more credible for me) and media
mogul Dorothy Brunson (president
of Brunson Communications).
Though Helgesen found some
simililarities between Mintzberg's
top males and her stellar women, she
also found a host of startling
differences.

Mintzberg's chief revelation was
the choppy nature of the executive
day. But while even his best bosses
were put off by the perpetual
interruptions, Helgesen's exemplars
see the same interruptions as natural
and fruitful. A man's annoying
interruption is a woman's sparkling
opportunity to work on cementing a
relationship with an insider or
outsider, to say thanks or otherwise
show respect for a valued subordinate.

Women also tend to put relatively
more emphasis on the long term
(Helgesen calls it "the ecology of
leadership"). This doesn't mean that
Helgesen's women have more or
better long-range plans. Rather, they
tend to see things in a larger, longer
context.

The Girl Scouts' Hesselbein
pictures herself as part of a continuum that links past, present and
future. Helgesen also notes that
Dartmouth business-school professor Leonard Greenhalgh finds
women to be better negotiators than
men. That's because men focus on
wins, losses and competition.
Women "treat negotiation within the
context of a continuing relationship," trying especially hard to make
the other party a winner in its own
and the world's eyes.

Helgesen's successful women are
much more apt than Mintzberg's
men to see themselves in the middle
of a tightly spun web. The women
emphasize closeness to, rather than
distance from, other members of
their team or department. They
practice inclusion rather than
exclusion. They are far more willing
than men to distribute and share
information. (Hoarding information
was a pronounced characteristic of
Mintzberg's male execs.)

Perhaps least surprising, but no
less potent because of that, women
tend not to make distinctions
between their jobs and lives. The
two are viewed as seamless. Values
of nurturing and caring lived in one
context (life) are naturally carried
over to the other (business). Again,
this is especially important today,
when relationships, teamwork and
value-driven management are
imperative to success. Mintzberg's
men at work — and this is probably
not surprising to women — literally
did not mention family from one
week to the next. Ouch.

Sally Helgesen is blunt: "What
business needs now is exactly what
women are able to provide." I could
not agree more wholeheartedly. To
make the statement, of course, is not
to say that women's so far slippery
ascent to the corporate pinnacles
(the hierarchy, subtle or on the
organizational chart, is still there in
most cases) is suddenly going to
become easy.

For one thing, men have begun to
wake up to the new needs, even if
they are clumsy in general at dealing
with them. Second, this is not,
though I have so far painted it so, a
story about black and white styles

— one good, one bad. There is a lot
to say for a new leadership mode
that blends the most useful male and
female talents.

When pressing my point with a
Silicon Valley corporate observer
recently, I got the following response: "All right, let women run
the companies about 90 percent of
the time. But when a bet-the-
company gamble is called for,
maybe that's the time to bring John
Wayne back for a cameo appearance." That overstates the case, to be
sure, and is hardly operational
anyway. On the other hand, traditional male impatience and abrupt-
ness still may have their place.

Helgesen herself talks of combining styles. She contends that her top
women executives do just that: They
are fully in control and insist upon
results, even though they go about
achieving control and results in
markedly different ways than most. I
buy her reasoning up to a point.

The fact is, as Helgesen and
many others before her have pointed
out, men and women do take
different approaches. Each can learn
from the other. But the trendy
androgynous manager of a few years
ago, male or female, is a myth, a
delusion and a trap. We've suffered
far too much utopian, "be all things"
advice. Sounds great, but by and
large it won't fly.

The greatest value of Helgesen's
book is that it puts a critical stake in
the ground at a critical moment. All
four of her champions took pleasure
in being women and in taking
advantage of their natural strengths
in an unabashed fashion.

There is, I believe, a female
advantage.Arguably it is becoming
more obvious each day. I hope that
Sally Helgesen's pioneering work
will give a few more women the
determination to "damn the torpe-
does" (as the very macho Admiral
David Farragut put it at Mobile Bay
on August 5, 1964) and do their own
thing. We males — and society at
large — will benefit if they do.

Reading 14.4

PAST TOKENISM[23]

By Marcus Mabry

Recently top managers at Ortho Pharmaceutical surveyed their black and female employees. To their dismay, they found that most of them were in positions beneath their qualifications. "It would be the same if we had a piece of equipment that was only producing 80 percent," says Conrad Person, human-resources manager. Eager to get a greater return on its investment, Ortho hired a consultant to learn why minority workers weren't advancing. The conclusion: bias. Today, all Ortho executives and most employees have gone through workshops designed to help understand on-the-job "diversity." A diversity advisory committee and a cooperative program for minority students have been created. Person says his company had no choice: "If you want to exclude women and people of color, you are going to have to look harder and longer to find the people who can be successful in your organization."

Ortho isn't alone. Businesses from oil companies to white-shoe consulting firms are beginning to respond to the demands of "Workforce 2000," the new buzzword for a labor force that is gradually being transformed by women and minorities. According to the U.S. Department of Labor, native white men now account for only 45 percent of America's 117.8 million workers. Over the next few

years, that share will decline to 39 percent. Only 15 percent of people entering the work force from 1985 to 2000 will be white men. Corporate America is beginning to realize that to make the most of nonwhite workers, it must move past hiring goals and tokenism and learn how to keep, motivate and promote minorities as well. "Just from an economic standpoint," says one recruiter from Amoco Corp., "if we're going to attract and keep those employees we're all going to have to change our attitude."

Not everyone is embracing the new talk of "diversity management." Some companies feel they don't have the time or money to give to sensitivity training. Others worry about alienating white male managers. Still others don't feel that the demographic changes will hit home. "I've heard things like 'we're in upstate New York and the population there is still pretty much white'," says Taylor Cox Jr., assistant professor of organizational behavior at the University of Michigan. Still, more and more companies are taking the challenge seriously. Over 1,000 organizations have bought consultant Lewis Grigg's seven-part video training series on "valuing diversity." Honeywell has stepped up efforts to recruit the best minorities on college campuses. Pillsbury has created a "vice president of cultural diversity and personnel development." Both those companies and others are also trying to make the new hires more comfortable and productive once they're on board. Says Ted Williams, affirmative-action compliance manager at US West, "As we compete for the best and the brightest among women and minorities, we start looking at them as assets and not as problems."

Companies usually start the learning process by hiring consultants to conduct "diversity seminars." Session leaders aim to show how subtle biases affect the level of support minority workers receive, as well as their prospects for advancement. Even people who thought they had no preconceptions learn something. After a three-day session at Ortho Pharmaceutical, manager Tracy Stanko says she "was embarrassed and pained to learn that I do bring some prejudices into the workplace." Stanko realized that she tended to see articulate black executive as exceptional, while she took intelligence in whites for granted.

'Pluralism councils': Digital Equipment Corp. is a leader in diversity training. As part of a company-wide "Valuing Differences" program, it organizes hundreds of "core groups," or small interracial discussion sessions aimed at airing grievances and improving understanding. "The outcome of those groups gets translated into policy- related work," says Digital spokesman Alan Zimmerle. Avon, the cosmetics giant, supports minority-group "networks" that can get the ear of upper management. US West runs "pluralism councils" in 14 states and also brings together employees in "celebration workshops" to eat ethnic foods, watch tribal dances and participate in other activities aimed at increasing awareness of various cultures.

Many companies don't just want to teach whites how to manage nonwhites better; they aim to give minorities the tools they need to move into management. McDonald's runs special "black career development" seminars. One goal, says affirmative-action director Pat Harris, is to "teach [black employees] how to identify and manage their 'black rage'" — the tendency to see any conflict or criticism as the result of racism. Al Bodero, a Hispanic product manager at Pacific Bell in San Ramon, CA, says Pac Bell's "efficacy training" taught him how to "redefine and use friction." When his white male boss commented that a female Hispanic manager would not get as far as her white counterpart, instead of accusing him of perpetuating stereotypes, Bodero sat him down for a quiet talk. The training helped give Bodero the "people" skills he needed to move up. "I knew how to put my nose to the grindstone," he says, "but networking was a skill I learned as part of efficacy training."

Finding mentors: Although most companies resist pressure to set precise quotas for minority promotions, some have had success with broad goals. In the 1970s, Xerox executives identified key positions across the company that they hoped to fill with minorities. As time went by, they refined the promotion process, creating targets in each of the company's job grades. Today 26 of Xerox's 270 vice presidents are black and the firm boasts one of the highest-ranking black executives in a major, white-run corporation, A Barry Rand, president of the U.S. marketing group.

Other companies have had success with "mentoring" — matching new hires with veteran employees, often of the same gender or ethnic group. Proctor & Gamble implemented an "Onboarding" program after a company study found that white men were quick to adjust to the corporate culture while minorities, particularly women, were slower. James Lowry, head of his own consulting firm, learned the value of mentors while he was an associate at a major Chicago-based company. After being sent to Tanzania on a project, Lowry complained to his boss that the assigning partner was deliberately trying to make him look bad. His boss replied, "Then I suggest you show him he's wrong." That's just what Lowry needed to hear. "I turned that project around," he says. "So often, if a black is blowing it, the white manager is afraid to tell him. The camaraderie and mentorship don't carry over between the races."

Some corporate leaders are intervening before Workforce 2000 even leaves grammar school. IBM funds bilingual education programs in schools across California and Florida. "Education is the key to success," says Mario Sanabria director of affirmative-action programs. Over the past decade, Big Blue has also earmarked an increasing amount of its education funding for minority schools. Says Donald Bush, a vice president of Harvard Industries, the manufacturing company, "American business is going to have to make a commitment to basic education and training."

Harvard is a good example of the demographic forces propelling the new management trends. It had tried newspaper ads, radio spots, employment agencies, even telemarketing to recruit skilled workers for its Farmingdale, NJ, electronics plant but it could only muster a skeleton crew. "All of the normal means of developing a pool of applicants dried up," says Harvard's Buss. Finally the company went directly to inner-city minorities. It set up an employment office in a vacant storefront in the nearby city of Asbury Park. Soon all the positions were filled. "Our survival [was] at stake," says Bush.

Less hard-pressed companies aren't always ready to go to such pains to find and motivate minority workers. Cost is one obstacle to diversity training: programs can run to six or seven figures. During a cash crunch last year, Avon placed a temporary moratorium on workshops and eliminated its diversity-coordinator position. Another sticking point is the potential resistance or resentment of some white men. "They need to understand that they are a valuable resource in this process, and none of them [stand to be] fired as a result of managing diversity," says Elsie Cross, head of her own Philadelphia consulting firm.

Yet companies that don't commit resources to making better use of minorities may pay a bigger price in the long run. "They will experience higher rates of turnover, differences in productivity and absenteeism," says Professor Cox. "They will sacrifice enormous benefits in problem solving, creativity and marketing to a diverse marketplace." A growing number of executive agree. "Unless [companies] take pro-active steps, they'll be behind the eight ball," says Bob Beavers, a black senior vice president at McDonald's. U.S. companies that learn how to understand differences at home may also gain an edge in doing business overseas. As Dallas consultant Thomas Raleigh puts it, the need for diversity management "isn't based on morality and being nice. It's based on sheer, raw economic necessity." And that's the only incentive that American business has ever needed.

Chapter **15**

Entrepreneurs

Me? an entrepreneur? No, I don't fit that. I break all the rules. I'm unconventional. I kept my board small — a little autocracy. I talk and talk and talk. I cajole and persuade and enlist possible supporters. I'm continually thinking of new strategies. I work around the clock. I worry and pace... Besides, I'm trying to promote and sell programs we've developed and get some commitment to the values by putting together the skills and resources needed. No, I'm no entrepreneur.[1]

Dreamers and rebels can accomplish great things, but they are not always neat and orderly.[2]

It is better to ask for forgiveness than to seek permission.
 — One of the Intrapreneur's Ten Commandments.[3]

1. Ken Hemmerick, Executive Director, British Columbia Humane Society, in conversation with Fiona Crofton.

2. Ted Rogers, Rogers Communications Inc., *Macleans*, (October 29, 1990), p. 53.

3. Gifford Pinchot III, *Intrapreneuring*, (New York: Harper and Row, 1985).

The term *entrepreneur* refers to the person who both owns and runs a business. In recent years such people have started many successful, visible companies. Apple Computer, for example, was started by Steven Jobs and Steve Wozniak back in the 1970s when they were making computers for themselves and their friends in the Homebrew Computer Club. The Body Shop International was started in the United Kingdom by Anita Roddick. Ben and Jerry's Inc., was founded by Ben Cohen and Jerry Greenfield. And Mrs. Fields Cookies, which was discussed in the chapter on operations and control, was started by Randy and Debbie Fields.

Countless other organizations, large and small, also had their beginnings in the dreams and rebellions of entrepreneurs. The U.S. automobile industry, for example, was essentially started with the ideas and energies of Henry Ford. In every era, many enterprising individuals are seeking new ways to do things that eventually define a field, a service or a product. Some ventures make it; others do not. What are some of the characteristics of successful entrepreneuring?

According to one writer, "The entrepreneur is a person who not only sees business opportunities, but is willing to take the risk and make the effort to make them happen. Entrepreneurs tend to be independent, self-reliant individuals with a high need to achieve. Most small businesses are started and run by such persons."[4]

There appear to be some distinctive characteristics of entrepreneurs. Entrepreneurs tend to indicate an interest in this activity early in life; do not enjoy working for other people; frequently come from families with a tradition of self-employment and do not delegate easily to others or retire readily.[5] Bill Paley, the driving force behind CBS, twice fired individuals who were his apparent successors. He stayed on as head of CBS for many years beyond his expected retirement dates.

Entrepreneurs tend to be independent, to have a high need for achievement, strong drive and a capacity to spend long hours working toward their goals.[6] They tend to be willing to take risks and engage in ventures others might even consider reckless. However, evidence from psychological testing, observation and interviews with entrepreneurs suggests that they are not reckless. They often have figured the odds, covered their bases and organized their efforts so that risks are reasonable rather than extreme.

Entrepreneurs usually focus on the positives and on the probabilities of success rather than on the chance of failure. Warren Bennis has coined the term "the Wallenda Factor" to describe a quality of individuals that links to this positive focus on entrepreneurs.[7] Bennis interviewed people who were organizational leaders in their respective fields and noted that in virtually every case they responded to failure in memorable ways. He noted that the word "failure" was never used. They didn't even think about it as a condition, instead they relied "on such synonyms as *mistake*, or *glitch* or *bungle* or countless others, such as *false start, mess, hash, bollix,* or *error*. Never *failure*. One of them said during the course of an interview that "a mistake is just another way of doing things." Another said "I try to make as many mistakes as quickly as I can in order to learn."[8] The term Wallenda Factor came from a phrase and an attitude of Kurt Wallenda, a world famous tightrope aerialist. He apparently said, "The only time I feel truly alive is when I walk the tightrope." His energies were devoted to walking the tightrope rather than *not falling*. His wife, discussing his death in 1978 in an attempt to walk a 75 foot high tightrope in downtown San Juan, Puerto Rico, observed that it was the most dangerous feat he had attempted. She said he spent the three months before the walk preoccupied with falling, "Something he had never even thought of before."[9]

4. Steven H. Applebaum et al. *Contemporary Canadian Business*, (Toronto: Holt, Rinehart and Winston of Canada, Ltd, 1987), p. 113.

5. William F. Glueck, *Instructor's Guide for Management*, (Hinsdale, IL: Dryden Press, 1977).

6. Applebaum et al., op cit.

7. Warren Bennis, "The Wallenda Factor," *New Management*, 1,3 (1986), pp. 46-47.

8. Ibid, p. 46.

9. Ibid.

We should not focus exclusively on the personality characteristics of entrepreneurs, however. People with such characteristics may offer an early advantage to an innovative effort and are probably significant for startups of new, small organizations. However, in middle-sized and large organizations, entrepreneurial behavior is due in large part to the way the system is set up and operated. Organizations that reward innovative practices tend to get entrepreneurial behavior from a wide range of managers and employees. Establishing the context for innovation contributes to the outcome.

The Entrepreneurial Process

What are the characteristics of the entrepreneurial process itself? Your text will probably discuss this topic. We would like to provide here a brief outline of the key ideas on the entrepreneurial business, drawing to a large degree from an important book on this topic, *Innovation and Entrepreneurship* by Peter F. Drucker. Drucker is one of the most influential thinkers and writers on modern organizations and their management.

Large businesses can innovate and exercise entrepreneurial leadership. Examples that come readily to mind are 3M, which creates highly engineered products for industrial and consumer markets, and Johnson & Johnson, which is a leader in hygiene and health care products. Interestingly, middle-sized organizations are best suited to be innovative since they have the range of managerial competence and the necessary resources, particularly human resources, to create new ideas and to stay the pace to get them to market. In addition, they may not be weighed down by a large bureaucracy. Size of organization is not an impediment to entrepreneurship, but bureaucratic systems and procedures and conservative attitudes are. It is the way the organization is run that makes the difference.

To yield results, entrepreneurship requires hard work and plenty of practice. Innate creativity is less important than effort. Every product and service innovation requires a matching dose of administrative innovation. While creativity might be "ten percent inspiration and ninety percent perspiration," the issue is not simply a matter of working harder, it also involves working smarter. Innovation can occur in organizations where some people and systems are entrenched in the status quo and where some people see change as a threat to their self interests, their pet projects and their careers. Managers, therefore, must recognize the practical nature of activities and processes and create mechanisms to deal with them.[10] The politics of entrepreneurship are readily seen in the *Tucker* videoclip that accompanies this chapter.

The Entrepreneurial System Policies

Peter Drucker points out several aspects of entrepreneurial systems. Needed are policies that:

1. Make innovation the norm in the organization — the routine everyday way of doing things. It requires "a systematic policy of abandoning whatever is outworn, obsolete, no longer productive, as well as the mistakes, failures and misdirections of effort."[11] It is not necessary that managers give up entirely what they are doing but that what is being done is seriously questioned and examined periodically to see if it is relevant to the needs of the company and the customer. Drucker observes that "every organism needs to eliminate its waste products or else it poisons itself."[12]

2. Make the company "greedy for new things."[13] When managers and their staffs accept that everything they do and produce has a limited life expectancy, then there is likely to be a greater readiness to think about ending old patterns and searching for new ones.

10. Peter J. Frost and Carolyn E. Egri, "The Political Process of Innovation," in *Research in Organizational Behavior*, L. L. Cummings and B. M. Staw, eds. (JAI Press, 1991), pp 229-295.
11. Drucker, op. cit. p. 151.
12. Ibid, p. 152.
13. Ibid.

3. Provide the organization with a system or systems for gathering information that allows managers to define and decide on the degree, focus and time frames for their innovative activities. Given that innovative efforts include likelihoods of failures, the level of these efforts in the organization needs to be high to ensure that some successes are registered.

Entrepreneurial Practices

Drucker discusses several practices that increase the likelihood of successful implementation of entrepreneurship. Included among these are:

1. A vision, articulated by leaders in the organization that reinforce attention on opportunity. People see what is emphasized and overlook what is left out of management presentations and reports. Typically what is presented in management meetings and in written reports are the problems facing the organization. "What went wrong on this project! Why is this effort falling short of its target?" Attending to these issues will often consume the time and energy of the management group. Unless prime time is also cleared for discussing opportunities, it is an aspect of management that is not developed. Drucker describes the practice of one successful entrepreneurial business. It presents an operating report with *two* "first pages," one that lists problems, the other that describes all the areas in the company that are ahead of expectations. Both get discussed and acted on in management meetings.

2. Management practices that generate entrepreneurial spirit across the organization. This might come in company retreats or in other general sessions where successful innovations are examined and celebrated.

3. Meetings between senior and junior managers in which the more junior members of the organization raise issues, challenge existing practices and describe what they see as new opportunities for action. In some organizations, junior people are expected to develop working papers on the issues they raise in these meetings. The reports are presented at subsequent joint meetings of managers. Some of these reports lead to new product and service ideas.

4. Systems for measuring innovative performance that are built into the overall business controls of the organization.

5. Arrangements that separate new from existing ventures. New ideas often trigger the organization's "immune system" and the result can be the destruction and elimination of those ideas before they are strong enough to see the light of day. Some companies develop "skunk works" where the ideas are developed in relative isolation from the main sections of the business. Steven Jobs set up the Macintosh group in Apple this way. The product was created and produced in a physically separate section of the Apple organization.

6. Champions and sponsors. Individuals who are in charge of innovation projects play an important part in their successful completion. Such managers protect those engaged in the project from distractions and harassment and ensure that they get the resources they need for the job. Steven Jobs played this role for the Macintosh group throughout the development of that project.

7. Compensation and reward systems for the individuals and groups in the organization who take the entrepreneurial risks and get the job done. Such systems need to be custom made. It is difficult to create a routine package of rewards when the task, entrepreneurship, has such unpredictabilities in the way work is done, when the length it takes for completion and the impact of the product or service are so difficult to predict. 3M and Johnson & Johnson both have arrangements in which "the person who successfully develops a new product, a new market, or a new service and then builds a business on it will become the head of that business and general manager, vice president or division president, with the rank, compensation, bonuses and stock options appropriate to that level."[14]

These are some of the steps that companies need to take to inject and sustain entrepreneurship in their operations. Given that change is a fact of life for most managers in the 1990s and that this will continue into the next century, the only way organizations can survive is to increase their ability to innovate. As a society, we need people who discover and invent new ways of doing things as well as help us keep what is valuable from the present and the past. We need systems and structures of organization that enable these energies and events to take place.

14. Ibid. pp. 165-166.

Name _____

ID# _____

Section _____

We'd like you to reflect on your own ideas and feelings about entrepreneurship. What does "entrepreneurial" mean? What is an "entrepreneur"? Don't look at your text or a dictionary. What associations do *you* have with the words, "entrepreneur," "entrepreneurial" and "entrepreneurship"?[15]

1. You've been challenged to be an entrepreneur. What will you do? What ideas do you have?

2. Would you want to become an entrepreneur or would you prefer to be employed with
   (1) a large established firm or
   (2) with a smaller firm?
   Why?

15. This exercise was developed by Fiona Crofton for *Management Live: The Video Book*.

MIRROR TALK: FOCUSSING ON ME

Do you have the characteristics of an entrepreneur? Researchers have attempted to define the characteristics shared by successful entrepreneurs. John Hornaday, after years of surveys and interviews, developed a list of traits common to highly successful entrepreneurs.

The characteristics identified by Hornaday's research follow.[16] Rate yourself on each of the characteristics using a -2 to +2 scale as described below:[17]

16. These items were reported in J. A. Hornaday, "Research about Living Entrepreneurs" in Kent, Sexton & Vesper, *Encyclopedia of Entrepreneurship* (1982).

17. This exercise was developed by Fiona Crofton for *Management Live: The Video Book*.

-2   I don't really have this characteristic
-1   I don't have very much of this
 0   Neutral or Don't know
+1   I have this characteristic a little bit
+2   This characteristic is very strong in me

Entrepreneurial Characteristics[16]

	- 2	- 1	0	+ 1	+ 2
Self-confidence	——	——	——	——	——
Energy, diligence	——	——	——	——	——
Ability to take calculated risks	——	——	——	——	——
Creativity	——	——	——	——	——
Flexibility	——	——	——	——	——
Positive response to challenges	——	——	——	——	——
Dynamism, leadership	——	——	——	——	——
Ability to get along with people	——	——	——	——	——
Responsiveness to suggestions	——	——	——	——	——
Responsiveness to criticism	——	——	——	——	——
Knowledge of market	——	——	——	——	——
Perseverance, determination	——	——	——	——	——
Resourcefulness	——	——	——	——	——
Need to achieve	——	——	——	——	——
Initiative	——	——	——	——	——
Independence	——	——	——	——	——
Foresight	——	——	——	——	——
Profit orientation	——	——	——	——	——
Perceptiveness	——	——	——	——	——
Optimism	——	——	——	——	——
Versatility	——	——	——	——	——
Knowledge of product and technology	——	——	——	——	——

1. Once you've completed your ratings, think about a couple of your strong characteristics. Think about situations in which you have clearly demonstrated these characteristics.

2. Certain items on this list may not be descriptive of you. Would you want them to be? Why or why not?

3. What characteristics (if any) would you like to be more strongly a part of you?

MAKING CONNECTIONS: IN-CLASS INTERACTIONS

Entrepreneurs face various crises in beginning a new venture that can be aligned with stages of the new venture's growth.[18] These stages and crises can be outlined as follows:

Stage	Crisis
Pre-start-up	Planning crisis of development
Start-up	Cash crisis of operations
Early Growth	Capital crisis of expansion
Later Growth	Management crisis of delegation

(More detail on these stages and crises can probably be found in your course textbook.)

1. Form a group of four or five people. Have available the list of the characteristics provided in "Mirror Talk" exercise.

2. Review the list of characteristics. Consider how each characteristic can be helpful or a possible hindrance at the stage/crisis point your instructor has assigned for consideration.

3. Describe the ways each characteristic may be a strength or a weakness. Write your list on a flip-chart. Share your group's ideas with other class members.

18. This exercise was developed by Fiona Crofton for *Management Live: The Video Book.*

Entrepreneurs   **293**

Lights

The film *Tucker* tells the story of Preston Tucker, a man with a dream he wants to fulfill and give to the American people; a dream of a revolutionary car: the 1948 Tucker. It's a story that reveals the strengths and weaknesses often part of an entrepreneurial character and provides us with a look at the opportunities, threats and crises that are faced in a new venture.

"No chance," "It won't work," "It's not possible," are statements that seem to encourage rather than discourage Preston Tucker. "Is there anybody who can look me in the eye and say it can't be done?" he asks. There weren't many who would. They didn't look him in the eye and say it couldn't be done even though financing wasn't initially forthcoming; even though modeling clay was unavailable and designers had to go directly to steel; even though bids to acquire a steel production factory were disallowed; even though various parts could not be machined in time and substitution parts had to be scrounged from a scrap yard; even though "The Big Three" (Chrysler, Ford and General Motors) who had greater access to resources, services and capital, had limited their redesign efforts because of the scarcity of these essentials; even though the government restricted Tucker's access to material and resources.

Preston Tucker is passionate about his idea — it's new, it's innovative, it's progressive — and it's causing a stir in the industry. But the passion, creativity, enthusiasm and determination he had and encouraged in others, and even the response to the car itself, weren't sufficient to prevent the death of the Tucker enterprise. But even with the confirmed end of the Tucker car, Preston's last words are "It's the dream that counts."

Camera

1. Introduction to the film and Preston's military vehicle.

2. Preston has an initial (and unsuccessful) meeting to acquire financial backing.

3. Since financial backing is not initially forthcoming, Preston launches a promotional campaign through a magazine and the response is tremendous. His next meeting with a banker is much more positive but not without its conditions.

4. Tucker is informed that the "Big Three" need nine months for prototype development. Ever confident, Tucker says it can be done in 60 days.

5. Design and time problems are faced in building the prototype.

6. The unveiling of the Tucker car.

7. Tucker's designer and other employees are given new specifications from engineers "upstairs." Tucker's supporters try to speak to the board to discuss reasons for changes.

8. Preston Tucker returns from his promotional tour to challenge the board and discovers his lack of legal control.

9. A secret investigation has been conducted and Preston Tucker is charged with fraud.

10. The court case concludes and people gather outside the courthouse and are getting into the Tuckers lining the street.

Action

Consider the questions that follow and be prepared to discuss them as directed by your instructor.

1. Focus on Tucker the man:
   a. What strikes you most about him? What words would you use to describe Tucker?
   b. Describe Tucker's strengths and weaknesses as an entrepreneur.

2. Focus on the exchanges between Tucker and others:
   a. What does Tucker rely on most?
   b. How are his interactions effective or ineffective? Why?

3. Focus on the development of the Tucker Corporation:
   a. What opportunities, threats and crises occur in the process?
   b. Is there a parallel between the growth stages and the crises that occur?
   c. What things supported the development of the Tucker Corporation as a viable company? What interfered?

COMING TO OUR SENSES: MAKING A DIFFERENCE

 It's time to reassess your thinking and feelings about entrepreneurs, entrepreneurial endeavors and entrepreneurship. To do this, we think it's helpful to involve as many of our senses as possible.[20]

Find a space alone and spend some time reflecting on the following questions. People differ in the sense they rely on most to interpret their environment. Therefore, you needn't answer the questions in any particular order. If you tend to be visual, do that question first. If what you feel is the first point of connection, answer the feeling question first. If you think things out first and then go to feelings and create images, consider the questions in that order.

1. What thoughts do you have about entrepreneurs, entrepreneurial endeavors and entrepreneurship itself? What do these mean to you? Write a brief description.

2. What pictures do the words "entrepreneur," "entrepreneurial" and "entrepreneurship" evoke for you? Draw or describe them.

3. Are there particular sounds that you associate with the entrepreneur? What kind of music or sounds would you expect to hear as a backdrop to entrepreneurial activity?

4. What kinds of feelings do you have about entrepreneurs, entrepreneurial endeavors and entrepreneurship? Are they positive? Negative? Neutral?

5. There are probably aspects of entrepreneurship that you would like to pursue or develop in yourself. What actions will you take toward this end?

20. This exercise was developed by Fiona Crofton for *Management Live: The Video Book.*

We expect that in the future the rate of change will be even faster than it is today. Only those organizations that are able to innovate and to adapt will survive. Steven Jobs, a founder of Apple Computer, observed "Technological advances are coming at a rate that is far more ferocious than ever. To me, it's staggering to contemplate the tools we're going to be able to put in people's hands in the next few years."[21]

We agree with this prediction. We think it has implications for the way organizations will use technology. It will also be an important impetus for the way people bring their creativity and entrepreneurial drive to their organizational lives. In that same interview, Jobs also asserted:

> I think humans are basically tool builders, and the computer is the most remarkable tool we've ever built. The big insight a lot of us had in the 1970s had to do with the importance of putting that tool in the hands of individuals.

> Let's say that — for the same amount of money it takes to build the most powerful computer in the world — you could make 1,000 computers with one-thousandth the power and put them in the hands of 1,000 creative people. You'll get more out of doing that than out of having one person use the most powerful computer in the world. Because people are inherently creative they will use tools in ways the toolmakers never though possible. And once a person figures out how to do something with that tool, he or she can share it with the other 999.[22]

The future, we believe, belongs to people who create management systems that enable those who work in them to use their creative energies and to share them with others. The "1,000 computers" analogy is relevant here. Innovation and entrepreneurship applies as much to the management of enterprises as it does to the production of new ideas, perhaps even more so. In an interdependent world such as ours, the skills of managers — your skills — will need to be highly developed in the art and craft of encouraging, protecting, rewarding and evaluating the innovative efforts of others. Fundamental to this view is that we are each in our own way, creative, contributing individuals. Managers need the social, political and organizational skills to enable the process of innovation to happen. What is desirable is the development of entrepreneurial drive and courage in each manager of the twenty-first century!

Courage is important. While we have emphasized the importance of entrepreneurship and innovation in this chapter, it should be recognized that these are not automatically good for society. Questions we must ask are: Innovation for what? For whom? Entrepreneurial drive toward what end? Given the delicate balances that are emerging in the late twentieth century between development and sustainability of this planet, there is a distinct need to examine and encourage entrepreneurship that helps solve the environmental crises we have created through the excesses of our past efforts. We need to find ways to nourish rather than exploit our environment. We think that the trend will be toward innovations within organizations that address this issue. The following article, "Keeping the Fires Lit under the Innovators," illustrates many of the facets of entrepreneurship in the modern organization.

21. "The Entrepreneur of the Decade," *Inc.*, (April 1989), p. 118.
22. Ibid p. 116.

Reading 15.1

KEEPING THE FIRES LIT UNDER THE INNOVATORS[23]

By Christopher Knowlton

Around this time of year, the noonday temperature in St. Paul, MN, is three degrees below freezing, so it seems an unlikely spot for a caldron of innovation. Nonetheless, new products bubble up at a rate of more than 200 a year from the research labs that crowd Minnesota Mining & Manufacturing's 435-acre St. Paul campus. Many of 3M's innovations are modest variations of such ordinary but ubiquitous industrial and consumer items as making tape, coatings for highway reflectors and sandpaper.

Some 6,000 scientists and engineers are continually stirring the pot, primarily in chemistry and applied science. In all, the company makes some 60,000 products that last year produced revenues of $9.4 billion, up 10 percent from the year before. Operations in 50 other countries accounted for 40 percent of those sales. Assisted by the ailing dollar, earnings rose 18 percent to $918 million. In *Fortune's* annual survey of America's most admired corporations, 3M most recently ranked No. 6 — out of 306 entries. The company is often cited for its ability to keep innovation alive in a large, necessarily bureaucratic organization.

The man responsible for seeing that the fires don't go out is Allen F. Jacobson, 61, known as Jake, who joined 3M as a chemical engineer straight out of Iowa State University in 1947. In contrast with his popular predecessor, Lewis Lehr, Jacobson is strict and a little cold. He once rebuked the minister at his Presbyterian church for preaching that one person's profit is another's loss. Collaring the young man after the service, Jacobson informed him tersely that his remarks were "not in line with our country's best economic thinking."

While hardly the type to encourage the entrepreneurial whims of 3M's researchers, this Calvin has a dash of the Good Shepherd. To be sure that his flock of innovators share their ideas, Jacobson keeps his organization relatively decentralized. Information flows to the top from clearly defined reporting relationships and lots of shoptalk. He says, "You can't make too many of the decisions on the executive floor. You have to depend on the people who are close to the market and the technology."

Under Jacobson, 3M continues to codify many of the practices that preserve the innovative spirit of its scientists and engineers. Researchers are encouraged to spend 15 percent of their time pursuing pet projects that might have a payoff for the company down the road — a pastime they call "bootlegging." The stick behind the carrot is that 25 percent of each division's annual sales are expected to come from products developed in the prior five years.

Small groups staffed with a researcher and a market push inventions through the design and development stage. It takes an average of seven years from a product's invention to its successful introduction, although the trek can be made in less. Though Post-it notes took six years, some tapes take only one. Ultimately, 60 percent of the ideas wind up on the lab floor, but Jacobson wryly notes, "Outsiders say we are very lenient in rewarding failure."

23. *Fortune* Vol. 117, No. 7 (March 1988), p. 45. Christopher Knowlton, *Fortune*, ©1988 The Time Inc. Magazine Company. All rights reserved..

One superior product fresh from the labs is the first videocassette tape for the Super VHS video recorder. The tape, which 3M hopes will be the industry standard by the 1990s, improves picture resolution by capturing 400 lines of broadcast information vs. the standard 230.

Besides coming up with new products, the labs are also supposed to protect and extend the product line against the encroachments of competitors. A case in point: In 1980, 3M developed the first water-activated synthetic casting tape used to set broken bones, but by 1982 eight other companies had brought out copycat products. When 3M researchers discovered that some of these tapes were actually easier to apply than 3M's, they retreated to their labs to develop and test 140 new versions in a variety of fabrics, before introducing the next year an improved product that was stronger and easier to use.

In 1985, 3M's earnings declined 9.5 percent when the lofty dollar pummeled sales. Though Jacobson responded by cutting costs 35 percent, he spared R&D spending. Through this period, it actually rose from 4.5 percent of sales in 1980 to 6.6 percent today, a figure roughly twice the U.S. average for manufacturers. Now the company is reaping the benefits of that investment.

Every so often the caldron produces a witch instead of a winner. Recently a line of air ionizers used to remove dust from the air in factory production facilities began leaking radiation. Though 3M maintains that the ionizers pose no serious health threat, it recalled them, fearing they would taint the company's reputation. When asked about that reputation, Jacobson dismisses all the business buzzwords and phrases save innovation and the pursuit of quality. "These are the tools for staying ahead in our increasingly competitive society," he says. For a man who goes one on one with God's anointed, he practices what he preaches.

Chapter ■16

Ethics, Environment and Social Responsibility

This is the kind of ethical theory you get into. It's not black; it's not white. You're not responsible legally; but you are responsible. The question is, what are you responsible for? (A quote from Frank McGraw, manager, purchasing.)[1]

Every week, it seems a new insider trading scandal dominates the headlines of the business press. Young Wall Street traders with a six-or-seven figure income seem oblivious to the law in their pursuit of the yuppie dream of "having it all."

Is the new generation of business leaders less ethical than its predecessors? Has greed become the chief motivating force in today's business world? Are American business schools adequately preparing their students for ethical business practice?[2]

1. Barbara Ley Toffler, *Tough Choices* (New York: Wiley, 1986), p. 181.
2. Amitai Etzioni, "Is Greed America's New Creed?" *Business & Society Review*, No. 61 (Spring 1987), p. 4

The key reasons for human survival as a species was our large, complex brain. The mind that emerged from that brain conceived of a *future* as no other animals have. By inventing the future, we also gained a unique consequence — *choice*. By projecting the effects of our actions into the future we could see there were different options that led to different consequences. So we deliberately chose the option that we thought maximized our survival. Today, with all the amplified brainpower conferred by computers, telecommunications, scientists and engineers, we seem incapable of choosing the best option to avoid catastrophic consequences. In large part, we are blinded by deeply held beliefs and values, while all around us the signs of environmental degradation are legion. We must invent a future free of blinders to that we can choose from real options.[3]

* * *

You have just completed a long hard year in college. You are moving out of your apartment and heading out of town for a summer job. You have been pretty good about looking after your apartment. As you prepare to leave, your landlord tells you he is keeping the damage deposit! You tell him this is unfair. (Besides, you had counted on the cash.) He says it's standard practice in his business, and walks away. Your reaction is unprintable!

* * *

You are sitting in class, your mind wandering pleasantly to thoughts that have nothing to do with this course, when the instructor suddenly gets your undivided attention by announcing that the midterm exam has been changed from two weeks away to the day after tomorrow! No reason is given for the change. You feel that the contract for exams specified in the course outline has been violated and are not sure what should or can be done about it. You are not happy at all about this.

* * *

It is lunchtime and as you join friends in the student lounge you come in on a conversation about the final exam in accounting, which is due next week. One of your classmates has gotten a copy of the first page of the exam and is suggesting that each of you get a head start by looking at the questions. You are asked if you want to see the page. Do you participate? Do you blow the whistle? Or do you walk away?

* * *

Choices, options, values and beliefs, self-interest, knowing right from wrong and acting on your options, these are all ingredients that enter into ethical decisions and socially responsible behavior. Environmental concerns are an important arena for ethics and social responsibility because many people believe that the environment—which can be taken as a synonym for the planet Earth—is in serious trouble. As a result, so are humans and most other species. Humans have become so powerful and human organizations have such impact on peoples' lives and on the environment, that unethical acts and socially irresponsible behavior by organizations can threaten our future and that of planet Earth. We need to discover ways that we, as future managers, can make a positive impact on the quality of life for all species.

3. David Suzoki, *Inventing the Future* (Toronto: Stoddart Publishing Co., 1989), p. xiii.

In the "Textbook Tie-In" that follows, we will discuss some of the managerial issues around ethics and responsibility, and then deal with managing the environment as a special case of social responsibility.

There is no universal consensus on what ethical management is. This is true for a number of reasons. First, there are significant differences between and among cultures as to what ethical behavior is. Second, even within a given society people often differ on the ethical appropriateness of given actions. The word "ethical," according to *Webster's Seventh New Collegiate Dictionary,* means "relating to what is good or bad, and [having to do] with moral duty and obligation." "Ethical" comes from the Greek work "ethos" which has a dual meaning, "character" and "sentiment of the community." The term concerns the way individuals conduct themselves and the way that others in the culture judge that behavior.

In her interesting book on managers' ethical behavior, Barbara Ley Toffler found that managers who were asked to define *ethical* tended to answer in ways that fit one of four different meanings of the word:

• As a basic truth: "Ethics are eternal verities of right and wrong."

• As rules of behavior: "They (ethics) are really rules—rules of behavior."

• As the integrated unity of an individual's character: "Integrity is what it means; it has to start from within [the individual]."

• And as institutional (or cultural codes) : "The most appropriate meaning of *ethical* is: conforming to the standard of a given profession or group. So any group can set its own ethical standard and then live by them or not."[4]

If you think back to the earlier example of ethical problems involving the landlord, the professor and the student, you may see how these different aspects of the meaning of ethics come into play. One can make the case that cheating on an exam is fundamentally wrong. This would be a basic truth within many cultures. One can argue that the landlord who withheld the damage deposit, the professor who changed the exam time and the student who looked at the exam page each transgressed the rules set up around each transaction. One might question the personal integrity of each of the individuals involved.

Each perspective on ethical behavior helps us to more clearly see complex and often subtle actions. They also help us get a sense how serious the unethical action is and how it might be dealt with. The central factor of the ethics of a policy or a practice in an organization is: Who benefits and who is harmed by that policy or action? You will find that there are frequently no clear-cut answers to these questions in organizations and that the issue of ethical or unethical action is often not directly addressed by a specific legal principle or rule.

Tension often exists in business between the pursuit of self-interest and the accomplishment of collectively beneficial actions. We talk about ethical action at this level in terms of **social responsibility** of corporations, by which we mean the attention they give to the social as well as economic outcomes of business decisions. There is an expectation that management has an "obligation to make choices and take actions that will contribute to the welfare and interest of society as well as to the organizations."[5]

Americans tend to accept the notion of the "invisible hand," which uses free markets to focus and channel individual self-interest into actions that serve the needs of a larger common good. This is key to the ethics of the free enterprise system. It is often called the "Profit Maximization" approach to social responsibility. Essentially, the assumption is that it is the long-run and "social" mission of business to maximize profits as long as the business stays within the "rules of the game." Society is expected to use other agencies and institutions to take care of social and environmental needs.

4. Toffler, op. cit. p. 10.
5. Richard Daft, *Management* (Chicago: Dryden Press, 1988), p. 80.

An alternative view to the profit maximization perspective is that the corporate mission must go beyond the economic realm. The argument is that there is an "iron law of responsibility," that in the long run society will strip power from any organization whose actions society judges to be unacceptable.[6] Therefore, it is in the interests of both society and corporate institutions for business to consciously try to meet social and environmental needs.

Take for example, the case of Hoffman-LaRoche which makes Accutane, a popular drug for the control of acne.

While effective in treating acne, Accutane has been shown to cause severe birth defects when taken by pregnant women. The common good appears to be better served in this and similar cases when some constraint is placed upon the corporation to ensure that the drive to sell large quantities of the drug and thus increase profits is tempered by actions that keep it out of the hands of people who may be harmed by it. In this case, an advisory panel of the U.S. Food and Drug Administration recommended in 1988 that the drug's availability to doctors be restricted and that some of the company's own recommendations be implemented for strengthening warnings about side effects. We can compare this case to that of Beech-Nut, which knowingly sold bogus apple juice for babies.

In the Beech-Nut case the corporation made no effort to prevent this action. Beech-Nut was eventually found out and the result was $25 million in fines, legal fees, and a settlement of a class action suit. In addition two top executives went to jail and the reputation of Beech-Nut was damaged. Profits were also diminished by a loss in market share to two other corporations, Gerber and Heinz.[7]

Think about three factors when you reflect on these two cases. First is the importance to individuals, the corporation and society (the common good) of a company's voluntary, proactive stance with respect to socially responsible action. (Hoffman-LaRoche acted to prevent misleading the customer. Beech-Nut did not.) Second, great damage can be done to humans and to the environment in the name of profit. Failure to control and prevent harm by Hoffman-LaRoche caused much misery for individuals and society. Actions by drug companies in earlier times were sometimes less ethical and led to human tragedy. For example, in the 1960s thousands of babies were born without one or more limbs. This was the result of sales to pregnant women a drug called Thalidomide. The drug was sold without adequate testing of its side effects.

Third, notice the harmful consequences to Beech-Nut for its actions. The corporation lost a great deal of money and, at least for a time, a significant part of its reputation. Also, executives lost their freedom, their reputations and, most likely, their jobs. These outcomes are important because negative consequences of unethical actions and positive outcomes for ethical behavior put pressure on corporations and their executives. Consider the problem of pollution in North American rivers and lakes. Until recently, the fines for dumping toxic wastes into these outlets have been much lower than the benefits companies received for simply dumping their wastes into the river. In the absence of any real concern or even awareness on the part of managers about what they were doing to the environment, the choice was simple and irresponsible: "Dump it down the toilet and flush!"

Of course, other factors, such as the culture of the corporation, are also important.

In October, 1982 Johnson & Johnson withdrew all its supplies of Extra Strength Tylenol capsules when eight people died after ingesting capsules that had been laced with cyanide. The J&J culture that emphasized social responsibility is believed to have been a factor in the speed and unanimity of that decision.

Education that clarifies and instills values supportive of ethical action is another factor.

6. Henry L. Gantt, *Organization for Work* (New York: Harcourt, Brace, Jovanovich, 1989).

7. James Stoner and R. Edward Freeman, *Management*, 4th ed. (Englewood Cliffs, N. J.: Prentice Hall, 1989), p. 109.

Ethics, Environment and Social Responsibility   **303**

This discussion has focussed on ethical dilemmas within the U.S. business culture. Remember that substantial differences exist across and between cultures, so managing ethically becomes even more complex when we are talking about global management issues. International managers must act with one set of ethical guidelines representing their home country and another set reflecting that of host nations. Does one take kickbacks, accept gifts or make payoffs to get contracts if one's own country and laws and ethics forbid this but the practices are common in the host country? What about situations in which one promotes a product in a host country that is banned as toxic or considered undesirable in one's own country. Is it ethical to promote cigarettes aggressively in developing countries when there is concern in the United States about the health effects associated with smoking? What are the ethics of treating men and women unequally in the work place anywhere? What are the ethics of this issue when the cultural practices of countries in which one's company operates treat men and women in dramatically different and, to our eyes, discriminatory ways? Is it acceptable to use land resources in other countries to feed North Americans, while people starve in the host countries for lack of land? These issues and other more subtle ones are difficult for managers to sort out. What is right or wrong and how to right the wrongs requires patience, understanding, courage and clear thinking. Effective action requires guidelines that are dynamic and sensitive to prevailing conditions. Ethical management also needs to be rooted in principles that protect human life and the planet's environment.

Ethics and the Environment

In their book *The Green Capitalists,* John Elkington and Tom Burke tell an interesting story that captures how times have changed where environmental issues are concerned. It goes like this:

> There was something distinctly odd about the photographs, recalled Charles Brookes, a senior vice president at W.R. Grace & Co, the U.S. chemical company. Someone had suggested that he decorate his office with a set of aerial photographs of the chemical company's Curtis Bay plant, in Maryland. To his dismay, he and his staff found a "two-square-mile red blotch staring at us," produced by a chemical Grace had been dumping into Chesapeake Bay. When Mr. Brookes asked a subordinate to "do something about the pollution," the man repaired to his office. He returned later with a new set of photographs in which the red areas had been neatly airbrushed out. "That was his solution," Mr. Brookes explained. "That was 1970," he added. "We didn't think about these things."[8]

Today, in many little and large ways, the impact of organizations on the environment and its effect on us have made it one of the most significant issues on the agenda of top management. One only has to think of the Three Mile Island or Chernobyl nuclear reactor accidents, the ugliness and toxicity of industrial waste disposal in the Love Canal, the pollution of rivers and lakes in the United States, Canada, Germany, Poland, Czechoslovakia and other countries, the enormous human suffering following the chemical spill in Bhopal and the destruction of animal and plant life following the Exxon Valdez oil spill in Alaska to get a picture of the industrial-environment battleground. By the time you read this, other such incidents may have occurred also. The problem transcends national and economic boundaries. Environmental disasters span both capitalist and Communist ideologies.

On a smaller scale, but equally significant, are the day-to-day environmental issues that occur because we have not recognized or have chosen not to recognize the social and environmental consequences of our actions. When we use plastic non-biodegradable coffee cups, when we toss out note paper and computer paper that could be recycled and when we drive cars that don't have pollution controls, we contribute to pollution and environment damage. Multiplied over millions of people, such actions create hazards to our health and that of others.

8. John Elkington and Tom Burke, *The Green Capitalists,* (London: Victor Gollanez, 1989), p. 13.

When you become a manager, you will make choices that will help or harm the environment. As with other ethical choices, the best decision will not always be clear, especially given pressures of short-run versus long-run effectiveness and the tensions between economic and social goals. However, your managerial decisions will be more beneficial to you and others if you factor in environmental as well as economic considerations. Elkington and Burke suggest that the key to a company's environmental excellence is for its managers to identify priority targets and to get people moving step by step toward these targets.[9] They suggest ten guidelines to help make this happen. Briefly these are:

1. **Develop and publish an environmental policy.** It can be short. It serves to legitimize environmentally aware action by managers.

2. **Prepare an action program.** This helps identify the immediate priorities for action and to allocate responsibility to do the job.

3. **Make managers responsible.** Top management needs to take the responsibility for environmental action. Managers on the line must act and know that success as managers includes their effectiveness on the environment front.

4. **Allocate adequate resources.** No money, no result. Companies signal commitment by allocating money to environmental initiatives. Without this action, environmental action by managers will only get lip service.

5. **Invest in environmental science and technology.** This is an industrial-level commitment, but it can be done by the company too. 3M has a Pollution Prevention Pays Program that has developed ways to dramatically reduce pollution and energy waste in their corporation.

6. **Educate and train.** Thinking and acting in an environmentally conscious way requires a shift in attitude and perception for many companies and managers. In some firms this has been translated into having all employees think of themselves as environmentalists.

7. **Monitor, audit, report.** Action without feedback, evaluation and adjustment will not enable managers to act environmentally and effectively. Regular assessment of a manager's environmental performance is important.

8. **Monitor the evolution of the green agenda.** This is a fast changing phenomenon. New ideas, findings and attitudes are emerging almost continuously on environmental issues and what is important to do about them. As Elkington and Burke put it, "The environmental agenda is constantly evolving. Any company which assumes the adequacy of information which it picked up two years ago, or even three months ago, may be in for an unpleasant surprise."[10]

9. **Contribute to environmental programs.**

10. **Help build bridges between various interest groups.** In the United Kingdom, British Petroleum, a major oil company helps train the staff of environmental charities and other nongovernment organizations in business management techniques. This is one way, among many, in which business firms can help make productive links between themselves, government and environmental interests. It meets the spirit of social responsibility in an important way. As you consider your career, keep yourself informed on which companies act in such responsive ways. The information will help you evaluate job offers.

Your textbook and course instruction will deal in detail with different approaches to ethics and social responsibility. What we want to communicate here is the complexity and challenge of being a manager who acts ethically and with a sense of social responsibility. There are many conflicting points of view as to what is the right way to act given the interests of stockholders, customers, employees, legislative bodies and management. Most of the ethical dilemmas managers face do not have an obvious right answer.

9. Ibid. p. 228-237.
10. Ibid. p. 236.

Ethics, Environment and Social Responsibility   305

READY FOR CLASS

Name _____

ID# _____

Section _____

11. This exercise draws on suggestions for class discussion noted in James A.F. Stoner and R. Edward Freeman's *Management* 4th ed., Annotated Instructor's Edition, (Englewood Cliffs, N.J.: Prentice Hall, 1989).

Since this is a course on management and organizational behavior, and this module is about ethics and social responsibility, we'd like you to think about these concepts before coming to class. The following questions provide a road map for thinking about ethical behavior in organizations.[11] Such behavior is both complex and critical in modern organizations. We'd like you now to start applying your own thinking and ideas to this matter. Please take a few moments to answer these questions.

1. Write down your image of what a "socially responsible" organization would be like. What might its goals be? What kinds of actions might it take? What might be rewarded and punished? (Think about it in terms of what social responsibility means to you.)

2. List those characteristics you believe an ethical manager should have.

3. What are the distinguishing characteristics of a successful organization? What makes an organization successful? (Draw on your own ideas and what you have gathered from discussions in your text, in class and other sources.)

MIRROR TALK: FOCUSSING ON ME

Often when we hear the words "ethics" and "social responsibility", they have a detached, abstract sound. We sometimes think of them as words philosophers and moralists use and worry about. We might notice in the press that some business executive has been accused of unethical actions in a business deal. But it is all "out there" — not something that affects us very much in our day-to-day life. Oh sure, we know it is unethical to cheat on exams or to plagiarize other writers' work in our term papers, but are ethics really something we have to worry about each day of our lives? Are there decisions you make, choices you face, actions you take over the course of your life that have ethical and socially responsible implications? We think there are. They come up frequently, usually in unexpected ways. You will have to wrestle from time to time with ethical dilemmas. So "ethics" and "social responsibility" are concepts that affect us directly.

We'd like you to take a few minutes to think about and answer the following questions. When you answer, pick an example that you feel comfortable writing down. Use this exercise as an opportunity to make this topic as real for you as you can.

1. Think back over your last couple of years in school or in the places where you have worked and recall a situation when you weren't sure what was the ethical or socially responsible thing to do. (For example, you might have been dealing with behavior in examinations, sharing course information with someone who was cutting classes, deciding what to do about a dishonest teacher, classmate or manager at work.) Once you have that recollection in your mind, describe the situation in as much detail as you can. What was the issue? What were the circumstances surrounding the issue? Who were the players?

2. What were the conflicts for you in the situation?

3. Why were they conflicts for you?

4. What did you do?

5. Did you think it was the right thing to do?

6. How did you know it was the right thing to do?

7. Looking back at the situation, would you change anything in the way you acted if you were to do it again? If so, what would you change and why? What three things have you learned about yourself and your approach to ethical action by revisiting this past situation?

Pick up virtually any business publication from the newsstand these days and you will likely find an article about management's efforts to come to grips with environmental issues. Many of these stories discuss the way such attempts, when successful, can lead to increased corporate profitability. It is a phenomenon called by some the "greening of corporate America." Many books that deal with business and environment make the same argument: that social responsibility exercised on environmental matters can be profitable for business firms. (One such example is *The Green Capitalists: How to Make Money And Protect the Environment* by John Elkington and Tom Burke.)

The video clips you will see today feature Ben Cohen and Jerry Greenfield of Ben and Jerry's Homemade Inc. This is a highly successful company that sells ice cream in over 30 states. It has received the Small Business of the Year Award and grossed over $45 million in 1988, more than 40 percent above the figure for the previous year. Behaving in a socially responsible way is a core belief about why a business exists, in the mission and strategies of Ben and Jerry's Homemade Inc. In the 1980s this translated into activities designed to make the company an enjoyable place to work and into contributions to social causes. In the 1990s Ben & Jerry's has added environmental concerns to its list of causes.

The first videoclip examines some of the ethical decisions the company has made to keep its internal operations consistent with its core beliefs. The second videoclip discusses the company's environmental actions. Watch both clips and then note your responses to the following questions.

1. Why are Ben and Jerry spending so much time and energy trying to find a "low priced" financial officer?

 a. What is the point of choosing an executive in this way?

 b. Is it a wise financial strategy? Why/ why not?

2. What are the benefits and the costs of making social responsibility a determining factor in selecting and managing people in a corporation?

3. What are your reactions to the initiatives Ben and Jerry are making to deal with environmental issues?

a. Are these just public relations gimmicks or are they genuine acts of environmentalism? Why do you say this?

4. Think of a consumer corporation with which you are familiar (for example, Proctor & Gamble, Coca-Cola, IBM or Ford Motor Company). Name one or two of the company's products.

a. List the ways this company could act in environmentally responsible ways. If you know some of the ways they do so already, note these and then think of other actions that could be taken.

b. What are likely barriers to implementation of these actions?

5. A final thought: Is it socially responsible to sell ice cream when it is widely believed that high cholesterol intakes can increase the risk of heart disease? What is the ethical stance an ice cream company might take to deal with this concern?

Note: At the end of this exercise, read the consultant's report on Ben and Jerry's Homemade, Inc., at the end of this chapter.

The focus of this class exercise is management decisions in a pulp mill. You will put yourself in the role of a plant manager focussing on the difficult issue of balancing financial goals and environmental pressures.

The Frond Lake pulp mill is a $3 billion operation of Conglomco Inc. and has been in existence since 1962.[12] Like the other facilities owned by Conglomco, Frond Lake operates as a semiautonomous organization. While the company mission and overall policies are set at the head office, each plant has virtual autonomy in all aspects of decision making as long as the financial integrity of the operation is maintained (that is, by achieving at least 100 percent of profit objectives).

The Problem: With general depreciation and rapid technological advances in the last few years, Frond Lake's capital equipment has become out of date. This is a problem faced by all of Conglomco's plants and threatens the company's competitiveness, particularly in light of foreign competition. Conglomco has been gradually replacing outmoded equipment to enhance viability in an increasingly competitive world market.

One area of concern is the introduction of antipollution equipment as a part of the modernization process. At present, the mill has a minimum of antipollution equipment and discharges into the lake 75 tons of toxic organochlorines every day.

Consider the positions and points of view of these managers:

The Plant Manager's responsibility is to lead the senior management team in its efforts to arrive at a solution. The plant manager must decide how to proceed on the antipollution equipment purchase. The decision will be an integral part of the plant's long-term environmental policy with implications for the financial, legal, public relations and engineering departments. The plant manager is under considerable pressure to meet the corporation's profit objectives. The past two years the plan has come in at 97 percent (two years ago) and 94 percent (last year) of the financial targets. Furthermore, foreign competition has been making significant inroads into the pulp and paper industry. The plant manager wants the plant to succeed and is aware that long-term career security and progress is tied to such a result.

The Chief Financial Officer has calculated that with current product demand, the plant would achieve only 50 percent of head office's profit objectives for this year should the equipment be installed. After this initial equipment investment, the plant would achieve only 92 percent of head office's profit objectives for up to four years given the resulting loss in efficiency. The inelastic price of the company's product make it virtually impossible to pass on to the consumers these added costs. In a speech made to the board of directors last year, Conglomco's CEO endorsed a clean environment in principle, but seemed to be clearly against reducing company profitability in order to combat pollution.

The Senior Engineer has determined that in order to reduce emissions by 18 percent per year, scrubbing equipment would need to be installed at a cost of $12 million. This equipment would further result in a loss of efficiency of 6 percent at the plant. The plant has already spent $200,000 developing and testing a new program for the plant employees. The project was undertaken to assess the amount of slack in present plant operations. Unfortunately, the final report is not due for four to eight weeks, and although there is no concrete data, there are indications that the plant's efficiency could be improved through training.

12. This exercise is adapted with permission from "The Pulp Mill of Frond Lake" developed by Larry Shetzer, Larry Moore and Richard Stackman.

The Senior Public Relations Officer has learned that a local antipollution group (The "Save Frond Lake Committee") is mounting an aggressive protest campaign and is submitting a petition containing 21,000 signatures demanding immediate action. Several members of this group's leadership were also instrumental in the successful campaign that made recycling mandatory at Frond Lake. Also, the officer has noticed that there has been renewed interest by the media in environmental and pollution issues. Newspaper editorials have called for "something to be done."

The Senior Legal Officer has read that unless the plant immediately takes identifiable steps to reduce emissions by 18 percent per year over the next five years, lawsuits are going to be launched in the next three months by the state government. If successful (estimated probability of 70 percent), these suits would result in fines for this fiscal year of about $8 million. The $8 million does not include added legal costs, which could reach another $1 million.

Now that you have read the case, please:

1. Write down what you would decide if you were the plant manager and had listened to the reports of your four officers. My decision as plant manager would be to ...

My reasons for this decision are:

2. Predict the responses of your management team to this decision. What do you predict will be the response of:
   a. the Senior Financial Officer:

   b. the Legal Officer:

   c. the Public Relations Officer:

   d. the Senior Engineer:

COMING TO OUR SENSES: MAKING A DIFFERENCE

 Managers have the potential to be ethical and unethical, responsible or irresponsible each time they make a decision to hire or fire, buy or sell, reward or punish, start or finish a task. Virtually everything they do affects other people for better or worse. To make it tougher, the personal instincts of a manager might differ from the way an employer might want us to think and feel. We often have to deal with having to contradict our personal intuition or instinct because "that's not how the company does it."

Managing can present a never-ending series of dilemmas. However, before you throw up your hands, let's take stock of what might be helpful to you in your journey to become a manager or professional.

Reflect on the ethical issues that were discussed in class and in your text. Pick the issue you felt most strongly about. Write the issue essentials in a single sentence.

Ethical Issue:

1. What is your stance on this issue? (For/Against)

2. What are your feelings about this issue?

3. Why?

4. What is the main argument you use to defend your stance or to attack someone with a different stance?

5. If you were given the task of resolving this issue and your career depended on resolving it:

    a. What would be the first thing you'd do to tackle the issue?

    b. Who would you turn to for help? Why?

    c. What information would you need to have available to deal with the issue?

6. Looking ahead to the real world, identify three things you need to do in the next six months to have you better prepared to deal with this issue so that you can be more aware and effective when you have to face it in a real situation.

Sir Adrian Cadbury, who headed the English chocolate-making company Cadbury's, discusses ethical management in the following article, "Ethical Managers Make Their Own Rules." His ideas are likely to anticipate part of the thinking of managers in the twenty-first century. Some essential points that Sir Adrian makes are:

• **No Simple Rules Exist for Managing Ethically**.

> Business is part of the social system and we cannot isolate other economic elements of major decisions from their social consequences....Those who make business decisions have to assess the economic and social consequences of actions as best they can and come to conclusions on limited information and in a limited time.[13]

This will certainly be the case in a world that is changing rapidly. At the same time, our future world will be highly interconnected. So it will be necessary to have available the best information, and have it easily accessible. Managers will need well coordinated networks of people and sophisticated and efficient data bases on computer.

• **Companies will need to be judged by their actions, not by what they say in their public relations pronouncements.** While PR will be an important aspect of the twenty-first century manager's world, so too will be the degree to which she or he is subject to scrutiny and skepticism by an increasingly educated public. The next century will likely be the century of environmental awareness and action. (It had better be this, or there is unlikely to be a twenty-second century!). Actions will speak louder than words. If they are unethical actions, the reactions are likely to be far more punitive than they are today, because the consequences to people will be more damaging than they are even today. Sir Adrian's comments in this regard are as follows:

> What matters most...is where we stand as individual managers and how we behave when faced with decisions which require us to combine ethical and commercial judgments.... The first (step) is to determine as precisely as we can, what our personal rules of conduct are.... (this means) looking back at decisions we have made and working out from there what our rules actually are. The aim is to avoid confusing ourselves and everyone else by declaring one set of principles and acting on another. Our ethics are expressed in actions, which is why they are usually clearer to others than to ourselves... (The) second stage, which is to think through who else will be affected by the decision and how we should weigh their interest in it.[14]

The twenty-first century manager will have to be very clear about what he or she really intends to do in an ethical dilemma. He will need to anticipate and incorporate a wide variety of other people's perspectives into that decision and action for the result to be seen as ethical and socially responsible.

13. Sir Adrian Cadbury, "Ethical Managers Make Their Own Rules," *Harvard Business Review*, (September-October 1987), p. 70.
14. Ibid.

• **Actions are unethical if they won't stand scrutiny.** The twenty-first century manager will not have many places to hide. Unethical behavior will come out into the open. There are many avenues for uncovering actions taken by organizations. In the information age, information is recorded more formally and can be assessed in a wide variety of ways.

Covering up unethical behavior will be difficult. The trend toward seeking out and prosecuting socially irresponsible behavior will accelerate, largely because more people are becoming aware of the damage to the common good these actions have. We are not suggesting that unethical behavior will cease to occur. There are so many perspectives and values at work that more and more of a manager's actions will be seen as controversial and subject to scrutiny. That factor alone will keep this issue alive. Also, we expect that greed will always play a role in the actions of human beings. We are saying that twenty-first century managers will have good reason to take the ethical implications of their actions very seriously, just as they have taken profit efficiency implications into account in the past. Whether they are then sensitive to ethics as a result of moral concerns (our hope), or self preservation, or economic concerns (our expectation) or due to some combination of all three reasons, the result will likely be a more socially responsible management philosophy and practice in the next century.

Sir Adrian Cadbury's advice here comes as two rules of thumb. (He is discussing payments by Cadbury's to companies to win orders and acceptance of gifts by employees from companies who want Cadbury's to take their product.)

1. Is the payment on the face of the invoice?

2. Would it embarrass the recipient to have the gift mentioned in the company newspaper?

In general terms, the first rule of thumb aims at keeping actions out in the open and on record. The second says that if the act became public knowledge, would the manager who gave or received gifts be embarrassed. The intent of Sir Adrian Cadbury's argument is to say to us as managers of the future, "Can you look yourself in the eye when you look in the mirror, after you have acted as a manager? Can you live without undue embarrassment, with a public discussion of your actions? Can you say to someone's face what you have said about her behind her back?" If the answer to such questions is yes, then you have some confidence in the ethical intent of your managerial action.

The second article, "Stinky B.C. Pulpmill Clears the Air," from the *Toronto Globe & Mail* newspaper, describes some of the problems and actions that are taking place on the frontlines of the war to save the environment. It makes interesting reading in light of the Frond case in this chapter.

The final piece in this chapter is a consultant's report — an employee survey — carried out for Ben & Jerry's Homemade, Inc.

Reading 16.1

ETHICAL MANAGERS MAKE THEIR OWN RULES[15]

By Sir Adrian Cadbury

In 1890 Queen Victoria sent a decorative tin with a bar of chocolate inside to all of her soldiers who were serving in South Africa. These tins still turn up today, often complete with their contents, a tribute to the collecting instinct. At the time, the order faced my grandfather with an ethical dilemma. He owned and ran the second-largest chocolate company in Britain, so he was trying harder and the order meant additional work for the factory. Yet he was deeply and publicly opposed to the Anglo-Boer War. He resolved the dilemma by accepting the order, but carrying it out at cost. He therefore made no profit out of what he saw as an unjust war, his employees benefited from the additional work, the soldiers received their royal present and I am still sent the tins.

My grandfather was able to resolve the conflict between the decision best for his business and his personal code of ethics because he and his family owned the firm which bore their name. Certainly his dilemma would have been more acute if he had had to take into account the interests of outside shareholders, many of whom would no doubt have been in favor both of the war and of profiting from it. But even so, not all my grandfather's ethical dilemmas could be as straightforwardly resolved.

15. George Adrian Hayhurst Cadbury is chairman of Cadbury Schweppes PLC. Article reprinted by permission of *Harvard Business Review*. "Ethical Managers Make Their Own Rules" by Sir Adrian Cadbury (September-October 1987). Copyright ©1987 by the President and Fellows of Harvard College; all rights reserved.

So strongly did my grandfather feel about the South African War that he acquired and financed the only British newspaper which opposed it. He was also against gambling, however, and so he tried to run the paper without any references to horse racing. The effect on the newspaper's circulation was such that he had to choose between his ethical beliefs. He decided, in the end, that it was more important that the paper's voice be heard as widely as possible than that gambling should thereby receive some mild encouragement. The decision was doubtless a relief to those working on the paper and to its readers.

The way my grandfather settled these two clashes of principle brings out some practical points about ethics and business decisions. In the first place, the possibility that ethical and commercial considerations will conflict has always faced those who run companies. It is not a new problem. The difference now is that a more widespread and critical interest is being taken in our decisions and in the ethical judgments which lie behind them.

Secondly, as the newspaper example demonstrates, ethical signposts do not always point in the same direction. My grandfather had to choose between opposing a war and condoning gambling. The rule that is best to tell the truth often runs up against the rule that we should not hurt people's feelings unnecessarily. There is no simple, universal formula for solving ethical problems. We have to choose from our own codes of conduct whichever rules are appropriate to the case in hand; the outcome of those choices makes us who we are.

Lastly, while it is hard enough to resolve dilemmas when our personal rules of conduct conflict, the real difficulties arise when we have to make decisions which affect the interests of others. We can work out what weighting to give to our own rules through trial and error. But business decisions require us to do the same for others by allocating weights to all the conflicting interests which may be involved. Frequently, for example, we must balance the interests of employees against those of shareholders. But even that sounds more straightforward than it really is, because there may well be differing views among the shareholders, and the interests of past, present and future employees are unlikely to be identical.

Eliminating ethical considerations from business decisions would simplify the management task, and Milton Friedman has urged something of the kind in arguing that the interaction between business and society should be left to political process. "Few trends could so thoroughly undermine the very foundation of our free society," he writes in *Capitalism and Freedom,* "as the acceptance by corporate officials of a social responsibility other than to make as much money for their shareholders as possible."

But the simplicity of this approach is deceptive. Business is part of the social system and we cannot isolate the economic elements of major decisions from their social consequences. So there are no simple rules. Those who make business decisions have to assess the economic and social consequences of their actions as best as they can and come to their conclusions on limited information and in a limited time.

As will already be apparent, I use the word ethics to mean the guidelines or rules of conduct by which we aim to live. It is, of course, foolhardy to write about ethics at all, because you lay yourself open to the charge of taking up a position of moral superiority, of failing to practice what you preach, or both. I am not in a position to preach nor am I promoting a specific code of conduct. I believe, however, that it is useful to all of us who are responsible for business decisions to acknowledge the part which ethics plays in those decisions and to encourage discussion of how best to combine commercial and ethical judgments. Most business decisions involve some degree of ethical judgment; few can be taken solely on the basis of arithmetic.

While we refer to a company as having a set of standards, that is a convenient shorthand. The people who make up the company are responsible for its conduct and it is their collective actions which determine the company's standards. The ethical standards of a company are judged by its actions, not by pious statements of intent put out in its name. This does not mean that those who head companies should not set down what they believe their companies stand for—hard though that is to do. The character of a company is a matter of importance to those in it, to those who do business with it and to those who are considering joining it.

What matters most, however, is where we stand as individual managers and how we behave when faced with decisions which require us to combine ethical and commercial judgments. In approaching such decisions, I believe it is helpful to go through two steps. The first is to determine, as precisely as we can, what our personal rules of conduct are. This does not mean drawing up a list of virtuous notions, which will probably end up as a watered-down version of the Scriptures without their literary merit. It does mean looking back at decisions we have made and working out from there what our rules actually are. The aim is to avoid confusing ourselves and everyone else by declaring one set of principles and acting on another. Our ethics are expressed in our actions, which is why they are usually clearer to others than to ourselves.

Once we know where we stand personally we can move on to the second step, which is to think through who else will be affected by the decision and how we should weight their interest in it. Some interests will be represented by well-organized groups; others will have no one to put their case. If a factory manager is negotiating a wage claim with employee representatives, their remit is to look after the interests of those who are already employed. Yet the effect of the wage settlement on the factory's costs may well determine whether new employees are likely to be taken on. So the manager cannot ignore the interest of potential employees in the outcome of the negotiation, even though that interest is not represented at the bargaining table.

The rise of organized interest groups makes it doubly important that managers consider the arguments of everyone with a legitimate interest in a decision's outcome. Interest groups seek publicity to promote their causes and they have the advantage of being single-minded: they are against building an airport on a certain site, for example, but take no responsibility for finding a better alternative. This narrow focus gives pressure groups a debating advantage against management, which cannot evade the responsibility for taking decisions in the same way.

In *The Hard Problems of Management,* Mark Pastin has perceptively referred to this phenomenon as the ethical superiority of the uninvolved, and there is a good deal of it about. Pressure groups are skilled at seizing the high moral ground and arguing that our judgment as managers is at best biased and at worst influenced solely by private gain because we have a direct commercial interest in the outcome of our decisions. But as managers we are also responsible for arriving at business decisions which take account of all the interests concerned; the uninvolved are not.

At times the campaign to persuade companies to divest themselves of their South African subsidiaries has exemplified this kind of ethical highhandedness. Apartheid is abhorrent politically, socially and morally. Those who argue that they can exert some influence on the direction of change by staying put believe this as sincerely as those who favor divestment. Yet many anti-apartheid campaigners reject the proposition that both sides have the same end in view. From their perspective it is self-evident that the only ethical course of action is for companies to wash their hands of the problems of South Africa by selling out.

Managers cannot be so self-assured. In deciding what weight to give to the arguments for and against divestment, we must consider who has what at stake in the outcome of the decision. The employees of a South African subsidiary have the most direct stake, as the decisions affects their future; they are also the group whose voice is least likely to be heard outside South Africa. The shareholders have at stake any loss on divestment, against which must be balanced any gain in the value of their shares through severing the South African connection. The divestment lobby is the one group for whom the decision is costless either way.

What is clear even from this limited analysis is that there is no general answer to the question of whether companies should sell their South African subsidiaries or not. Pressure to reduce complicated issues to straightforward alternatives, one of which is right and the other wrong, is a regrettable sign of the times. But boards are rarely presented with two clearly opposed alternatives. Companies faced with the same issue will therefore properly come to different conclusions and their decisions may alter over time.

A less contentious divestment decision faced my own company when we decided to sell our foods division. Because the division was mainly a U.K. business with regional brands, it did not fit the company's strategy, which called for concentrating resources behind our confectionery and soft drinks brands internationally. But it was an attractive business in its own right and the decision to sell prompted both a management bid and external offers.

Employees working in the division strongly supported the management bid and made their views felt. In this instance, they were the best organized interest group and they had more information available to them to back their case than any of the other parties involved. What they had at stake was also very clear.

From the shareholders' point of view, the premium over asset value offered by the various bidders was a key aspect of the decision. They also had an interest in seeing the deal completed without regulatory delays and without diverting too much management attention from the ongoing business. In addition, the way in which the successful bidder would guard the brand name had to be considered, since the division would take with it products carrying the parent company's name.

In weighing the advantages and disadvantages of the various offers, the board considered all the groups, consumers among them, who would be affected by the sale. But our main task was to reconcile the interests of the employees and of the shareholders. (The more, of course, we can encourage employees to become shareholders, the closer together the interests of these two stakeholders will be brought.) The division's management upped its bid in the face of outside competition, and after due deliberation we decided to sell to the management team, believing that this choice best balanced the diverse interests at stake.

Companies whose activities are international face an additional complication in taking their decisions. They aim to work to the same standards of business conduct wherever they are and to behave as good corporate citizens of the countries in which they trade. But the two aims are not always compatible: promotion on merit may be the rule of the company and promotion by seniority the custom of the country. In addition, while the financial arithmetic on which companies base their decisions is generally accepted, what is considered ethical varies among cultures.

If what would be considered corruption in the company's home territory is an accepted business practice elsewhere, how are local managers expected to act? Companies could do business only in countries in which they feel ethically at home, provided always that their shareholders take the same view. But this approach could prove unduly restrictive, and there is also a certain arrogance in dismissing foreign codes of conduct without considering why they may be different. If companies find, for example, that they have to pay customs officers in another country just to do their job, it may be that the state is simply transferring its responsibilities to the private sector as an alternative to using taxation less efficiently to the same end.

Nevertheless, this example brings us to one of the most common ethical issues companies face — how far to go in buying business? What payments are legitimate for companies to make to win orders and, the reverse side of that coin, when do gifts to employees become bribes? I use two rules of thumb to test whether a payment is acceptable from the company's point of view: Is the payment on the face of the invoice? Would it embarrass the recipient to have the gift mentioned in the company newspaper?

The first test ensures that all payment, however unusual they may seem, are recorded and go through the books. The second is aimed at distinguishing bribes from gifts, a definition which depends on the size of the gift and the influence it is likely to have on the recipient. The value of a case of whiskey to me would be limited, because I only take it as medicine. We know ourselves whether a gift is acceptable or not and we know that others will know if they are aware of the nature of the gift.

As for payment on the face of the invoice, I have found it a useful general rule precisely because codes of conduct do vary round the world. It has legitimized some otherwise unlikely company payments, to the police in one country, for example, and to the official planning authorities in another, but all went through the books and were audited. Listing a payment on the face of the invoice may not be a sufficient ethical test, but it is a necessary one; payments outside the company's system are corrupt and corrupting.

The logic behind these rules of thumb is that openness and ethics go together and that actions are unethical if they will not stand scrutiny. Openness in arriving at decisions reflects the same logic. It gives those with an interest in a particular decision the chance to make their views known and opens to argument the basis on which the decision is finally taken. This in turn enables the decision makers to learn from experience and to improve their powers of judgment.

Openness is also, I believe, the best way to disarm outside suspicion of companies' motives and actions. Disclosure is not a panacea for improving the relations between business and society, but the willingness to operate an open system is the foundation of those relations. Business needs to be open to the views of society and open in return about its own activities; this is essential for the establishment of trust.

For the same reasons, as managers we need to be candid when making decisions about other people. Dr. Johnson reminds us that when it comes to lapidary inscriptions, "no man is upon oath." But what should be disclosed in references, in fairness to those looking for work and to those who are considering employing them?

The simplest rule would seem to be that we should write the kind of reference we would wish to read. Yet "do as you would be done by" says nothing about ethics. The actions which result from applying it could be ethical or unethical, depending on the standards of the initiator. The rule could be adapted to help managers determine their ethical standards, however, by reframing it as a question: If you did business with yourself, how ethical would you think you were?

Anonymous letters accusing an employee of doing something discreditable create another context in which candor is the wisest course. Such letters cannot by definition be answered, but they convey a message to those who receive them, however warped or unfair the message may be. I normally destroy these letters, but tell the person concerned what has been said. This conveys the disregard I attach to nameless allegation, but preserves the rule of openness. From a practical point of view, it serves as a warning if there is anything in the allegations; from an ethical point of view, the degree to which my judgment of the person may now be prejudiced is known between us.

The last aspect of ethics in business decisions I want to discuss concerns our responsibility for the level of employment; what can or should companies do about the provision of jobs? This issue is of immediate concern to European managers because unemployment is higher in Europe than it is in the United States and the net number of new jobs created has been much lower. It comes to the fore whenever companies face decisions which require a trade-off between increasing efficiency and reducing numbers employed.

If you believe, as I do, that the primary purpose of a company is to satisfy the needs of its customers and to do so profitably, the creation of jobs cannot be the company's goal as well. Satisfying customers requires companies to compete in the marketplace, and so we cannot opt out of introducing new technology, for example, to preserve jobs. To do so would be to deny consumers the benefits of progress, to shortchange the shareholders, and in the longer run to put the jobs of everyone in the company at risk. What destroys jobs certainly and permanently is the failure to be competitive.

Experience says that the introduction of new technology creates more jobs than it eliminates, in ways which cannot be forecast. It may do so, however, only after a time lag, and those displaced may not, through lack of skills, be able to take advantage of the new opportunities when they arise. Nevertheless, the company's prime responsibility to everyone who has a stake in it is to retain its competitive edge, even if this means a loss of jobs in the short run.

Where companies do have a social responsibility, however, is in how we manage that situation, how we smooth the path of technological change. Companies are responsible for the timing of such changes and we are in a position to involve those who will be affected by the way in which those changes introduced. We also have a vital resource in our capacity to provide training, so that continuing employees can take advantage of change and those who may lose their jobs can more readily find new ones.

In the United Kingdom, an organization called Business in the Community has been established to encourage the formation of new enterprises. Companies have backed it with cash and with secondments. The secondment of able managers to worthwhile institutions is a particularly effective expression of concern, because the ability to manage is such a scarce resource. Through Business in the Community we can create jobs collectively, even if we cannot do so individually, and it is clearly in our interest to improve the economic and social climate in this way.

Throughout, I have been writing about the responsibilities of those who head companies and my emphasis has been on taking decisions, because that is what directors and managers are appointed to do. What concerns me is that too often the public pressures which are put on companies in the name of ethics encourage their boards to put off decisions or to wash their hands of problems. There may well be commercial reasons for those choices, but there are rarely ethical ones. The ethical bases on which decisions are arrived at will vary among companies, but shelving those decisions is likely to be the least ethical course.

The company which takes drastic action in order to survive is more likely to be criticized publicly than the one which fails to grasp the nettle and gradually but inexorably declines. There is always a temptation to postpone difficult decisions, but it is not in society's interests that hard choices should be evaded because of public clamor or the possibility of legal action. Companies need to be encouraged to take the decisions which face them; the responsibility for providing that encouragement rests with society as a whole.

Society sets the ethical framework within which those who run companies have to work out their own codes of conduct. Responsibility for decisions, therefore, runs both ways. Business has to take account of its responsibilities to society in coming to its decisions, but society has to accept its responsibilities for setting the standards against which those decisions are made.

Reading 16.2
STINKY B.C. PULP MILL CLEARS THE AIR[17]

By Kimberley Noble

PORT MELLON, B.C.—For decades, residents of scenic Howe Sound have wished the Port Mellon pulp mill would somehow disappear. To a certain extent, their wish is about to come true.

In a week or two, the billowy plumes of stinky smoke that make it possible to see — and often smell — the Port Mellon plant from up to 100 kilometers away are expected to be gone. They will be replaced by clear and practically odorless emissions that will turn a local eyesore into an almost invisible clump of buildings hidden by a bend in the British Columbia shoreline.

And that's not all. Port Mellon's owners, partners Canfor Corp. of Vancouver and Oji Paper Co. Ltd., a major Japanese paper producer, have spent more than $100 million in the past two years on environmental improvements designed to clean up every aspect of the mill's operations.

Canfor and Oji have managed to turn one of British Columbia's worst polluters into the cleanest pulp mill in Canada — one that even draws praise from the environmentalists crusading for a clean-up of the pulp and paper industry.

"They have not gone all the way to meeting what we have asked companies for, which is a total elimination of chlorine in the pulp system," said Brian Killeen, West Coast pulp and paper campaigner for the environmental group Greenpeace. "But they are moving in the right direction, and Port Mellon is one of only a few mills that will be under government standards" for pulp and paper pollution when new federal and provincial regulations come into effect over the next few years.

The clean-up program is part of a $1 billion program to expand and upgrade the Port Mellon mill into an operation its partners hope will be the first step in a successful and long lasting international alliance.

The joint venture, called Howe Sound Pulp & Paper Ltd., is this cycle's Cinderella story in the B.C. forest products business. Since Canfor and Oji formed their joint venture in late 1987, this plant has been transformed from the oldest and smallest operating pulp mill in the province to one of the most modern and efficient.

So far, the partnership has spent $860 million of the $1.14 billion it has pledged to the site, where, in addition to making environmental improvements, it is expanding pulp production, adding a newsprint mill and building a power plant that should provide the mill with 70 per cent of its energy needs before the middle of the decade.

What distinguishes Howe Sound from the other B.C. pulp and paper companies that have launched environmental improvement programs in the past several years "is that we are spending much more than anybody else," said Howe Sound president William Hughes. "Quite frankly, one of the things that Oji has brought to the table is access to the capital markets of Japan.

"We've borrowed our money in yen and U.S. dollars from Japanese banks," said Mr. Hughes, who was Canfor's vice-president of pulp production before moving over to head up the joint venture. "If we had to pay Canadian interest rates, on the money we've needed, I don't think we'd have a project. We certainly would not have as big a project."

Vancouver-based Canfor, the largest lumber company in Canada and one of B.C.'s biggest pulp producers, had known for years it had to overhaul operations at Port Mellon, a small and inefficient chemical pulp mill it had owned since the early 1950s.

By 1986, the plant was making 650 tons a day of bleached kraft softwood pulp — well below the 1,000 or more produced at most of the province's chemical pulp mills, an output that still ranks far below that of market pulp manufacturers in competing countries.

Moreover, it posed one of the worst pollution problems on the B.C. coast and was increasingly the target of criticism from Vancouver-based environmental groups and area residents.

While pulp mills in the B.C. Interior, all built since 1965, have been required to install at least rudimentary treatment systems for water discharged back into rivers, coastal mills are only now facing similar rules. Until last year, Howe Sound, like every other mill on the Pacific, dumped untreated effluent straight into the ocean.

This practice culminated in a federal government order-first made in December, 1988, and still in effect-to close Howe Sound to commercial fishing because of high levels of chemical contamination caused by Port Mellon and the Western Pulp Ltd. Partnership's Woodfibre pulp mill at the east end of the sound. The ban has since been extended to a total of eight areas of British Columbia where pulp or lumber mills operate.

17. *Toronto Globe and Mail.* (October 1, 1990), p. B-1 and B-7.

The discovery of dioxins and furans in pulp effluent spurred Ottawa and Victoria to draft new regulations aimed at eliminating these contaminants-caused when chlorine bleach or wood preservatives come into contact with the organic material in the wood-as well as significantly reducing related forms of water pollution.

As they are now written, these regulations require Canadian companies to outfit their mills with a variety of environmental systems by 1992, and are expected to cost the industry up to $5 billion by the 1994 deadline.

But, by the time the governments started to clamp down, Canfor's clean-up program was already well under way.

The company had decided that the answer to Port Mellon's problems lay in a joint venture with a Japanese paper company. At the end of 1987 Canfor and Oji reached a deal that required Canfor to put up the Howe Sound operation and a Vancouver sawmill, assets that the Japanese matched with $307.5 million in cash. In exchange, each company got 50 per cent of Howe Sound.

The partners immediately announced their intention to expand the pulp mill to produce 1,000 tons a day and to add a newsprint machine, which when it starts up in April, 1991, will make 585 tons of paper a day.

Under their agreement, Canfor continues to operate the pulp mill and market its output in Europe and Japan, while Oji will be responsible for running the newsprint machine and selling the paper. Moreover, they have already marked the spot where a second paper machine will some day be installed beside the first one.

As soon as the pulp expansion is finished and the old equipment torn down, the company will begin construction of a new power boiler and two turbo generators that will use steam and wood waste from the pulp plant to generate 85 of the 125 megawatts of electricity the expanded mill will need.

"This in itself will have a major environmental impact," Mr. Hughes said. For one thing, it will enable B.C. Hydro to delay development of its Site C dam on the Peace River, and secondly, it will use the equivalent of two scows a day of wood waste that currently go into Vancouver landfills.

But the biggest environmental improvements will be in air and water quality. Port Mellon's complete overhaul enabled Canfor and Oji to start installing the latest effluent and emission controls years before Canadian regulators - and, Mr. Hughes stresses, environmentally-minded foreign customers began to demand them.

Most of this technology is designed to reduce or eliminate the use of chlorine bleach to remove lignin, the natural glue that binds cellulose fibres in the wood and gives unbleached paper its brown color.

To do this, state-of-the-art pulp mills now use a combination of extra cooking and oxygen delignification to take out most of this glue before the mulched-up wood fibres go to the bleach plant. At this point, a percentage of the chlorine is replaced with chlorine dioxide, a less dangerous chemical that bleaches the fibres but does not create dioxins and furans.

The left-over mixtures containing re-usable chemicals are sent to a recovery boiler, while water with mostly soaps and wood residue goes to primary and secondary treatment lagoons that settle out the solids and "reactivate" waste water so it does not damage water quality or rob marine life of oxygen.

Howe Sound now has all this, and then some. It has become the second company in Canada to install an oxygen bleaching system (the other is E. B. Eddy Forest Products Ltd. of Ottawa) and the first of B.C.'s coastal mills to put in secondary treatment lagoons. It has replaced a full 50 per cent of its chlorine with chlorine dioxide, and is in fact making a "chlorine-free" pulp for European customers, using 100 per cent chlorine dioxide substitution.

And it has built the world's biggest recovery boiler, a $100-million, 75-metre structure scheduled to start up at Thanksgiving. It is designed to process 5.6 million pounds of so-called "black liquor" a day, and in such a way the emission of stinky sulphurous gases will be reduced by 70 per cent, Mr. Hughes said.

Moreover, the giant boiler will be fitted with modern electrostatic precipitators designed to remove virtually all the particles that until now went straight up the chimney into the air. It is these last two steps that are supposed to render the pulp mill's emissions invisible and almost odorless.

Company officials are hoping the federal government will soon give commercial fishing the go-ahead, a move that would signal the success of their water pollution clean-up.

"Our last test showed no dioxin and a 99.4 per cent reduction of furans," Mr. Hughes said. Crabs taken from Howe Sound in May were shown to have 4.4 parts per trillion of the contaminants in their muscles, compared with 141.2 ppt at the time the federal government banned commercial fishing. Their digestive glands, where the chemicals accumulate, contained 123 ppt, down from 1,442 ppt in January, 1989.

Meanwhile, the company expects that by November it will have reduced the amount of chlorinate organic compounds in its effluent below 1.5 kilograms a tonne-the target the federal and B.C. governments hope to set for 1994 — compared with 6.5 kilograms in early 1989.

And after that? Mr. Hughes wants to start work on a new pulp for the discerning international customer. "It will be chloro-free — no chlorine, no chlorine dioxide." And how will he do that? "I don't know," he laughed. "But we think there will be a market for it, so we hope to figure it out by next year."

WORK LIFE AT BEN & JERRY'S

Dear Ben & Jerry's Employee:

This report summarizes the results of the employee opinion survey taken in January 1990 by some 250 of you. Most employees participated and 96% said that they took the survey seriously.

These results come from people at Waterbury (67% of the surveys), Springfield (22%), and from Company Stores and field locations (11%). All departments are represented. The overall findings are made up of the opinions of hourly people (61% of the work force), managers and supervisors (24%), and salaried people who are not managers (15%).

Here you will see very impressive results, compared to those of the average US employee, and compared with results from excellent and progressive companies. For example, 96% of you really care what happens to the company and 88% are proud to work at Ben & Jerry's. 90% of you are satisfied with your jobs and like working here. Your ratings of the quality of the company's products and services, the friendliness and helpfulness of co-workers, and your own pay and benefits are much more favorable than those found in national polls and surveys of other tops companies.

18. Reprinted with permission of Ben & Jerry's Homemade, Inc., and Philip H. Mirvis for educational purposes.

Still, there are some areas for improvement. 58% say that things run smoothly in the organization but 32% say they don't run smoothly. This creates frustration, makes some people's jobs harder, and means that many have too much to do to everything well. Plant equipment is not satisfactory; there are concerns over chances for advancement; and many find that their work load takes too much away from home and family life.

This report is only a summary. More detailed findings are available for your examination and results for major work areas of the company will be reported to you and your work groups. However, no data will be reported that can in any way identify individuals or small groups of employees. No one in the company has seen the surveys and we have taken every step to ensure the confidentiality of your individual opinions.

We hope you find this report, and any briefings you might attend, to be interesting and thought provoking. You also can read the "comments" report to see what your co-workers say, in their own words, about Ben & Jerry's.

We affirm that this report is a fair and representative summary of employee opinion.

Philip Mirvis

Amy Sales

Dennis A. Ross

Independent Researchers

1. Jobs at Ben & Jerry's

This part of the survey measured how people rate the work they do. Most B&J people have good jobs...

• The great majority of employees find variety (88%) in their jobs and meaning and challenge (77%).

• Most (72%) have the responsibility to decide how to do their jobs.

• The majority say their work load is reasonable but 41% have too much to do to do everything well.

2. Job Resources and Information

This part asked whether or not people have the resources to do their jobs well. Most B&J people have high levels of training and job support. But there are problems with equipment and getting job-related information...

• Most people get the help they need from supervisors and co-workers and most have enough authority to do their jobs well.

• Problems with quality of equipment and its reliability and maintenance. 50% of hourly people dissatisfied with equipment. Most trouble in Waterbury Production, Shipping & Receiving, and Springfield.

• 44% of the work force has trouble getting information needed to do job well. Some find that their jobs are harder because other departments don't do their part (46%) or because of management interference (28%).

3. Supervision

This part asked about people's immediate supervisors. In general, supervisors get high marks on handling people and work. Less favorable on communication...

• Most say that their supervisor trusts them to do a good job and has high performance standards.

• 74% say supervisor encourages teamwork and makes sure people know what has to be done. 63% say supervisor does a good job planning and organizing work.

• About half the employees say their supervisor regularly lets them know how well they are doing and lets people know when they are performing poorly.

• 35% say the supervisor does not give regular feedback.

4. Human Relations at Ben & Jerry's

This part measured people's attitudes about the "human side" of the company.

• High levels of satisfaction with the friendliness of co-workers.

• Two-thirds say managements cares about what people think and feel and is truly interested in their welfare and well-being.

• Is the work you do valued and appreciated in this company?

Hourly People   61%

Rest of work force   80%

5. Participation and Communication

This part measured people's participation in decisions and ratings of communication in the company. Participation is very high. Communication gets mixed reviews...

• Most (79%) say their supervisor encourages them to take part in decisions and 84% say work group members exchange ideas and opinions.

• Some 58% are satisfied with their chances to participate in decisions. 31% are not.

• Most are comfortable with the upward communication, but 30% don't hear about change before it takes place.

• Favorable ratings on suggestions and how they are acted upon. Less satisfaction with how complaints are addressed.

II SATISFACTION, REWARDS AND CLIMATE

1. Job Satisfaction

Overall job satisfaction is very high. Satisfaction with pay, benefits, and security equals ratings in most progressive and effective companies. Great majority of employees say the company is committed to providing safe and healthy working conditions and agree that women are treated fairly. 80% of B&J people are happy with their life off the job. However 43% don't have enough time to spend with family and friends or in leisure.

2. Work Rewards

Two-thirds of B&J people say that if they perform especially well on their job they'll be given more responsibility and nearly as many say they will gain the respect of co-workers and recognition and praise from their supervisor.

About half say that they are quite likely to get a much better pay increase and close to a third expect to get a promotion or better job. 67% of B&J people say that their pay is fair compared to what other companies in the area pay. 55% find it fair compared to what other employees in B&J earn.

3. Organization

This part of the survey asked about how the organization operates and how things get done. B&J people find too much fire-fighting and some have problems with internal "politics."

• Most people understand what other departments do and say that other departments do their fair share.

• 51% say there is too much "fire-fighting" in the company and 26% have difficulty working with people from other departments to solve problems.

• Over one-third of B&J people are troubled by "politics" in the company — they see too little openness and honesty from management and too many supervisors playing "favorites."

Still, two-thirds find a lot of "family feeling" in the company.

4. Values vs. Practices

Two-thirds of B&J people say that the company "really practices what it preaches." The great majority understand and support the company's social mission. 61% say it is "in tune" with their own values (12% say too conservative and 27% say too radical).

5. Views of the Future

By and large, B&J people are very confident in the future of the company. About one-third don't feel well informed about the future plans but most are confident B&J's will keep its social mission strong, stay ahead of the competition, and remain a good place to work.

Chapter 17

Going Global: International Management

Capital raised in London in the Eurodollar market by a Belgium-based corporation may finance the acquisition of machinery by a subsidiary located in Australia. A management team from French Renault may take over an American-built automotive complex in the Argentine. Clothing for dolls, sewn in Korea on Japanese supplied sewing machines according to U.S. specifications, may be shipped to Northern Mexico for assembly with other components into dolls being manufactured by a U.S. firm for sale in New York and London during the Christmas season. A California manufactured air bus...is powered by British...engines, while a competing air bus...flies on Canadian wing assemblies. A Frenchman is appointed president of the U.S. domiciled IBM World Trade Corporation, while an American establishes...a Swiss-based international mutual fund.[1]

1. Nancy J. Adler, *International Dimensions of Organizational Behavior*, (Boston: Kent Publishing Company, 1986).

The business world used to be rather simple. U.S. companies owned by U.S. shareholders were located on American shores, and typically employed all U.S. workers and managers — perhaps occasionally drawing from off-shore suppliers or setting up off-shore manufacturing sites. Competitors, while not necessarily located across town, or even in the same state, were usually based in the United States. And more often than not, the majority of the customers whom these businesses tried to woo were Americans, too.

But today, international enterprises have become commonplace, and the very way in which many products are designed and made has been "globalized." Take hockey gloves, for example. Although these would seem to be a fairly straightforward product, one particular brand is designed in Scandinavia, manufactured in Korea using materials from Spain, distributed by the Japanese, and finally sold in North America. And, by the way, the headquarters for the company that makes the gloves is in Canada!

Joint ventures and collaborations spanning the globe are becoming a normal part of doing business. Competitors can crop up in any part of the world, and companies must learn how to appeal to customers in cities ranging from Boston to Bangkok to Berlin.

This unprecedented surge of global economic activity has fundamentally altered the makeup of many U.S. corporations. In addition, those companies that have become truly international are facing some extraordinary new challenges: How do you coordinate the activities of a company that has ever-changing boundaries and affiliations? How do you communicate with the various pieces of the organization, including suppliers, subsidiaries and partners? And how do you manage the cross-cultural differences that must exist as you cross so many borders and time zones?

It is this last question, perhaps more than any other, that we must answer in order to groom a generation of managers with the sensitivity and skills to take on the global challenge. A London-based recruitment firm came up with a list of credentials for the "ideal" executive to run a pan-European operation.[2] The search firm identified such a model executive — perhaps only partly tongue-in-cheek — as "a half-Irish, half-French ad exec married to an American, living in Brussels, who speaks three languages and has worked as a manufacturing salesman and an organizer of Paris social events."

2. "When in Europe, Firms Want the Euro-Exec," *The Wall Street Journal*, (April 20, 1990).

While we would argue that this definition is unnecessarily narrow, there are unquestionably certain skills, attitudes and characteristics that would stand today's "international" manager or executive in good stead. And as the globalization of the business world continues, those managers who have the ability to thrive in a variety of environments and cultures will be a hot commodity, indeed.

Let's assume for a moment that you've landed a good job out of college in an international company, you've put in a few years of hard work and now your boss has called you in to her office to discuss your future with the organization. As a reward for your commitment and dedication, she is offering you a promotion, a raise…and a three-year managerial post at the company's Tokyo subsidiary.

For many young managers, an overseas assignment such as this would be seen as a coup: an exciting and promising opportunity to live abroad, to experience a new culture and, perhaps, to perform well enough to get on the fast track for future promotions. Although in today's globalized business world such opportunities are becoming more and more common, managers are only beginning to understand the special challenges that will confront them when they work overseas. The same intriguing cultural differences that induce vacationers to travel to foreign countries can — in a business setting — frustrate and baffle the best-intentioned overseas manager. In fact, it has become increasingly well recognized that culture has a profound influence on organizational behavior.

The miscommunication that so often arises from cultural differences can take a variety of forms: A prompt German executive arriving for a scheduled meeting with an Arab official may be forced to wait stewing for hours, for example, while the government official, who doesn't place the same importance on punctuality, takes care of other business and visitors. Or representatives from Canada and China may flounder in a cross-cultural meeting, as one side pushes for a speedy resolution and the other tries to avoid direct confrontation. Or, in a more extreme case, an entire business unit may languish after its management fails to understand the needs and expectations of the host country.

Although cultural differences exist to a certain degree even between close neighbors, such as Mexico and the United States or France and Germany, one of the starkest contrasts — and one of the most well documented — is the cultural gap between the U.S. and Japan. Even the way Japanese and Americans play baseball reflects the vast cultural discrepancies: While American players thrive on stolen bases, home runs and other feats stressing the glory of individual endeavor, Japanese teams play a careful, cautious game typified by walks, sacrifice bunts in the first inning and lengthy strategy sessions.[3] As for the business world, the American manager who takes a post in Tokyo, or the Japanese manager who transfers to Detroit, must make some very profound changes in how they operate.

For example, a member of a Japanese team that established a Panasonic subsidiary in Vancouver, WA, Atsushi Kageyama, reported that although the venture was largely a success, the American employees nevertheless experienced "culture shock," and expressed a number of criticisms at the firm's first anniversary.[4] Workers complained, among others things, that Japanese managers didn't trust American workers and were too secretive; that American managers were given too little authority; that job descriptions were fuzzy; and that Japanese management was slow to make decisions and overly negative.

In response to these criticisms, Kageyama offered the following insightful summary of some of the differences that may have contributed to the Americans' sense of culture shock: Managers in Japan he wrote, are

3. Robert Whiting, *You Gotta Have Wa: When Two Cultures Collide on the Baseball Diamond,* (New York: MacMillan, 1989).

4. Atsushi Kageyama, "Looking for the Real Thing in Sony," *The Wall Street Journal,* (October 2, 1989).

…rarely given the kind of individual authority that is common in American companies. Americans value an aggressive, quick, individualistic decisions-making style. But for the Japanese it is more important to have consensus than to have a quick decision. Working relationships in Japanese companies are long-term, and loyalty, cooperation, and harmonious interpersonal relationships are very important. A participative management style has developed in Japan to induce better cooperation. This means less individual authority and a much longer decision-making process than Americans are used to. In this system the nail that sticks out tends to get hammered down.

Maybe some Americans who were used to standing out and who expected praise as a result were bewildered when no praise came. But it is important for Americans to understand that Japanese rarely praise others because they are uncomfortable when others praise them. Praise is confused with flattery, and flattery is a cause of mistrust.

Cultural differences such as the ones Kageyama identified can profoundly affect expectations of what a given job entails in a different country. One study, for example, maintained that because of a fundamental difference in "thinking style," Asian and American CEOs vary both in *what* they typically do, as well as in *how* they accomplish their tasks.[5] As a generalization, the study's author argued, Asian CEOs are "systems" thinkers, focussing on the interrelationships of all elements in the puzzle, while Western CEOs have a more analytic, cause-and-effect orientation. Table 17.1 which breaks down the progression of a typical day for an American and Japanese CEO responding to the same events, shows the vastly different actions that can result from these different management approaches.

5. Robert H. Doktor, "Asian and American CEOs: A Comparative Study," *Organizational Dynamics*, (Winter 1990).

Table 17.1 American and Japanese CEOS: A Comparison of a Typical Day

American	Japanese
6:30 a.m. Mr. Mann, president of Eastern Oil, begins his day with a cup of coffee.	
7:15 To beat traffic he leaves early for work.	
7:15-7:45 Along the way he uses his minicassette recorder to dictate instructions to his secretary and employees.	
7:45-8:00 Mr. Mann's mobile phone rings as he pulls into Eastern Oil. His refinery production manager tells of an oil leak at the Indonesia plant. The manager wants instructions on what to do next. The president says he will call him back with a plan of action.	
8:00 Mr. Mann has his secretary call in all necessary personnel for an 8:30 meeting and his assistant gathers all related files.	8:00 a.m. Mr. Nakamura, president of Congee Oil, begins his day with a limousine ride.
8:20-8:30 He asks the legal department about legal problems that could result from the spill.	
8:30-8:50 He briefs subordinates on what is known so far about the spill.	
9:00-9:15 The legal staff submits reports on what can and should be done.	9:00 Mr. Nakamura arrives. He proceeds to have tea and read the newspaper.
9:17-10:00 Mr. Mann meets with plant and design engineers and discusses suggestions on how to contain the oil spill.	

10:03 The VP of marketing and communications says the press is calling for a story. She wants to know what the angle should be.

10:10-10:25 The Indonesia plant manager calls back, asking what the plan of attack is.

10:31-10:47 The plant engineers at the headquarters decide to shut down the plant until the leak is contained.

10:55-11:15 The accounting department is asked how much the plant shutdown will cost. The comptroller says he will have the figures in an hour.

11:30 The Indonesia plant manager calls back, saying that only the affected area of the plant has been shut down, so production will continue at 60 percent capacity.

11:45 a.m.-12:15 p.m. Mr. Mann holds another meeting with the chief assistants to get an update on the situation.

12:15-12:30 He has a hurried lunch while talking on the phone to the legal department about insurance clauses.

12:30 At this point Mr. Mann already has had many times as many meetings as his Japanese counterpart in half the time. The remainder of his day is a mirror image of his morning.

9:45 Mr. Mann finishes his day, having had a grand total of 18 meetings, 20 phone calls, 2 vending machine meals, and a late night at the office.

10:00 a.m.-12 noon He meets with subordinates to discuss why the planned effort in the South China Sea isn't working. (Earlier the CEO was made aware of the problem and informed his subordinates indirectly of his solution. The subordinates then met and developed a consensus of opinion on the solution.) At the same time, the subordinates, already aware that there has been an oil leak at an Indonesian plant, do not mention the leak to the CEO. Rather, their staff makes a considerable effort to develop an appropriate response plan to the leak problem.

12:15-12:30 The subordinates and staff inform Mr. Nakamura of the oil leak and the plan of action already in place to address the problem. Mr. Nakamura acknowledges the information and compliments the staff on their quick action.

12:30-2:30 He meets with an MITI (Ministry of International Trade and Industry) representative for lunch to discuss long-term production goals.

3:00-5:50 He meets with two department heads to discuss the 25-year plan for the Yokohama refinery.

6:30 p.m.-1:00 a.m. He has cocktails with a supplier, followed by dinner and evening entertainment at a private restaurant club in the Ginza.

This table is excerpted from Robert H. Doktor's, "Asian and American CEOs: A Comparative Study," *Organizational Dynamics*, (Winter 1990).

Considering the disparity in managerial style and substance demonstrated by these two examples, it is not hard to imagine how clashes could occur when Americans and Japanese try to do business together. But cultural clashes are by no means limited to East-meets-West transactions. When brash General Electric Co. took over the sedate French medical-equipment maker Cie. Generale do Radiologie (CGR) in 1988, for example, sparks began to fly almost immediately.[6] The combination of GE's aggressive "all-American" style with CGR's reserved culture made the process of assimilation doubly hard. Even GE's morale-boosting ploy of asking all CGR European managers to wear T-shirts sporting the GE slogan "Go for One" to a training seminar backfired: French managers found the exercise humiliating and overbearing.

6. Mark M. Nelson and E. S. Browning, "GE's Culture Turns Sour at French Unit," *The Wall Street Journal*, (July 31, 1990).

Of course, Americans aren't the only ones who sometimes appear "ugly" in their business dealings with other countries. Companies based outside of the U.S. are just as likely to stumble with their American operations if they try to enforce their own methods and beliefs without a proper appreciation of the culture they are facing. After Britain's Blue Arrow employment agency took over Milwaukee-based Manpower in 1987, for example, friction between the two cultures became an immediate issue.[7] As a symbol of his distaste for the way Blue Arrow was trying to run things, Manpower's chairman, Mitchell Fromstein, even refused to distribute the Blue Arrow company newsletter, which, he told *Time* magazine, was "poor in quality, provincial and British in nature with little articles about the soccer team in South Wales." In an ironic twist, Fromstein ended up in charge of the combined company after a battle for control.

No one knows exactly what percentage of overseas ventures fail as a result of cultural misunderstandings. But a major study of Swedish expatriates found that 25 percent of managers sent abroad returned before the end of their contracts.[8] Moreover, one estimate suggests that as many as one of every five American managers sent overseas will return home before successfully completing an assignment.[9] The cost of these failures, both in personal terms and in what it costs companies in time, energy and salaries, is staggering.

Working overseas is a challenge that more and more managers must meet. In fact, the ability to adjust to new cultures and to flourish abroad is becoming more important each year. Given that cultural differences are unavoidable, what can managers do to ready themselves for the new era of globalization? Following are a few suggestions that may help managers prepare for the demanding task of doing business abroad:

• **Acknowledge and Understand Cultural Differences** Ignoring the concerns and behaviors of a foreign culture is counterproductive to working within it effectively. But neither is it realistic for managers to feel they must adopt the styles or actions of every country they are dealing with. Instead, they must recognize where important cultural differences lie, and then find a way to allow for these differences in their dealings. Even if such "cultural compromises" may sometimes require managers to negotiate more slowly than they might like, for example, or to handle conflicts indirectly instead of head-on, a manager who understands the cultural beliefs behind different behaviors will be able to handle such situations with diplomacy and skill.

• **Tailor Management Styles to Specific Situations** Many young managers in the United States have been barraged with course work or texts advocating the adoption of a particular "best" management style. But most of these organizational behavior theories have been developed with American companies in mind. The same approach that might have brought stellar results in the United States could prove disastrous in Argentina or the Philippines. "In moving from domestic to international management, leaders must develop a wider range of thinking patterns and behaviors along with the ability to select the pattern best suited to the particular situation," wrote Nancy J. Adler. "Effective international managers must be chameleons capable of acting in many ways, not experts adhering rigidly to one approach."[10]

• **Develop Respect for Different Cultures** Many observers of U.S. culture have complained that Americans are naturally more isolated and parochial than, for example, Europeans, whose homelands typically share borders with several different countries, and who are often fluent in at least two or three languages. But even though many Americans may not have grown up with as much exposure to foreign cultures, they can operate just as effectively if they approach new situations and cultures with respect and a willingness to learn. Peter Kuin, former vice-chancellor of the International Academy of Management, wrote that "the magic of multinational management lies not so much in perfection of methods of excellence...as in developing respect for other nationalities and cultures and for the determination to succeed in foreign markets."[11]

7. William McWhirter, "I Came, I Saw, I Blundered," *Time*, (October 9, 1989).

8. Yoram Zeira and Moshe Barai, "Selecting Managers for Foreign Assignments," *Management Decision*, (1987).

9. John S. McClenahen, "Why U.S. Managers Fail Overseas," *Industry Week*, (November 16, 1987).

10. Adler, loc. cit.

11. Peter Kuin, "The Magic of Multinational Management," *Harvard Business Review*, (November-December 1972).

Task I: Am I Cut Out for Working in Another Country?

Find someone who has lived and worked in a country other than their native one. Interview them and identify what obstacles they faced; what successes and failures they had; how the international assignment affected their career; and what skills they think are needed to be successful abroad. After the interview, answer the following questions:

1. What did I learn about the challenges of living and working in another country?

2. What are the major difficulties and barriers that have to be overcome?

3. What are the skills, values and attitudes that I must have in order to succeed?

4. Are there some limits to how accommodating I would be in another culture?

5. How would I prepare for such an assignment differently based on what I learned from the interview?

Task II: Prejudice Analysis

Everyone has prejudices. Do you believe you don't hold any biases? Think again!
Maybe you have a bias against royalty, or rich kids, or illegal aliens, or men, or
athletes on scholarship, or, just perhaps, university professors. Your task is to do
some careful self-examination and reflection. It is not easy to confront this issue
honestly, but prejudice is real and it can have a profound impact on your performance as a manager. The prejudice may or may not be directed at another culture,
but examining this issue should help you understand how such prejudices operate.

1. I have a bias against the following group(s):

2. Why do you think this prejudice developed within you?
   How did such a view become ingrained?

3. What function does it currently serve for you to think this way?

4. Do you want to hang on to this bias?

5. How would you go about deleting this from your views? What information and/or experience
   would lead you to think differently?

Task III: Create a Cross-Cultural Experience

12. This exercise was adapted from "A Painless Approach to Integrating 'International' into OB, HRM and Management Courses," *OBTR*. vol. XIII, No. 3, (1988-89).

One way to learn more about living and working in "foreign" cultures is to experience—if even briefly—a local version of a very different world than your own. Your task is to plan, carry out and then analyze a cross-cultural experience. This could range from visiting an ethnic neighborhood unfamiliar to you to spending time with a rival fraternity or sorority. The purpose is to seek out a situation where you might experience some "culture shock."[12]

1. What other cultures did you experience?

2. What seemed different than the way you would normally behave, think, and look?

3. How did you feel as an outsider?

4. Could you ever become comfortable in that culture? Why or why not?

5. If you were asked to live, work and operate within this different culture, what would you want to do to ensure that you would be welcomed and effective?

Lights

We have already looked at some of the cultural differences that exist between the U.S. and Japan, and have talked about how these differences may affect organization behavior. The videoclip you will see in class today lays out some of these cultural clashes. *Gung-Ho* features Michael Keaton as Hunt Stevenson, a working-class hero intent on salvaging Hadleyville, a struggling Rust Belt town where he lives. After traveling to Japan as an emissary for the town, Stevenson convinces Japanese car manufacturer Assan Motor Co. to reopen Hadleyville's recently shut down car manufacturing plant. The segment you are about to see opens as workers arrive for their first day under new management, with Stevenson as the new employee liaison.

Camera

The segment begins with the workers out on the field the first day for morning exercises, and concludes with a Japanese manager chiding an American worker, and saying, "There is one way to run this company!"

Action

After watching this video clip, think about the following questions:

1. What traits of the Japanese managers would you characterize as positive, or good for the company? Could these approaches ever work in the United States?

2. What mistakes did the Japanese managers make in dealing with the American workers?

3. What about the American workers; what were the positive aspects of their approach to the job?

4. Did the Japanese managers identify some real failings on the part of the employees?

5. What are some examples of racial bias on either side?

6. What could have been done to make this a smoother transition from the start?

Name _____

ID# _____

Section _____

The following case addresses some of the issues we considered earlier in the chapter and poses the kinds of troubling questions that face organizations and managers as we move toward a more global business world. In preparation for class, read the case and answer the following questions.

Reading 17.1

SHOULD CHEMICALS GROUP POST A WOMAN SALES MANAGER TO ASIA?[13]

Oscar Hofer, managing director of Austrian-based chemicals group Schaub, had been procrastinating for weeks over the appointment of a regional marketing manager for Asia. His initial choice had been Claus Dietrich, a tireless if unspectacular performer, who had serviced customers and suppliers in East Europe for the past decade.

But at the executive committee's regular Monday morning meeting it soon became obvious that a majority of Hofer's management team opposed the selection of the 45-year-old Dietrich. Moreover, there seemed to be a consensus that the best person for the new post was Gertrud Wagner, Schaub's star sales performer who had trebled business in Scandinavia since joining the company two years ago. The ambitious 35-year-old Wagner had been lobbying for the Asian appointment and had hinted that if she didn't get it, she would be looking for a new job.

"Breaking with our policy not to send women managers to Asia is not a decision I take lightly," Hofer said. "I have no qualms about Wagner's qualifications. But this is a new and sensitive posting. In Dietrich we have an equally competent and loyal candidate whom we can send to Asia without having to worry about the unknown cultural factor, not to mention Wagner's dual-career family problems."

"That need worry no one," said personnel director Heidi Polzin. "The Wagners are a model dual-career couple. Her husband is very supportive, and both he and their two children are keen about the move to Asia. He believes it will create new opportunities for his job as a freelance writer."

"All Wagner's qualifications may count for nothing if she runs up against traditional barriers to women in male-dominated societies," interjected finance director Norbert Esser. "No doubt she'll be able to service existing customers, but what about her ability to develop new business?"

Marketing director Walter Mayer noted that "judging by her performance in Scandinavia, Wagner should have no problems on that score."

"Ah, but Nordic companies have very liberated attitudes towards women in senior management positions," Esser pointed out. "Asia is a different ball game. I remember my grandfather telling me how Chinese families used to venerate their sons and drown their infant daughters."

Raising his hand to silence the chorus of laughter, Hofer remarked: "Comments like that only serve to fuel myths. But they reinforce the reservations shared by some of us: namely that Wagner may be ready for Asia, but is Asia ready for her?"

"I'm afraid that the only way we're going to get the definitive answer is to get Wagner out there," said Mayer. "We take a risk if we do. We risk losing her if we don't."

13. The fictional case was developed by Jules Arbose. It appeared in *International Management*, (July/August 1989).

1. Is Gertrud Wagner the right choice for the Asian post? Why or why not?

2. How strongly should organizations weigh possible racial biases in making a personnel selection?

3. If Wagner is the choice, what steps could either she or her company take to smooth her entry into the Asian marketplace?

4. If Schaub doesn't choose Wagner, what can the company offer to retain her?

MAKING CONNECTIONS: IN-CLASS INTERACTIONS

Instructions

1. Break into groups of three for role playing:

One person take on the role of Gertrud Wagner, arguing why she should receive the new managerial position;

One person assume the role of Norbert Esser, finance director, who questions Wagner's ability to be effective in Asia,

And one person adopt the role of Heidi Polzin, the personnel director who believes Wagner is the right choice for the job.

2. Spend a few minutes debating the pros and cons of Wagner's selection.

3. As a group, reach a consensus on what you believe to be the right decision.

4. Choose one person to report to the class.

5. After all the presentations have been made, vote — as a class — on the decision that Schaub's managing director, Oscar Hofer, should make.

In the past, getting an overseas managerial assignment wasn't necessarily seen as a plum job. At many companies, managers posted abroad often came to feel that they had become "invisible" to the executives back at headquarters running the "real" business. "Out of sight, out of mind" was an expression that struck terror into the hearts of ambitious managers sent to foreign countries.

But the sense that going abroad can prove a costly detour in a manager's upward mobility is rapidly being replaced by the belief that overseas experience is one of the key qualifications that companies will be looking for when grooming their chief executive officers. Indeed, the flexibility, responsiveness and adaptability that a manager must demonstrate to thrive in a foreign clime are all key leadership qualities.

The following excerpt details some of the changing ideas about the growing importance of international experience.

Reading 17.2

GOING GLOBAL: THE CHIEF EXECUTIVES IN YEAR 2000 WILL BE EXPERIENCED ABROAD[14]

By Amanda Bennett

Since World War II, the typical corporate chief executive officer has looked something like this:

He started out as a finance man with an undergraduate degree in accounting. He methodically worked his way up through the company from the controller's office in a division, to running that division, to the top job. His military background shows: He is used to giving orders — and to having them obeyed. As the head of the United Way drive, he is a big man in his community. However, the first time he traveled overseas on business was as chief executive. Computers make him nervous.

But peer into the executive suite of the year 2000 and see a completely different person.

His undergraduate degree is in French literature, but he also has a joint M.B.A./engineering degree. He started in research and was quickly picked out as a potential CEO. He zigzagged from research to marketing to finance. He proved himself in Brazil by turning around a flailing joint venture. He speaks Portuguese and French and is on a first-name basis with commerce ministers in half a dozen countries. Unlike his predecessor's predecessor, he isn't a drill sergeant. He is first among equals in a five-person Office of the Chief Executive.

As the 40-year postwar epoch of growing markets and domestic-only competition fades, so too is vanishing the narrow one-company, one-industry chief executive. By the turn of the century, academicians, consultants and executives themselves predict, companies' choices of leaders will be governed by increasing international competition, the globalization of companies, the spread of technology, demographic shifts, and the speed of overall change.

"The world is going to be so significantly different it will require a completely different kind of CEO," says Ed Dunn, corporate vice president of Whirlpool Corp. The next century's corporate chief, Mr. Dunn adds, "must have a multienvironment, multicountry, multifunctional, maybe even multicompany, multiindustry experience."

The changing requirements bemuse some who hold, or once held, the top slot. "I'm glad I lived when I did," says William May, who was chief executive officer of American Can Co. between 1965 and 1980. "I'd have to really learn a whole lot of new tricks" to be a chief executive today.

With the 21st century slightly over a decade away, many companies are already trying to figure out just who the chief executive of the future ought to be.

14. Amanda Bennett, "Going Global: The Chief Executives in Year 2000 Will Be Experienced Abroad," *The Wall Street Journal*, (February 27, 1989).

To study the question, Dow Chemical Co. is setting up a worldwide panel of senior executives. "We want to know what kind of skills and knowledge will be needed so we can give the heirs apparent that training in the next few years," says Willard B. Maxwell, a senior training consultant at Dow. Whirlpool, which until recently identified potential chief executives about five years in advance, now believes that the selection process may have to begin as early as 25 years ahead. "We're thinking more about development throughout someone's career," Mr. Dunn says.

Until recently, the road to the top in a big corporation has been fairly well marked. General Motors Corp., for example, has been run by a finance man for 28 of the past 32 years. More than three-quarters of the chief executives surveyed in 1987 by search firm Heidrick & Struggles had finance, manufacturing or marketing backgrounds.

Donald Frey, recently retired chairman of Bell & Howell Co., started in product engineering and product planning at Ford Motor Co. "It was a fairly conventional route for the sacred few in my generation. We became CEOs by virtue of being able to design and get products made."

In the future, however, specific functional backgrounds such as marketing or finance are becoming less important for chief executives. "Where they come from won't be at all relevant," says Jerry Wind of the University of Pennsylvania's Wharton School. With creative financing techniques that turn financial decisions into marketing questions, manufacturing processes that center on computer technology, and product designs that depend on rapid market feedback, the chief executive will, instead, need a varied background.

"It will be very difficult for a single-discipline individual to reach the top," predicts Douglas Danforth, former chairman of Westinghouse Electric Co.

Specific industry experience will also become less relevant because there will be few one-industry companies. More than two-thirds of chief executives in a survey to be released later this year by executive-search firm Korn/Ferry International and Columbia Graduate School of Business said their companies would be involved in several different industries by the year 2000, compared with fewer than half who described their companies that way today.

Intensifying international competition will make the home-grown chief executive obsolete. "Global, global, global," is how Noel Tichy, a professor at University of Michigan's graduate school of business, describes the wider-ranging chief executive of the future. "Travel overseas," Mr. Danforth of Westinghouse advises future chief executives. "Meet with the prime minister, the ministers of trade and commerce. Meet with the king of Spain and the chancellor of West Germany. Get yourself known."

With over half of Arthur Andersen & Co.'s revenue generated outside the U.S., the company's next chief executive "will be a person with experience outside the borders of the U.S., which I have not," says Duane R. Kullberg, the head of the big accounting and consulting company. "If you go back 20 years, you could be pretty insular and still survive. Today, that's not possible."

Dow Chemical figures that mere international exposure isn't enough. It wants chief executives who have run foreign businesses for a long time and foresees the day when many other companies will, too. "About five years of international experience" will do, says Dow Chemical Chairman Paul Orrefice, who worked for Dow in Switzerland, Italy, Brazil and Spain and was its first president of Latin American operations in 1966. "It should be long enough to really run it."

Others predict that by the next century, overseas executives will be equal contenders in the race for the top. This year, for the first time, Merck & Co. won't segregate its senior-executive training programs by country. "We have internationalized our training," says Art Strohmer, Merck's executive director of human resources. "We have high-level employees from Europe, Latin America, the U.S. and the rest of the world rubbing shoulders with each other." The model many cite for future chief executives is Coca-Cola Co.'s chairman, Roberto Goizueta, who started out with the company in Havana, Cuba, in 1954.

COMING TO OUR SENSES: MAKING A DIFFERENCE

Opportunities for managers to gain international experience are expanding every year. At the same time, businesses are placing more and more value on the very skills that help managers prosper overseas: a flexible management style; an appreciation of differences in behaviors and cultures, and respect for other people. Managers who become skilled at understanding the demands of foreign market-places, and at recognizing the range of organizational behaviors that follow from cultural differences, will be well equipped to prosper in our increasingly global marketplace.

In light of the issues raised in this chapter, and the *Gung Ho* video clip, think about the following questions:

1. How easy or difficult would it be for me to accommodate to other cultures?

2. How easy or difficult would it be for me to learn other languages? Are there other ways to "fit in" to a foreign culture?

3. How easy or difficult would it be for me to manage people who are "foreign" to me, or to be managed by people who are "foreign"?

4. How can I be sure that I don't become too ethnocentric like the classic "ugly American"?

Chapter 18

Managing Change

It was 1960 and Simplex Basic Products Co. was in trouble. Employee morale had unaccountably begun to slip and quality control on the company's four lines of rubber bands was slipping too. At the same time, a new competitor was beginning to encroach on the tri-state area that Simplex had always dominated. Desperate for advice, Max Capable, Simplex's president, CEO and chief financial officer, called in a bright young consultant to help redirect the company. With the consultant's help, Capable launched a comprehensive restructuring, using many of the tactics thought to be most effective in managing change.

For example, Capable gathered his four key line managers together for a brainstorming session and impressed on them how serious Simplex's dilemma was. For their part, the managers reported that employees were discontent because they felt excluded from all decision making, even in product areas where they could have good input. After encouraging workers to come forward with new ideas, Capable gradually geared up to add bobby pins and barrettes to the Simplex offerings. Workers, pleased that they had been consulted about the problem yet frightened by the possibility of losing their jobs if Simplex didn't prosper, rallied behind the vision of becoming the most comprehensive hair care products company in the region.

To drum up enthusiasm for the new product lines, Capable instituted a generous reward system, giving bonuses to employees who came up with innovative ideas for hair care products, such as glow-in-the-dark head bands and edible barrettes. With this new array of products, Simplex easily overpowered its closest competitors. Moreover, at the end of two years, many of the same Simplex employees who had formerly spent their coffee breaks shooting rubber bands at each other now worked right through lunch hour to achieve their quality and production goals. Capable had presided over a resoundingly successful turnaround.

Break to some 30 years later. As a result of its restructuring, Simplex has experienced unprecedented growth and left rubber bands far behind. In fact, after acquiring British competitor Comfort Skincare, Simplex has changed its name to Complex International, and now offers products ranging from genetically engineered wrinkle removers to 24-hour diapers. Capable has retired a millionaire and although Complex still has a U.S. headquarters, its British operation functions semiautonomously, and there are sales outposts in more than a dozen foreign countries.

But all is not well at Complex. Once again, the company faces pressures for change. More to the point, it faces pressures for multiple changes. Animal rights activists are picketing the laboratory where Complex tests its wrinkle remover on puppies. The head of the British operations has begun to offer free child care to all workers, and the U.S. employees are clamoring for the same benefit. The manager of the diaper division, a stout environmentalist, has resigned following news reports that the 24-hour diaper is the least biodegradable product on the market. And Complex's largest competitor has just introduced an inexpensive cream that reverses baldness.

In an effort to respond to these pressures, Complex's board of directors calls back out of retirement the now aging consultant who had helped Simplex so many years before. Unfortunately, faced with this daunting array of challenges, the consultant begins to hyperventilate and must be carried away from the room before he can devise a change strategy. In his place, you are called in to help.

But will you know how to manage change in today's world? Will you be able to help an organization develop a strategy for responding to multiple changes? Furthermore, can you orchestrate a process by which the company can respond to its competitive pressures?

The example of Simplex/Complex is obviously fictitious. But it does represent how managing change has become more complicated than it was two or three decades ago. As this case illustrates, today's companies often are confronted with a bewildering array of internal and external forces for change that their earlier counterparts simply didn't face.

Are you prepared for this challenge? Are you flexible enough? Will you be effective at introducing strategic, cultural, technological and human resource changes as they are needed? Will you know when to change? What to change? How to change? And, who to help you make change happen? Managing has virtually become synonymous with managing change. It means that you will be spending a lot of time at work instigating changes affecting other people and coping with multiple changes affecting you.

Name _____

ID# _____

Section _____

In preparation for class, think back on some of your own experiences with change.

1. What does "change" mean to you? Circle the words below that you would most frequently associate with change:

Improve	Transition	Upheaval	Learn
Alter	Fun	Different	New
Transform	Birth	Deteriorate	Opportunity
Exchange	Stress	Redo	Disruption
Exciting	Fearsome	Transfer	Replace
Challenging	Chance	Better	Youth
Vary	Modify	Initiate	Awesome

2. What pattern do you see in your descriptors of change in your life?

3. Do you think your "associations" with change are typical?

Managing Change   349

Suppose you arrive in class today and the professor announces that everyone is going to have to move to a new seat in the classroom. What would be your reaction? "Great news, I really wanted a change of scenery," — unlikely. "What a marvelous opportunity to meet some new students,'' — also unlikely. "If that's what the professor wants, it's OK with me," — unimaginable!

Your reaction would probably be more like the following: "What a pain in the neck, I really liked my seat,'' or "What's next? I'll probably get called on to talk!" or "What a waste of time and energy.'' Even though this example is trivial, the reactions are symptomatic of how we often feel in the face of change. We are more often resistant, angry, befuddled or disappointed than we are elated, energized and challenged.

And yet the twenty-first century manager will likely face a steady barrage of change. How will you react and handle it? Befuddled or elated? Will the glass seem half full or half empty to you? Managers and organizations are going to have to build a strong capability for anticipating and adapting to change; indeed, some have even advocated "thriving on change and chaos."

Viewing change as opportunity rather than threat and even seeking out change is antithetical to how many of us generally operate as human beings. We are, after all, creatures of habit. We generally prefer control in our lives and some predictability. Most of us operate according to the principle that says, "We don't change things unless they are broken." The new credo for the twenty-first century, however, may sound more like, "If it ain't perfect, you better be improving and changing." And since individuals and organizations are never perfect, the challenge of managing change will be a constant.

It hasn't always been this way, however. Many of your parents' generation worked in organizations that had stability as their hallmark. The deal was pretty simple: a job for life in return for loyalty and a "fair day's work." This is the way it was for many industries such as banking, insurance, oil, steel, auto, telephone, food service and transportation. These stalwarts of yesterday have become among the most turbulent of industries today. Why? Many forces are reshaping the business landscape:

1. "Global business": This is now a redundant phrase. To be doing business means to be global because global threats and opportunities have become standard fare.

2. Technology: Today's speed and remarkable innovations make obsolescent last year's state-of-the-art achievements, and so it will continue into the twenty-first century.

3. World financial markets: Economic swings are now more frequent and more dependent on geopolitical and geoeconomic factors. The infusion of Japanese and other Far East investment in the United States and Europe is only one example of how the value and exchange of money more readily will affect a company's profitability and ability to invest.

4. Competition: There is more and more competition for fewer resources, especially in mature markets. Even as new markets open up, competition quickly becomes fierce.

5. Organizational capability: A new source of competitive advantage is an organization's culture, competencies and systems. For example, increasingly the excellent companies have attacked major areas such as quality and customer service through comprehensive programs. These become new ways of doing business and require major changes in attitudes and practices.

When you put these five forces together and add in various other idiosyncratic factors, you find a work place that is rife with turbulence and uncertainty. These forces for change, however, are often equaled by forces of resistance to change.

Kanter identified 10 common reasons for resistance: (1) loss of control, (2) excess uncertainty, (3) being surprised, (4) perceived differences from normal habits and routines, (5) perceived indictment of the "old way," (6) concerns about future competence, (7) ripple effects on personal life, (8) more work, (9) past resentments from other changes or actions, and (10) real threats to one's values, status or position.[1]

An effective change process is one that tries to mitigate these common sources of resistance and allows people the time and the support to "work through" their reactions. Often these reactions approximate the overall experience of "loss." When any of us lose something near and dear to us, we react in predictable ways. In its most dramatic form, it is as if we are in bereavement. As such, we first react with denial and shock, then anger and resentment, and perhaps depression, followed by acceptance and acknowledgement of the new reality.

The loss typically has the following four dimensions:

1. Loose ends: People become confused, temporarily lost and disoriented. In essence, they are at "loose ends."

2. Out of it: People pull back, withdraw and become disengaged. In essence, they step "out of it."

3. Sad: People are depressed by what has occurred. Familiar routines, comfortable relationships and known support systems are disturbed.

4. Sour: People are irritated, upset and angry.[2]

Consider these reactions and stages when viewing the video segment from the movie *Broadcast News,* which will be shown in conjunction with this module.

In managing change, it therefore becomes critical to help people overcome their resistance and reactions. This requires both a sensitivity to people's intellects and emotions. Both levels coexist inside individuals who are being subjected to change. Individuals need to be aware and, it is hoped, convinced of the need for change. They need to develop or be provided a sense of what the new conditions will be like. And finally, they need some sort of transition plan for getting themselves prepared, competent and excited about the new circumstances. These three factors can be aggregated and understood in organizational terms.

There are three phases of the change process in organizations that are generally described by management observers. First, organizations need a reason to change. This is relatively easy if and when a crisis occurs. Yet, while we may assume that everyone seeing the same data interprets it the same way, we often learn later that the so-called crisis is more evident to some than to others.

Thus, managers must spend time convincing others, or even themselves, that there is good reason to change. No change occurs without this sort of driving rationale. And the more one tries to institute change before its need is undeniable, the more difficult it is to get people to pay attention. Diagnosing and identifying the need for change — what is sometimes called "unfreezing" or energizing the organization — is a necessary but not sufficient condition for making change happen.

A second key ingredient is to develop a vision of what should be changed. In other words, once you recognize that things can't stay the way they are, you need to have a reasonable image of how things will be better in the future. And this vision needs to be shared as widely as possible.

1. Rosabeth Kanter, "Managing the Human Side of Change," *Management Review,* (April 1985), pp. 52-56.

2. George Truell, *Helping Employees Cope With Change,* (Buffalo, NY: PAT Publications, 1988).

For example, a vision could be to become an organization that is "the best at serving customers" or "the most cost efficient." This may not be that different from what you do when you aspire to and dream of becoming a marathon runner or "a friend who'll always be there" or a more caring family member. These go far beyond the idea of a goal because they are dreams that can never be completed.

The final piece of the process is to create a transition plan, a way to get "from here to there." Sound easy? No, not really. Letting go of things we are familiar with, even if we recognize we must, is never easy. And being motivated to change to become something (or someone) else who we don't really "know" is always difficult. So, we need some "enabling mechanisms" for helping us along.

These might include the following: new incentives, training in new skills, finding role models of the new behaviors, hiring or promoting people who are more receptive to the changes we want, experimenting with new behaviors and gaining permission from "the powers that be" to do so and, finally, preserving the will to persist despite what are likely to be substantial obstacles.

Change occurs when all three of the above conditions are met:

1. When the need for change is well understood and communicated;

2. When there develops an image or vision of how things could be better, and

3. When the transition from the old to the new is well implemented.

But these must be done in such a way that the costs are minimized. That is, if the costs of losing skills, confidence, power, rewards or any other valued part of one's work life are perceived to be greater than the value in changing, the change is likely to be stymied.

The process of change then becomes critical, perhaps more critical than the nature of the change itself. Sometimes relatively little changes, poorly introduced, will be far more disruptive and painful than bigger changes that are well managed. What are the common characteristics of companies that have been successful at renewing themselves? A comparative study of six companies identified key elements in the process leading to successful change:

1. Ownership: Unit management and employees must have complete ownership of the changes they were trying to bring about. Programs driven from the corporate offices undermined this.

2. Business-problem focused: Local management identified a change relating to a core business issue.

3. The process and structure of the change effort was key: A critical business issue was attacked through the help of multiple stakeholders and included the development of an engaging vision.

4. Changes in behaviors were thus driven by changes in informal organizational arrangements: Attitudes and skills shifted after people participated in crafting a new form of management.

3. Michael Beer, R. Eisenstat and B. Spector, *The Critical Path to Corporate Renewal,* (Boston, MA: Harvard Business School Press, 1990).

5. Accountability: Top management held people accountable for the changes and the change process, not just the financial and operating results.[3]

Typically, changes break down because there is a disconnect and conspicuous inattention to the varying needs of the senior management (often key to the development of the reason for change and the vision of the change), the middle management (often key to the implementation and transition process) and the majority of employees or recipients of change who must enact the changes.[4] Ultimately, successful changes occur when and if there is attention to the individuals involved and their particular needs and reactions, and to the demanding pressures for change.

Managing change is a delicate process that must be carefully yet flexibly fashioned if organizations are to become as adaptive and responsive as they must be to remain competitive. It takes a major long-term commitment of time, energy and talent to undertake major changes. There is already an enormous tendency on the part of companies to push faster, to spend less and to stop earlier than the change process requires. But no changes will "stick" and provide enough good will for the future unless and until the recipients of change come "on board."

What you will probably appreciate after this chapter is the magnitude of these challenges. We also hope however that you will become more confident that change can be managed well and that you can help an organization to become more effective.

4. Rosabeth Kanter, B. Stein and T.D. Jick, *The Challenge of Organizational Change*, (New York: Free Press, 1992).

Lights: Budget Cuts at *Broadcast News*

One of the issues in managing change is how you react to the change itself. This depends on a number of factors: your personality, your previous experiences with similar situations, your personal circumstances and, of course, how the change is presented to you. We are now going to view another segment from *Broadcast News*. This segment portrays the announcement of budget cuts and layoffs at the station and shows the way various individuals react to the news.

Camera

Bill (Jack Nicholson) arrives as the station manager (Paul) is about to inform a number of individuals that they have been fired due to budget cuts. Carefully observe the reactions of each individual and how they were told of the changes. The cast of characters is as follows: Bill (Jack Nicholson), the national news anchor; Paul, the station manager; Paul's secretary; Tom (William Hurt); Jane (Holly Hunter); Albert Brooks; Ernie (the older fellow); Donny (wearing the bow tie); and the tall redhaired woman..

Note the reactions of these employees:

	Reactions
Tom (William Hurt)	
Jane (Holly Hunter)	
Albert Brooks	
Ernie (older fellow)	
Donny (bow tie)	
Tall redhaired woman	

Action

In debriefing the segment, you can examine two issues: First, how did people react to the news? Second, how well was the news of the change introduced?

Reactions

1. Why did people react as they did?

2. Why is change so difficult here?

3. How might you have reacted?

4. Why was this so traumatic even for the "survivors"?

The Management of the Change:

1. How was the change introduced?

2. How would you have managed things differently?

3. How would you have conducted the farewell party?

4. How can people be helped to cope with changes like these?

MAKING CONNECTIONS: IN-CLASS INTERACTIONS

Individual Task

Think of one thing during the past month that you tried to change in your personal life. (For example: "I tried to take more initiative;" "I tried to diet or do more recreation;" "I wanted to change my roommate's habit.")

1. What behavior in yourself (or in others) did you try to change?

2. Why were you trying to make this change?

3. How difficult did you think this change would be? Why?

4. How did you go about changing yourself or others?

5. How successful were you?

6. What prevented you from changing as quickly or as smoothly as you would have liked? (And what might lead you or them to return to the old way?)

7. What would you do differently if you had to do it all over again?

Group Task

1. Have each person describe the change they attempted, the process and the results.

2. As a group, discuss and identify those factors that enabled change to happen and those that impeded change.

3. What were the most common mistakes made in trying to make a change?

4. What lessons for managing change would you draw from your collective experiences?

MIRROR TALK: FOCUSSING ON ME

 It takes a lot of personal flexibility as well as organizational flexibility to handle the change challenges of twenty-first century organizations. Are you "countercyclical," doing the reverse of what is *au courant* just for the fun of it? Do you make a habit of trying new foods, magazines or activities? Do you engage in new projects without assurance of success? Are you open with friends and associates about your failings? Are you comfortable with a wide diversity of friends and relatives? Do you believe that if change does not occur, you would lose your zest for the future? If you are not this way, do you think you can change?

Take a look at yourself now:

The Change-Friendly Quotient Survey

In the situations described below, four reactions or coping methods are given. Put yourself in each scene and check all those responses you would actually use, leaving blank the ones you would rarely or never use. Also, write the number "1" by your favorite response.[5]

1. If my company reduced our insurance benefits package, I would:

   a. _____ talk to the benefits officer about it.

   b. _____ discuss it with others to see if they feel as I do about it.

   c. _____ seek additional insurance to compensate for lost benefits.

   d. _____ wonder if my company is in financial trouble; review my career options.

2. If a friend/colleague canceled our luncheon at the last possible minute, I would:

   a. _____ confront the person about his or her behavior.

   b. _____ ask around to see if this person has canceled with others.

   c. _____ think what to do with the free time and how it affects my schedule.

   d. _____ assess whether there was a good reason for canceling.

3. If I were sent for training in a field totally new to me, I would:

   a. _____ look forward to learning something entirely new.

   b. _____ get information from others who've had the training.

   c. _____ bone up on information that would help me with it.

   d. _____ evaluate how useful it would be to me.

4. If I were transferred to another city, I would:

   a. _____ picture myself living and working there.

   b. _____ find out more about the place by talking to everyone.

   c. _____ call a realtor to settle the housing issue.

   d. _____ review the social, personal and financial pros and cons.

5. If I were to notice one of my parent's health declining, I would:

   a. _____ contact my parent's doctor for an opinion.

   b. _____ talk it through with parents, relatives and friends.

   c. _____ read up on the illness and its symptoms.

   d. _____ try to determine how serious it really is.

5. Excerpt from Jacquelyn Wonder and Priscilla Donovan, *The Flexibility Factor*, (New York: Doubleday, 1989), pp. 16-19. Copyright ©1989 by Jacquelyn Wonder and Priscilla Donovan. Used by permission of Doubleday, a division of Bantam.

6. If an important relationship suddenly ended to my surprise, I would:

a. _____ become more active socially; plunge into new interests; develop a new skill.

b. _____ join a support group on breakups; talk to others who've "been there."

c. _____ transfer my energy to areas of my life that are going well.

d. _____ figure out what caused the breakup and, perhaps, consult an expert.

7. If my favorite newspaper columnist were dropped, I would:

a. _____ call the editor and ask for an explanation.

b. _____ read the replacement column and compare with my favorite.

c. _____ begin a letter-writing campaign to get the column reinstated.

d. _____ recall past columns to find reasons for the cancellation.

8. If a project I had devised were rejected, I would:

a. _____ protest and try to dissuade objectors.

b. _____ confer with others, then go "back to the drawing board."

c. _____ give it up if objections seem legitimate and move on.

d. _____ study the project design for possible flaws.

9. If a friend wore an inappropriate outfit, I would:

a. _____ smile and say "more power to you."

b. _____ ask others for their reactions to it.

c. _____ caution him or her about wearing it to work.

d. _____ worry about my friend but do nothing.

10. If I were delayed in traffic 30 minutes on my way to an important appointment, I would:

a. _____ try to find a shortcut or new route.

b. _____ rehearse explanations in my mind.

c. _____ try to find a phone to notify someone of my delay.

d. _____ assess how to turn the situation to my advantage.

11. If I were asked 20 minutes before a meeting to describe a project for which I'm responsible, I would:

a. _____ welcome the chance to make an impact; dream up a dramatic way to present it.

b. _____ ask others on my team for their input; conceptualize a brief overview.

c. _____ tune out everything going on around me; outline the essential information.

d. _____ decline until I had time to prepare more fully.

12. If I were challenged when discussing a topic I know well, I would:

a. _____ relish the controversy if the challenger is witty and friendly.

b. _____ ask the challenger to say more about his or her views, then paraphrase to further clarify.

c. _____ compare our points of view and attempt to get consensus.

d. _____ review how I came to my conclusions; wonder if the challenger has more data.

Self Assessment: Computing Your Scores

Four different reactions are offered for each situation. All of them are valid, normal and effective ways of managing change. Now it is time to compute your scores:

1. Add the number of *first* choices you checked in a, b, c and d and enter below.

_____ a. The Risker

_____ b. The Relater

_____ c. The Re-Focuser

_____ d. The Reasoner

Now, what do your scores mean? You may be predominantly one of the change styles below:

a. The Risker: Your change style is usually enthusiastic, spontaneous and daring.

b. The Relater: You rely on your friends, family and others for information and advice in processing change.

c. The Re-Focuser: You focus your energies and like to finish one thing at a time.

d. The Reasoner: Your attitude toward change is studied and careful and your style logical and orderly.

2. Enter the grand total of all the responses you checked.

The larger the grand total, the more flexible your change style. That is, checking all four alternatives on a given question indicates that you are very flexible in the type of situation described and have many options in dealing with that kind of change.

Here is some more explanation of the different types of styles, their strengths and weaknesses:

Risker If most of your first choices are in line a, you are a Risker, someone who is decisive about making change. You are a risk taker either mentally or physically (and sometimes both). You are the leader who has learned to lead by leading, the changemaker who has learned how to do by doing. Your comfort with risk allows you to make great leaps forward when massive changes are required. Generally an extrovert, you are visual and action-oriented and may find yourself being impatient with gathering details. Your energy and intuition will often help you handle changes easily, but when you make an error, it can be a whopper.

Relater If most of your first choices are in line b, you are a Relater and are rather like a poll-taker. Since you relate well to people, when faced with change you will seek out the opinions of others instead of researching facts and focusing on details. You alter your own attitudes in response to others. Because of your sensitivity to people, you are especially successful in influencing others to change. You consult with professionals, friends, family and the person on the street. This approach is effective as long as you stop at some point and actually make the necessary change. But excessive poll-taking can leave you confused and dispirited; if you get too many conflicting views, the task of sorting them out can become overwelming.

Re-Focuser A preponderance of first choices in line c means that you are a goal-oriented Re-Focuser. While you have strongly held attitudes toward change, you periodically review and revise your way of doing things, usually in response to a problem. When involved in change, you are practical and focus on achieving tangible benefits. Even when interrupted or offered a pleasant diversion, you can quickly refocus on your task. Your intense concentration makes you extremely effective in getting things done and unshakable even under pressure. But occasionally you may overlook important details or circumstances. You might behave like the plumber who was so intent upon installing the new plumbing and appliances during a kitchen renovation that he failed to notice clues that the water heater is building pressure. Just as he completed the beautiful designer kitchen, the hot water tank blew up, spattering the pristine white decor with rusty water.

Reasoner Line d is most often checked by the analytical Reasoner, who approaches change thoughtfully. If you are a Reasoner, you base your attitudes and responses to change on past experiences and on information you carefully search out. Before undertaking change, you spend a great deal of energy on this research, making sure you have a thorough understanding of all the implications of the change. You are particularly skillful in dealing with change that requires organization. If you were planning a cross-country move, you'd have inventories and flowcharts for each phase. While others find this kind of planning for change tedious, you thrive on it. Your tendency to over-plan can be a pitfall when you irritate those you're working with or when you become so enamored with information-gathering that you never act.

COMING TO OUR SENSES: MAKING A DIFFERENCE

 How do you view change now — as threat or opportunity? Do you still associate the same words and images of change as you thought earlier? The materials of this chapter point to how important your answer will be. First and foremost, your answer will determine how flexible you personally might be to the prospect of a career filled with the unexpected and how open you might be to creating change around you. In addition, your attitude will undoubtedly influence your ability to institute change in a company, to help others to be more receptive and responsive. And finally, your view of change will influence how able you will be to see the need for change.

1. What's your biggest personal concern about a prospective working career with far fewer anchors than ever before experienced?

2. What excites you most about living and managing in fast changing organizations?

3. Where can you start experimenting with initiating change? Pick an opportunity that involves you or something you really care about.

Think about the year in your life in which you experienced the largest number of or greatest magnitude of changes. For example, perhaps you moved to a new community, started a new school, changed majors, had a death in the family and worked on a new project. It probably was a stressful year, maybe exciting in some respects but exhausting as well. This kind of intense period, with lots of emotions and lots of demands, was probably a difficult personal experience.

Imagine for a moment, however, that this was followed by another set of changes... and then another year of changes... and on and on. Continuous change, one might call it. This is exactly what people are saying that life in organizations will be like, if it isn't already — a string of continuous changes, substantial in nature, fast-paced in their onset and demanding.

Managing and surviving in this ever-changing type of organization will be challenging. Your job will change, the skills required will change, the organization structure will change, your goals may change, the competition will shift, your geographic location may change, you may lose valued work mates and gain new ones. Whether it be changes that you perceive as "good" or "bad," you will be working in a company where change will be constant — or your company won't!

What will be required to survive and succeed in such a work world personally and managerially? What seems to spell the difference is the capacity to remain flexible: flexible enough to see the need for change, flexible enough to develop new aspirations, and flexible enough to enable changes to occur. Unless you are flexible, you will be overwhelmed and paralyzed by the pace, the multiple "intrusions," and the lack of orderliness in it all.

Some organizations already seem to have recognized the importance of being flexible and responsive. The MCI company is often identified as an organization that has weathered a tremendous amount of change rather successfully. Its chairman, Bill McGowan, identified a list of tenets for the flexible organization of the future:[6]

1. We move fast; individuals have the power to make decisions and take actions; a minimum of reports and studies.

2. We are countercyclical; whatever is normal, expected or traditional, we change.

3. We institutionalize change; employees change jobs every two years and there are no organizational charts or job descriptions, no rule books or policy pronouncements.

4. We encourage initiative by giving both responsibility and authority.

5. We like employee turnover because when people get stale in a job they should move on to another. They can find another job in another area or leave the company and return when the time is right and not lose any benefits.

6. We sometimes decide not to decide; sometimes the pace of change is so fast, it is better to watch and wait for the right opportunity or the right product to arise.

7. We are not pretentious know-it-alls; we know we can't do everything well all the time. We will make mistakes and we will learn from them. We are egalitarian.

8. We insist that work has to be fun; you must feel you can make a difference.

9. We encourage all thinking and change styles; diversity on the staff leads to more innovation.

10. We know that nothing is forever except change; we realize that decay sets in as soon as an idea or organization is born.

6. Wonder and Donovan, op. cit.

11. We learn more from the future than from the past; imagine you are five years hence and speculate what you wished you had done the year before.

This is an organization unlike most you would see today but one that many companies are aspiring to become. It probably sounds a bit like some small club or project you may have have once experienced, a high performing system that was very fast-paced, fun and responsive. But to create such an experience in a large organization, on a wide scale, over an extended period of time is a real challenge. That's the challenge in managing change in the decades ahead.

For many companies, this challenge will evolve over time as we approach the twenty-first century. It will likely become less a matter of large transformations and more a matter of constant improvement, so that large, painful changes are rarely necessary. One company that appears to model an approach of "continuous improvement" is Toyota. The article that follows, "Why Toyota Keeps Getting Better and Better and Better," highlights Toyota's efforts to ensure that success breeds more success and not "large corporation disease" of stagnation and unresponsiveness.

The resounding incessant theme will become obvious — improve, improve, and, guess what, improve some more; adapt, adapt, and, guess what, adapt again. In other words, never be comfortable with things as they are and you are already getting prepared for twenty-first century managing.

Reading 18.1

WHY TOYOTA KEEPS GETTING BETTER AND BETTER AND BETTER.

by Alex Taylor III

Of all the hortatory slogans kicked around Toyota City, the key one is kaizen, which means "continuous improvement" in Japanese. While many other companies strive for dramatic breakthroughs, Toyota keeps doing lots of little things better and better. Consider the subcompact Tercel, the smallest Toyota sold in the U.S. The car contributes modestly at best to profits. Even so, Toyota has made the 1991 model faster, roomier, and quieter than its predecessor — with less weight, equally good mileage (32 mpg on the highway), and, remarkably, the same under-$8,000 price for the basic four-door sedan. It's $100 cheaper than GM's new Saturn and as much as $1,600 less than other competing models.

One consultant calls Toyota's strategy "rapid inch-up": Take enough tiny steps and pretty soon you outdistance the competition. By introducing six all-new vehicles within 14 months, Toyota has grabbed a crushing 43% share of car sales in Japan. In the just-ended 1990 model year, it sold more than one million cars and trucks in the U.S. for the first time — strengthening its position as No. 4 to the hard-pressed Big Three. Californians buy more Toyotas than Fords, Chevrolets, or any other make. Another half dozen new Toyotas are due in the U.S. in the next 12 months, including a sporty two-door based on the Tercel, a V-8-powered coupe version of the top-of-the-line Lexus, and bigger, more American-ized editions of the bread-and-butter Camry and the upscale Cressida.

The magnitude of these accom-plishments may surprise anyone who thinks of Toyota mainly as a builder of competent sedans, renowned more for reliability than pizazz. The company simply is tops in quality, productivity, and effi-ciency. From its factories pour a wide range of cars, built with unequaled precision. Toyota turns out luxury sedans with Mercedes-like quality using one-sixth the labor Mercedes does. The company originated just-in-time mass production and remains its leading practitioner.

In short, Toyota is the best carmaker in the world. And it keeps getting better. Says Iwao Isomura, chief of personnel: "Our current success is the best reason to change things." Extensive interviews with Toyota executives in the U.S. and Japan demonstrate the company's total dedication to continuous improvement. What is often mistaken for excessive modesty is, in fact, an expression of permanent dissatisfaction — even with exemplary performance. So the company is simultaneously restructuring its management, refining its already elegant manufacturing processes, planning its global strategy for the 21st century, tinkering with its corporate culture, and even becoming a fashion leader.

Toyota is putting to rest its reputation for fuddy-duddy design. Its Sera, a glass-topped minicoupe with gull-wing doors, is this year's fad favorite in Japan. The jellybean-shaped Previa, a hit with U.S. buyers, proves that minivans can be stylish as well as utilitarian. The $44,700 Lexus LS400 has become the first Japanese car to show that prestige doesn't have to wear a German or British nameplate. After only 14 months on the market, it outsells competing models from Mercedes-Benz, BMW, and Jaguar in the U.S. Japanese buyers have to wait a year to park one in the driveway.

Leading this juggernaut is President Shoichiro Toyoda, 65. Only 5 foot 2, this unlikely samurai is a grandson of the founder of Toyota's predecessor, Toyoda Automatic Loom Works, started in 1926. (Toyoda means "abundant rice field," inappropriate for a carmaker, so the company changed its name in 1936, three years after it got into the auto business.) A Ph.D. in engineering who enjoys being called

"Doctor," Shoichiro Toyoda has worked at the family company since 1947 and succeeded his second cousin Eiji, now 76, as president in 1982. The whole family owns less than 1% of the company's stock, worth some $450 million. (The Ford family's holdings amount to 8% of their company's common stock and 40% of the voting stock.) Though relatives abound on the Toyota payroll, none seems likely to succeed to the presidency.

At an age when many American executives have one foot on the golf course, Shoichiro Toyoda keeps driving his company ahead. In recent months he has ripped out two layers of middle management, stripped 1,000 executives of their staffs, and reorganized product development, putting himself in charge. He explains, "We felt we suffered from large-corporation disease. It had become extremely difficult for top executives to convey their feelings to our workers. So we embarked on a cure. We have a saying: 'A large man has difficulty exercising his wits fully.' We wanted to recertify that customer satisfaction is our first priority."

Globalization is a close second. Toyota is tightening its grip on Southeast Asia, making inroads in Latin America, and mobilizing for an assault on Europe from a new assembly plant in Britain. Any day now it will announce plans for a third U.S. assembly plant. No. 3 among the world's automakers since 1978, Toyota could sell nearly five million vehicles worldwide in 1990 (vs. about eight million for General Motors and six million for Ford). It is well on its way to its goal of six million cars and trucks a year by 1995.

Global expansion and waves of new models haven't dented Toyota's profitability. It made a net profit of 4.7% on sales of $64.5 billion in fiscal 1990, which ended June 30. Toyota enjoys the highest operating margin in the world auto industry, according to Gerard Paul of New York's Sanford C. Bernstein & Co. In Japan it earned a healthy 9% profit in fiscal 1989, vs. 8.4% for Nissan and 6.5% for Honda. Toyota netted 2.9% from U.S. sales, partly because its new Georgetown, Kentucky, plant wasn't running at capacity. (Ford made 4.3% from North American auto operations last year, while GM earned a scant 0.7%.)

Japan's No. 1 automaker is so rich that it makes more money on financial investments, including lending to other companies, than it does on operations. Jokingly known as the Bank of Toyota, it sits on $22 billion in cash — enough to buy both Ford and Chrysler at current stock prices, with nearly $5 billion to spare.

For years Toyota was the most conservative of Japan's automakers. Its heart remains in congested, provincial Toyota City (population: 327,000) in Japan's industrial belt. Four of Toyota's five car assembly plants are there, along with factories for nearly 140 of its parts suppliers and company housing for thousands of employees. Top executives work out of a flat-roofed three-story structure smaller and less prepossessing than a typical U.S. high school. The lobby is tiled in vinyl. Silver-plated cigarette boxes shaped like cars dot the conference tables.

Lately competition for Toyota's soul has started coming from Tokyo, 300 miles to the northeast. While Nissan and Honda are headquartered there, Toyota has shunned the bright lights and high prices of the capital. But in the past year it opened a design center in Tokyo to feed back data on fashion trends, as well as the world's biggest new-car showroom — a five-story, high-tech display where nearby office workers can kick tires as well as eat lunch. A fleet of four helicopters shuttles executives back and forth from Toyota City. (Toyota's only company plane — prop-driven — is based in Long Beach, California, to serve the U.S. sales operation.)

Like chrysanthemums in a rock garden, other signs of a new Toyota are popping up. A few executives — though not Dr. Toyoda — have traded in their blue sack suits for tailored double-breasteds and designer ties. Beige colored jumpers have replaced the traditional blue uniforms for the women who serve as receptionists and offer visitors orange juice and hot washcloths. Toyota today appears more open to outsiders, even boastful. The company distributes reprints from the Harvard Business Review praising product development methods like Toyota's. Says Satoshi Nakagawa, a research manager: "The mood is definitely different. There is a feeling among the younger engineers that they can take things on their own and change them. That wasn't there before."

After years of leaving technological innovation to Nissan and Honda, Toyota is moving to grab the lead. Between 1984 and 1989, R&D spending tripled from about $750 million to $2.2 billion. Rather than develop flashy consumer items such as four-wheel steering, the company concentrates on practical manufacturing technology — for example, new ways to stamp sheet metal. Toyota spends about 5% of sales on R&D, a slightly higher percentage than GM or Ford.

Many automakers, notably Honda, exude dedication and purpose. But Toyota is 2 1/2 times the size of Honda — and functions even more efficiently because of its unparalleled mastery of kanban, the just-in-time system conceived by Eiji Toyoda and perfected by legendary production boss Taiichi Ohno. In appropriating Ohno's ideas in the early 1980s, Detroit used just-in-time only to manage the delivery of parts to the assembly line. Toyota builds its entire production process around just-in-time. It aims to manufacture only what is needed, when it is needed, and in the quantity needed, whether it's a water pump or a complete car.

With traditional mass production, parts and finished cars are turned out in large batches and pushed downstream, ending up in inventory on dealer lots. Under just-in-time, parts and cars don't get built until orders move upstream to request them. Japanese dealers use on-line computers to order cars directly from the factory. Thomas Hout, a vice president of the Boston Consulting Group who spent six years in Japan, says the system works like airline reservations: In placing an order, the dealer essentially reserves a portion of factory capacity. Rather than wait several months, the customer can get his built-to-order car in a week to ten days. That leads to savings all along the line. The factory can balance production and stay in touch with shifting demand; the dealer keeps almost no inventory.

Under Toyota's management, just-in-time has produced remarkable results. The company makes 59 passenger-car models from 22 basic designs. Ford, which sells about a third more cars, produces only 46 passenger-car models. Using data collected by the International Motor Vehicle Program at MIT, professor Michael Cusumano estimates that Toyota needs only 13 man-hours to assemble a car in its best plant, vs. 19 to 22 hours for Honda and Nissan. Ford performs about as well as Honda and Nissan; GM lags behind. Toyota's high-volume family cars — Corolla, Camry, and Cressida — all rank tops in their class for assembly quality, according to the latest ranking by J.D. Power & Associates, the automotive research and consulting firm near Los Angeles.

Like all great ideas, just-in-time sounds simple. But Ohno spent 20 years perfecting it. Toyota's system is fed by a network of suppliers whose competence and close ties to their parent are the envy of the world. Toyota owns two suppliers outright; 228 others produce everything from jigs and molds to general contracting services for new plants. The suppliers also perform more R&D than American ones. That fact, along with higher productivity, helps explain why Toyota's payroll looks so skinny, with 91,790 employees vs. 766,000 at GM.

To feed its superb production system, Toyota reorganized product development in February. A council headed by Toyoda took over long-range product strategy. Under him were placed 240 members of the product planning division, arrayed in three groups: small front-wheel-drive models (for example, Tercel); big rear-wheel-drive cars (Lexus); and trucks.

The reorganization was driven by changing marketing requirements. Back in the 1950s, U.S. automakers turned out cars in one size — big. Today full-line manufacturers produce five basic sizes (mini, subcompact, compact, midsize, and full-size), with several variations of each (two-door, four-door, three-and five-door hatchback, fastback). "We have learned that universal mass production is not enough," says Kazuo Morohoshi, head of Toyota's Tokyo Design Center. "In the 21st century, you personalize things more to make them more reflective of individual needs." The winners will be those who target narrow customer niches most successfully with specific models.

To manage each new model, Toyota created the position of chief engineer and gave him unusually broad responsibilities: He has charge of everything associated with the development of a car. First he determines its physical dimensions and suitability for its potential market, then how it will be made and who the suppliers will be. He even helps design marketing strategies and talks frequently with car buyers. In January, for example, the Tercel's chief engineer will travel to Boston, Chicago, and Florida with six assistants to find out what dealers and owners like about the 1991 model — and to begin planning the 1995 version.

Besides getting the cars out, the chief engineer has to stay on top of social, political, and environmental trends. Toyota is grappling with issues that will affect future models, including fuel economy, alternative fuels, exhaust emissions, recyclability, highway congestion, and safety — both active (antilock brakes, traction control) and passive (air bags, reinforced bumpers). While it is behind Chrysler in adopting air bags, Toyota should catch up quickly.

The chief engineer system differs sharply from Detroit's product development practice, where a new-model boss has narrowly defined responsibilities and limited power. The Detroit chief usually works under specific instructions from the product planning and marketing departments. Even if he stays with the project through the manufacturing launch, he almost never has direct contact with dealers and customers.

Toyota's system has many advantages. Speed is No. 1. Toyota takes a new car design from concept to showroom in less than four years, vs. more than five for Detroit (and seven for Mercedes-Benz). That cuts costs, allows quicker correction of mistakes, and keeps Toyota better abreast of market trends. Gains from speed feed on themselves. Toyota can get its advanced engineering and design done sooner, says Yoshio Yunokawa, a manager of corporate R&D, because "we are closer to the customer and thus have a shorter concept time."

Teamwork also accelerates the process. Product and manufacturing engineers work closely together under the chief engineer, so factory machinery gets developed in tandem with prototype testing. Typically prototype testing leads to changes in the car that require alterations in the assembly line. Since Toyota completes the two processes simultaneously, no last-minute changes stall the production plan.

The Toyota system also drives down factory tooling costs, the biggest chunk of any development budget. Tools and machinery can account for about three-quarters of the $1-billion-plus required to design a new model and ready a plant to build it. Among the highest-cost items are the custom-designed dies that punch out each piece of frame and sheet metal, and the big stamping presses that hold them. Donald Smith, a researcher at the University of Michigan, estimates that Toyota designs and manufactures dies and presses for one-half to two-thirds less than the Big Three.

Here again, just-in-time cooperation is critical. Car engineers design parts with the body engineers, the manufacturing engineers, and the stylist so they can be made with about 35% fewer strokes of the stamping press, by Smith's calculation. Fewer strokes mean lighter, less expensive dies, lower operating costs, shorter shutdowns, and reduced maintenance.

Body panels that emerge from Toyota's stamping operation are as precisely cut "as the works of a Swiss watch," says Smith. In some competitors' plants, he adds, "I've seen people force panels into compliance. If the parts are not consistent, the welding guns have to operate almost like C-clamps to force the parts together. Toyota parts usually just lie in the fixtures and require no force from the welding guns."

Because of model proliferation, Toyota needs twice as many dies as it did ten years ago. So it has automated the die manufacturing process. Computers drive numerically controlled machining tools that cut dies faster and more accurately than mechanical methods can. Giant cranes carry die castings to the machining tools and retrieve the finished dies. The whole system can run for ten days without human intervention: The plant can make dies "lights out" while workers are on holiday.

Using Pascal's law describing the behavior of fluids under pressure, Toyota has adapted a remarkable stamping process to make the production of small-volume niche models more efficient. In this flexible press system, the bottom half of the metal die is replaced with — of all things — water. A fender, say, gets stamped between a curved metal die and a tankful of water, which serves as a smooth, flexible bottom die. The system cuts die costs by nearly one-third, improves yield, and reduces piece costs by 18%. Toyota says it makes a better fender because the die is more accurate and can bend the metal more than conventional two-piece dies. Drawbacks: The forming process takes 80 seconds, vs. three to five seconds with conventional dies, and finished pieces must be dried.

On the assembly line, Toyota's guiding principles shine through the grit and haze. Quality is defined not as zero defects but, as another Toyota slogan has it, "building the very best and giving the customer what he wants." Because each worker serves as the customer for the process just before his, he becomes a quality-control inspector. If a piece isn't installed properly when it reaches him, he won't accept it. His first act is to alert his supervisor by tugging a rope that turns on a warning light. If the problem isn't corrected by the time the next piece comes down, he can stop the line by pulling the rope a second time.

Toyota's Japanese workers also perform feats of agility never seen in a U.S. factory. In the 50 seconds or so it takes for a car to pass their station, they climb inside the front and rear passenger compartments to install electronic equipment or interior trim. One man has to clamber into the trunk to affix a wiring harness. A few workers wear leather cushions belted around their waists to protect them when they sit down inside the car.

Like all employers in Japan, Toyota faces a stringent labor shortage because of slowing population growth and a national reluctance to import workers. So it is trying to enrich assembly line jobs by "making work more creative," says personnel boss Isomura. He adds: "We want work to be pleasant and vivid for our employees, because when they grow, the company grows." Already a pioneer in quality circles, where workers discuss ways to improve their tasks, the company is working to eliminate what it calls the three D's: the dangerous, dirty, and demanding aspects of factory work. It is also investing $770 million over the next four years to improve worker housing, add dining halls, and build new recreational facilities. Single men live dormitory-style with shared bathrooms, while married workers with families qualify for their own small apartments. At least 24,000 Toyota employees in Japan live in company-subsidized housing.

Across Japan, on average, there are 1.37 jobs available for every worker. The squeeze is even tighter around Toyota City, where the figure is 2.13. Toyota's assembly plants in Japan all run on overtime, with workers logging an average of 1 1/2 extra hours every shift (for which they are paid time and a half). Over the course of a year, Toyota figures its workers spend about 2,300 hours on the job — the equivalent of more than 57 standard 40-hour workweeks — vs. 2,200 for Nissan and only 1,960 at Honda. And that's not counting 25 vacation days. By 1993, Toyota wants to reduce the workload to 2,000 hours. It also wants to hire more women, who account for about 9% of all employees but do not work in the plants.

To reduce overtime, Toyota is investing heavily in automation. Capital spending will rise 39% to nearly $4.2 billion for the current fiscal year, according to Automotive News, a trade weekly. In final assembly, where the car body is fitted with its engine, transmission, electronics, and trim, Toyota has added robots that apply adhesive to the windshields and drop spare tires into trunks. Still, only 5% of the assembly line jobs are automated, vs. 30% at some Volkswagen and Fiat plants in Europe (which has long experience with labor shortages).

White-collar workers, who might otherwise have boarded the bullet train to shop for new jobs in Tokyo, are also getting a dose of job enrichment. Says Toyoda: "We are still slow in movement. But we are making ourselves more attractive to younger people." Employees are being retrained to work with less supervision, accept more responsibility, and move projects along more quickly. Instead of getting up to ten sign-offs on a new program, in many cases they now need only three. But Toyota has not given up its longtime emphasis on decision-making by consensus. Says Junji Numata, who used to help out as a translator in the public-affairs department and now heads European operations: "We still work together as a team. You can't just wave your flag and go."

A nine-month training regimen for new white-collar workers provides plenty of opportunity to imprint the company culture. College graduates embarking on a Toyota career spend four weeks working in a factory and three months selling cars. They get lectures from top management and instruction in problem solving. Their supervisors make them keep reworking solutions until they produce one that's suitable.

Developing cadres of independent-minded team players should serve Toyota well as it tries to develop integrated worldwide production. Until recently executives found it hard to leave the supportive network of suppliers and well-established manufacturing practices of Toyota City. Not until last year did the company set up Japanese plants outside its friendly confines.

Toyota was especially cautious about starting U.S. production. It tiptoed in via a joint venture with GM in 1983 to build Corollas in Fremont, California. Its biggest problem was replicating just-in-time parts delivery. Since most auto suppliers are based in the Midwest, Toyota set up a warehouse in Chicago to accept deliveries, then shipped parts to California by train. Just-in-time was redefined from several hours to 3 1/2 days, but the discipline of the system was maintained. Toyota will add trucks to the Fremont operation in 1991, and is expected to expand its production further in 1996 by buying GM's share of the venture.

With the California facility up and running (and Nissan and Honda already established in their own U.S. plants), Toyota in 1988 opened the Georgetown, Kentucky, facility, where it will build 220,000 compact Camrys this year. Several hundred American supervisors went to Japan for training. The plant abounds with imported techniques, among them big electrical signs called andon boards that track daily production, signal overtime requirements, and identify trouble spots along the line. Individual workers have their own smaller versions that tell them, for example, whether they have attached a bolt tightly enough.

Quality is high at Georgetown but productivity runs about 10% below Japanese levels. Toyota production boss Susumu Uchikawa blames the lag on U.S. suppliers, which he says aren't up to European standards, much less Japanese. To defuse political objections, Toyota buys American parts anyway. In some cases it keeps identical Japanese-made components on hand as insurance against defective American materials.

By the mid-1990s Toyota could be selling 1.5 million cars and trucks in the U.S., half of them made in North America. It is building one of the world's largest test tracks on 18 square miles of Arizona desert; the proving ground should be ready by 1994. The company is also doubling the size of its California design center, which sculpted the exterior of the Previa minivan and the upcoming Lexus SC400 coupe, and is expanding its technical operations in Ann Arbor, Michigan, and Torrance, California.

With five separate subsidiaries reporting back to Japan, Toyota's North American operation is overdue for reorganization. Some top U.S. executives have to make the 24-hour round trip between Los Angeles and Japan as often as nine times a year, frequently to discuss future product plans. Changes may be forthcoming when U.S. sales head Robert McCurry, 67, retires in three years.

Western Europe presents Toyota with a fresh set of obstacles. With Peugeot boss Jacques Calvet as their chief spokesman, inefficient European automakers are waging a protectionist battle to limit Japanese car sales until the next century. Some compromise will likely be worked out, but Europe still won't be a pushover. French, Italian, and German buyers are more resistant to non-European cars than Americans are. Toyota has set up a design center in Brussels and is building a plant in Derbyshire, England, with a capacity of 200,000 cars annually. European boss Numata expects that Toyota will have only 3% of a 20-million-vehicle market by 2000, vs. 2.5% now.

The smaller nations on the Pacific Rim provide a glimpse of Toyota's skills at operating overseas. These countries have some of the world's toughest local-content laws, but their populations aren't big or skilled enough to support integrated manufacturing. So Toyota put together a clever scheme to build carmaking expertise.

This fall it started casting cylinder blocks in Indonesia, and it will soon begin making other parts in Thailand, Malaysia, and the Philippines. For now the parts are being shipped back to Japan, but eventually they will be assembled into cars at a more central location. Labor costs in Asia's less developed countries are one-third to one-fifth of Japan's, but workers require more intensive training and factories run more slowly. By 2000, Toyota expects to be operating one or two assembly plants in the region and selling one million cars and trucks annually in a 3.5 million vehicle market.

Southeast Asia is a paradigm for how Toyota would like to operate in the future — buying parts, building cars, and selling them around the world regardless of national boundaries. Dr. Toyoda has a plan for globalization, as he seems to for everything else. It has five steps. Toyota is on the cusp of step four, which calls for turning overseas operations over to local managers. In the final stage, perhaps in 20 years, the company "optimizes its operations by planning and managing all of them from a global perspective," Toyoda says.

That would mean turning the world into a giant Toyota City and establishing operations wherever they make economic sense. To pull that off, Toyota needs to loosen further the ties that bind its overseas operations to the home office, while making production function as smoothly in Thailand as in Toyota City. But having written the book on automotive manufacturing, Toyota appears well placed to update it with a new global edition. Momentum is clearly on its side. Thanks to *kaizen* and *kanban*, continuous improvement and just-in-time, Toyota's lead over the competition — American, European, and Japanese — keeps growing and growing and growing.

You have now come to the conclusion of *Management Live!* And surely you have come to your own conclusions about management and the exciting challenges and opportunities ahead for you. "All" you have to do now is put it together and implement it.

What we have presented has been organized by topics that help to focus attention on critical management issues. However, in a real time setting, the issues do not emerge with "chapter headings." Rather, they appear as problems, symptoms and opportunities which require multiple skills and analytic tools. The most successful managers are able to see the world in complex terms, drawing from a broad combination of the topics in this book.

This is what the Toyota story reminded us. A continuously successful company is always growing and changing in a variety of ways. If you think about what Toyota is doing, you see the potential of integrating all that you've been exposed to and learned through *Management Live!* and your course. And you see how fulfilling and exciting the experience of management can be.

What's the secret of Toyota's managerial success? Managers are always examining and refining their structure and systems, their operation and their global reach. They are broadening the leadership roles and responsibilities of their people, while using teamwork to accelerate results. They are trying to motivate their employees by enriching jobs and they invest heavily in inculcating a corporate culture dedicated to problem solving. In short, they are managing change all the time. And we could go on and on, reviewing the key concepts you've been learning.

We hope that you too will be able to approach your task as a manager with similar vigor and sophistication. And we hope that your tool kit will always include recollections of the video clips, exercises, self-awareness and analytics that we have provided you through this course. If you relied on us throughout this course to help you see some of the critical issues in organizations and management, now we rely on you to make the twenty-first century life in organizations more effective, more efficient and more healthy than ever before.

THE NASA SPACE SHUTTLE LAUNCH DECISION
To Launch or Not to Launch: That was the Question

by Roger Boisjoly

The final decision to launch the Challenger on January 28, 1986 rested on the coordination of hundreds of prior decisions made by thousands of contractors, subcontractors, and three space centers. Decisions were not only those concerned with the ability of the rocket to fly but included decisions about cargo space, crew training, flight-plan designs, schedules, experiments, and computer programs.

Data and decisions moved up through successive levels, and at each point in the succession, fewer people were involved in assessing increasingly reduced data summaries, adding their own particular views and concerns and passing their evaluations and decisions up to yet another decision level. The Mission Management Team, the last in the chain of command, took over management 48 hours prior to the launch and encouraged launch officials at lower levels to report any new problems or difficulties. Unfortunately, these lower-level individuals report through the chain of command and, like a game of pass-it-on, information gets distorted as it passes up the hierarchy, often as a result of the reflected interests of bosses along the way. It was such a distortion, along with a number of other factors, that contributed to the disaster of January 28, 1986.

Roger Boisjoly, ``Ethical Decisions — Morton Thiokol and the Space Shuttle Challenger Disaster,'' paper presented at the December, 1987 meeting of the American Society of Mechanical Engineers; and R. Marx, C. Stubbart, V. Traub, and M. Cananaugh, ``The NASA Space Shuttle Disaster: A Case Study,'' *Journal of Management*. Vol. 3, pp. 300-18. Appearing in D. H. Holt, *Management* (Englewood Cliffs, NJ, 1990), pp. 125-27.

Various changes in NASA reflect the other factors contributing to the tragic decision to launch that day. Reorganizations in its history included the development of a stronger headquarters team to coordinate efforts among field centers in 1961, a decentralization in 1963, a recentralization to integrate decision-making and increase emphasis on safety in 1967 as a result of a tragic fire that resulted in the deaths of three astronauts, and, finally, another reorganization in 1983 that reclassified the shuttle program from developmental to operational.

Such reorganizations were not only the result of the internal workings of NASA but also reflected both the degree of financial support that could be garnered and the goals and agendas of presidents along the way. On the heels of a time of great support through the Kennedy-Johnson administration, where NASA was perceived as "an organism that was more responsive to its own internal technological momentum than externally developed objectives," the Nixon administration called for more practical goals to provide tangible benefits to science, the economy, and national security. This shift from a technological focus to a more political one was followed by President Reagan's two 1982 policy priorities — to maintain U.S. leadership in space and to expand private-sector involvement and investment.

The shift in political tone brought NASA face-to-face with several new challenges: commercialization, meeting the needs of military and civilian agencies, developing private sector activities and meeting customer commitments. NASA was no longer its own customer; it had to serve the needs of private industry. The primary stakeholders were now a close-knit network between NASA, Congress, the Department of Defense, and private industry. With the needs and priorities of commercial customers essentially driving the program, cost and schedule constraints received greater emphasis, and soon safety issues took a back seat as personnel were pushed beyond their endurance limits to meet deadlines. The organization moved from one dominated by scientists and engineers to one dominated by bureaucrats and administrators.

While the Kennedy-Johnson administration provided NASA with its greatest period of support, the Kennedy administration was also responsible for opening up NASA to the public and moving NASA away from its concern to maintain secrecy. With this shift an eager press followed. The benefits of media coverage were soon recognized — especially as space flights became more common place, as worn out notions of astronauts as fearless daredevils had to be replaced with new images, and as contractors, performing 80-90 percent of NASA's design and development work, lobbied to promote their interests.

All these factors led to various changes. By the mid 1980s a distinction was made between engineering and program management decisions. An engineer who had been with NASA since 1960 spoke about this change from years past: "At the beginning all the decisions were made at the lowest possible level.... It was simply inconceivable that one person could have thought something was wrong… and everyone else not know about it." Another engineer said, "People making the decisions are getting farther and farther away from the people who get their hands dirty." It was just such a distinction in decision-making responsibility that was ultimately responsible for the tragic decision to launch that fateful January.

In an evening telecon meeting between MTI, MSFC, and KSC, presentations of data were made by engineers expressing concern regarding seal integrity at particularly low temperatures. According to R. Boisjoly, a senior engineer on the project at MTI, the data supported a no-launch decision. At the end of the engineering presentation, Larry Mulloy of NASA asked MTI for a launch decision; launching was not recommended based on the engineering position. Mulloy then asked G. Hardy of NASA for his launch decision. While Hardy said he was "appalled" by MTI's recommendation, he said he would not launch over the contractor's objection. Mulloy then gave his views and concluded that the data presented were inconclusive.

Based on NASA's earliest rules that forced contractors and themselves to prove it was safe to fly, Mulloy's statement about the inconclusivity of the data should have been enough to stop the launch. However, it was likely that this statement prompted MTI vice-president Kilminster to request an off-line caucus to reevaluate the data. As soon as MTI was off-line, J. Mason, MTI General Manager, said, "We have to make a management decision." It was clear that an attempt would be made by executive-level management to reverse the no-launch decision.

Two engineers, A. Thompson and R. Boisjoly, attempted to make themselves heard as managers began a discussion among themselves. No one in management seemed to want to discuss the facts, and with cold and unfriendly looks to the engineers they struggled to make a list of data that would support a launch decision. A vote poll was taken by only the four senior executives present; engineers were excluded from both the discussion and the poll. Returning to the telecon, Kilminster read the launch support rationale and recommended that the launch proceed as scheduled. NASA accepted the launch recommendation without any discussion or any probing questions — the recommendation was consistent with their desires. In fact, NASA had placed MTI in the position of proving that it was not safe to fly instead of proving that it was safe to fly.

CHANGING THE SHUTTLE LAUNCH DECISION PROCESS

Date: January 28, 1986
Time: 11:38 A.M. eastern standard time
Event: Space shuttle Challenger lifts off from Cape Canaveral

Exactly one minute and 14 seconds later NASA's worst fears were realized when Challenger exploded in a huge ball of fire, killing all seven crew members. Prior to the disaster there had been 24 shuttle flights without injury to any crew member, and NASA was confident in its procedures. Since then, however, the procedures and processes surrounding shuttle missions have been thoroughly reexamined.

Technically, the Challenger explosion was caused by the failure of an O-ring on one of the solid fuel booster rockets. However, subsequent investigations have placed the responsibility squarely on NASA's launch decision. That decision was made despite repeated warnings by engineers at Morton Thiokol, the company that manufactured the boosters, that it was dangerous to launch the shuttle in cold weather. In the aftermath of the disaster, NASA significantly overhauled the decision-making process leading to the shuttle launches.

The new system involves a number of reviews by several committees and uses much more information than in the past. Under new procedures, the deputy director of National Space Transportation System Operations, astronaut Robert L. Crippen, has the final responsibility to launch or to hold a shuttle. He will receive support and management inputs from the Launch Team, the Mission Management Team, and the Space Shuttle Management Council as he makes his decision. The Management Council is comprised of directors of the Kennedy, Johnson and Marshall Space Centers in turn receives input from the National Space Technology Laboratories.

D. H. Holt, *Management* (Englewood Cliffs, NJ, 1990), pp. 127-28.

Once a preliminary launch decision has been made, a number of critical reviews take place before the terminal countdown is started. The most important of these reviews is the Flight Readiness Review (FRR), which addresses all aspects of flight preparation, especially any that can cause problems at the time of launch or during the flight. Technical matters that are likely to endanger the flight in any way are addressed by a committee of NASA engineers with inputs from relevant outside contractors. The engineering committee assesses the likely impact of the technical problem and decides on how to solve them. Their assessment is then considered by the review committee, which decides whether to proceed with or delay the launch and formally recommends the same to the Mission Management Team.

The FRR also takes into account the preparedness level of the crew. Special attention is given to crew members who will be going into space for the first time. The crew also are assessed on their ability to handle problems that might occur in space. If a particular crew member is believed to be not sufficiently capable of handling his or her duties, especially in a crisis, the committee recommends that either the individual be dropped from the flight or the launch be delayed until such time that the astronaut is more fully trained.

Another important review is the constraints review. This review involves all supporting organization (the National Space Technology Laboratories and the three Space Centers); possible constraints on a particular launch are analyzed and ways are devised to cope with them. For example, constraints might include inclement weather causing a risky launch or landing, solar flares that could disrupt communications, or other aspects of the mission, like deploying a satellite in a particular orbit, that would involve unusual shuttle maneuverings. The constraints committee also reviews the preparedness of alternative landing sites if their use is considered possible.

Two days before the scheduled launch date a final review, under Crippen, takes place. At this time the mission Management Team verifies that all actions from the FRR and any other actions recommended by other review committees have been completed successfully. Finally, nine minutes before launch a poll is taken by the Launch Director and head of the Launch Team, Robert B. Sieck. The engineering support team, Air Force meteorologists at Cape Canaveral, NASA's test director, and the chairman of the Space Shuttle Management Council are polled for final concurrence. Sieck then formally recommends to the Mission Management Team Chairman, Crippen, that they go ahead with the launch. However, any member of the Launch Team is authorized to interrupt the mission countdown until the moment of launch (T minus zero).

In retrospect, the Challenger disaster is seen by many experts as the result of top management's isolation from the technical personnel closest to the launch. The Presidential Commission that investigated the accident concluded that those who gave the launch order did not have a clear understanding of the engineering and weather objections that should have stopped the launch.

The current decision-making process involves checks and verifications by over 300 NASA personnel as well as by numerous outside contractors. Although viewed by some as cumbersome, the system has been adopted in order to insure the safety of NASA personnel and equipment. The current process is intended to keep NASA's management in touch with lower-level engineers and others with technical expertise. To date, revised launch procedures appear to be working successfully. Only time and subsequent launches, however, will prove the long-term effectiveness of the changes made.

Recommended Answers and Scoring to the Decision Style Questionnaire Using the Decision Style Model

Abbreviations:

S-A = Autocratic Style

S-P = Participative Style

S-C = Consultative Style

S-L = Laissez-Faire Style

1) S-C. yes: time, S-A OR S-C: information, S-A OR S-C: acceptance, S-C: capability. Use a consultative style (S-C), 3 points, 2 points for the autocratic style (S-A), 1 point for the participative style (S-P), 0 points for the laissez-faire (S-L).

2) S-P. yes: time, S-P: information, S-P OR S-C: acceptance, S-L OR S-P: capability. Use the participative style. 3 points for S-P, 2 points for S-C, 1 point for S-L, 0 points for S-A.

3) S-L. yes: time, S-L OR S-P: information, S-A: acceptance, S-L: capability. Capability takes precedence over acceptance, they have no choice but to come in as requested. This is a good situation to let the group decide. 3 points S-L, 2 points S-P, 1 point S-C, 0 points S-A.

4) S-C. yes: time, S-A: information, S-C OR S-P: acceptance, S-C: capability. In this situation a consultant was hired because your employees were not capable in this situation. You want to "sell" them on the idea. 3 points S-C, 2 points S-A, 1 point S-P, 0 points S-L.

5) S-P. yes: time, S-P OR S-C: information, S-L OR S-P: acceptance, S-C: maturity. Acceptance takes precedence. Use a participative style. They will most likely want to participate in this situation, if not change to the consultative style.

6) S-A. no: time. When there is no time, time takes precedence over the other variables. 3 points S-A, 2 points S-C, 1 point S-P, 0 points S-L.

7) S-A. yes: time, S-A: information, S-A: acceptance, S-P: capability. Information takes precedence. You have to implement top management decisions in most cases even if you do not agree with them. 3 points S-A, 2 points S-C, 1 point S-P, 0 points S-L.

Adapted from *R.N. Lussier, Human Relations in Organizations: A Skill-Building Approach — Instructors' Manual* (Homewood, IL: Irwin, 1990), p. 1A-135-136.

8) S-L. yes: time, S-L: information, S-L: capability. In this situation acceptance is critical to meeting the contract. If employees make the decision they will most likely meet the contract. If they have no input they probably will not. 3 points S-L, 2 points S-P, 1 point S-C, 0 points S-A.

Ch. 6, Reading 6.1, "The New Breed of Leaders...." Reprinted with permission from *Working Woman Magazine*. Copyright © 1990 by WWT Partnership.

Ch. 6, Reading 7.2, "Continuum of International Decision Making Style." Pearce and Robinson, *Management,* © 1989, McGraw-Hill, Inc. Source: From L. Copeland and L. Griggs, G*oing International* (New York: Random House, 1985), p. 123.

Ch. 7, Carter Racing case. "Facts, Figures and Organizational Decisions: Carter Racing and Quantitative Analysis in the Organizational Behavior Classroom," *OBTR* (1990), p. 62-81, used with permission.

Ch. 8, Reading 8.1, "Work Teams Muffle Labor's Voice." Copyright © 1989 by the *New York Times Company*. Reprinted with permission.

Ch. 8, Reading 8.2 "Is Teamwork a Management Plot?" Reprinted from February 20, 1989 issue of *Business Week* by special permission, copyright © 1989 McGraw-Hill, Inc.

Ch. 8, Reading 8.3 Brian Dumaine, "Who Needs a Boss?" *Fortune,* May 7, 1990. Reprinted by permission.

Ch. 8, Team development model. Reprinted with permission from NTL Institute, "Developing a Productivity Team: Making Groups at Work Work," by Jane Moosbruker, pp. 91-92, *Team Building: Blueprints for Productivity and Satisfaction,* edited by W. Brendon Reddy with Kaleel Jamison, copyright © 1988.

Ch. 9, "The Far Side" cartoon, by Gary Larson, copyright © Universal Press Syndicate Company. Reprinted with permission.

Ch. 8, Team bulding. William G. Dyer, *Team Building,* © 1987, by Addison-Wesley Publishing Company, Inc., Reading, pp. 68-70. Reprinted with permission of the publisher.

Ch. 9, Reading 9.1. Fred Luthans, "Successful vs. Effective Real Managers," *The Academy of Management Executives,* © 1988, Vol. II, No. 2, pp. 127-132.

Ch. 10, Reading 10.1. Reprinted by permission of *Harvard Busines Review*. "The Coming of the New Organization," by Peter F. Drucker, (Jan/Feb 1988). Copyright © 1988 by the President and Fellows of Harvard College. All Rights Reserved.

Ch. 10, Reading 10.2. "At these Shouting Matches...." Reprinted from June 11, 1990 issue of *Business Week* by special permission, copyright © 1990 by McGraw-Hill, Inc.

Ch. 13, Reading 13.1, "Forever Young," by Erik Larsen, *Inc. Magazine*. Reprinted by permission of Georges Borchardt, Inc., and the author. Copyright © 1988 by Erik Larson.